LAY BARE THE HEART

AN AUTOBIOGRAPHY OF

THE CIVIL RIGHTS MOVEMENT

JAMES FARMER

A PLUME BOOK

NEW AMERICAN LIBRARY

NEW YORK AND SCARBOROUGH, ONTARIO

Library of Congress Cataloging-in-Publication Data

Farmer, James, 1920-
  Lay bare the heart.

1. Farmer, James, 1920- 2. Afro-Americans
Biography.   3. Civil rights workers—United States—
Biography.   4. Afro-Americans—Civil rights.   I. Title.
E185.97.F37A35   1985b   323.4'092'4 [B]   85-29770
ISBN 0-452-25803-0 (pbk.)

First Plume Printing, March, 1986

1 2 3 4 5 6 7 8 9

PRINTED IN THE UNITED STATES OF AMERICA

"WITHOUT JAMES FARMER'S PERSPECTIVE, THE SAGA OF THE CIVIL RIGHTS MOVEMENT IS AN UNFINISHED STORY."—*Charleston News & Courier*

"An essential book, one that lends credence to the argument that holds James Farmer . . . as the rightful heir to Martin Luther King's legacy."
—*Los Angeles Herald Examiner*

"An invaluable contribution to the history and literature of the unfinished civil rights movement. Anyone who wants to deepen his or her understanding of America's struggle to free itself from racism—or who wants to learn more about a compassionate, human-hearted man—is well advised to read this book."—Julian Bond, in *Atlanta Magazine*

"Powerful . . . inspiring . . . weaves songs, convictions, emotions, personal travails and on-the-scene reporting into a rich tableau that draws us deeply into the 1960s tumult . . . gives us insights into Martin Luther King, Presidents Kennedy, Johnson and Nixon, Malcolm X and other leaders."
—*Cleveland Plain Dealer*

"James Farmer, the only survivor of the movement's 'Big Four,' vividly tells his fascinating, no-holds-barred story, the good and the bad, breakthrough and betrayal, sparing no one, including himself."—*United Press International*

JAMES FARMER, the founding director of the Congress of Racial Equality, was one of the "Big Four" leaders of the civil rights movement along with Martin Luther King, Roy Wilkins, and Whitney Young. He is now a visiting professor at Mary Washington College in Fredericksburg, Virginia.

To Lula

THIS BOOK IS FOR HER MEMORY.

Contents

Acknowledgments

IN ANY UNDERTAKING of this magnitude, noting all indebtedness would exceed the limitations of space. I would be remiss, though, if I did not especially thank Dr. William Haddon, president of the Insurance Institute for Highway Safety, for permitting the institute's word processor to be used in the drafting and editing of the manuscript.

My gratitude also goes to Rea Tyler, a good friend, writer, and editor, who spent countless hours applying her professional skills in helping to craft this book, staying with it through late evenings and weekends, through numerous debates with the author on content and style, but persevering until the job was finished. Appreciation also is due her husband and daughter for their forbearance throughout.

Two young historians, Rebecca Rogers and Joel Treese, helped greatly by validating my assertions and checking my recollections against historical sources. They dug up names and dates I had forgotten and detected certain errors in chronology, which, uncorrected, would have damaged the authenticity of this work.

Another writer/editor and friend, Scottie Dalsimer, gave encouragement and advice throughout, especially during my tussles with the particularly troublesome portions of the book.

Dee Wilson took weekend respites from her administrative job to resurrect superb shorthand and typing skills as I raced to meet final deadline. Jackie Linsdell, my former secretary, typed and retyped the early chapters and, despite my season of sadness, forced me to go on.

A student intern in history, Richard Marcolis, did the initial research, piling up documents to refresh my memory as I contemplated writing this book.

Several friends, in addition to those already mentioned, who shared various parts of my life and work, read the draft manuscript and came together for no-holds-barred discussions and criticism. Among those participating in that constructive free-for-all were: Val Coleman, a splendid writer and literary technician; Ruth and Antoine Perot, Jr., both fine thinkers with encyclopedic knowledge of the black experience; and Donald Wendell, in whose perceptive mind disparate events always seek a rational linkage.

In the early processes of the book, Professor John Pearce, a historian who shared a daily commuter bus with me, read the first eight chapters, providing penetrating observations and highly useful suggestions. Finally, another historian and movement scholar, Dr. Lawrence Reddick, carefully went over the manuscript and gave me many lively comments and helpful suggestions.

From all of their efforts, the book has benefited immeasurably. Its shortcomings, however, are mine alone.

"Man was not born to solve the problem of the universe, but rather to seek to lay bare the heart of the problem and then to confine himself within the limits of what is amenable to understanding. The question to ask is not whether we are perfectly agreed, but whether we are proceeding from a common basis of sentiment."

—JOHANN WOLFGANG VON GOETHE
1749–1832

PART ONE

Mississippi Revisited

CHAPTER 1

WHEELS OF TERROR

CAPTAIN RAY'S INDEX FINGER shot through the air. "Follow that police officer," he said with professional aplomb, "and get into the patrol wagon."

That was a gesture and those were words destined to be repeated by Jackson's police chief hundreds of times in the next three months as Freedom Riders from twenty states saturated Mississippi jails.

Captain Ray's stabbing finger came to symbolize his role in the drama being played out—that of the little Dutch boy of legend vainly trying to plug a breach in the dike of segregation in order to hold back the floodwaters of resistance—to save his city, his state, his way of life.

Scarcely four hours earlier on that day in May 1961, the Greyhound bus had left a riot-torn Montgomery, Alabama, where mobs of white men had rampaged and held Freedom Riders prisoners through the night in the First Baptist Church. Martin Luther King had flown in from Atlanta to join us for a rally at the church and he, too, was caught in the siege. Robert Kennedy had flown in U.S. marshals. Martial law had been declared and the Alabama National Guard called to duty.

The next day, curfew had been enforced and sporadic gunfire could be heard, shattering the quiet. Now, jeeps patrolled the streets. The atmosphere was warlike. As thirty or forty nonviolent black youths readied themselves for their ride into bigotry's main den, to beard the beast lurking there, individual apprehensions were eclipsed by collective determination.

The eclipse was only partial, though; fear shone through. If any man says that he had no fear in the action of the sixties, he is a liar. Or without imagination.

If there are those who think that the leaders were exceptions to that and were strangers to fear, let me quickly disabuse them of such a notion. Frankly, I was scared spitless and desperately wanted to avoid taking that ride to Jackson. Alabama had chewed up the original thirteen interracial CORE* Freedom Riders; they had been brutalized, hospitalized, and in one case disabled—by flame, club, and pummeling fists. Across the Alabama line from Georgia, blacks had been brutally pistol-whipped and clubbed with blackjacks and fists and then thrown, bloodied, into the back of the bus. Whites had been clobbered even worse for trying to intervene—one suffered a stroke as a result and was paralyzed forever.

A bus had been burned to the ground in Anniston, Alabama, and the Freedom Riders, escaping with their lives, were hospitalized for smoke inhalation. In the Birmingham bus depot, Jim Peck, a white man, had been left for dead in a pool of his own blood. His head required fifty-three stitches. How many stitches could repair the heart that bled for the nation?

And, fortuitously, I had missed that carnage on the ride from Atlanta to Montgomery due to the death of my father. But how would I escape Mississippi? If Alabama had been purgatory, Mississippi would be hell.

Black students from Nashville, members of SNCC,** their numbers augmented by youthful black CORE members from New Orleans, had dashed in to catch in midair the baton dropped by the initial thirteen. They had not asked if I would ride with them: they assumed that I would.

I had different thoughts, though. I had decided not to ride. Definitely, at any cost, not to go. Catalogued in my mind were all the necessary excuses. When the inevitable question came, I was ready with answers.

But that decision had not come without inner pain. After all, when I took over the helm of CORE, four months earlier, I had said that I would be no armchair general, tied to the tent. I would not *send* troops, but would go with them. But that was bravado born of remoteness from reality. Who would expect me to risk being cut down so early in the promise of a leadership career? Everyone would understand when they thought about it. There would be many other battles, much time to show courage. And how could I let myself be wiped out now, before anyone outside the inner circle of the movement even knew I was there? Not now, maybe later. And my father had just died. I should not follow him so soon. Two deaths in two weeks would be too much for my mother. The family needed me now.

Yet, a grain of ambivalence stuck in my craw. Maybe a "still, small voice" would speak. A part of me hoped so. But if it spoke, I was certain that I

*Congress of Racial Equality
**Student Non-Violent Coordinating Committee

would close my ears. Though, just in case, I had packed my suitcase and tossed it into the trunk of a staff car. And along with it my inner turmoil.

When the kids boarded the buses, I watched as a father seeing his children leave the home, as they must, and race into an uncertain future. Typically, the father was sad because he could not go with them; they had to go alone.

On the first bus, the Trailways, they were not alone. With them was a young black Methodist minister, the Reverend James Lawson. A man of much imagination, Jim Lawson must have had the same apprehensions that I had. But he had decided to go anyway. Courage, after all, is not being unafraid, but doing what needs to be done in spite of fear. He fairly leaped onto the bus, with a grim gladness. The students on board smiled and gave me a "thumbs up" gesture and shouted, "See you later, Jim." I returned the gesture and the smile, hoping that they would see me later, *much* later.

The second bus, the Greyhound, was boarded by some SNCC people, but mostly by CORE people. The CORE contingent had come at my urging, transmitted by my staff in New York, to keep the "revolution" going. They fully expected the protection my presence would provide. They filed in and took seats. I stood outside and waved farewell. The windows were open and I extended my hand through to shake hands with a pretty seventeen-year-old CORE girl from New Orleans. She took the hand with some puzzlement. "My prayers are with you, Doris," I said. "Have a safe trip, and when it's over, we'll get together and decide what we have to do next to finish the job."

Doris Castle's eyes, strafed with fear, became huge balls of terror. "You're coming with us, aren't you, Jim?" she whispered. I went through my prearranged litany of excuses: I'd been away from the office for four weeks; my desk was piled high with papers. People would be angry with CORE if they got no timely response to their letters, would not contribute money. Someone had to raise money to fuel these buses, to keep the revolution going. As national director, I had a solemn responsibility to mind the store. All of us want to be where the action is, but no such luck. Some of us are stuck with the dull jobs, the supportive ones. I could not be there in person, but she knew I'd be there in spirit.

Eyes wide, she shook her head slowly, brushing away all my words. Brain did not believe what ears were hearing. She spoke softly, in a stage whisper. But the words hit like a trip-hammer, driving me, it seemed, partway into the pavement. "Jim. *Please.*"

"Get my luggage," I shouted to a CORE staffer standing nearby. "Put it on the damn bus. I'm going."

Doris didn't smile, she just looked. And she suddenly looked tired. Kids grow up fast under fire, and sometimes grow old. Like in war.

In addition to the kids, six reporters were aboard. This was *the* story of the day. The headlines. TV. No reporter worth his salt would miss it, whatever the risk. On their faces was the expectancy of great by-lines, immortal photos.

Six Alabama National Guardsmen were on the bus, too. With rifles and fixed bayonets. Their hearts, no doubt, were on the other side. Which way would they point their guns? I wondered.

Helicopters chopped overhead, scanning the woods and roads. Attorney General Bobby Kennedy had moved at last. He had ignored the Freedom Ride until the bus was burned at Anniston and blood was splattered over Alabama and headlines screamed the tale all over the world. I had rejected his call for a halt and a cooling-off period.

But he had moved. State police sirens howled up and down the highway, warning Klansmen that they were outgunned. The feds were watching.

As wheels pounded concrete, a lavender haze fogged my brain. I longed for rest. Some of the kids were writing something. Diaries? No. We don't write; we talk. I looked, and it was names and addresses of next of kin. The young men stuffed those grim messages in their pockets; the women, in their bras.

I dozed. When the senses can endure no more, mercifully, they cut off.

Later, I was told that we had not stopped at Selma as planned for there had been a mob waiting—with chains, clubs, and guns. We would have to stop at Jackson, for that was our destination. What would be waiting there?

Mississippi's governor, Ross Barnett, had been on the airwaves and television for several days, urging the rural folk, the "red-necks," to stay home and let the law take its course. Whoever violated their sacred segregation laws would be duly punished. But by the law. I felt, of course, that Governor Barnett was not concerned for our lives, but for his state's image while he romanced northern industry. If we got ourselves killed, let it be not on his turf, but across the state line.

But who or what could control the haters? The governor? The president? The spirit of Gandhi? Or the barrel of a gun!

The wheels rolled and I tossed in the reclining seat. The state line, and that fabled sign: "WELCOME TO THE MAGNOLIA STATE."

The bus pulled off the road onto the shoulder and stopped. We had no forewarning of this, so anxiety reigned. The Guardsmen showed no concern. The reporters and photographers stiffened to an alert, their pads and pencils and cameras at the ready. The Freedom Riders all looked at me, searching for a cue. I tried to remain emotionless.

The driver of the bus left and was replaced by another. The Alabama National Guardsmen left and were replaced by a Mississippi contingent. The director of public safety of the state of Alabama, Floyd Mann, boarded the bus and whispered a message into the ear of one of the reporters. He then left the bus and the privileged reporter passed his new knowledge on to the other five. Those five then left the bus.

The door was closed and the wheels rolled again. I asked the remaining reporter what the message had been.

"I was informed," he replied, "that this bus will be ambushed and destroyed inside the Mississippi border." The Freedom Riders' eyes were on me, questioning. I relayed the ominous report.

I forced a smile, as though everything were under control. They smiled back.

We rolled on. One young man, Hank Thomas, burst into song to break the tension:

> I'm a-takin' a ride
> On the Greyhound bus line
> I'm a-ridin' the *front seat*
> To Jackson, this time.

Everyone joined lustily in the chorus:

> Halleluja, I'm a travelin'
> Halleluja, ain't it fine?
> Halleluja, I'm a travelin'
> Down freedom's main line.

The next stanza:

> In Nineteen Fifty-four,
> The Supreme Court has said,
> Looka here, Mr. Jim Crow
> It's time you were dead.

And we felt better: song stiffens the spine. Sleep was gone. This was Mississippi.

We reached a heavily wooded area. On both sides of the road, great forest. One could almost see the water moccasins and hear the rattlesnakes. Huge oak trees rose in majesty from the swamplands, laden with moss. The foliage was dense.

I imagined runaway slaves a century ago, sloshing through water and hiding behind trees as they fled pursuing hounds. Visions of Harriet Tubman and the Underground Railroad. Visions, too, of black bodies swinging, with bulging eyes and swollen tongues.

National Guardsmen flanked the highway, rifles pointed toward the forests. Audible to us in the bus was an order shouted by an officer over a bullhorn: "Look behind every tree!"

This clearly was where the ambush was expected. It did not come.

When the bus pulled into Jackson, there was an eerie stillness. The streets were nearly deserted. Maybe Ross Barnett had succeeded. Or maybe everyone was at the bus terminal. Waiting for us.

We pulled into the terminal. And there it was. The huge crowd of white men, standing there. Solemn, unexpressive faces. Just standing.

"This is it," I thought. "But it's what we came for; we can't sit here and hide."

I made my way down the steps of the bus. A Nashville student, Lucretia Collins, followed me out the door and linked arms. Her soft nearness was reassuring, and her faint fragrance comforted me.

The crowd curiously did not attack, but divided, forming a passageway to the "white" waiting room. They knew where we were going. Head high, I looked to neither side, trying to conceal my apprehension.

(That crowd, I later learned, was made up of federal agents, plain-clothes policemen, and media people. Ross Barnett's appeal had worked.)

Lucretia and I, arm in arm, crossed the "white" waiting room, sipped from the "white" water fountain, and walked to the "white" restaurant entrance.

And there was Captain Ray, blocking the doorway. He asked my name and nodded slightly when I told him. Three times he ordered us to "move on," and three times I refused, on grounds of the Supreme Court decision in the Boynton case.* He asked me if we understood his order and I replied, "Perfectly."

It was all very civilized; the nation was watching through newsreel cameras. Bigotry had many faces, and unlike Alabama, where Klan hooliganism had been allowed to run amok, Mississippi was putting its best face forward.

When the captain ordered the arrest and commanded us to the patrol wagon, a grimace swept Lucretia's features and quickly vanished. "What are the charges?" I asked.

He looked at the ceiling momentarily, then replied, "Disturbing the peace, disobeying an officer, and inciting to riot."

My companion and I turned, followed the waiting policeman, and climbed into the patrol wagon. The wagon filled quickly with youthful Freedom Riders directed there by Captain Ray's thrusting forefinger. The doors were slammed shut and latched, and the wagon leaped forward toward jail. The quiet of the city was violated by the siren of the squad car escorting us. Somehow, the sirens of Jackson seemed fiercer and angrier than any I'd ever heard.

Suddenly, the air was rent with another sound exploding through the barred windows of the paddy wagon. "We Shall Overcome" came first, and we sang at the top of our lungs, as though shouting to straining ears in cotton fields and shacks on plantations in the far reaches of the state. It was Lucretia who had said, "Let's sing," and then, "Louder, louder."

The greatest fervor was reserved for the stanza "We are not afraid. We are not afraid. We are not afraid, today. Oh, deep in my heart, I do believe, we shall overcome, someday."

*Boynton v. Virginia, 1960, in which the Court ruled that segregation according to race in the use of bus terminal facilities used by interstate passengers was unconstitutional.

I wished, I must confess, that singing it could make it so. It almost did. We sang loudly to silence our own fears. And to rouse our courage. There is no armor more impenetrable than song.

The wagon drew to a halt. Its doors were unlatched and we filed out. Camera eyes blinked. Two dozen policemen with rifles stood at alert. We were silently motioned through the door of the Jackson City Jail. In single file, we entered through the cordon of protectors.

As the door closed behind us, it shut out the smell of magnolia blossoms.

It also locked out civility.

CHAPTER 2

WHICH SIDE ARE YOU ON?

THE FOURTH ESTATE, OUR chief protection, was not there in the Jackson City Jail. The pads brought out when we entered were not note pads of reporters, but ink pads for fingerprinting. The only camera, for mug shots; the only interviews, interrogations—bristling and hostile.

The police processing us made no attempt to hide their hatred and frustration at being forced to exercise even a modicum of restraint. Their habit, beyond doubt, was to beat and even kill blacks with impunity, and they baited us, digging for an excuse to indulge the habit. No real provocation was needed. Our presence, challenging what was beyond challenge, was provocation enough. But Washington was watching now, and they had their orders. They had better not take liberties with the hated Kennedys.

They needed no excuse, though, to hurl epithets. We were called niggers and black bastards and threatened with billy clubs. A particularly red-faced cop fingered his holstered revolver when one youth breathed up into his face, "I'm not a nigger. I'm a *Negro.*" I froze, and relaxed only when one of the policeman's peers tapped him on the shoulder, shaking his head. I cautioned our group to patience and forbearance, for we had a long ordeal ahead of us.

A young minister in clerical collar smiled when called "boy" by his interrogator and quietly said, "My church generally ordains *men*, not boys." The officer leaped to his feet, billy club aloft: "I'll knock yo' fuckin' black nappy head through that goddamn wall if you don't shut yo' goddamn mouth, nigger." I held my breath. The minister, the Reverend C. T. Vivian, smiled even more broadly, looking the officer coolly in the eye. The policeman sat down, deprived of the opening he sought.

That we were making this challenge in Mississippi was beyond the comprehension of our interrogators. They tried to extract from each one of us a confession that we were communists, drug addicts, homosexuals, we didn't know what we were doing, or we were being paid by some organization to do it. "Niggers don't do things like this," they kept saying.

I was treated with a kind of sullen caution, if not a begrudging deference—almost like a captured general. The word evidently had come down. I was called neither "nigger" nor "boy"; not even "uncle," a favorite appellation for older black males. In fact, they didn't call me anything; they just spoke, looking everyplace except at me.

The photographing, fingerprinting, and questioning seemed interminable. Shortly, as other buses arrived, more Freedom Riders came in. They only fanned the fury of these minions of the law. The hole in the dike had not been sealed by Captain Ray's finger; it was growing bigger.

Some of the new insurgents were whites who had been recruited by CORE. They were arrested by Captain Ray in the "colored" waiting room, but were processed separately. Segregation did not end at the jailhouse door. Two of the white Freedom Riders paused at the open door of the room where we were, started to walk in, and were jerked back. They grinned and gave us the V for Victory sign before being roughly shoved on.

Our group broke into loud applause and shouts of "All right." Then the irrepressible and thunderous singing. It was the second stanza of "We Shall Overcome."

> Black and White together
> Black and White together
> Black and White together, now,
> Oh-oh, deep in my heart,
> I do believe,
> We shall overcome someday.

Like an echo, the same words blasted back at us from down the corridor. Then there was scuffling down there and some poundings of fists against flesh and the singing stopped.

In *our* room, our tormentors began rushing around in panic, waving billy clubs over their heads, shouting, "Cut out that noise. Cut it out, *Now!*"

When we finished the chorus, we stopped singing. And we felt good. There were lumps, I'm sure, in all of our throats, and tears in more than a few eyes. That we had obeyed the command to stop singing did not bother us at all. The cops suddenly seemed irrelevant. We had the boost we needed. We could face anything now. We were not alone.

Soon, there were too many of us for the Jackson City Jail, so they prepared to move us to the Hinds County Jail. Though it was only across the street, the preparation was as if for doomsday. It was a midnight operation and our pathway was flanked by Jackson's finest, shoulder-to-shoulder, armed with rifles, shotguns, and submachine guns—wary, no doubt, of a sudden Klan attack. Other police stood in readiness down the streets, and silhouettes were visible on rooftops. An ambulance idled at the curb.

I led the procession, trying my best to exude confidence for the benefit of those who followed. The sweat dripping from my face was from the Mississippi heat, I hoped all would believe, not from anxiety.

Still cameras flashed and television cameras whirred under blazing lights. Yes, the nation was watching now, and the state wanted no accident to happen.

In the county jail, we black male Freedom Riders occupied one cell block, with enough two-bunk cells and a common room. There was a john in the quarters and one wash bowl in the common room. So inadequate were the sanitation facilities, that body odors soon permeated the place. It was not long before nostrils rebelled and stopped sending their messages of offensiveness to our brains.

I wondered aloud how our white counterparts were faring, somewhere in the same jail.

One Nashville student sneered, "Oh, they prob'ly have a suite of rooms with hot and cold running maids; 'If you're white, you're right; if you're brown, stick around; if you're black, get back.'"

Others jumped in, all talking at once. "Man, you gotta be from the North; you don't know nothing about the South. If they're on our side, they'll get their asses kicked more than us. They always do. Man, the whites caught more hell riding through Alabama than the Negroes did. They almost got killed. Ain't that right, Jim? You tell him about it, Jim," said a slight, bony youth, Bernard Lafayette, whom I called "Little Gandhi." He looked exactly as Gandhi must have looked at twenty, and he sat on the floor, cross-legged, contemplating like the little brown man of India who, with passive resistance, had brought the British Empire to heel.

I agreed with his observation.

Each one had an anecdote to prove it: "On our picket line last month in Memphis, we got pushed around by the red-neck cops, but the whites got their heads split open."

"Remember that sit-in in Nashville in March? When they got through with us, all we needed was some Band-Aids and some rubbing alcohol. But, man, the whites had to go to the hospital."

"Yeah, man, the whites are looked at like traitors to their race, on top of everything else."

That settled, I wondered about the women, black and white, also somewhere in the building—and also segregated.

One skinny youth said, "Well, they better not touch *my* girl."

No one wanted to talk much about what might happen to the women. Imaginations were running wild.

A Nashville Bible student, James Bevel (referred to as "Bible Student" throughout) began clapping his hands in rhythm, and his song filled the room, spilling out the windows onto the 2:00 A.M. Jackson streets. And everyone joined in, hands clapping.

The jailer rushed to our cell block, eyes red from lack of sleep. Trembling with nervousness, he shouted, "Y'all will have to stop that singing. It's two o'clock, and if you wake up those people out there in the city, no telling what they gonna do to you. Now we don't want nothing like that to happen. And the other prisoners wanna sleep, too, and they can't sleep with all that noise."

An athletic youth from Nashville, LeRoi Wright, six foot two and 190 pounds (referred to as Six-Two throughout), swung his fist toward the ceiling and yelled, "Come on, let's sing some more. Let's let 'em know we're here and let 'em know who we are."

They needed no urging:

> If you can't find me in the backa the bus;
> You can't find me nowhere,
> Oh-h, come on up to the fronta the bus,
> I'll be ridin' up there.

> I'll be ridin' up there—up there,
> I'll be ridin' up there.
> Oh-h come on up to the fronta the bus;
> I'll be ridin' up there.

We sang it over. And over. Women's voices wafted through the doors and crevices of another wing, with the same song. From another floor, white Freedom Riders answered, changing a few words:

> If you can't find me in the fronta the bus;
> You can't find me nowhere,
> Oh-h, come on back to the *backa* the bus;
> I'll be ridin' back there.

> I'll be ridin' back there—back there;
> I'll be ridin' back there.
> Oh-h, come on back to the *backa* the bus;
> I'll be ridin' back there.

Sound then blasted from still another corner of the jail, the white women's quarters—some voices breaking as *they* belted out the song.

The jailhouse rocked with songs of the Freedom Riders. Predawn Jackson had never heard the likes of it before.

We were all hyper from the adrenaline pumping madly through our bodies. We had raced into the bowels of the never-never land. And we were still alive. If only we could keep the momentum of this drive going, southern segregation was doomed!

A black jail trusty watching us from outside the cell came close to the bars and whispered, "Come here close. I can't talk loud."

Everyone went to the bars.

"Don't you tell nobody who told you this. If you do, they'll kill me."

We promised, then the trusty related his extraordinary tale. Some officials of Mississippi had tried secretly to get hardened black convicts in the state, long-termers, to meet the Freedom Ride buses at the terminal and beat the riders severely as they disembarked. In return, the prisoners would be given reduced sentences or early parole. One lifer had agreed to the deal, but all of the others had refused. So the plan was aborted.

"I know it was true," whispered the trusty, "cause a friend of mine, my boon coon, my main man, was one of those asked, and he told me about it. And he don't lie. Not to me."

The men in the cell block stood in stunned silence.

What a coup that would have been for Mississippi. What a public relations bonanza for the state. Imagine the nationwide headlines: "FREEDOM RIDERS AXED BY MISSISSIPPI BLACKS." The whole South would have been vindicated. "Our colored people are happy the way things are," they always said; "they don't want those outside agitators coming down here stirring up trouble." This would have proved it!

What words could I have found to counter that stroke of tactical brilliance? The explanation would have been simple, yet nothing could have erased the indelible image such a tragedy would have stamped on the movement.

The cell block was sobered, and I suggested that we try to get some sleep. Our adversary was crafty and tomorrow might hold more surprises. We had to be alert.

Morning came early with a breakfast of cold grits with a dab of grease and a piece of fatback. And biscuits so hard that the men tossed them around the common room in mock baseball double-play action.

Lunch was no better. It was so bad that it inspired several to announce a hunger strike—a fast "till death" to protest segregation on the buses or segregation in the jail, or simply to protest our imprisonment.

The enthusiasm of these college students ran high and they were full of Mahatma Gandhi and imbued with a sense of history in the making. But clearly there was too little discipline and not enough maturity for such a decision. I tried to talk them out of it by reminding that "till death" meant not until some romantic, fictional tomorrow, but *until you die.*

That persuaded most, but two persisted in the idea—one's fast lasting two days, the other's two meals.

Our trial was perfunctory, and the verdict instantaneous: one year in jail for everyone. I urged all who could to remain in jail for forty days, the maximum one could serve and still file an appeal in Mississippi. We wanted to fill up the jails and place as great a burden on the state as possible, for as long as we could. Perhaps segregation would be seen as too heavy an albatross for the ship of state to bear.

All were aware of the jail-filling tactic of the Ride—a step beyond the lunch counter sit-ins of the year before, where the jailed were sprung as soon as bail could be arranged—and most eagerly agreed to stay in. The "forty days and forty nights" seemed somehow symbolic. A few, of course, had personal commitments and obligations that precluded a long stint behind bars. CORE bailed them out as quickly as needed.

For those who stayed, the days wore heavily with boredom and the youthful longing for the sensory excitements of the world outside. Tempers grew short; arguments and even fights occurred. A smaller man, for instance, raised a chair to smash Six-Two. How our captors would have loved the spectacle of a Freedom Rider hospitalized by Freedom Rider violence. I jumped between the two. The chair was returned to its place on the floor and the warriors separated.

Each day during the first week was an eternity. Bible Student announced categorically that if we continued to sing and shout, like Paul and Silas, the jail doors indeed would open and we, too, would walk out. This miracle, he informed us, would be wrought within forty-eight hours.

"Where're the bail bonds coming from?" I asked.

"God don't need no bail," Bible Student replied.

The more the others taunted and laughed their disbelief, the more withdrawn and brooding he became. As the deadline approached, and passed, Bible Student sat alone most of the time, apparently feeling betrayed by the God of biblical miracles.

A few who had pledged to stay inquired of me privately if CORE could bail them out right away because they wanted to go home.

On one of his daily visits to us, I instructed our lawyer, Jack Young, to bail out two Riders—one black, one white—every other day and set up a press conference for them. In addition to releasing those who wanted to get out, the controlled bail-out also would provide us with a protective shield; any brutality in jail would be quickly exposed. Our numbers inside would continue to grow, for I had sent instructions to my staff to keep Riders coming into Jackson on virtually every bus. Some came by train or plane and then rushed to the bus terminal restaurant to keep their rendezvous with Captain Ray.

Morale got a boost with each new arrival. Applause and singing accompanied every lift of spirit. Many of the new recruits were not schooled in nonviolence. So the Reverend Jim Lawson proposed a daily workshop in the common room on nonviolence and Gandhi. This was promptly instituted and he and I alternated in leading the sessions.

Early one morning, after breakfast, the jailer came to the bars of the cell block slightly bug-eyed. "Mr. Farmer," he called.

I walked to the bars.

"You got a visitor," he announced in hushed tones.

"You mean Jack Young, our lawyer?" I said.

"No," he replied. "Somebody else."

"But I thought we weren't allowed any visitors except our lawyer."

"That's what I thought, too," he shrugged, "but they let *this* man in. They sent him over here from across the street."

I glanced at the other Freedom Riders, and they stood still, or sat upright, braced for trouble. Who was this mystery caller? Friend or foe? Was this another cunning ploy by our captors?

"Maybe it's the KKK with machine guns," Six-Two said, "and we ain't got no place to run." I motioned him to silence.

Moments later, my visitor walked to the bars. Roy Wilkins, smiling. Nattily attired in a crisp, white Palm Beach suit, tan shirt and shoes, and white tie, striped with red.

I stood still, looking at Roy, my face surely mirroring my surprise. Why had they let him in? Were they awed by the head of the vaunted NAACP? Or maybe they thought this established leader would tell us to come out of jail and stop this "wild stuff" and go back to familiar terrain—working in the courts.

As I stood there, flashing through my mind was the vision of Roy twenty years earlier, along with Thurgood Marshall, disguised as a sharecropper, investigating a lynching on a plantation in Mississippi. Then, his long, artistic fingers—a dead giveaway despite the field hand's clothing— had blown his cover. Furthermore, this proud man could not possibly have shuffled convincingly.

Roy had not thought the Freedom Ride a good idea. He thought it would be suicidal and had tried tactfully to dissuade me. How well I remembered that conversation. I'd made an appointment with him and gone to his office at 20 West Fortieth Street in New York. He sat behind his huge mahogany desk piled high with papers, all in neat stacks. The desk was on a slightly raised platform so he peered down at his guests. He leaned back in his high-backed executive chair, swiveled to one side, and his long fingers gracefully moved an expensive cigar to and from his mouth.

After I'd explained the plan of the Freedom Ride, he frowned. "Jim," he said, "I respect your intelligence and admire your guts. But this plan of yours will mean, at the very least, mass arrests with high bail bond, exorbitant lawyers' fees, and enormous costs for multiple appeals piled on top of multiple appeals.

"Why? Why do you want to do that when money is scarce? All we really need is one good test case so we can fight it out in the courts and put an end to segregated travel in this country, just as we reduced the concept of segregated schools to ashes."

"Roy," I answered, "we've had test cases and we've won them all and the status remains quo. I have a dozen letters on my desk from Negroes saying that they had tried to ride in the front of the bus or use terminal facilities without segregation as the Supreme Court has said they have a right to do, and they were jailed, or beaten, or both. Despite the court rulings, nothing has changed. We've got to force the federal government to act to enforce its laws over state laws."

"Is Martin going?" he asked.

"I don't know," I replied. "I haven't asked him yet, but I probably will in a few days."

The next day, Wilkins called to say that he'd spoken by phone with his Mississippi staff leader, Medgar Evers, and Medgar thought the Freedom Ride a bad idea and hoped we wouldn't come to Mississippi. I told Roy that I'd send a member of my staff into Mississippi if we got that far, and hoped that my man and Medgar could work well together.

Roy replied softly, "You're making a big mistake, Jim. Give it a lot of thought."

And that had ended the conversation.

Yet, here he was, with a full heart and two books in his hand as gifts to help me pass the prison hours. One was Harper Lee's *To Kill a Mockingbird.* I walked to him and we embraced through the bars.

He said, "You look all right, Jim, but you need a shave."

I smiled and thanked him for the books.

"You've really shaken them up, fellow," said he. "I'm watching closely and if I can be of any help, if you need anything at all, just have Jack Young give me a call."

Everyone in our cell block came up and shook his hand. He and I embraced again and he turned and walked out. We all stared after him.

As soon as Wilkins had left, the jailer came back in, still bug-eyed. "That man, Wilkins, he's a *big* nigra, ain't he?"

"One of the biggest."

"Like Martin Luther King?" he asked.

I nodded.

He was clearly impressed as he slowly shook his head and departed.

Once again there was an explosion of song, joined by the other groups in other quarters—black females, white females, white males. We sang and sang, and then paused to catch our breath.

We heard a voice softly calling from upstairs: "Hey, Freedom Riders."

We all rushed to the window nearest the sound.

"Freedom Riders" the voice continued, "if you teach us your songs, we'll teach you ours."

Needless to say, we complied. They were taught freedom songs and we learned work songs, protest songs, unfamiliar gospel songs. One man upstairs had a magnificent voice and a style that defied description. I asked his name, wrote it down, and promptly lost it.

Earlier, I had requested that the jailer put us in with other black prisoners; we did not like being isolated from our brothers—separated like lepers, from the other prisoners. The jailer had replied, "No, we can't do that. Them other nigras would kill y'all. They know their place and they hate y'all for coming down here stirrin' up trouble."

I didn't believe that and said we would gladly take our chances with our brothers. His answer still had been emphatically no. (I had suspected, of course, that the real fear was that we might contaminate the convicts, turning them into Freedom Riders.)

Now, contact had been made with our anonymous brothers, at their initiative. We felt good. We knew which side they were on.

Our communication with the floor above did not escape the notice of the authorities. The jailer rushed to our cell block, shouting, "If you boys don't stop that singing right now, the store ain't gonna come to this cell block no mo'."

What a compelling threat! The "store" was a cart of goodies for sale, wheeled in by a trusty. It dispensed candy, chewing gum, potato chips, pretzels, pork skins, and most other junk food. And cigarettes. This little luxury each day made the next day somehow more bearable in anticipation.

When the threat was made, some faces fell. It was Little Gandhi this time who started our musical response.

> Ain't gonna let nobody turn me 'round,
> Turn me 'round, turn me 'round.
> Ain't gonna let nobody turn me 'round.
> Gonna keep on decidin'
> To keep on a-ridin'
> Ridin' to the Promised Land.

"That does it," yelled the jailer as he walked out, "no mo' store!"

Bible Student said, "I have a plan."

Rushing to the communication window, he called upward, "Hey, upstairs!"

"Yeah, Freedom Riders."

Bible Student explained our punishment and learned that they faced no similar reprisals. He disclosed a simple plan: each day before time for the store, we would make a list of desired items, and that list and the money, wrapped in a handkerchief, would be pulled upstairs by a string, which our friends would lower from their window to ours.

The scheme was accepted and it worked. We even got our change back. The goodies never tasted so good before.

The next day's mail brought a letter from my wife. It was a joyous letter. Lula had known my fears and understood them and was filled with pride when informed by my staff that I had taken the ride to Jackson. And when she learned from the news that her husband was safely behind bars, that pride was mixed with overwhelming relief.

Friends had come over to our Greenwich Village apartment and had celebrated. Lula related that one had said, "Jim really did it. I know he was scared, but he did it anyway." Another had raised his glass for a toast—a toast to Thoreau—and recounted the familiar Emerson-Thoreau anecdote: "Emerson, seeing Thoreau in jail, cried, 'Thoreau, my dear friend. What in the world are you doing in there?' Thoreau replied, 'Emerson, my dear friend. What in the world are you doing out there? This is the place for honest men in times like these.'"

Then my wife's guest had lowered his glass and asked, "How many of you have your bus tickets?"

"Buses are too slow," came one response. "Let's fly down and then go to the bus terminal." Three friends left the party to pack their bags.

In the civil rights movement jail was not a punishment, but a triumph. This perception had rubbed off on my two-year-old daughter, Tami. I could almost hear Lula chuckling as she wrote.

> I was taking Tami for a walk and every time we passed someone, she would look up at them and announce excitedly, "My daddy's in *jail*." Most of the people we met, of course, were neighbors, and they knew who Tami was and had seen your picture in the papers being arrested in Mississippi.

> They all smiled or laughed and patted Tami on the head and wished me well. The others, thinking the little girl's father must have committed some crime, frowned and clucked their tongues. They looked at me and shook their heads, and seemed astonished by the smile on my face. I didn't bother to explain, for if there is anyone today who is not aware of what is going on in this country, words would be wasted.

All the riders enjoyed Lula's letter. They enjoyed equally the cover of *Jet* magazine, with its pictures of Wilkins, King, Elijah Muhammed, and me—and the title: "WHO SPEAKS FOR THE NEGRO?" I was so glad I'd boarded that bus in Montgomery. Thank God for Doris Castle and her pleading words.

The jailer came to the cell block, a little tentatively this time, and called me: "Mr. Farmer, there's a preacher in town who comes here every Sunday to preach to the inmates and to pray for them. Well, he'll be here tomorrow, and he'd like to preach to you so-called Freedom Riders when he comes. Will y'all listen to him?"

I consulted with the other men, and we agreed to hear the preacher if he would entertain questions at the conclusion of his sermon.

"Why does he want to preach to us anyway," asked Six-Two, "when he prob'ly doesn't even think we have souls?"

The next morning, the preacher came. With him were several others, with Bibles and hymnals. They sang and prayed, and we joined in. One read the Scripture. Then the minister preached a sermonette.

"Are you ready for questions, Reverend?" I asked, when the sermon appeared to be finished.

"Yes," came the reverend's drawl.

"Are you a minister, sir?" was my first question.

"Yes."

"Do you have a church?"

"Yes."

"Does your church have any black members?"

"No."

"Well, now. Could a black Christian join your church if he wanted to?"

"No."

The preacher was not at all shaken when the Freedom Riders snickered their contempt. Bible Student was hard-pressed to hold his peace, but all had agreed that I would do the questioning. And I had not finished.

"Can black Christians worship in your church if they wish?"

"No."

"Didn't Jesus preach that all men are born of one blood?"

"Yes."

"Do you see any contradiction there?"

"No," the preacher answered. "The only question is, do you *believe?* Have you been washed in the blood of the Lamb?"

Bible Student stood and stamped his foot hard in disgust, spun around once, and sat back down violently, a frown furrowing deep in his forehead.

"Thank you, sir," I said and left the bars and walked back into the common room. The preacher and his coterie departed.

Inevitably, that encounter produced a spirited discussion on the absurdity of fundamentalist Christianity's basic dichotomy between faith and works, belief and deeds. Those young, black college students were stunned by the hypocrisy of loving Christ and unashamedly viewing un-Christlike social behavior as irrelevant. The discussion was interrupted by the appearance of the trusty at the bars.

He looked behind him to be sure there was no one else within earshot. His message riveted the men to their seats: "They haven't told you guys, yet, and they won't tell y'all till the last minute, but tomorrow midnight they gonna transfer y'all to the Hinds County Prison Farm."

"Is that bad or good?" somebody asked.

"The food's good, but the treatment's terrible. It's one of the worst places this side a hell. They're gonna whip yo' asses out there. Try to break you."

We thanked him. When our lawyer, Jack Young, came the next day, he had not heard of the transfer and responded with a low whistle of concern.

"That place is rough. You're going to have trouble there," he said.

I asked him to arrange to get one person out on bail within a few hours after our arrival at the prison farm and to set up a press conference for him and see that he called the FBI, if necessary.

Jack had two interesting bits of intelligence for us. He reported that the Mississippi Bureau of Investigation had sent agents throughout the nation seeking derogatory information on each Freedom Rider who had come into the state. He also informed us that Mississippi was hurting: the state had announced that its auto-use tax—one of the nuisance taxes scheduled for early elimination—could not be canceled because the Freedom Rides were costing them so much money in beefing up their police, investigation, and prison forces. And no end was in sight.

That news evoked a lusty cheer from the cell block.

Time passed heavily on that Monday afternoon as we awaited some official word on the transfer. I thought of Hamlet's soliloquy: We hated our present abode, but at least by now it had the comfort of being known to us. Now we were about to race into the unknown. What horrors would it hold? Why did they speak of the prison farm in hushed voices? We would rather "bear those ills we have than fly to others that we know not of."

Little Gandhi called upstairs from the window, "Hey, upstairs."

"Whatcha want, Freedom Riders?"

"They're going to send us to the Hinds County Prison Farm."

A long silence from upstairs increased our anxiety. Finally, a voice: "Aw, y'all'll be all right. I been there. Jus' don' give them screws no cause to do nuthin' to ya."

The jailer came to the cell block. We thought, of course, that he had come with the official word. But, no, he just wanted to talk.

His usual salutation summoned me to the bars. "How y'all feeling?"

I told him not bad, but we'd feel a lot better if they'd just let us all out, drop the charges, and serve us in the bus terminal restaurant without any commotion. Then I told him that I could stop the Freedom Rides, at least on buses in Mississippi.

"Mr. Farmer, you know good'n well they ain't gonna do that," he said, a bit sadly, I thought. He quietly continued: "Maybe when my grandchildren grow up, they'll do something like that. Lot 'a the young people down here don't feel like the old folks do; these things ain't goin' to go on forever. They cain't.

"Them boys with you is good boys," he continued. "They ain't criminals. They hadn't oughta be in jail here. They ain't done nothing—they ain't killed nobody, or robbed, or raped. They just wanta be treated like everybody else." He lowered his eyes and his chin quivered. He knew of the imminent transfer, no doubt, but was not aware that I shared that knowledge.

He went on: "If I was a ni—If I was colored, I'd be doin' the same thing as them boys is. I understan' these boys. But I cain't understan' them white boys up there. They can go anywhere they wanna go, they're white. What they come down here for?"

I ventured an answer: "Well, they believe, as Jesus said, that all men are brothers."

His glance was still averted and his shoulders shook. Reaching my arm through the bars, I patted his shoulder. The *jailed* comforting the *jailer!*

Our jailer shook his head slowly and walked out without looking back.

Thirty minutes later, a policeman entered the corridor. As he approached the bars, he commanded, "Get y'selves ready. Y'all gon be takin' a ride in a half hour."

CHAPTER 3

I'LL KEEP MY SOUL

A CARAVAN OF POLICE vans moved swiftly through the night with an escort of state and county police. Arriving at the county prison farm, we filed into the prison on order. Surrounded by guards, armed and ominous, we were herded together while the superintendent spoke to us.

Like an army sergeant spitting out orders, he told us that we were going to be put in our cells and the lights turned out for the night and there wasn't going to be any singing or any other noise. None at all! At six in the morning, we'd get breakfast. Then, one at a time, we'd be processed, and when asked questions we were going to answer "yes, sir" and "no, sir." There wasn't going to be any "yeah" or "naw." If anybody disobeyed this order, the guards standing by would correct his manners immediately. That was all.

As the cell gates slammed shut, I fervently hoped that attorney Jack Young remembered my request that he bail someone out quickly. Surreptitiously, we held a strategy conference, with each person's comments relayed from cell to cell. We readily agreed to forego singing for a day, and to reassess on the morrow. Then we tackled the issue at hand.

"I'd die before I'd say sir to these crackers," declared Six-Two. "I ain't gonna kiss *no* red-neck's ass."

"What's the big deal about saying sir?" asked Little Gandhi. "We say sir and ma'am to our professors and our parents and to a lot of people we don't even know, don't we?"

"Yeah," said someone else, "but these ain't our professors or our parents. These creeps want to see us dead."

"Right, but why you wanna take the bait and give them an excuse to kill us?"

"Man, they ain't going to kill nobody. They're just trying to scare us. If they killed any of us, Bobby Kennedy'd be down here the next day."

"Man, you know Bobby Kennedy ain't go'n bring his skinny ass down here. Or his brother, neither. They'd whip their butts, too."

"How they gonna whip their asses when they got the whole United States Army, Navy, and Marines to back 'em up?"

"They ain't never goin' to use all that to help *us.*"

"They might use it to help themselves, though."

"Well, if they don't come, I bet they'd send somebody. And that'd be the same thing."

Someone asked what I thought. Clearly, this was no time to pontificate; the pros and cons were both compelling, and the best response unclear to me. And broken heads were at stake.

I did not know what to do, but my gut reaction was to comply rather than be savaged over an issue of protocol instead of principle. But was this mere protocol when the method of addressing one another was the very essence of southern caste: the enforcement code of a racist society? Could we yield to this command and at the same time maintain dignity? Or would the next compromise, whatever it was, then come easier? Protocol could force one to bend the knee. Would there be a step-by-step process, eroding dignity and dragging us over the brink into the chasm of bowing and scraping, shuffling and scratching like many of the blacks down there? Who was strong enough or wise enough to draw the line where it could be moved no farther?

The fundamental issue was dignity. With that in mind, I tried, without confidence, to formulate an acceptable compromise.

"Let us keep our dignity at all costs. Why not say yes or no loudly. Then, after a brief pause, even more firmly, say sir. We will have complied with the letter of the command. But not its spirit. The *spirit* is the important thing."

Several riders said "Uh-huh." But Six-Two demurred: "Naw, I don't wanna compromise with no nigger-killin' racist bastards. Let's die like men insteada livin' like dogs."

Silence followed. No one else felt like venturing an opinion.

Clearly, there was no consensus. A unified policy was not available to us. Each was left to the counsel of his conscience and his God. I did ask, though, that each man processed reply loudly enough for us to hear, so we could prepare our response.

We slept fitfully and breakfast came early. Scrambled eggs, thick sliced country bacon, grits with a chunk of butter, hash brown potatoes, bread with a slab of butter, milk and coffee. And strawberry preserves.

"Maybe they're fattenin' us up for the kill," drawled Six-Two.

Two beefy guards lumbered down the corridor, stopped at one cell, and called out the name of one of its occupants. The Rider summoned walked out of the cell and disappeared down the corridor between the two guards.

None of us spoke a word, but all ears strained. We did not hear the question, but the answer came clear. "No," and then a louder "sir." The latter word was spat out with a vengeance. A long pause followed. Then the questioning continued.

After the interrogation, the Freedom Rider walked down the corridor accompanied by the guards, blackjacks in hand. "I did it, man," he whispered as he passed my cell. His meaning eluded the guards.

Next came the Reverend C. T. Vivian. This time, we heard the question: "Do you live in this state?" The answer was in a firm voice. And "sir" did not follow "no."

Almost instantly, came the sound of weapons against flesh. The thud of a slight body falling to the floor. Rapid voices, and the beating stopped. There was panic in the interrogation room. Moments later, male nurses were seen running through the corridor.

When C.T. was led back down the corridor, there were bandages over his right eye and his T-shirt was covered with blood. The huge guards, half carrying him, appeared frightened. There was a smile on C.T.'s face.

Those blackjacks—flat leather thongs stuffed with lead—were designed to beat into unconsciousness without leaving any telltale signs. But C.T.'s assailants had been overeager, striking with the edge of the weapon instead of its flush side. Blood had been shed.

After that, the processing was halted.

An hour later, Jack Young came with $500 bail-bond money for one Rider who had previously indicated a desire for release. The timing was exquisite! The Freedom Rider bailed out had his press conference and called the FBI.

Two hours after the bail-out, the FBI arrived, and the lions of the county farm became mice, scurrying about. There was a hang-dog look about them as they kowtowed to their superiors.

That night, we were transported back to the Hinds County Jail in Jackson without incident.

Our return to the county jail cell block was like a homecoming. A half-dozen new occupants were there, having arrived during our absence. They had been informed of our transfer to the county farm by the trusties and the upstairs prisoners—those non-Freedom Riders who now sang Freedom Rider songs. The homecoming was celebrated with more singing, joined by the other three Rider groups and, occasionally, by the upstairs inmates.

Some in our group swaggered triumphantly, like conquering heroes. We had met the enemies at the dreaded county farm, and they were *ours.* We had survived it with a minimum of brutalization. We had forced them to retreat. Our tormentors were tormented. We had twisted the tail of the lion and lived to tell the story. Even the upstairs fellows were impressed.

The new Riders had come from all over. One, a tall, skinny kid in his senior year at Howard University, possessed an infectious smile and enormous charm. We instantly felt that we'd known him always. But he seemed so pliant and easygoing, so quiet and so shy, that I told myself he would never make it in this world. His name was Stokely Carmichael.

Our new cellmates brought us current on the outside world. The Freedom Ride, we learned, had captured the nation's imagination more than we'd ever dreamed. Front pages were still full of it. It was the most popular topic of conversation at meetings, cocktail parties, and in the streets. A common greeting among both whites and blacks had become, "Hi. Got your bus ticket?" Buses had become instruments of the struggle.

We also were told that several prominent persons had demonstrated their solidarity by flying into Jackson to have their encounter with Captain Ray. They jailed in, bailed out, and returned to their respective labors. Among them were Percy Sutton, who later became borough president of Manhattan; Mark Lane, then a rising New York politician; and the Reverend Wyatt Tee Walker, executive secretary of the Southern Christian Leadership Conference (SCLC), Dr. King's organization.

That night, once again, we slept little. There were too many fast-moving experiences to recount, too many mental notes to compare.

When breakfast came, we thought of the county farm, maybe a bit wistfully this time. The trusty who brought those tin plates of outrage also brought something else: information that, during the next night, we would be taking another ride. This time to the state penitentiary at Parchman.

We'd all heard of Parchman, of course, the most fabled state prison in the South. But it held no terrors for these victors in the Battle of the County Farm.

The ride, as usual, was a fast one and the drivers of the vans less than gentle. Sudden stops sent us tumbling to the front, and jack-rabbit starts returned us in a heap to the rear.

When we arrived, we were ordered out, under heavy guard, as dozens of red-necks stood by, staring. In a negative kind of way, we were celebrities and they had come to watch, some somber-faced and some grinning. It would be something to tell their children and grandchildren.

We were led into a large basement room and told to take all our clothes off, including shoes and socks. We stripped off our clothes, and with them a measure of dignity. The red-necks outside jostled for position at the barred windows, gawking. We were consumed by embarrassment. We stood for ages—uncomfortable, dehumanized. Our audience cackled with laughter and obscene comments. They had a fixation about genitals, a preoccupation with size.

"Holy Christ," said one, "look a' that lil' nigger there! He got one like a hoss." A touch of envy was in his voice.

"But look a' that one," said another. "He ain't hardly got nuthin'. And that one there—ya cain't hardly see it."

"His ain't no bigger'n Jeff's."

Jeff demurred: "You know ah got more'n that. Ask yo mama!"

The sound of brief scuffling ensued outside the window. And a few shouts. Then more guffaws.

An old stereotype had just been exploded. Could it be that a few sexual fears were also allayed?

Fleetingly, I recalled a conversation with Whitney Young, head of the National Urban League. He'd said, "Jim, I see in the papers that you've been running all over the country demolishing racial myths. Well, there's one myth I don't want you to mess with; leave that one alone." We both had laughed.

Deputy Tyson, who was in charge, obviously enjoyed his role as impresario of this scene. He twanged his orders repetitively in a penetrating voice, amazingly high-pitched for his ample size.

"Awright," he sang out, "y'all all a time wanna march someplace. Well, y'all gon' march right now, right t' yo cells. An' Ah'm gon' lead ya. Follow me. Ah'm Martinlutherking."

Naked, in single file, we trekked through corridors and up a short flight of stairs. That march of the naked Freedom Riders took an eternity; clothes were an invention, I think, to conceal man from his own perception of himself. Their absence stripped off all pretense, and shorn of the make-believe, who can strut and posture?

We were given time to wallow in our nakedness. Eventually, guards brought clothing—a pair of undershorts for each of us. Unerringly, they were the wrong size—little ones for the large men, big ones for the small. All of us, large and small, had to grip cloth at our navels to keep shorts from dropping to the floor.

Little Gandhi shouted, "If your cellmate is a different size, switch shorts." A great idea, but it didn't work; our jailers had planned too well. Small men were bunked with small men. My roommate was two inches taller and four inches broader than I.

"It's indecent," Six-Two exclaimed.

"Makes us feel like animals," moaned someone else.

Bible Student said, "What's this hang-up about clothes? Gandhi wrapped a rag around his balls and brought the whole British Empire to its knees!"

His profundity silenced all grumbling. I had underestimated Bible Student. Ill-fitting shorts were transformed miraculously into a symbol of our mission.

That obsession with clothes eliminated, we examined our cells. About six by seven in size, each had two steel bunks, with thin straw mattresses, a john, and a washbasin. Period.

This was death row, and it had been cleared out for us. We were allowed no paper (except a roll of toilet paper), no pencils, no books. Neither were there goodies from a store. No cigarettes either, and some of us were chain smokers. The guards took pleasure in sauntering down the corridors, puffing deeply and blowing the smoke painstakingly into our cells.

Nicotine fits! Maybe, faced with necessity, we could quit. We'd all planned to do it before, but now our persecutors were our unwitting allies.

The food was worse than in the Hinds County Jail. I would not try a hunger strike; I was not convinced that was the appropriate tactic at this time. I would just stop eating, except for a taste of this or that. And a sip of the coffee, which was more like dishwater. Maybe I'd lose weight, if I could exercise, too. Without anything else to do in those tiny cells, at least exercise would kill time.

Hank Thomas, a lanky six-foot-four Howard University sophomore with the best voice in the whole place, became our impromptu song leader and director of calisthenics.

The singing went on at Parchman, and the group calisthenics, cell-to-cell, became a daily routine after breakfast. Each day, our numbers increased. We *were* filling up the jails.

Incoming white Freedom Riders were put in our cell block—at the far end, only partially segregated. This fact did not escape our attention. It provoked the anthem "We Shall Overcome," with emphasis on the "black and white together" stanza.

For Mississippi, that was not a surrender of principle. It was simply an acknowledgment that they were fast running out of cell space.

The white male Riders told us that the women were also in the same prison, in this maximum security unit, semisegregated. And their numbers were growing faster than that of the males. Each of them had been given a vaginal search by a female guard using the same rubber-gloved finger, without washing between searches.

We sighed. And ate the putrid meal served through the opening in the bars of each cell. Taste buds rebelled.

The quality of the repast drove Bible Student to prayer: "Let us all bow our heads. Father, forgive us for not offering thanks to Thee for the food we have just received. But we know that Thou hast allowed us to eat that slop in order to test our faith. Thou hast made us descend into hell that we might better appreciate heaven when we get there. Forgive us if we spew it off our tongues, and give us strength to survive even this punishment dished out by this God-forsaken state. We ask it all in Freedom's name. Amen."

Throaty amens echoed around the cell block.

"It oughta be against the law to give anybody crap like that," moaned Six-Two. "They hadda go out of their way to make food that bad."

"That's right, man," came several responses.

"Whatta you guys expect?" countered Hank Thomas. "This ain't the Waldorf-Astoria."

But Six-Two was irrepressible. "I know it ain't," he said, "but just the same, I think we oughta protest. Let's go on strike. Let's refuse to eat and refuse to talk and refuse to recognize any orders they give us until the food gets better."

"Yeah," shouted several others. "Let's protest prison segregation, too. And the way these people *talk* to us. And let's demand a voice in making some of the decisions in this hell-hole."

"Look, men," said Bob Singleton, a Freedom Rider from UCLA. "We didn't come here to improve the food or reform the prison system. We came to fill up the jails. Let's stick to one thing and take whatever this damn state can throw at us." He expressed my views precisely.

Hank Thomas boomed out, "Paul and Silas, bound in jail. Had nobody to go their bail. Keep your eyes on the prize. Hold on." Everyone joined in, including Six-Two.

Deputy Tyson rushed into the cell block, scooting around the corridor rapidly, shouting, "Now you boys goin' hav' to cut out that singin'. We ain't goin' have none of that here!"

That command, of course, was an invitation. The singing became louder. We went through our entire repertoire of Freedom Rider songs with Hank leading, until he called for me to start "Which Side Are You On?"

Tyson and his guards scurried about in confusion. The decision on how to stop our singing clearly had to be made higher up. There would be no repetition of the county farm, summoning the feds. They fairly ran out the door, expelled by the overwhelming sound enveloping the cell block. Someone would have to tell them what to do.

We sang until we were tired. Then sleep came easily in our bare cells, whose only luxury was the thin mattress on each steel bunk.

The next morning, we had an unannounced visitor who walked slowly around the U-shaped corridor that wrapped the rectangular cell block, looking into each cell. He paused in front of my cell. He was a small-boned man with an enormous potbelly and the sun-reddened, wrinkled neck of many middle-aged white southerners. Neatly dressed in a pale blue-gray seersucker suit, white shirt, and blue tie, he had an air of supreme self-assurance.

"What's your name?" he drawled, without rancor.

As I answered, I grasped in my fist the two ends of the unbuttoned waistband of my undersized shorts, holding them tight. He nodded and asked, "Are they treating you all right?"

"Well, there's been no physical brutality, if that's what you mean," I answered.

Again he nodded and asked, "No complaints?"

"Oh, there are complaints, all right," I said. "The biggest complaint is that we are *here*. We never should have been arrested for doing what the Supreme Court said we have a right to do."

Our visitor was too sophisticated, too genteel, too different from the men who had gawked through the barred windows of the basement room to be shocked by that statement. His face remained expressionless as he nodded again and walked slowly out the door without looking back.

"Jim," shouted one of the white Riders at the far end of the block. "Do you know who that was?"

I didn't know, so he yelled the answer, loud enough for all to hear: "Ross Barnett."

We sang a good-bye serenade to the governor: "Ain't Gonna Let No-

body Turn Me 'Round." Just in case Barnett was still within earshot, Hank
Thomas bellowed out my song, "Which Side Are You On?" We all thundered the second stanza:

> They say in Hinds County,
> No neutrals have they met.
> You're either for the Freedom Ride
> Or you Tom for Ross Barnett.

Deputy Tyson came back in, walking slowly this time and puffing on a
gargantuan cigar. Blowing billows of smoke into each cell, he spoke with
tight-jawed deliberation: "Now y'all gon' cut out that singin'! I ain't gon'
tell y' no mo'. But if y' don' cut it out, you'll wish you had! Now cut it out
right now!"

He said it several more times as he walked around the U-corridor and
back again. I wondered if he now had a plan. I could almost hear him
pleading with the governor. "But, Guv'nor, how we gon' stop their singin'
if we cain't go up 'side their heads?"

We stopped singing. Not because he ordered it, but because we were
hungry and it was chow time. Bad as the food was, it was better than
nothing.

Lunch came, delivered by black trusties, smoking cigarettes. Six-Two
asked a trusty in a loud whisper, "Hey, brother, how 'bout givin' me a
cigarette?"

The trusty looked away, embarrassed, and walked to the next cell. This
was Parchman, not Hinds County.

On the way back, the trusty stopped at Six-Two's cell, looked both ways,
then handed him not one cigarette, but two. Six-Two asked for a light.
The trusty lit both.

Six-Two took a long drag on both his prize possessions, then passed
each around the partition to the next cell—one right and one left.

When the butt reached me at the end of the row, little remained but the
filter. I inhaled deeply, filling my lungs. There was an immediate sensation
of giddiness as nicotine-starved cells soaked it up.

That night, I tossed on my thin-mattressed bunk, brooding about what
the prison response to the singing might be. Solitary confinement? That's
the penal system's supreme reprisal. They won't beat us. The feds from
the FBI would be down here. Yes, of course, it'll be solitary. How can I
stand that? A three-by-three hole with a hole in the floor—and not high
enough to stand up. I'll be screaming to get out. I'll go stark raving mad. I
can't even stand a small room if it's closed in, or a small airplane where I
can't stand up and stretch. I've been claustrophobic since I was seven,
since daddy punished me by locking me in a dark closet. I screamed then
and I'd scream now. And how will it be when they bring me back to my
cell, cowering, tail between my legs. Oh, God, maybe I can bite my tongue
and live through it—or die . . .

All thoughts were banished at last by the sweet embrace of sleep.

In the morning after the calisthenics ritual and breakfast, we sang some more, the songs summoning Deputy Tyson and his guards.

"I'm gon' tell you boys jus' one mo' time," he said. "If y' don' stop that singin' we gonna take away your mattresses. I asked ya nice an' ya wouldn' listen. So if there's any mo' singin' yo' mattresses gon' fly away." All the while, he was blowing smoke into each cell.

I thought, "Great. No solitary. At least not yet." But the singing stopped abruptly, and no one spoke for a long time.

Then Little Gandhi faced the malaise. "Look, men, we're all worrying about these thin, hard, stupid mattresses, because that's all we've got in this place. But these mattresses ain't anything but *things*. Things of the body. And we came down here for things of the *spirit*. Things like freedom and equality. And brotherhood. What's happening to us?"

"That's right," said Bible Student. "Satan put us in here for forty days and forty nights. To tempt us with the flesh. He's sayin' to us, 'If you'll just stop your singin' and bail outta there, I'll give you anything you want— soft, thick, cotton mattresses and down pillows and everything. Be good boys and I'll let you keep your mattresses. I'll let you have your lollipop.'"

The booming basso profundo of Hank Thomas thundered forth, "Guards! Guards! Guards!" Each time, the volume grew, and the bars almost rattled.

Tyson came through the door as if catapulted from a slingshot. He must have thought one of us was having a seizure.

"Come get my mattress," roared Hank. *"I'll keep my soul!"*

Instantly, song bounced off the walls and nearly split our own eardrums.

"We Shall Overcome." And this time, it was not slow like a funeral dirge, but quick and upbeat. Never before had I heard it sung with such powerful emphasis. Each beat was John Henry's sledgehammer. The prison walls were thick, so when we drew breath at the end of each line, we could scarcely hear the answering sound from the women's quarters of the maximum security unit.

Guards rushed around like ants, with black trusties obeying their every order, removing mattresses. One Rider lay on his mattress, hugging it, refusing to move. A heavily muscled black prisoner was brought in to remove him and pin him to the floor while the mattress was taken out.

When the mattresses were gone, it was like a heavy load lifted from our shoulders. We didn't have to sing for uplift. Our hearts sang.

After lunch, Deputy Tyson came into the corridor: "If you boys ain't gon' sing no mo', y' can have yo' mattresses back."

"Hey, Deputy Tyson," Little Gandhi called.

Tyson walked toward him and asked, "What you want, boy?"

"Since those mattresses are so valuable," Little Gandhi taunted, "why don't you auction them off and tell people that the Freedom Riders slept there. In that way, you can get back some of the money the Freedom Rides are costing you. And, we'll sing a little song at your auction, too." There was smile on the small one's face.

"You shut yo' mouth, boy." Tyson walked out, a bit crestfallen.

"Why does he always call us boy?" asked Six-Two. "Next time he comes in here, I'm gonna tell him I'm a *man*, not a boy. And if he don't stop callin' me boy, I'm gonna call him Deputy Boy."

Bob Singleton from UCLA cautioned, "Now, wait a minute, you guys. Tyson doesn't mean anything derogatory by it. That's just the way they talk down here."

Little Gandhi asked, "Do you think so? Well, I'm going to ask him the next time he comes in here."

"Let's ask him now. I know how to get 'im here." It was Hank Thomas and he started singing.

Deputy Tyson took the cue. "This the las' time I'm gon' tell you boys. There ain't gon' be no mo' singin' in here."

"Quiet, you guys," yelled Little Gandhi. "I want to ask Deputy Tyson something."

The singing stopped as Tyson looked toward Little Gandhi's cell.

"Deputy Tyson," asked Little Gandhi in a most serious voice, "do you mean anything derogatory when you call us boy?"

"I don' know nuthin' 'bout no 'rogatory," replied Tyson. "All I know is if you boys don' stop that singin', y'all gon' be singing' in the rain."

Hank led off with "Which Side Are You On?" and made up a new stanza as he went along:

> Ole *big* man Deputy Tyson said,
> I *don'* wanna cause you pain,
> But *if* you don't stop that singin'
> > now
> You'll be singin' in the rain!

The words had barely left our throats when a fire hose was dragged in and we were washed down.

"Next time you're gonna do that," sputtered Six-Two, "let us know so we can have the soap ready."

That night, everything in the cells was wet, spirits included. My cellmate and I wrung out our shorts and hung them over the washbasin to dry. Lying on my wet bare bottom on the wet bare lower bunk, I was freezing. Cold in July. In Mississippi. They had opened windows and turned on powerful exhaust fans to draw the chilling draft over our goose-pimpled bodies. By morning, many of us had sniffles and didn't feel like singing much. Maybe the punishment fit the crime!

A few days later, we learned that the state's director of prisons was coming to inspect things at Parchman. When Tyson came by, blowing his smoke, I asked for an appointment with his big boss when he arrived.

"Ah don' know, Mr. Farmer," he said. "Ah'll check it out and let y' know."

The other men and I conferred, cell-to-cell, on an agenda, just in case I got the appointment. I would not raise the question of the food; we had gotten used to that. Furthermore, some of us on the portly side were losing weight; the fare did not tempt us to overindulge. Nor would I complain about our mattresses or the drenching or the exhaust fans. It was singularly important to us that we sing. And, for whatever reasons, it was equally important to the prison authorities that we not. So far, we seemed to be winning that contest of wills; at least we were not losing. In fact, I would not gripe about any prison conditions or regulations, per se. As Singleton had observed a few days ago, our objective was to fill up the jails, not reform them. One thing at a time. Prison reform was a different struggle. Some other day some other troops must fight that war. But this was *our* fight.

All that we'd ask would be the same privileges other prisoners had. One that stuck in our minds was the right to the sun, to the out-of-doors. We were sick of the dank, cold, concrete-and-steel cells. Prison pallor had crept into our faces and we wanted to fill our lungs with fresh air, to feel the sun on our backs. We even wanted to work; we could learn to chop cotton, or pick it, or whatever else other prisoners did. And we needed the exercise.

Tyson unlocked my cell gate and said, "Awright, Mr. Farmer, come on. He'll see ya now."

I walked behind him, waving with one hand to the men in the cells up the row behind me. With the other hand, I held my undersize unbuttoned shorts up, padding barefoot along the concrete floor.

The director of prisons was a stereotype of the cotton-belt plantation owner. His middle-aged face and neck were wrinkled by exposure to the sun. The white Palm Beach suit was wrinkled, too. Small eyes squinted through gold-rimmed spectacles and white hair peeped from under the Panama on his head.

He lounged in a huge, overstuffed chair, legs crossed, flicking ashes from the inevitable cigar into a floor-standing ashtray.

I stood before him, holding my shorts up and trying to salvage what dignity I could. There was no other chair in the room, but I would not have been invited to sit anyway.

"Yes?" he drawled with rising inflection and, it seemed, without parting his lips.

I told him that we had just one request: to be allowed to go outside and work, along with the other prisoners.

"Naw, you all wouldn't las' two minutes out there. The other nigras'd kill you. If you want to get y'selves killed, it's all right with me. But y' ain't goin to do it here."

I said that we would gladly take our chances with the other prisoners; that we would like sunlight and the exercise.

"Naw!" he shouted. "We ain't goin' to let y'all go no place." His face reddened perceptibly and lips quivered with hatred. "We didn' tell you all t' come down here, but y' came anyhow. Now, we want y' to stay in there an' *rot!* We've got to feed ya, but we can put so much salt in y' food that y' won't be able t' eat any of it. And that may be just what we're gonna do."

He twisted his body in the chair and looked away. A signal to me that the meeting was over.

I thanked him for his time. He made no reply. Deputy Tyson, waiting outside the door, led me back to my cell where I reported the failure of the mission. The next few meals were so loaded with salt as to be inedible.

We had learned to sleep on steel, to eat slop, to sing when we must, and to make a game of periodic floods. We also learned to count the days till bail-out.

My fortieth day was just beyond the coming night. I lay down early to contemplate. Outside, as night began to fall, lightning knifed through heavy clouds and the skies opened up and dumped oceans on Parchman.

While the summer storm raged outside, my heart was at peace. Not one of the men and women who shared the Freedom Ride could ever be the same. Nothing would ever again be routine. No more humdrum. A Promethean spark somehow had been infused into the soul of each of us.

The younger ones had left a little of their youth in the prison cells. They had aged, matured. The older were surely younger now, more enthralled with freedom, imbued with its quest.

Freedom Ride imprisonment was almost over for me. But the state's ordeal would end only when I willed it. (I smiled at my own arrogance.) Nor could Mississippi soon recover its sleepy delta ways. Those who grew up in its closed society must now damn the light that filtered through the splintering door; but their children would be healthier, less myopic.

I myself, when a small child, had bumped my head on the closed door. The collision left a wound that never ceased reopening. It would have been worse had I not been in a home with abundant bandages of love. And still worse, without the armor of my father's position in our proscribed community, sheltering me from the fiercest barbs from behind that door.

Tomorrow as a mature adult of forty-one I would face for the first time the world outside without dad. How different would it be? How would it be, leaving this place after forty days locked in our own closed society?

If I had been able to look ahead twelve hours, I'd have seen myself standing outside the door of the building, with my rumpled and dirty suit hanging on me like a tent (I had lost twenty-two pounds), awaiting the opening of the van door for the ride to Jack Young's home in Jackson. On the ground beside me would have been a large suitcase and a huge box containing forty copies of the *New York Times* and the two books from Roy Wilkins. If I could have looked ahead, I would have seen a van of white female Freedom Riders, including a pretty teenage redhead, pulling up to begin their Parchman stint. They would have recognized me, waved through the bars, and sung "We Shall Overcome." Two nondescript white men would have been standing by, staring at me murderously, chewing tobacco and spitting its juice precariously close to my feet. But my brain would not let the feet move. One would have said to the other in a voice I could hear, "He mus' be the big shit." The other would have responded, "Yeah. If Ah cud git mah hands on 'im he'd be a dead shit."

But this was tonight, not tomorrow. Tonight without the man who had been a Gibraltar in my life. My mind went back to the earliest days I could remember with dad.

Sleepless dreams. Sleep finally arrives, but dreams do not depart: a small boy holding onto his mother's finger as they trudge along an unpaved red dirt road on a hot midsummer day. The mother shops at the town square and they trudge homeward, the child still clinging to her finger. She removes a clean handkerchief from her purse and pats her son's face and then her own. The boy looks up at his mother and says, "Mommy, I want to get a Coke."

"You can't get a Coke here, Junior," the mother replies. "Wait till we get home. There's lots of Coke in the icebox."

"But, mommy," says the boy, "I don't want to wait. I want my Coke now. I have a nickel; daddy gave it to me yesterday."

"Junior, I told you you can't get a Coke now. There's lots of Coke in the icebox at home."

"Why can't I get a Coke now, when I have a nickel?"

"You just can't."

The child sees another boy enter a drugstore across the street. "Look, mommy," exclaims Junior, "I bet that boy's going to get a Coke. Come on, let's go see."

He pulls his mother by the finger across the street, and they look through the screen doors, closed to keep out the flies. Sure enough, the other kid is perched on a stool at the counter sipping a soft drink through a straw.

"See that, mommy," said the small boy. "We *can* get a Coke here. He got one. Let's go get ours."

"Son, I told you to wait till we get home. We *can't* get a Coke in there."

"Then why could he?"

"He's white."

"He's white? And me?" inquires the boy.

"You're colored."

I came awake; I knew the rest of the dream. In fact, I knew it all; it had recurred so many times through the years, and each time my chest filled up. Several years ago, I'd mentioned it to my mother and she remembered the incident just as clearly. The dream had been a reality.

We had walked home silently that day under the oppressive sun. I no longer held her finger; my hands were at my sides, and we kicked up red dust as we trudged along. She had thrown herself across the bed and wept. I didn't want the Coke anymore and had sat on the front porch steps with dry eyes, a little brown boy alone with his three-and-a-half-year-old thoughts. Thoughts of the present and of the future. I don't recall the thoughts, only the thinking.

My father had come out and sat beside me in silence.

Would the man have been in a cell in Parchman in 1961, if the child had not been denied his soft drink in Holly Springs thirty-eight years before?

PART TWO

PK (Preacher's Kid)

CHAPTER 4

HOLLY SPRINGS

SOMEDAY, SOMEONE WILL DO an illuminating book on PK's in the black experience. Preachers' kids. What becomes of them and what do they become and why? They lead lives unlike any others: exposed to merciless scrutiny, spared no censure, even denied most of the childhood mischief indispensable to growing up. Being forced to sit still through their fathers' sermons is the least of the agonies preachers' kids must endure.

The black preacher, especially in the South, is king in a private kingdom. Whether learned or ignorant, he is both oracle and soothsayer, showman and pontiff, father image to all and husband-by-proxy to the unattached women in the church and others whose mates are either inadequate or missing. More than a priest, he is less only than God.

Growing up under such a man can be psychological mayhem. The old thesis about maternal dominance in the black family has no validity here whatever. The PK lives with a dominant male image.

The black preacher's wife would disappoint modern feminists: she is mother, cook, housekeeper, and unobtrusive helpmate—laughing at his wit no matter how stale, nodding dutifully at his sermons, and clinging to his arm when he decides that she should be there. She cannot be aggressive or the women of the church will resent her. She mustn't be jealous lest she deprive some pillar of the church of his presence. Above all, she must take care not to detract from his image of power, or the hypnotic spell will be broken, the mystique shattered.

Every part of the PK's life is colored by the fact that he is a preacher's child. He breathes it in the air, suckles it from his mother's breast. Relentless eyes and ears and tongues demand that he be somehow larger than childhood.

For that reason, PK's are generally distrusted by their peers: they are fashioned in the goody-goody mold. Naturally, rebellion is a most common response to the unnatural life-style of PK's—rebellion of all sorts. Adam Clayton Powell, Jr., wore the cloth with an impudent nonchalance. Malcolm X moved from Harlem vice-lordship to militant black nationalism. Deviation from society's accepted conventions has high incidence among PK's—alcoholism, homosexuality, profligacy, promiscuity, protest action.

There is also a high incidence of all kinds of talent: the environment of the black churchman's home is an oven, firing to white heat any incipient abilities put there.

Loneliness shrouds the lives of PK's, too. Their closest bond is to each other; when they meet, they understand, for each sees himself in the other's eyes.

This world of preachers and preachments is, in a sense, a world of endemic hypocrisy. No one can be as good as the preacher's aura would make believe. It is also a breeding ground for politicians; the Machiavellian thrust of black church politics would make Democratic and Republican Party shenanigans look like a Boy Scout jamboree.

Yet, being the son of a preacher does not really define my early childhood. Daddy was a minister, it is true, with all that implies. But he had another mystique, equally definitive in Holly Springs, Mississippi, in the early 1920s. He was an authentic scholar at a time and place in which scholarship was mysterious and a Ph.D. degree magical—among both blacks and whites.

He had been the first black Ph.D. in Texas, where I was born on January 12, 1920; and may have been the first in Mississippi, where we moved six months later. Faculty and students alike at Rust College, a Methodist school for blacks, were dazzled by this man, educated at Boston University, who could read, write, and speak Hebrew, Greek, Aramaic, and Latin, not to mention French and German.

Whites in the small Klan-ridden town, I'm told, spoke with incredulity of a "nigger up there at that Rust College who's got a pee-aitch-dee." On the rare occasions when they had to speak to him, he was called "Doctor." In the southern code of the time, that was permissible, whereas calling him "Mister" was not.

I sensed in those early years that there was something extraordinary about my father and without knowing what it was, accepted it. It set him apart. It set me apart, too, on two counts—PK and PhDK.

Daddy's family was poor. He told me that when he was in first grade he would run home from school to sit in his mother's lap and suck at her breast. In that way, food for one could feed two. They were, he often quipped, as poor as Job's turkey, which had to lean against a fence in order to gobble.

Like any black boy of his time, not of the "free Negro aristocracy," he got an education the hard way. He was born in 1886 of ex-slave parents in Kingstree, South Carolina. He finished grade school in Pearson, Georgia, but there were no high schools for blacks in that state. The legendary Mary McLeod Bethune gave him a working scholarship to the private school she'd founded in Daytona Beach, Florida, known then as Cookman Institute. The school was financed partly through the sale of sweet potato pies. It was there that he met my mother, romance flowering as he helped her with math problems.

He was a straight-A student and upon getting his diploma, was accepted at Boston University. He walked to Boston (there was no money for transportation, and nothing to hitch a ride with except an occasional horse and wagon), sleeping en route in barns of kind farmers.

At the university, he worked full-time as valet and carriage boy for a wealthy white woman, sending money home to support his impoverished parents. (His father was blind—blinded, so they say, by looking up at the sun while working in the turpentine forests. His mother, a mulatto offspring of slave and slaveowner, sometimes worked as wetnurse in white homes.) Still, he completed the four-year bachelor of arts curriculum in four years, magna cum laude. Then, from the university's theological school, he earned a bachelor of sacred theology (STB) degree with a record unmarred by anything less than A. He completed all work on his doctorate in one year, including a dissertation entitled, "A Rediscovery of Deutero-Isaiah," but due to a two-year residency requirement, had to wait twelve months for the coveted degree.

For three years Methodist bishops assigned him as pastor of black churches in Texarkana, Texas, where my sister was born, and in Galveston, Texas. That, however, was soon considered a waste, and his ministry was given its natural dimensions, religious and academic, in Methodist-related schools.

Because those colleges were short of money, highly trained faculty, and clerics who could preach to the bookish, daddy had to be versatile. At Rust, for instance, he was campus minister, dean of the college, and professor of philosophy and religion. At times, he taught sociology and even psychology. (They believed that anyone with a Ph.D. should be able to teach anything.)

My mother, Pearl, had also taught at one time. After graduating from Bethune-Cookman Institute, she had gotten a "normal" (or teaching) degree and had spent several years teaching in her hometown, Jacksonville, Florida, while daddy was away in Boston. They were married after he received his doctorate and she joined him as a rather typical minister's wife in Texas.

She was a mother and wife of the first rank. My memories of her from the early years are much clearer than of my father. She was always there;

daddy was there by image only. In person, he was much more remote, wrapped up in his library—in fine points of scholarly disputation—getting his kicks, so to speak, from the awesome acclaim of those who heard his sermons and benefited from his ministerial counsel.

Students benefited from his extracurricular assistance, too. Several septuagenerians who had studied under dad tell me that they would go to him with problems in physics or analytical geometry or calculus. (They thought he knew everything.) He would sit in his desk chair, feet crossed at the ankles, picking hairs from his prematurely balding head, as he always did when deep in thought. Moments later, with a flourish, he would write the correct answer and his method of arriving at it.

Though an intelligent and sensitive woman, mother was not an intellectual or an academic. Basically, she was a homemaker, a supporting actress for her star-husband and an "upbringer" for two children. It was she who kissed the bruised elbow, felt the forehead for fever, comforted when sister and I needed comforting, and disciplined when we stepped out of line. She was always there.

But daddy was present in a more mystical way—like a god who could reward and punish from afar, who could cause lightning to flash and thunder to sound, but if you tried to reach him with the senses it was often thin air.

I remember mother as a sweet and beautiful woman, and her photographs bear out the latter. She had long, wavy hair, which she could sit on if it hung loose. After all, her maternal grandmother was a full-blooded Seminole Indian.

From early childhood, I'd seen photographs of a handsome woman with long black hair, seated on the veranda of a large frame house in Florida. Asking mother who she was produced only changes of subject. Only much later, after my mother's death in 1966, I put that same question—"Who is she?"—to Sadie, my youngest maternal aunt.

Sadie said, "Don't you know? She was your mother's grandmother, your great-grandmother."

"But why didn't mother tell me that?" I asked.

"You know your mother," Sadie smiled. "She was the greatest Puritan in the world. My mother, Louisa, was an illegitimate child. That Seminole beauty—my grandmother, your great-grandmother—was seduced by a visiting Frenchman. Pearl, especially after she married a minister, considered the fact that her mother was born out of wedlock to be a skeleton in the family closet."

"And the great house?" I asked.

"That," replied Sadie, "was the Seminole lady's house. Her husband, our stepfather, had money."

"Where is it? Why don't we have some of it?"

Sadie smiled with no trace of bitterness. "Well, after her love-child with the Frenchman, your great-grandmother married and had children by a black farmer and real estate man. He was land wealthy, collecting rent from a dozen houses and marketing vegetables from his farm. But *their* children, the 'legitimate' family, got the money.

"Your grandmother, Louisa," Sadie went on, "married a black school-teacher with Indian blood in Live Oaks, Florida. And she taught in Live Oaks, too, until the family moved to Jacksonville, where he got a job as a mailman and my mother, Louisa, worked as a nursemaid, taking care of white folks' children."

The Roaring Twenties didn't roar very much at Rust College; they just purred, and rather demurely at that. Flappers of the day may have been at home in Harlem hot spots, but they were alien to Rust College in Holly Springs. This was, after all, the Bible belt for blacks as well as whites. It was also a citadel of moralistic Methodism. Coeds wore skirts below the calves and I would guess that virgins were the rule rather than the exception.

But I would not bet on it; children of tender age are unaware of much that goes on. One thing I was aware of, though, was the soft drink episode. Every black child in the South has an early experience of racism that shafts his soul. For the lucky, it is sudden, like a bolt of lightning, striking one to his knees. For others, a gradual dying, a sliver of meanness worming its way to the heart.

Another awareness was school. On campus, there was an elementary laboratory school where Rust students preparing to be teachers were given practical experience. The pupils were children chiefly of college professors and the few other middle-class blacks in town. It was superior in quality to the public schools for blacks in Holly Springs, and only the privileged or gifted got in.

My sister, Helen, seventeen months my senior, was in the second grade, and I wanted to be in school, too. So, at four and a half, I entered first grade. I already knew how to read and write and count, having learned as sister studied aloud while I bounced a ball against a wall at home, absorbing.

During the first week, it was quickly established that I was far ahead of the other children in 1-A (low first), so I was moved to 1-B. Soon, I was skipped to 2-A, catching up with my sister, to her great displeasure.

To add to the other sweet curses of my early childhood, I also became the campus pet. I was serious, unsmiling, brooding. My memories of life within the campus community are of almost no negatives, only positives—being praised as a paragon, a repository of all virtues and gifts. I do not recall in those early years ever needing reprimand or receiving punishment.

My environment was entirely supportive, except on the rare occasions when I left the cocoon, as in the Coca-Cola incident. How well, or how poorly, was I being prepared to accept my own frailties when I learned them, and to relate interpersonally to my fellows, or to face a world that would take my head off?

* * *

When the Rust College football team, in daily workouts, ran past our house on campus, one of the players would yell, "Come on, Junior" (as I was called). Excitedly, I would ask mother for permission, then run to them while they jogged in place, waiting for me. I would be hoisted onto a burly shoulder as they trotted on. When the shoulder tired of its burden, I would be passed on to another, and another.

The players all seemed enormous to me—incredible black hulks. Actually, they were small by today's standards. Then, anyone over two hundred pounds would be a tackle, whereas today he would hardly qualify in size as a running back.

The team won games. The campus was exuberant in victory and depressed in defeat. I went to home games; daddy or some college students would take me. Only one cheer song, sung with gusto by everyone, remains vivid in my mind:

> Good e-e-ve-ning Mister Tougaloo [the
> name of the opponents' college]
> Your *hair* is just as *rough* as—
> Your *hair* is just as *rough* as—
> Your *hair* is just as *rough* as—
> *Mine.*

On the heels of that bleacher-buster, laughter and banner waving swept the crowd. Being a contemplative sort of child, I always puzzled over the song's meaning. I asked my mother, but she would not tell me. Forty years later—in the days of the rediscovery of black pride—the song's significance struck me with force. What it meant, of course, was that we were not afraid of them; we could beat them because they were black like us.

Sister and I shared much of life in Holly Springs. She tried to remember not to study aloud, to avoid doing me the favor of relieving me of the homework chore. Yet, we got along. She was very protective, as older sisters usually are. On rare occasions when other children would quarrel with me, I would simply stand there with a frown, brooding. Invariably, with hand on hip, she'd rise to my defense: "You leave my brother alone." Invariably, also, the other child would back off.

She and I posed for interminable pictures for college students and visiting families who wanted to take with them something of Rust College and of Dr. Farmer. Sister, in crisp, starched dress with ruffles and a ribbon in her hair, always posed—hand on hip, head cocked to one side, impudent expression. In short pants and middy blouse, I just stood there looking bored.

At college functions on holidays, she and I always had to perform, either in individual recitations or in a duet. One was unforgettable: "Jesus Loves Me, This I Know." Even then, I could not sing. As soon as I, in a loud voice, had sung the first notes, the most hysterical outburst of laughter I'd ever heard shook the rafters. I stopped singing and looked up at sister in confusion. A born ham, she was still singing as though nothing unusual had happened. The laughter was uncontrollable, but I continued the song, glancing up at my older sibling every few seconds to make sure she was still unperturbed, wishing with all my heart that the song's end would come swiftly.

The laughter did not cease. It increased when we finished singing, and merged with the applause. We left the stage—she with her head high, apparently still unperturbed, I embarrassed.

I snuggled up to mother in the audience, where she had joined unrestrainedly in the hilarity. Whispering in her ear, I asked, "Why were they laughing, mother?"

"Because you were singing so well, Junior," she answered, as she put her arm around me, still chuckling.

I didn't believe that; it did not make sense. And I wondered why my mother lied. To protect my feelings, I suppose. But not telling me the truth didn't protect my feelings; it hurt them more, for it also insulted my intelligence. People don't laugh at a good performance unless it is intended to be funny.

Perhaps that is why I have never been able to sing. But if singing was a disaster to me, so was the endless picture taking. People always wanted me in places and in poses I did not want to be in.

One occasion especially comes to mind. Aunt Sadie was living with us at the time and going to college at Rust. A thin, pixieish young lady of twenty-one, Sadie always seemed like a child-woman. Only five feet one, she talked with a lisp, which added to the puckish impression. "She's not a lady," I always said. "She's nothing but a little girl." (Daddy constantly teased her about not being able to talk clearly, so, being a woman of action, she went to a doctor and had the offending tongue membrane clipped and came home speaking as well as anyone.) But little girl or not, everyone loved Sadie. To us, she was almost like a big sister.

One bright Sunday afternoon, she, mother, sister, and I dressed up in our dandies and went for a walk to see the sights in that metropolis of five thousand souls. And, naturally, to take pictures.

We stopped on a railroad overpass, and the adults decided that was a perfect place for a few photographs, because in the distance on a hill the buildings of Rust College could be seen. So, I was placed upon the four-foot-high iron platform that walled the overpass from the tracks below. I glanced down behind me and it was the Grand Canyon, with curving and crisscrossing ribbons of steel beckoning me.

Terrified I was, but I was a big boy, four years old, and could not cry and did not want to show fear. But it welled up in me and I protested that I wanted to get down. I do not think the wall was more than a foot wide, and there was nothing to hold on to or keep me from falling backward.

Mother and Sadie assured me that it was all right, and I should just stand still.

I was not convinced.

That shutter took forever to click. I was lifted down and my legs felt weak. As long as I can remember, I've been afraid of heights. (And neither have I ever been comfortable with picture taking.) Was my panic on the railroad overpass the cause? Or was it the result of that phobia?

The smallish, boxlike, two-story frame house with yellow clapboard siding where we lived on campus, and beside which my sister and I posed for so many pictures, became a permanent part of my consciousness. Permanent, because it was the first home in my recollection, having moved there when I was only six months old.

The memory is as clear and loving now as the smell of jonquils in the front yard, almost as indelible as the Coke that eluded me.

In the spring of 1925, however, daddy informed us at the dinner table that in a few months we would be moving. He had just been assigned by the bishop to the post of registrar and professor of religion and philosophy at Samuel Houston College (now Houston-Tillotson) in Austin, Texas.

Mother simply smiled and nodded. (She must have already known about it. Ministers' wives must take transfers with equanimity; and if it is a step up, with enthusiasm.) Sister had many questions. I chiefly listened, with solemn face and solemn, childish thoughts. Where was Texas? How far away? What was it like? What kind of a place was Austin? And Sam Houston College; was it like Rust?

All the answers to our questions were framed in the most favorable light. Texas was in the robust West and it was the largest state in the nation—over six times as big as Mississippi. Austin was ten times the size of Holly Springs. Our new college was greater than Rust and had a better football team. (Bigger somehow meant better.)

Aside from the four members of my immediate family, the only other person at the dinner table was Bessie, an older cousin from Georgia, who had come to Holly Springs to live with us and go to college. (Sadie had graduated a year before and gone somewhere—New York, I think—to take up her life or to study at a higher school.)

Bessie and my mother vied with each other in showing enthusiasm for the pending move. She was daddy's niece, twelve years my senior, and like all members of his family, she worshipped him. He was the first of the Farmers to go to college. And he had that rarest of academic credentials, a Ph.D. They gloried in his string of degrees when no one else had even *one:* A.B., S.T.B., Ph.D., and D.D. (honorary). He was a minister and a professor. Their pride and joy.

Daddy felt close to her, too; for she was his dead sister's only child. He supported her and put her through school. In fact, when any of his relatives needed help or advice they turned to him, and he always came through. Mother was proud of daddy because he was her husband. But to Bessie, he was husband to all in his blood family and they did not relish sharing him. Naturally, there was some tension between the two, and without understanding its roots, I sensed it even at that green age. But it remained low-key, rumbling below the surface.

Dominating everything at the dinner table that day was the coming change in our lives. We were all thinking about how it would affect ourselves. Sister inexplicably seemed elated at the prospect of a change. As usual, I brooded. Mother knew my mind was whirling, so she let me leave the table early to be by myself. For a boy of five, leaping into the unknown possessed an element of adventure. And of apprehension.

On a Sunday afternoon, Bessie took sister and me for a long walk. Sister grew tired, so we rode back on the bus.

Walking down the aisle of the bus, Bessie held our hands, my sister in front and I behind.

"Let's sit here," I said, stopping at an empty seat midway down the aisle.

Bessie smiled, shook her head, and pulled me on.

"But I don't *want* to sit in the back," I complained.

Sister looked back at me with disdain, as though I was dumb for not knowing where to sit. We sat on the empty rear bench.

"Why, do we have to sit here?" I asked. "Because we're colored? Is it like this everywhere?"

"Yes, except for the North," Bessie replied.

"Texas, too?"

She nodded and hugged us both tightly about the shoulders.

Fifty-five years later, I was looking back with some nostalgia to those months preceding the uprooting in Mississippi and the replanting in Texas. I had returned to Rust College in June 1980, for the first time since leaving as a small child.

I'd been invited to deliver the commencement address, and the college president had made it the occasion for a reunion of the class of 1925. The class members were all in their seventies, of course. Some were spry and some decrepit, and some were not present because they were no longer living.

Many had anecdotes about my father, and a few had photographs they had saved all those years—pictures of sister and me, of mother and daddy.

Preparing to leave Holly Springs again in the spring of 1980, I wondered how the town had changed. How it had been affected by the civil rights movement, which had slipped into high gear after the Freedom Rides in 1961? Before the commencement ceremonies there had been no time, so afterward, I walked alone through the town to see what I could remember and what I could recognize as having changed.

Entering a gin joint, the acid test of any social transformation, I walked up to the bar, sat on a stool, and watched the bartender polishing glasses.

"Yes, sir," he said, without looking at me. "Can I help y'all?"

Gripping the bar's edge tightly so as not to fall off the stool, I replied, trying not to sound as tentative as I felt, "Yes. I'd like a martini, please. Beefeater, extra dry, with a twist. Straight up."

He didn't even blink as he said, "Ain't got no Beefeater, sir. How 'bout Tanqueray?"

I nodded and then tasted the drink cautiously. Then the sips came routinely and without hesitation. Occasionally, I would glance at the bartender and would see him looking at me with no apparent hostility. Quickly, his eyes would shift.

Outside, a motor revved and died. A tractor trailer had pulled in front. When its driver came in, I stiffened, expecting trouble. The mirror behind the bar told me that he was a typical red-neck, rough-hewn and roughly clothed, dirty hands and face, chewing hard on a chunk of something ballooning his jaw. I thought of the gawkers outside the window at Parchman.

He sat beside me. Elbows on the bar, he buried head in hands. The bartender drew him a beer without being asked. Removing one beefy hand from his head, he gulped the foam, wiping his mouth with his forearm.

I ventured conversation. "You seem upset. Is something wrong?"

Without looking up, he drawled, "Yeah, I got problems. Bad problems."

Then, he glanced at me and did a double-take. With a startled expression and a finger pointing, he fairly shouted, "Hey, I know *you*. I seen you on TV!"

"Farmer," I said.

"Yeah! *James* Farmer. I use ta see you alla time on TV!"

I smiled and relaxed a bit.

He seemed to relax, too, and went on. "Well, as I wuz sayin', I got a real problem. Mah young daughter had a baby. An' now she done run off to live with th' man. An' they ain't even *married*."

"So," I shrugged, "what else is new?"

"Yeah, but he's a ni—" he mumbled. "Ah mean he's black."

"Where're they living?" I asked, holding my breath.

"Raht here in Holly Springs."

It was my turn to gawk, mouth wide open.

"But don' get me wrong," he continued, feeling talkative now that he'd gotten that burden off his chest. "I ain't mad 'bout it. I jes don' lak the way they done it."

I gasped. And the hairs on the back of my neck crawled and itched. But he was not through yet.

The words tumbled out: "But, Ah'll tell y' one thing. It ain't gon las'. The Lawd did'n intend for the races to mix thet way. It says so in the Bible. Look at thet Sammy Davis, Jr.; he married thet white actress from Europe. Whut wuz her name?"

"Mae Britt," I said.

"Yeah. Mae something or other. That didn' las'. It never do. It sez so in the Bible. An'—"

I interrupted, aware that I was being patronizing, and despising myself for it: "Well, I'm kind of a jackleg preacher and I don't remember that Scripture. Where *is* it in the Bible?"

"I don' know where it's at," he came back, faith undaunted. "But it's there someplace."

I stared at him with indescribable astonishment. I could not have been more astounded with this conversation had he told me that after a sudden eclipse of the sun one day Old Sol had reversed the field and started rising in the west.

But the man was not through baring his soul, and a second beer made it easier for him: "Uh, Mr. Farmer, I ain't never seen thet baby yet, but mah wife seen it. She seen it when she went t' the hospital when mah daughter wuz havin' it. An' you know whut she said? She said thet baby looks almos' white."

Words eluded me, but I felt a certain warmth for this man. I, too, am a father. He had a real problem. His peers would give him no rest. I could hear them now: "Yo daughter's fuckin' a nigger, an' you cain't do nothin' about it." No wonder there were bags under his bloodshot eyes. Social change does create personal tragedies.

In the old days, he would have called the boys together and had a necktie party. The boys—like those outside the basement window at Parchman, and like the two outside the prison when I was leaving! But if he did that now, the feds would be down there the next day and someone would do time. For conspiracy, probably; murder is only a state crime.

Holly Springs *had* undergone a transformation. But fifty-five years earlier, at age five, my preoccupation was not with future changes in the town; it was with the unfathomable changes about to come in my own life.

CHAPTER 5

GROWING UP IN TEXAS (STAGE ONE)

REVEREND WYATT'S SHOVEL STRUCK again and again, penetrating the muck. With a loud grunt, he tossed each shovelful over his shoulder onto a pile. His wife stood at the edge of the rectangular hole, peering in. The stench spread everywhere.

On that August day in 1925, mother and I stood inside the screen door at the back of the one-story white frame house, looking out. A lilting breeze swept our way.

"I don't see how Mrs. Wyatt can stand that odor." Mother whispered the words, even though the Wyatts were well out of earshot.

The Reverend Wyatt was cleaning out the hole in the ground over which the outhouse sat. The little whitewashed structure had been moved aside for this operation. The refuse inside the hole was dried, but still maggot-infested; the house had stood vacant for some months and was now being prepared for our occupancy.

Samuel Houston College had no houses for faculty, so we rented a house owned by Reverend Wyatt. It was in a black section of Austin, of course, and the streets were unpaved and there was no sewage system. There was running water, though—a faucet in the kitchen sink and one outside the house. There was a portable porcelain washbasin for hands and face and a tin tub for bathing. There was a wood and coal-burning cook stove in the kitchen and a heater in the house burning the same fuel.

The house in Holly Springs, being on the campus, had possessed a few amenities. But the one in Austin, off-campus, shared the primitive facilities of most of the houses in the communities where "colored" people lived. The few affluent black families lived well—doctors, lawyers, businessmen. But college professors, though prestigious, were not well paid. Daddy got about a hundred dollars a month, so there was not enough to rent a big house. Mother budgeted carefully and there were no extravagances. We had food and clothing and an occasional small luxury, and apparently still saved a few dollars each month. We never wanted for necessities. And emergencies never floored us, so far as I knew.

If the absence of modern conveniences was disconcerting to mother, she never showed it; she went cheerfully about the task of making our surroundings into a functional and pleasant home. For sister and me, the outhouse and the tin tub were new experiences that we faced with eagerness. And *our* outhouse had a certain distinction; it was a three-holer. That, I was told, meant status; the neighbors had only two-holers!

Reverend Wyatt filled four crocus sacks with the shoveled excrement and then stood under the chinaberry tree nearby, mopping his forehead with a checkered handkerchief. His two boys, Tom and Sam, had come into the backyard now. Tom was my size, but older. I felt an immediate affinity for Sam, who was my age, but smaller. When his father introduced us, he greeted me with an embrace and a big smile of welcome.

Except for smaller size and a more outgoing nature, Sam was *me*, a mirror of myself. He was bright and well mannered and also a PK. My spirits sagged when I learned that Sam and Tom would not be in my school in September, for they lived on the other side of town.

There were other children on the block, though. In fact, just down the street, there was a boy of eight and his sister, six: Buddy and Sis Smith. Their mother was without a doubt the fattest woman I'd ever seen. At least four hundred pounds. She was a jovial, motherly type, but firm with discipline. She took in washing and soaked and scrubbed the clothes in a large iron pot over a charcoal fire in their backyard. She made her own charcoal in that yard, and in the laundry pot she made her own lye soap. And she dipped snuff. And sat on the front porch nursing her infant at a gargantuan breast.

Theirs was a fun yard to play in, but only with great reluctance did mother allow me to go across the street and play. For some reason, she did not want me to become close with the Smith children. Maybe because their house and yard were dirty. Or because they were noisy and had loud arguments. Or that they were not churchgoers. Or were not polished. But whatever the reason, mother was a kind person and would not offend neighbors by forbidding her child to play with theirs.

Mr. Smith always seemed to be sleeping when I was over there—or just getting up or just going to bed. He was a truck driver. When he was not on the road, his van was parked in front of his house, and the company advertised its services boldly on each side of the van. When awake, he drank beer and smoked cigars. Almost always, there was a cap on his head. One time it fell off, revealing a lump the size of a small grapefruit. Kicked by a mule, they said.

Buddy Smith was proud of his father. Not everyone's father gets kicked by a mule. And how many boys can boast a private playground in a truck big enough to carry an elephant.

That truck was an enchanted place, especially after dark. It could become whatever a child's imagination wanted it to be, concealing or revealing any fantasy conjured up. It was a cave, shutting out the adult world, beckoning adventure.

One evening after nightfall, Buddy, Sis, and I sat huddled together on the floor of the truck. Moonlight crept stealthily through branches and leaves of trees outside and snaked through the partly opened door of the van—shadows and breezes joining in an entire pantomime of ghosts and monsters. After a while, we ran out of imagination and sat still.

Buddy spoke: "J. Leonard [that is what I was called; no more Junior], nobody can see us. Do it to Sis."

Sis nodded her head, lay back on the floor, and pulled up her skirt. I jumped up, backed away, shaking my head and whispered, "Uh! uh! I better go home now. Mother'll be calling me."

"Aw, c'mon," Buddy urged. "Don't ya know how? Just lie down on top of her and stick it in."

I shook my head again and wanted to go home. But also wanted to stay.

"Here, I'll show you," said Buddy.

"Yeah," whispered Sis, "c'mon and show him."

He lay down on top of her and made rhythmic up-and-down motions. "Is that the way you do it?" I asked.

"Yeah," Buddy said.

I had known, of course, that there was sex in life; I'd learned that even in Holly Springs. Probably at school. But somehow, I'd always thought you did it standing up; nobody had told me you were supposed to lie down.

"Is it *in?*" I asked, my interest momentarily overcoming shame.

"Yes," answered Buddy. Sis answered yes, too.

In a minute, Buddy got up and buttoned his pants. I didn't look closely; maybe not looking would lessen the shame. Sis lay there expectantly.

"How'd you learn how, Buddy?" I asked.

"From mama and papa. We hear 'em in the next room at night."

"Yeah," added Sis. "And then we look through the hole in the wall and see 'em."

"Tha's right, J. Leonard," Buddy said. "And then we practice what we seen."

As if to confirm my suspicion that mother knew and saw all, I heard her voice on the front porch across the street calling, "Junior!" (She and daddy still called me that.)

The back doors of the moving van were partly open and I could hear plainly. Her call came as a relief, releasing me from the compulsion to try to "do it."

I jumped out of the van before answering, "I'm coming, mother." Without saying good-bye, I ran home.

Going in the house, I was eaten up by guilt. Never before or since have I felt the likes of it. The only thing that rivaled it was more than a decade later: my first sexual experience. But that time, guilt was laced with pride and manhood.

Though I'd done nothing, not even unbuttoned my pants, I had nevertheless thought about it. I was sure mother could read in my face what I'd *almost* done. So, I kept averting my eyes.

Mother's look moved from questioning to accusing.

"What's the matter, Junior?" I was sure the guilt was on my face and I could not hide it.

"Nothing," I said, without looking at her.

She seemed to accept that answer. Because she wanted to. To my enormous relief, her face said that she'd dismissed the thought of my having done dirty things.

"You've been running barefoot in the street with Buddy. You're full of dirt and dust. I'll heat some water and fill the tub. Take a bath and go to bed. You have to go to Sunday school tomorrow."

Eagerly, I obeyed.

But Texas was more than a moving van and Buddy and Sis. It was also school.

At the grade school for "colored people" in Austin, the principal's son, Irving, was in my class. He quickly became my best friend, because my father was a muckety-muck at Sam Houston College and also a professor there; and his father was a teacher at our school as well as the head man. I gravitated toward him, for he was my link to the school, to the fourth-grade class, and to its pupils—my security blanket.

Irving was three years older than I, but he was not as tall. He was stronger and heavier though; we wrestled in play and he always won. Except once, when he thew me to the ground and sat astride me, fist poised over my face for the benefit of the crowd of schoolmates during recess, who knew that it was all in fun because we were the best of friends.

I remembered a maneuver I'd seen in a Tom Mix cowboy movie. Quickly, I raised my legs and locked my heels against Irving's forehead and pulled his head backward to the ground.

Irving yelled with pain because the steel plates on my leather heels had kicked his brow, raising a lump. (I had persuaded mother to let me have the steel brads put on the shoes to make the heels last longer. My real reason, though, was to walk with a metallic clink like the cowboys in the movies.) I was filled with remorse at Irving's pain and helped him up off the ground. I was also full of joy at having beaten someone, finally, in a physical contest. It was the only time I ever defeated Irving, or any other boy, in the games or the realities of combat.

I could never outrun Irving. In fact, I couldn't outrun any boy in the class; I always came in last in the almost daily foot races during recess.

But easily the brightest in the class, it took no effort for me to maintain that status. I did not study much at home, but still knew the answers to the teachers' questions when none of the others did.

Sister was outraged. She once blurted out before the whole class, "But, brother didn't study his lesson last night. He just played ball and shot marbles in the house while *I* was studying."

To her dismay, the teacher was even more impressed. "Helen," said Professor Hurdle, with a ghost of a smile, "remember this: it's not the process but the product that counts."

Yet my deportment was not consistent with my academic performance. Everyone knew that I was a PK and occasionally teased me about it, so I tried hard to prove that I was a regular kid, one of the boys.

Irving sat across the aisle from me in his father's classroom, and scarcely a day went by that both he and I did not get a strapping across our backsides from his father for talking in class.

If it was not talking that brought on the punishment, it was spitballing staples and shooting them with rubber bands at the back of another boy's head. The spitball staples didn't really hurt. They felt something like a mosquito bite. The yelps they sometimes produced were provoked more by surprise than pain.

The rubber band snipings caused fights at recess and after school, fights I never won. But sometimes sister would win them for me. Once, as a boy named Clarence, one of my victims, confronted me on the way home after school, he closed in, saying that he wanted to know if I was as good with my fists as I was with the rubber band.

But Sister was there. She said, "You leave my brother alone."

Clarence tried to push her aside, saying, "Get outa the way, Helen. I don' wanna fight you. I'm gon' fight J. Leonard."

Sister stood her ground. She had her lunch bag in her right hand, with an empty half-pint jar, a half-eaten apple, and an untouched orange. She swung it right on target. Clarence staggered back from the suddenness of the blow to his head and then slunk away.

I thought Clarence had learned his lesson, so over the next days, the rubber band went back to work on his head. One day after school, however, he caught up with me when sister was not there.

I tried to imitate my sister's performance and swung the lunch bag. But I swung too hard and the bag broke, its contents flying off harmlessly into space. In my hand was left only crumpled brown paper. Clarence slapped me silly with both hands before I could organize any response. I tried vainly to strike back. I was dazed and embarrassed when he recoiled and walked away, saying, "I don't wanna hurt J. Leonard. I ain't gon' hit 'im no mo'. He don' even know how ta fight."

But I had a plan. The boy who sat directly in front of me may have been the dumbest kid in class, but I was sure that he was the strongest boy in the world. And the toughest. In the play yard during lunch recess he would demonstrate his prowess by bending metal pipes, unbending horseshoes, and snapping twine. Everyone knew his reputation by now, and on rare occasions when he had to prove his toughness, it was no contest. He once fought two boys at once—and beat them.

Nelson could lift anyone in the class over his head and dump him on the ground. He was ten, one year older than Irving, and four years older than me. He helped his father deliver ice in a wagon drawn by a bony horse on Saturdays. According to Irving, when Nelson was four, he carried sixty-pound chunks of ice and lifted them into iceboxes. Hence, his strength and barrel chest. (Much later, when I learned that Joe Lewis had been an ice boy in his childhood, I thought of Nelson.) He was from a large, dirt-poor family and had to fight older brothers for his share of food. If he couldn't fight, he wouldn't eat. That had to make him tough.

Nelson's clothes were ill-fitting hand-me-down overalls, plentifully patched but clean. His fingernails were dirty, and despite the clean overalls, he sometimes had a ripe odor. Yet, though preteens are often cruel, nobody teased Nelson.

I cultivated Nelson by slipping him the answers to questions that Professor Hurdle asked. Nelson would hold up his hand, hesitantly at first, for it was a new experience for him, and then wave it excitedly, snapping his fingers to get the teacher's attention. When, to the astonishment of all, he would give the correct answer, a smile actually labored across Nelson's face. After a few such occurrences, Professor Hurdle began looking at me suspiciously, but he let it go. He could not catch me at it, or perhaps did not want to.

Nelson showed his gratitude by keeping a protective eye on me during recess. And after school, he, Irving, and I walked home together. I explained to Nelson that I wasn't very good at fighting, but he was; and he wasn't very good at studies, but I was. So, I would help with his homework if he'd help me with my fighting when necessary.

"Okay, J. Leonard. If ya he'p me with m' homework, ain' nobody gon' bother you."

The agreement was made and we kept it all through grade school. He did not have to do much to keep his side of the bargain; he seldom had to fight. It was usually enough for Nelson to mumble simply and without emphasis, "Leave J. Leonard alone."

Hardly a Saturday passed that Irving and I did not find ten cents apiece and go to the movie house. It was a small theater—the "colored" one. The larger one, for whites only, was around the corner. In ours, there was the inevitable popcorn and candy bars and cockroaches. Maybe in the other one, too.

Saturday was for school kids. There was Tom Mix, our cowboy hero who could outfight anyone. And Tarzan, the weekly cliffhanger serial. And Rin Tin Tin, the super German shepherd.

And there was also Maxine. Her father was a doctor, Irving said. A small taffy-colored girl of six, she was so sophisticated, so knowing, that her running commentaries were as intriguing as the shows themselves. She could anticipate every move of our heroes: "Knock 'm down the stairs, Tom Mix!" "Watch out, Tarzan, that leopard's gonna leap!" "Come on, Rin Tin Tin, kill that wolf!" She was always there in the front row when we arrived and sat beside her, so she must have seen the show once already. And she orchestrated each episode with grunts and moans and other delicious sounds.

As she stretched her short legs in front of her, practically lying down in the seat, she led the booing of the villains and cheering of the heroes. I thought of Buddy and Sis Smith and their father's van, vaguely perceiving her movements as sexual.

I dreamed of Maxine many nights, and had wet dreams, if that is possible for a six-year-old. (There were, indeed, wet dreams. I had never stopped wetting the bed. That was my deep dark secret and I lived in constant fear that someone other than mother, daddy, and sister would find out about it.) In the movie house, though, there were no wet dreams, because Maxine was ineluctably there. She shared the stage with the movie.

As Irving and I and Maxine chewed our gum and ate our popcorn, we sat on the edges of our seats watching the missionary in the pot, sweat dripping, the fire building up beneath. Eyes anxiously scanned the distant trees on the screen for Tarzan's swinging rope. Ears strained for his haunting yell. Africans were dancing around the pot to the rhythmic tom-tom beat. A lone African face, painted and fierce, moved toward us on the screen, enlarging as it came, until, it almost leaped into our laps.

"Oh, God," cried Maxine and she wriggled.

I elbowed Irving and said, "Irving, that's you."

Maxine broke up with laughter and nestled deeper into her seat.

"Naw, man," Irving growled, "that ain't me. I ain't no *African.* Don't call me no African. I'm an *American!*" (I was only amused then. Four decades later, I would be outraged at the self-rejection implicit in his rejection of Africa.)

Before we had left Holly Springs, a neighbor had promised me a puppy when her collie gave birth. As the months dragged on into the spring of 1926, I asked mother about it and she said that maybe something had happened to Scottie.

Scarcely a week had passed, when Daddy brought home a puppy. He was not a collie. But a puppy. And mine. White with a yellow spot around one eye and on both floppy ears. A cute mongrel. Like most puppies, he was frightfully frisky. And that became his name.

Mother had asked me to housetrain Friskie. But I was not successful at it; I did not scold him convincingly enough. (Maybe I empathized with him for, after all, I still wet the bed.) She did the job herself, with newspapers and a switch from the chinaberry tree. He learned to obey her much more than me. When he got outside he'd run like the wind. I'd call and he'd run faster. Mother called him and he made a U-turn, running back without breaking stride.

At my next birthday, January 12, 1927, I was permitted to have a party, with the usual ice cream and cake and punch. Irving was there, of course. And Buddy and Sis. And Maxine and her brother, Charles. I invited Nelson, but he had to work. Everyone else came who'd been invited, and everyone was invited except Stanley, the boy who lived in the house at the end of the block, whom I didn't like.

Stanley felt slighted. The day after the party, I passed him on the sidewalk and said, "Hi, Stanley." He merely grunted and dropped his head and walked on.

The next day, Friskie was suddenly stricken with violent convulsions. He fell on the ground in the backyard, writhing, kicking, jerking, and screaming with pain. Mother and I were dragged helplessly into his pit of pain. When daddy came home from the college an hour later, the dog's crying had become more mournful, his terrible spasms less wild. The end was near. After a violent last convulsion, he was dead.

I was shattered. As the poison stopped the little dog's living, a small bit of it transferred itself to my existence.

Daddy dug a hole in the backyard for burial. On the back steps, I sat alone, as I always did when troubled, looking at Friskie on the ground. His mouth was still open, as though his agony were not yet ended. I tried to understand two incomprehensibles: death and cruelty. I had known of people who died, and I knew, of course, that animals died, too. But at age seven, death was remote. Never before had it invaded my life.

And never had I experienced such unmitigated meanness before.

As we laid Friskie in his grave, daddy tried to console me with one thought. Dogs, he explained in true religious fashion, did not have souls; so it was as though he'd never lived, had never been born.

I thought about that, but it did not help. After all, I had played with

Friskie and I had memories of that which I would never lose. I had memories, too, of his circling back home when mother called him. So how could it be as though he had never lived? The thought that he could live no more because he had no soul made it harder. Not easier.

The hole where Friskie lay was covered up and a hole in my life was torn open.

CHAPTER 6

GROWING UP IN TEXAS (STAGE TWO)

THE CAVERN WAS FILLED almost as soon as it had opened. As if they'd heard my inner cries, a letter arrived in a fortnight from the Freemans of Holly Springs.

In about ten days, a crate would arrive at the railroad freight depot.

The winter days crept by in February 1927. It was cold, but I did not notice. And school was only a time of tedious waiting.

"J. Leonard, are you sick?" asked Professor Hurdle. "You haven't done anything wrong this week."

"No, sir," I replied. "I was just thinking." (Daydreaming would have been more like it.)

I was not sure the day would ever come. But it did. Professor T. B. Echols (I'd already learned that T.B. was for Timothy Bertram and not tuberculosis), who taught religious education and youth work at Sam Houston, pulled up in front of our house in his Buick roadster. Daddy was in the car with him and they were both smiling

Mrs. Echols sat in the rumble seat, Persian lamb coat buttoned at the neck and a black wool scarf enveloping her head and ears. In her lap, wrapped in a blanket, was an eight-week-old collie pup.

The next few weeks were pure ecstasy. All of us helped train Carl. (It sounded like "collie.") He learned fast. And his growing even outpaced his learning.

Carl became more and more an extension of my life. Like every boy with a cherished dog, I ascribed superpowers to my collie and supreme attributes. He could run faster, leap higher, fight better, think quicker, love deeper, and guard more tenaciously and with greater heart than any dog that ever lived.

I had begun to feel comfortable in my enlarged cocoon in Austin, Texas. There were disappointments: I saw no cowboys except in movies, no horses but those pulling ice wagons. There had been traumas and juvenile triumphs. Yet I had friends and at least one perceived enemy. And Carl.

No longer did I live on a self-contained black college campus, but it was still an all-black world contiguous to a mysterious white one. There were thousands, tens of thousands, of shadowy white figures out there. If we were "invisible men," they, too, were invisible—to us.

There were occasional white speakers from the Austin board of education, but they were not *people:* they were figurines in a charade we did not understand. Their words bounced off our heads, for there was no basis for listening. Then there were the Eisenbergs, who owned the neighborhood grocery store around the corner, a "mom and pop" affair, and lived above it. But they might have been robots, filling paper bags, making change, and making the cash register ring. The two separate worlds were intertwined somehow, yet they seemed not to touch.

I was curious about that other world, which seemingly pulled the strings on mine by remote control. How did its people live? Were they stronger or weaker, meaner or kinder?

That curiosity lent special intrigue to the pleading of Alfred, a classmate, that I join him on Saturdays in caddying at the country club. Irving's parents had said he, too, could go if I went. With some reluctance, mother and daddy gave their permission.

It was a long walk, maybe three miles. The caddy yard was a walled-in area of about one hundred square feet with long benches on two adjoining sides. There was a latrine and a shed in case of rain. A heavy odor hung over the yard, a maelstrom of smells—of tobacco and wet sneakers and sweat and urine and discarded scraps of food.

There were about equal numbers of white and black boys. Some of the blacks were from my school, including Nelson. Alfred was a regular in the yard, and everybody knew him, even the whites. He also seemed to be every golfer's favorite caddy. On every Saturday, the most familiar sing-song call of the caddy caller was "Heah y' go, Alfred."

Irving and I were newcomers, so it was two or three weeks before either of us got a caddy call. Mine came unexpectedly and I was elated, but also more than a little afraid. I knew nothing whatever about golf, and Alfred hadn't told me much. In fact, the only thing he *had* told me was that the caddy should never touch the ball and must not move it, but just remember where it is at all times.

The caddy caller did not know my name, so he just pointed at me and motioned. I was assigned to two golfers and followed them to the driving range. They told me where in the distance to stand. They began driving balls in my direction. They must have driven six or eight. I was confused; I had not thought that was the way golf was played. I ran to each ball that was hit and saw where it came to rest. But how was I to remember the location of so many balls? I wished Alfred were there.

The two golfers soon called me to them and asked for their balls so they could drive them again. They were merely practicing their drives, but how was I to know? I'd never seen golf played in my life before. There was no television to record events at opens and no golf course in the black section.

They looked at each other in disbelief, if not in anger, and gave me a dollar and sent me back to the caddy yard.

I did not tell anyone what had happened. I didn't want to be laughed at. I walked back into the yard with a forced smile on my face, showing my dollar—generous pay for so brief a job. (Especially for having done nothing.)

There was no segregation in the caddy yard, except the voluntary sort. One bench was fully occupied by blacks; the other, occupied by whites, had a few spaces left. I sat in one of them.

I could feel the eyes of the boy to my left on me. He slid two inches closer until he touched me. Perspiration began to bead up on my forehead. Conversation in the yard had stopped. All eyes were on us.

Suddenly, the boy on my left jabbed me sharply in the ribs with his elbow. It hurt, but I made no sound and did not move. He poked again, harder. And again. My mind worked furiously as I searched in vain for acceptable responses. A few on the white bench tittered.

I heard someone on the other bench murmur "*Shi-a-t*". In a swift movement, Nelson left his seat and strode over to me. He said "Take mah seat, J. Leonard. Le' *me* sit heah."

There was no way I could have run from the situation, but I gave my seat to Nelson with untold relief. Nor could the bully avoid poking Nelson. The silence in the caddy yard deepened. No one tittered. A minute passed. Then the elbow dug into Nelson's ribs. Immediately, Nelson's answering thrust ripped into the boy's side like a pile driver, nearly knocking him off the bench.

The white boy sprang to his feet. Nelson stood to face him. Two other white boys jumped up and one said "Awright, c'mon. Le's go out t' th' lot."

Nelson and his foe followed them. Both benches emptied and everybody went to the lot, a vacant area away from the buildings and the golfers. The palms of my hands were wet and they trembled.

As we approached the lot, I whispered to Alfred "Do you think they'll gang up on Nelson?"

"Naw," whispered Alfred in reply. "They b'lieve in fair! They wan' a fair fight. One ag'ins' one."

I was reassured. But not convinced. Neither was Irving. "If they do, J. Leonard, we're all gonna have ta fight 'em," Irving said. "You take that little one there; he's older than you, but I know you can whup him. I'll get the one next to 'im." I gulped. We formed a circle, one half its circumference white, the other black.

They faced each other, Nelson standing straight, long arms relaxed at his sides. The white boy, in a semicrouch, circled. Nelson kept turning to face him.

The white boy elected to wrestle. He charged. They grappled for a moment. Nelson deftly maneuvered his right leg behind the other boy's legs and flung him heavily to the ground. He came up with a grin on his face and an open switchblade in his hand. Nelson stiffened. With adrenaline pumping hard, even I, who had never won a fight—except the one friendly tussle with Irving—felt ready for a do-or-die effort. I eyed the smaller white boy and planned my attack. The two whites who appeared to be leaders leaped in front of the boy with the knife, took it away from him and broke the blade under foot.

The defeated warrior dropped his head, turned, and walked through the circle and back to the caddy yard. We all followed. But the boy did not stop in the yard. He went on out, home—embarrassed.

Later, when I recounted the caddy-yard incident to daddy, my caddying career came to a screeching halt. Irving's too. Not only was I not allowed to take Carl to protect me, I was not allowed to go again by myself.

There had to be more to the enigmatic white world than the caddy yard. Those ragtag boys didn't live in the fancy houses I'd seen while riding wide-eyed in the rumble seat of Professor Echol's roadster. But maybe some of the golfers did. Or the cyphers who spoke to us in the assembly at school. What were their lives like?

Next door was a link of sorts. Mrs. Vandyke worked at the governor's mansion—maid or housekeeper or cook. Her husband "ran on the road," a pullman porter or dining car waiter. Their son, Elbert, was seventeen, and his sister, Juanita, several years older.

One summer day in 1927, Mrs. Vandyke called me to the fence separating our backyards. Elbert was sick in bed and the doctor would be coming by. She and Juanita would be at work, and Mr. Vandyke would be on the road. Would I come over and spend the next few days looking after Elbert until the weekend?

I agreed, and it enabled me to see a whole new world through a tiny peephole.

Elbert crept painfully into the kitchen in his nightgown and opened the icebox crammed with things I'd never tasted before, and never even knew existed (all taken from the governor's mansion as "totes," part of Mrs. Vandyke's pay). Avocados, papayas, mangoes, and a foul-smelling, greattasting, juicy morsel called a durian fruit. "It smells like hell," Elbert said, "but tastes like heaven." I tried holding my nose as I ate the durian, but found myself robbed of the taste. Then there was limburger cheese, another clash of taste and smell.

Elbert was delirious. Not with pain, but with delight at my fascination over the exotic goodies he pulled from the icebox like rabbits out of a hat. There was even a dab of caviar, the taste of which repelled me. And cream cheese and a kind of pink fish he said was smoked salmon. (I later learned it was lox.)

There was vintage wine in an elegant bottle. It tasted like vinegar, but I loved the uncorking process. There was dark German beer—the bitterest thing I'd ever tasted, except for the quinine powder I was given when I had a cold or fever.

That icebox was an enchanted cornucopia. But even more enthralling were the photographs of the mansion's interior. There was no television then, so such elegance and grandeur was without parallel in my experience. I thought of the London home of Tarzan's woman, Jane, as the Ape Man stood bewildered in the midst of such luxury. The Oriental carpets were luxurious, even in black-and-white photographs. The dining room table—the scene, no doubt, of many state dinners—would never fit in our house, even with all the inside walls removed. The great regal chandelier hung over the polished wood of the table like a constellation of stars dancing on a mirror lake. I dreamed of sitting full-grown at the far end of the table, laden with Mrs. Vandyke's casseroles, all heads around it bowed while I intoned words of blessing: "O Father, we thank Thee for this food which Thou has prepared for—"

A knock at the door interrupted my thoughts. The doctor with his black bag had come. He scolded Elbert for being out of bed. After examining his pelvic area and observing its sensitivity, the doctor lanced a boil on Elbert's groin, half the size of a tennis ball. No anesthesia was used; he simply scrubbed the area with alcohol and cut boldly into the center of the swelling. Elbert screamed as the scalpel thrust home, and the blood and pus ran out of the incision. After medicating the wound, the doctor taped a bandage over it. Ordering Elbert to remain in bed and take aspirin as needed, he departed.

I wanted to get back to the photographs to see more of how the important people in the mysterious other world lived. But as I reached for the photograph album, another knock came at the door, a rhythmical one: "dum-da-da, dum-dum—dum-dum." Two of Elbert's friends, older boys like himself, had come to visit.

I got a bottle of beer for each of them and Elbert, feeling a twinge of sinfulness at handling the alcohol. They all seemed to talk at once and laugh at the same time. In the merriment, Elbert forgot his pain. They talked about girls, and it seemed that most of the girls had been with all of them. Sexual smells dominated the mirth.

"Oo-oo-ee," squealed Elbert, screwing up his face and holding his nose, "that girl of yours sho do smell awful!"

"Yeah," one of the boys laughingly agreed. "But how 'bout that other broad? The one you wuz with just 'fore ya got sick. How did *she* smell?"

"She smelled the very same way," Elbert acknowledged with a sheepish smile.

The hilarity then subsided. I wondered what the odors were like. Like durian fruits? Didn't the girls bathe? Or was it something from inside the organs that bathing would not remove? If it was so offensive, why did they go back to seek it?

I also wondered if that last girl had caused the swelling on Elbert's groin. I'd heard whispers about something called a "social disease." Maybe that's what Elbert had. I hoped I wouldn't catch it.

When Elbert got well, and I didn't have to take care of him any more, Mrs. Vandyke gave me a heavy, knitted yellow wool slip-on sweater as a gift in payment. Probably from the "Big House," it was incredibly warm, though a bit large, and I longed for winter so I could show it off.

That winter brought two events of importance to me. One, of course, was the wearing of my "new" sweater as I romped with Carl on the sidewalk. Carl would sit and "stay" at the corner. I would run halfway up the block and then call him. The majestic animal would run like a streak, silken hair flowing with the wind, easily overtaking me before the end of the block. Then he would jump happily around, proud of his achievement. Other boys watched with envy. Even the children from the Big House, where Mrs. Vandyke spent her days, would have been consumed by envy. I had their sweater and it went with my color much better than theirs, and their dog, if there was one, could not match Carl.

The second important event came in December 1927: the birth of my brother, Nathaniel.

For months I had known it was coming. In fact, I'd wished for it, having told my parents for more than a year that I wanted a brother. But now that the time was at hand, I was torn by competing thoughts. I wanted a brother, for he could be my alter ego, sharing my innermost thoughts. Yet, eight years younger, what sharing could he do?

I knew nothing about babies (puppies, yes, but not babies) and, not knowing, pushed it aside. My brother would somehow spring from the womb my age. We would be contemporaries.

On the other hand, did I really want another sibling, a boy "sister"? And worse, one who would usurp my position as the youngest, the "fair-haired boy," as it were.

I'm sure that I loved my sister. We shared many joys of our childhood lives, one of which was a new family car—a boxlike, top-heavy 1927 Dodge sedan that could cruise at thirty-five miles per hour. The car made the country accessible. Though daddy was the worst driver in the world, often thinking of something else and crossing the center line, many Sundays after church we would drive ten miles into the country to visit the Alexanders, an elderly black couple, at their farm. We would enjoy a country dinner of fried chicken or home-cured ham and fresh vegetables of every variety—all from their forty acres. The Alexanders were rough-hewn, kind, gentle, and proud.

"This whole place," mused one visiting city slicker as he filled his lungs with country air, "is so—so—*rustic.*"

"That's right," rejoined Mrs. Alexander, biting the words off as she clamped her jaw tightly. "We're *all* rusty out here—old place and old people, too!"

Sister and I had great fun playing with the ducks and baby chicks, running from geese, trying to milk a cow, and riding bareback on a slow and ancient nag—a work horse, not a riding horse. Once when I fell off the animal, sister was at my side, holding me in her arms almost before I hit the ground.

Late one Sunday afternoon, driving home from the Alexanders', daddy pulled the high-top Dodge off the macadam road and came to a stop. The four of us and Carl walked about fifty yards across a field of bluebonnets to a welcome patch of shade beneath wild-growing pecan trees and spreading poplars, and we all sat down in the shade on the grass.

I carried the gallon jar of lemonade and the basket of picnic lunch Mrs. Alexander had prepared—fried chicken, boiled eggs, potato salad, and peaches from her own trees.

"I hope that pig we hit doesn't suffer," Daddy said. "If it's badly hurt, I hope it dies quickly."

About three miles back, shortly after we had left the Alexanders' forty acres, the animal had run out of the bushes onto the road in front of us. Daddy had braked hard, and the square sedan screeched and shuddered and rocked precariously as he swerved to try to avoid contact. Despite his efforts, there had been a dull thump at the front end of the car and a squealing pig had hobbled into the bushes on the other side of the road. The squeals had followed us, fading as we lumbered on.

"Don't you think you should have stopped?" mother had asked, looking worried.

"No," daddy had replied with a frown. "Out in these rural parts, Negroes are killed for less."

I was sorry daddy had mentioned the pig; I wanted to forget those squeals.

The fried chicken was still crisp and warm, and the lemonade cool enough to be refreshing. As I bit into a drumstick, Carl, lying panting in the grass, waited patiently for his bone.

A black pickup truck with a crumpled front fender chugged noisily in front of the Dodge and stopped. Two overall-clad white men got out. One was tall and gaunt and the other two inches shorter, but wider.

The taller man had a shotgun, which he held by the barrel with one hand. Both looked grim. The heavier one shouted in a deep, throaty voice, "Hey!"

Carl's hind legs flexed, quickly and smoothly, flinging him to a standing position, alert. A low rumble rose in his throat. Daddy jumped to his feet as if jerked by a rope and walked rapidly to the men.

Mother made Carl sit and stay and, at the same time, grabbed sister's hand with one of hers and with the other reached for mine. She was too late. I had already gotten up and was following daddy toward the men.

"Brother, come back! You come back here!" sister yelled after me, to no avail.

The tall man had no lips; his mouth was a narrow slit. Like his eyes.

Damp black hair fell over his face, and he threw it back with a toss of the head. A cigarette dangled from his mouth.

The heavier man was wet with sweat; a red stubble covered his face, and a double chin was lost in a thick neck. His thick lips parted in a snarl as his tongue moved in a circle clockwise, licking them. He shoved his hands into his overall pockets.

The tall one spoke, seemingly without moving his lips, cigarette ashes undisturbed: "You done kilt mah hawg, nigger." The ashes fell now. "Y'all gon pay fer that hawg," he drawled. "Ah wuz gon show that hawg in the county fair. Y'all gon pay a purty penny fer that hawg."

Daddy was the picture of contrition. The straw summer hat he always wore in the sun was in his hand. When he spoke, he was looking down, and I thought his voice a trifle higher-pitched than usual.

"I'm sorry, sir," he said. "I did hear a thump two or three miles back, but I wasn't sure I hit anything. If I killed your pig, I'll gladly pay for it. How much do you want for it?"

"That'll cost y'all forty-five dollars, nigger," replied the tall one.

"Well, sir, I don't have any money with me right now," daddy began, "but—"

The thick man interrupted, circling his lips again with his tongue: "Well, now, ain't that jes too bad."

Daddy continued: ". . . but I do have a check with me—a salary check from Samuel Houston College up there in Austin. A check for fifty-seven dollars. You may have that. I'll endorse it over to you."

"Le' me see it," the gaunt man drawled through unmoving lips.

Avoiding sudden movement, daddy reached with his left hand for his wallet in his hip pocket. Squinting eyes followed daddy's hand; the dark-haired man raised the stock of his gun from the ground. When nothing but the wallet came from the pocket in daddy's hand, the gun descended again to rest.

Daddy started to put his hat on his head to free the right hand to manipulate the wallet, thought better of it, and placed it under his arm instead. When he got the check out, he handed it to the tall man, who promptly dropped it.

As it fluttered to the ground at the man's feet, he said, "Pick it up, nigger."

Everything in me silently screamed, "Don't do it, daddy. Don't pick it up. He dropped it. Let him pick it up."

But daddy stooped and picked up the check, that curious frown-grin still on his face.

I was overwhelmed with anger. And shame. I turned and walked back to the patch of shade and sat down. I was silent, but I thought, "I'll never do that when I grow up. They'll have to kill me."

Mother looked at me and said nothing. Sister scolded, "You stay right here, brother. They'll hurt you."

Minutes later, after endorsing the check for the men, daddy walked back to our shade and ate in silence. In fact, none of us spoke, except sister, who said with a frown, "Brother, you're crazy—going up there. Didn't you see those men had a gun?"

I didn't reply. And I couldn't even look at daddy. Nor did he want to look at me. My heart swelled with rebellion.

Sister was protective like a mother hen. But she was still a tattletale, still jealous of my outperforming her in school. Once I hit her, punching her in true cowboy fashion. No sooner had I delivered the blow than daddy knocked me to the floor with a slap, and as I lay there stunned—he had never struck me before—with one swift movement he removed his belt from his trousers and walloped me. I was more shocked and embarrassed than hurt. Mother just stood there looking sad. Sister didn't gloat; she stared in wide-eyed amazement. But daddy was not finished yet. He locked me in the clothes closet as final punishment and let me out only when I screamed and banged on the door and shouted that I could not breathe and was dying.

My relationship with daddy was permanently altered on that day. Throughout the years, whenever I looked at him or talked to him, I remembered the whipping and the closet—not really with anger, but with incredulity. It rankled. The embarrassment never completely went away. Between us a fence was erected—which I peered over, looked under, reached through, but was never able to remove. I learned the lesson well, though. Never again have I struck a female.

In retrospect, I think that perhaps with that punch to my sister's stomach, I was trying to kill my brother, then growing in my mother's.

Would my brother be a tattletale, too? Would he be smarter than I or resentful at my being smarter than he?

I viewed the coming event with a dreamy excitement, but also misgivings. On December 16, 1927, it occurred while I was at school. We knew it was coming that day. All preparations had been made. A practical nurse was at our house and a doctor was coming. Daddy—yes, daddy—bustled around, getting us off to school.

After school, sister and I rushed home, literally running all the way. The doctor had gone, and the nurse would not let us touch the baby. He was wrinkled and bald and ugly, but he had a great throat. Carl was nervous at the screaming and rushing around, but they wouldn't let him come close to the baby. Somehow that dog seemed to understand and did not press his curiosity. Carl always understood. It was he, no one else, who was my best friend. As I stood there with inexplicable feelings, he pushed his nose into the palm of my hand as if to say, "It's all right, don't worry." I hugged Carl tightly about the neck even as I looked at my brother.

* * *

It seemed that Nathaniel had just been born when five months later, he faced death. He contracted bronchial pneumonia—in those days pneumonia was still a dread killer, long before the "wonder drugs" penicillin and sulfa had been discovered.

A very large, very dark woman, a registered nurse, was in the house for several days, around the clock. She was in total command. She ordered mother around and even daddy. Her directives were absolutely authoritative. She was Nathaniel's link to life, and all of us were her servants.

The treatment by today's standards was primitive. A large pot of boiling water was always on the stove. There were mustard plasters and hot poultices, and the smell of rubbing alcohol, Vicks', and other curatives permeated the house.

Frequent, terrifying coughing fits from the crib yanked mother from her chair and hurled her to cribside. But the nurse was always there first. For all her bulk, she moved with the quickness of a cat. Once mother collided with the large woman and almost fell as she was brushed effortlessly aside. With beads of perspiration glistening on her dark skin, she was instantly transformed from a juggernaut into a soft and gentle guardian angel, lifting the convulsing baby into her arms and turning him over, face down and head lowered, as she stroked and patted his back until the coughing stopped and the phlegm was expelled. She wiped his nose and mouth and returned him to his bed.

During those anxious days, that woman was *God*—all-powerful, ever-present, and all-knowing—holding life and death in her huge hands. On the rare occasions when she took a nap on a nearby cot or in an overstuffed chair, she sternly instructed mother as to what to do in every contingency. And to wake her if in doubt.

Before dawn on Saturday, the big lady awakened those of us who were sleeping and announced that it was now in the hands of God. That day, she informed us, the crisis would come. I had no idea how she knew except that, being like God, she knew everything.

Her words drove me into a state of suspended animation, standing around like a zombie. I thought of Friskie. I felt like death and almost wished that I could die in my brother's place, for then I'd be spared the horror of seeing him go.

Mother bit her lip and fought back tears. Sister sat immobilized by worry. The nurse hovered over the crib like a giant mother hen—calm, self-possessed. Daddy prepared breakfast. Oatmeal, toast, and milk. Afterward, he put his hand on my shoulder. I flinched and he removed it.

"Junior," he said, "there's a track meet at the ball park today—Sam Houston against Tillotson College. Let's go. I think you'll enjoy it."

I didn't think I would enjoy anything, but I said I would go.

"When we get back," daddy assured me, "everything will be all right."

"Are you sure?" I asked anxiously, hopefully.

"No, I'm not absolutely sure," he replied, "but I think Nathaniel will be fine if we pray hard enough."

"Daddy," I asked, "what did she mean when she said the crisis will come today? Did she mean she thinks Nathaniel is going to die today?"

"No," he replied, "she meant that by evening we will know whether he will continue to be with us."

We walked to the ball park, about a mile away, instead of going by car. As we walked along, he grasped my hand. My impulse was to pull it away, for I thought of the strap and the closet. Daddy must have read my mind, for he held my hand more tightly.

Eyes open, so he could see where we were walking, he began a prayer:

Our Heavenly Father, who knowest all things, and who controls the living and the dying of all Thy creatures, have mercy on us this day. Permit our loved one to remain with us and brighten our lives.

But, Heavenly Father, not our will but thine be done. In Christ's name, we ask it. Amen.

We walked more briskly now, and daddy squeezed my hand even more tightly. I tried to squeeze back, but something inside wouldn't let me. The fence was still there.

My eyes watched the running, the jumping, the hurdling, the vaulting, the throwing of the discus, and the shotput, but only a small part of my mind was with it. The sound of the cheering voices, the shrieks and yells, were good for me. Especially since we won most events. The joyousness of our crowd was contagious. At times, it dragged me out of my moodiness, lured me away from my dread of the return home. There were popcorn, peanuts, and Coca-Cola, and daddy allowed me to gorge myself that day.

In midafternoon, we turned homeward. Daddy let me set the pace. At times I walked fast, for I wanted home and good news. At times it was a funeral trek. As we approached the house, my feet dragged. I did not want to go in.

"Come on, Junior, let's go," said daddy, and he took my hand again.

Up the steps and onto the porch. Then we heard Nathaniel crying as though the world were ending. Or beginning. Daddy smiled and so I thought that even though the cries were agonizing, the signal must, inexplicably, be good.

The gentle Amazon swung the door open. Heavy lips were bent in a huge bow, edges upward. I'd never seen her smile before. She spoke four words: "The fever has broken."

Mother sat in a rocker with the baby in her lap. The long ordeal was etched in her face, but relief shone through.

I felt closer to Nathaniel through the years that followed. It was for me as though our beings had merged by sharing triumph over death.

In March 1930, another move was in the works for the Farmer family. This time, daddy would be professor of Old Testament and Hebrew at Gammon Theological Seminary in Atlanta, Georgia. He rolled the school's name off his tongue with relish; I knew that it was a step upward and something to his liking.

Mother scolded me for complaining in a moment of rashness that every time I started feeling at home, feeling that I belonged somewhere, we had to pack up and go. "When your Aunt Helen and Uncle Fred come to visit us next week," she added, "please don't let them hear you say anything like that."

Inwardly, I bridled at not being allowed to express the feelings I had. But what I said was simply, "I won't."

Aunt Helen, another of mother's three sisters, was five years older than Sadie and three years younger than mother. An aggressive woman in command of every situation, Aunt Helen brought to mind the giant nurse. But Helen Jones was not a giant. A small woman, like all the women in my family, she was nevertheless a domineering type, dominating everyone around her.

Everyone, that is, except her husband, Fred. No one dominated him. A hard-working, hard-drinking, heavy-eating, loud-talking man of ample proportion and warm heart, Fred Jones was a good provider for Helen and their daughter. He worked for the Grand Central Railroad in New York at their offices there. Evenings and weekends, he moonlighted on the streets of Harlem, selling tickets for something he called the Irish Sweepstakes, which I later learned was the ghetto stock market—the numbers game. Uncle Fred did well.

Muriel, their daughter, was not really their daughter. Actually, she was the child of my mother's other sister, Louise. But since Aunt Louise was not married when Muriel was born, the baby was given to Aunt Helen and Uncle Fred, who were childless. They raised and loved her as their very own.

I had seen Muriel's baby pictures before I met her and thought her an adorable baby, the prettiest I'd ever seen. But all of mother's relatives were of striking appearance, with large black eyes staring knowingly at the world. I never knew where those eyes came from, the Frenchman or the Seminole woman. When they came to visit us, Muriel was three, and her looks put the earlier photographs to shame.

Muriel had not been able to have a dog in their two-bedroom Harlem apartment, so she could not stay away from Carl. One day when Uncle Fred had walked downtown to buy a roast of beef for our dinner, he also brought back beef scraps and bones for Carl. As always, Carl was being fed outdoors at the side of the house. Gulping down the meat and saving the bones for dessert, he was totally absorbed with his feast. Muriel ran to him and threw her arms around his neck and hugged him. Before I could utter a word to stop her, Carl, with a snarl, swung his head toward her, his teeth hitting her forehead and opening a half-inch bloody gash. Muriel started crying.

I gasped, expecting Uncle Fred, who was watching, to scream at Carl and make a scene. So, I yelled at Carl first, as Aunt Helen ran to Muriel and took her into the house, where she and mother cleansed, medicated, and bandaged the cut. I hoped that there would be no permanent scar to mar her pretty face.

"No, Junior," said Uncle Fred, "don't scold Carl. It's not his fault. Muriel should know better than to grab hold of a dog while he's eating meat. Maybe she'll learn a lesson from it."

When the dog had finished his meal, Uncle Fred walked up to him and stroked his head and back. Aunt Helen joined him. But Muriel kept her distance.

"Come here, Muriel," Uncle Fred said. "Tell Carl you're sorry you got in the way of his food."

Muriel did, and Carl sniffed her forehead and licked it, wagging his tail. She threw her arms around his neck and squeezed him tight, and Carl washed her face with his tongue. His apology was fully evident.

As the time came for our guests to plan their departure, I glimpsed something of the complexity and absurdity of southern caste in 1930.

Uncle Fred, Aunt Helen, and Muriel had come down from New York by Pullman. A bedroom, they said. They had no problem getting the Pullman reservation from New York going south, but they expected difficulty getting a bedroom from Texas, going north. Also, had they come by coach, they said, they would have had to move to the front coach nearest the engine when they crossed the Mason-Dixon line. That sounded strange to me. The back of the bus and the front of the train.

The problem being discussed at dinner then, over steaks bought by Uncle Fred, was how to get a Pullman reservation from Austin, Texas. With a shrewd smile and a wink at Uncle Fred, daddy said he thought he could arrange it. He would have to go down to the railroad station and talk with the station manager. I asked if I could go along. Mother frowned and shook her head. But daddy thought for a moment, plucking hairs out of his balding head, and said, "Yes, I think you should come, Junior. I have no classes tomorrow, so we'll go in the morning."

It made me feel that I was growing up now. Important conversations were no longer being concealed from me. At ten, I was becoming a man, and I felt eager and strangely prepared for it.

The next morning, I felt as I had when I looked at the white boy at the golf club come up off the ground with a knife in his hand.

I clenched my jaws when daddy said, "Come on, Junior. Let's go."

This time, we went in the car. Daddy wore a dark suit, white shirt, and black tie. And a hat, brim turned up. I had on my Sunday best. The high-top, square-shaped Dodge whirred angrily, as if it would be part of the confrontation and was itching for a fight. Daddy and I didn't talk as we rode to the station.

"Awright, whatcha want, uncle?" asked the ticket agent.

"I'm Dr. Farmer, registrar of Sam Houston College," daddy replied. "I would like to speak to your station manager."

"Well, whutta ya wanna talk t' him about? Is sumpin wrong?"

"No, not exactly," daddy replied, "but we have a very important visitor in town from New York, and he's been called back home for a big meeting. And if we can't make arrangements to get him back in time, we may have a lot of serious problems down here."

"Well, he ain't here now. But jus set down ova there," he said, motioning us to a bench in the "colored" waiting room. "I gotta make a phone call."

We sat on a bench. The agent's phone conversation was not loud enough for us to hear. Then he looked at us and asked loudly, "Whut y'all say yo name wuz?"

"Dr. Farmer. J. L. Farmer, registrar at Sam Houston College."

After a few more moments of conversation, the agent hung up and said to us, "Awright, y'all jes set there. Th' manager's gon' call me back in a minute." (We later learned that the manager had called the president of the college to ask if he had a registrar named Dr. J. L. Farmer.)

When the call back came, the agent's eyes widened, and he turned to us and said, "Y'all jes set there. Th' manager, he's gon' be heah in a few minutes."

He must not have had far to come, for he was there in ten minutes. He motioned us into a small, cluttered office. Daddy and I sat down without being asked. I noticed, though, that Daddy removed his hat before entering the office. I wondered why.

"Well, now, Dr. Farmer," said the manager, "who's this big important visitor who's come down heah to Austin?"

Daddy answered, "Mr. Frederick Jones. From New York City. I *know* you've heard about him."

"Yeah, ah have," said the manager. "He's one of them big nigras from New York, ain't he? Editor of one a' them nigra newspapers up there or somethin', ain't he?"

"That's right," Daddy said, "and he's got to leave here tomorrow for an emergency meeting of all the editors. He's chairman of it."

I looked at daddy, puzzled by the lies and shocked that he would tell them. He avoided my eyes.

"Tha's right. We don' want no trouble down heah," the manager said, "but whut's the problem? We got several trains goin' north an' east tomorra."

"I know," said daddy, "but Mr. Jones can't ride in a coach like the rest of us do. He's got to go first class, Pullman."

The manager let out a low whistle and then was silent for a minute.

"Awright, I c'n give 'im a Pullman reservation fer tomorra. But ah'd rather have 'im git on th' train at night 'stead a' in th' day. Ah know you understan' cause you're from down heah. What do he want? An upper berth or a lower?"

"Yes," said daddy, "I understand. But he can't use an upper or lower berth; he has to have a bedroom, because Mrs. Jones and their daughter are down here with us."

"Awright," replied the manager. "I got a bedroom on the train tomorra night. He c'n have that, but it'll cost more. A bedroom'll be better th'n a berth, anyway, ain't too many people gonna see 'im that way, doctor."

Daddy paid him the money, got his receipt and Uncle Fred's reservation, and we left.

On the way home, daddy read my thoughts. "Junior," he said, "I had to tell that lie about your Uncle Fred. That was the only way we could get the reservation. The Lord will forgive me."

I was deeply troubled by my father's accommodation to a system that made him less than a man. I despised that within him that would not fight, perhaps because I saw the same survival instinct in myself. But I swore that when I grew up, scared or not, I'd never kowtow to meanness. Though I could not be Nelson, so help me I would find some way to defeat the boy in the caddy yard when he, too, grew up. And the men with the shotgun on the road from the Alexanders' farm.

The time *would* come. But first I sensed, without really knowing, I would have to escape from my jail. In a prison, locked behind bars of conformity in my father's house, I wanted to break down the doors, to spring out, to be myself.

If the boy is father of the man; and if, as they say, one's character and direction are formed in the first ten years, then my course was set in Holly Springs and Austin. The places were incidental; they could have been anywhere in the South.

In the precocious child, two warring natures had emerged. One gentle, even timid; the other hotly rebellious. One repelled by the violence that everywhere abounded, the other impelled to rebel aginst twin conformities: that of the PK—the too-good child of the preacher—and that of accommodation with the racial etiquette of pre–Martin Luther King America.

Even as a child, I hated the lying, the dissembling, the subterfuge, the pretense—the squeezing of one's soul into a room too small.

Symbolizing both conformities I despised was my father, so in a sense the rebellion was against him. A highly complex man, he projected three images, three distinct faces: to the black community, a savant and solon; to the whites, a "good" Negro, compromising if not subservient, who knew his place; and to his son, a strong father who, perhaps unknowingly, fostered the spirit of rebellion.

What course would my rebellion take? In 1930, at the age of ten, I could not have predicted war. Yet, when it came I was bound to resist it, and the resistance just as surely would shape the contours of my revolt against the vagaries of race.

PART THREE

Drawing Board

CHAPTER 7

THE WINDY CITY AND WINNIE

"JIM, FOR GOD'S SAKE *turn on your radio,*" the shrill voice of Bernice Fisher screeched over the phone. "The Japanese have attacked Pearl Harbor! We're going to war!"

I slammed down the receiver and nearly broke the knob off the radio turning it on.

The following day, the president addressed the nation: "December 7, 1941, a day that will live in infamy . . ." The sonorous voice of Franklin Delano Roosevelt slowly hammered that date into history.

We were at war.

Bernice, a white student at the University of Chicago Theological School, was a passionately committed religious pacifist and a Norman Thomas socialist. She called me as soon as the speech was over.

"My God, Jim, what does it mean? Does this kill the nonviolence movement before it gets started?"

"No!" I shouted in a voice of protest, not confidence.

"We can't let it stop us!" cried Bernice.

I removed the receiver from my ear and could almost see her gritted teeth and tiny, clenched fists, remnants of chewed fingernails biting into palms, as she hissed the words into the phone.

I had met FDR six months before. In April, a letter had come on White House stationery:

For a long time, I have thought that it would be a good idea for some of the leading young people of the country to meet with the President to discuss a number of matters of mutual concern.

I am, therefore, inviting you and about thirty other national youth leaders to have a buffet supper with me at the White House at 5:30 P.M. on June 5th, 1941.

Afterwards, you will have three hours with the President. He will speak briefly, after which you will be free to raise any questions you wish.

R.S.V.P.

It was signed by Eleanor Roosevelt.

I went. What twenty-one-year-old wouldn't have? Especially if he were, as I was, national chairman of the Youth Committee Against War at a time when war was imminent.

On the portico of the White House, there were card tables, each with four folding chairs, arranged for the supper. I sat at one with two other youths, both white, whom I did not know.

Mrs. Roosevelt took the fourth seat. I had seen her picture many times in papers and newsreels, but I'd never seen her in person. She was a tall, large woman, broad-shouldered but not fat. Her teeth protruded slightly, forcing her lips out when she closed them. Eleanor Roosevelt was homely, but magnificently homely. She brought to mind the great black woman Mary McLeod Bethune, who also lacked physical attractiveness. Ugliness has its own splendor when it houses a soul of beauty.

She looked tired, drained, and unhappy, but radiating from her was a ferocious dedication. She and I monopolized the conversation at our table. I think there were no other blacks there, and she moved toward me to prevent me from feeling strange and uncomfortable. I was flattered and immediately felt at ease with her. I liked her. There was no subterfuge, no patronizing. She listened to my views with seriousness and responded as an equal. I was being accepted as a peer, not an inferior, by a person of supreme importance in the scale of things: the wife of the most powerful man in the world.

It was, therefore, with excitement but also some regret that I heard the announcement that the president was ready to receive us and we should proceed into a designated room. I hated to leave her.

We went to the room and took seats. Mrs. Roosevelt sat in a front seat. I sat in a middle row. The door at the back opened, and all our heads turned. There sat the president, paralyzed by polio, in a wheelchair; that seductive smile, his trademark, electrified his face; a long ivory cigarette holder tilted upward in uneven teeth.

We rose, and suddenly all of us were paralyzed, too. An aide rolled the wheelchair down an aisle and behind a table in the front of the room and secured the brakes. The frozen smile thawed and drained from his face as his gaze moved from one side of the room to the other, eyes pensive.

Harry Hopkins, adviser and assistant to the president, announced that we should file by the president and shake his hand and tell him our respective names and organizations. Hopkins then retired to a chair in the back of the room with a sneer that twisted his gaunt, anemic face and curled the full lips.

Roosevelt's smile returned in all its majesty. With his left hand, he removed the cigarette holder from his lips as our single-file line approached and wafted smoke rings into the air. At intervals, the ivory appendage returned jauntily to his teeth as he nodded benevolently when each person identified himself. When it came my turn, he removed the cigarette holder, and I thought that the smile was dimmed ever so slightly by curiosity. His eyebrows arched as he asked me to repeat my name and organization. Then the smile and the cigarette holder returned simultaneously as he reached for the next hand.

Formalities done with, President Roosevelt made his remarks in his usual, beguiling manner. Like an abbreviated fireside chat, it was only five minutes in length and held all—even those of us who disagreed with its essence—prisoners of its charm. Its substance was that the war in Europe was an Armageddon, the final struggle between the children of darkness and those of light, and that our moral obligation was clear: to go to the rescue of Britain and France, who were the "defenders of freedom and democracy."

Upon finishing, he nodded with satisfaction: a maestro ending a hackneyed ditty at a children's party, confident that anything from the baton of a master is a masterpiece.

Immediately, a score of hands waved in the air. Gesturing with the cigarette in holder, he selected me for the first question. Out of the corner of my eye, I saw Eleanor's face turn toward me encouragingly. I stood with some trepidation; I was not sure the words would come. Maybe I would stutter or stammer or my mind would go blank.

"Mr. President," I began, with more pomposity than I'm afraid a twenty-one-year-old should have, "in your opening remarks you described Britain and France as champions of freedom. In light of their colonial policies in Africa, which give the lie to that principle, how can they be considered its defenders?"

FDR's smile disappeared. He blew smoke through pursed lips and studied its drift to the ceiling. Ten seconds went by before the president broke the quiet of the room. He pointed his cigarette holder at me, stabbing the air to emphasize each word: "Let's not put it that way. Let's put it this way. In which country would *you* rather live today—France or Nazi Germany?"

The smile returned as he eyed me with self-satisfaction, ivory prop tilted upward in his teeth.

I stood again to respond, but before I could utter a word, Eleanor had leaped to her feet, aiming her finger at the president like a pistol.

"Just a minute," she shouted, voice rising from a contralto to soprano crescendo. "You did *not* answer the question!"

Her accusing finger froze. FDR, visibly angered, lit a cigarette and bit the ivory mouthpiece with a vengeance, puffing streams of smoke.

"The question was *this*," he hissed, rewording my question. "Why do I consider Britain and France to be more on the side of freedom than Nazi Germany, despite their colonialization laws? And I answered it thus. You will please let *me* handle the questions!"

As Eleanor sat down, her face was saying, "I'll see you later."

I mumbled something in response to FDR's rephrasing of my question. But it didn't matter; I'd been defeated by an expert. But at least I'd gotten the question out. Later—was it Teheran or Casablanca or some other wartime summit?—the press reported that Roosevelt had chided Churchill about British imperialism in Africa while fighting for freedom, and the prime minister had turned on him angrily, saying, "Franklin, you don't know a bloody thing about Africa, so keep your damn nose out of it!" I wondered if the president had remembered or if Eleanor had prodded him further.

After fielding a few more questions, smiling genially, the great man looked at his watch and announced that he was late for a meeting with Cordell Hull, secretary of state, regarding critical new developments in Europe, and would have to go now. "But *you* don't have to leave," he said. "Stay as long as you like. Harry Hopkins will take over."

Roosevelt was wheeled out, waving and smiling as we stood, and Harry Hopkins came to the front. He was a very ugly man, who, unfortunately, lacked Eleanor's inner radiance and reminded me of a spitting cobra.

"You kids have your nerve. This is the greatest president we've ever had, and you acted like you were trying to embarrass him with your juvenile questions."

"Just a minute, Mr. Hopkins," Mrs. Roosevelt said calmly. "These young people have done exactly what I asked them here to do. And I'm glad they came. I want them to know that."

Hopkins averted his eyes to hide disgust as he ignored the intervention. I had the feeling that Eleanor had fought and overcome Hopkins to get the meeting scheduled and to keep it on the calendar.

The questions and answers went on for another twenty minutes or so. But everyone soon tired of it without the verve and drama of Franklin Delano Roosevelt.

On the way out the door of the White House, as I shook hands with Mrs. Roosevelt, I said: "I hope you do not feel that we were too presumptuous in the questions we asked the president."

"Not at all," she replied in her contralto-soprano. "The questions you asked needed to be asked. I'm glad you asked them, and I'm glad you came."

In August 1941, I had left the family nest for the first time and moved to Chicago. At twenty-one, fresh out of theological school at Howard University and filled with the social gospel, I had a job as race relations secretary of the Fellowship of Reconciliation (FOR). It was a kind of nondenominational Quaker body, eschewing all violence and rejecting all war. I was assigned to work out of the regional office in Chicago, instead of headquarters in New York, because it was more centrally located and I'd be traveling a lot. Like most full-time jobs, some weeks it was part-time and others no-time.

My salary, which came with regularity, was fifteen dollars a week. But of youthful age and full of vinegar, raring to take on the world, acknowledging no limits to the possible, dying to stop war, longing to keep an eighteen-year covenant with myself, I'd gladly have worked at that job for nothing. I would have paid for the privilege.

I'd never been away from home before, except for short trips. The Windy City was a challenge, and I felt ready for any challenge or adventure whatsoever. Chicago was for me the beginning of life. All else was prelude.

I was awed by Lake Michigan and intimidated by the thundering el's. Southside slums with their layers of alley-fronting porches, joined together by flights of rotting stairs, dragged me into fits of depression and jerked me out in fury. The ageless, heavy-stoned buildings of the Loop seemed to plunge a needle of raw power into my veins. The city itself, a rip-snorting behemoth spanning it all, told me somehow that the time had come.

I was not the only youth who had come to Chicago that year to tilt at the windmills churning the nation's air. There was, for instance, Ben Segal—an intellectual, pipe-smoking, tweed-wearing, small-statured Jew in his middle twenties—who ran the Midwest office of the Keep America Out of War Committee, a Norman Thomas Democratic Socialist group.

When Ben heard that I had come to town and was staying at the Y and looking for an even cheaper room, he called and told me that he had a small apartment, one bedroom, on Fifty-third Street in the heart of Chicago's Southside. I was invited to share it at no cost; he was paid enough to cover rent and his own food. I could have the other single bed. Or the couch. Whichever.

I jumped at it. My fifteen dollars would stretch much farther with a free roof over my head. And there would be the warmth of a home, not the coldness of an institution. Crackling conversation of people of like mind, even if no crackling fire in a fireplace.

Ben and I got along well in this flat just west of Cottage Grove Avenue. He kept office hours, but I didn't because my work was largely traveling to make speeches with schedules arranged from New York. So, most days, I had the apartment alone. To think. And to plan.

It was the best of all possible worlds for me. I had shelter and money for food. I gave speeches across the nation to bounce ideas off people of like mind. There was leisure to plan an assault on the demons of violence and bigotry, which had shaped my outlook on life. Above all, I was away from my father's home and free to become myself.

There had to be a "master plan," a blueprint for winning equality. So, with all the pretentiousness of youth, I began preparing the grand scenario. I didn't imagine that I was not experienced enough for that task and lacked the knowledge or the sophistication. I did not want to hear that the problems were more complex than my mind could conceive. No matter that others of greater maturity and scholarship had broken their heads on the walls I now clawed at with the irrepressible fingernails of youth. What could be mightier than the fierceness of wanting and the fervor of feeling?

What I wrote and rewrote was entitled, "A Provisional Plan for Brotherhood Mobilization." "Provisional" because it was going to evolve with the loving thoughts of those who shared the same sentiments. "Brotherhood" because that was the religious perception of progress, dictated by my own upbringing. "Mobilization" for there was a climate of war, and that was how war was waged. And this, too, would be war.

When my mind became a muddle of disarrayed thoughts, I put on my brown windbreaker and, bucking the already chilling fall wind off the lake, went down the street to the Bronzeville Drugstore just east of Cottage Grove Avenue. The heady aroma of a cigar would clear the head.

I selected the cigar, panatela-style, sleek and elegant. Like the svelt, olive-complexioned beauty behind the tobacco and cashier's counter, whose languorous eyes and quizzical smile stopped me in midsentence, openmouthed, as I asked for a White Owl panatela.

"One?" she asked, in a voice that matched the languor of her eyes, brows above them lifting a bit.

"No, two," said I, the last of the big spenders, mentally counting the days before the next paycheck.

Our eyes met for a moment, as the little smile played at her lips. Her dark hair lay in twin braids over firm, boyish breasts and extended nearly to her waist. At the end of each braid was a red rosebud set off against the navy blue smock. Artistic women held a special attraction for me, and I could picture her before an easel under a garret skylight, matching color with form.

Her long, tapered fingers caressed the petals of one rosebud gently, as I, with effort, tore my eyes away and turned and walked out. My walk from the drugstore had a touch of swagger, for I knew that the eyes were pursuing me, and I wanted to conceal my uncertainty, to exude confidence, and to show that quality, acceptable at the time, called *machismo.* The swagger came easily, for I was one inch over six feet tall, 190 pounds, with wide shoulders and slim waist.

The weeks that followed were sheer intensity. They were days in which everything seemed to be falling into place in my life. My brain waltzed between two preoccupations: the lined yellow legal pad on the kitchen table before me, and the twenty-year-old girl with the turned-up nose in the drugstore.

In a sense, the two things consuming my interest were really one. At least they converged in important ways. This knight had slain no dragons yet, but he was about to. Would that not make him more attractive to the maiden? And with this composite of all my favorite movie actresses— Lamar, Garbo, Tierney, Leigh, and Horne—this mixture of all my love fantasies wrapped in a coffee-with-cream skin at my side, how could bringing a dragon down be difficult? Seizing upon an instrument of battle would bring her within grasp and, conversely, her embrace would make my victory in the conflict all but assured. The two were inexorably joined.

A day did not pass that I did not stop work to go to the drugstore, sometimes for cigarettes or chewing gum to break the monotony of the cigars. But always to see Winnie Christie. (When I had asked her name and been told, I merely thanked her and walked out.)

On one of the early visits, she left me standing at the counter with an "Excuse me, please" and trotted gracefully from her station to pick up and caress a mewing cat that had wandered in from the street. I leaned against the cashier's counter and watched her get a saucer of milk from the lunch counter and place it on the floor for the cat. Her smock, light blue this time, was knee-length, revealing tailored tan slacks and tasseled loafers below it.

When Winnie returned to the counter, her eyes were fluid and her lips moist and smiling. So was my heart.

"Two White Owl panatelas?" she asked, sitting on a stool with elbows resting on the counter and hands clasped under her chin.

"No," I answered, "just chewing gum this time."

Her eyes searched for mine and found them. Obviously, she had come to expect my daily visit, and, I hoped, to look forward to it. I was embarrassed at the transparency of my interest. And she, I think, was curious and a little disappointed at my failure to approach her.

But I was imprisoned within my own shyness and inexperience with things romantic. Physically and intellectually an attractive young adult, socially I was somewhat less developed than average. In college days, I had been so much younger than the girls—having entered at fourteen, when the girls were seventeen, and graduated at eighteen—and more inhibited and less worldly than they. At seventeen, a girl is a woman; at fourteen, a boy is a child. A wallflower at dances, when I dared to go, I was uncomfortable even asking for a date. I should have been playing stickball in the street.

Winnie was my first serious attraction. I would have to make my move, but one that failed could slam the door. Delaying the approach might delay the closing of that door. And I wanted it to remain open. Indefinitely.

On one of my visits, her smile changed to a faraway look as she gave me my change. She hummed the tune of a popular song: "I Guess I'll Have to Dream the Rest."

Walking home, the words of the melody came to me:

> I guess I'll have to dream the rest
> Of honeymoon cruises so near to my heart . . .

She had given me a message. The ball, so to speak, was in my court now. My step quickened, and the cool wind was exhilarating. I went back to my pencil and yellow pad on the kitchen table with more zest than ever.

The yellow pad was my element, but as I studied the empty page, Winnie's face emerged on it. I got a beer from the refrigerator (it was Ben's, but he wouldn't mind) and paced the uncarpeted living room floor, removing my shoes to avoid bringing the banging of a broomstick against the ceiling downstairs.

The vision of the girl at the cashier's counter blurred and for the moment was obliterated by the pacing. In its place, I was gripped by a mental collage, a composite of bits and pieces and many images searing my thoughts and coming into focus—pictures of empty and angry and hopeless black faces swarming out of greasy spoon joints and seamy bars on Forty-seventh Street, while slick-haired, zoot-suited, sidewalk dandies shuffled by to the beat of jukeboxes splitting eardrums inside storefronts. Pictures of walk-up tenement slums floating in an aroma of chitterlings and collard greens and hamhocks, teeming with people and shared by cockroaches and beady-eyed rats. Pictures of sharecroppers' shacks on southern plantations patrolled by red-necked, tobacco-chewing, riding bosses with their whips, visible and invisible. Pictures of hooded Klansmen. And of guns. And ropes. Of "FOR COLORED" and "FOR WHITES" signs, and back seats of buses and Jim Crow coaches on trains. And Jim Crow neighborhoods and Jim Crow schools. And drinking fountains and toilets. Of plant gates of defense industries, many with invisible signs saying, "WHITES ONLY."

The montage, once formed, froze, and thoughts licked around its edges as I paced the floor. None of this is chiseled in stone, I thought. Then why has it all persisted? Despite NAACP and the Urban League; despite Fred Douglass; despite DuBois and James Weldon Johnson; despite Charles Hueston, Thurgood Marshall, Bill Hastie, and a whole battery of superb lawyers; despite the bombardment of the nation's ears by writers who can stride into the human heart and orators who put Demosthenes to shame. Despite it all, segregation persists.

Something, then, is missing. Anyone who says that all we need is more of the same is a liar or a fool. Thoreau put his finger on it: "Most of all, I must see to it that I do not lend myself to the evil which I condemn."

Segregation will go on as long as we permit it to. Words are not enough; there must be action. We must withhold our support and participation from the institution of segregation in every area of American life—not an individual witness to purity of conscience, as Thoreau used it, but a coordinated movement of mass noncooperation as with Gandhi. And civil disobedience when laws are involved. And jail where necessary. More than the elegrant cadre of generals we now have, we also must have an army of ground troops. Like Gandhi's army, it must be nonviolent. Guns would be suicidal for us. Yes, Gandhi has the key for me to unlock the door to the American dream.

The American dream? It is essentially the Hebraic-Christian ethos— brotherhood. The objective is the method. As Gandhi put it: the means are not justified by the end; they determine it. We cannot achieve a

raceless society through racist methods. We must demand of all who believe—whites, too—that they must, as a matter of conscience, as well as
strategy, withdraw from participation in racist practices.

Precisely how? That is yet to be determined in detail. The first step is
forging the sword. The next step is exactly how to wield it.

I drained the last gulp from the beer bottle, left the parlor, and attacked
the yellow pad on the kitchen table. Words surged onto the paper. The
movement must have "a distinctive and radical approach. It must strive
. . . not to make housing in ghettos more tolerable, but to destroy residential segregation; not to make Jim Crow facilities the equal of others, but to
abolish Jim Crow; not to make racial discrimination more bearable, but to
wipe it out. . . . We must effectively repudiate every form of racism. We
must forge the instrumentalities through which that nationwide repudiation can be effected. We must not stop until racial brotherhood is established in the United States as a fact, as well as an ideal."*

The thinking, the pacing, the writing, and the walks to the Bronzeville
Drugstore went on through a blustery November and an icy first week of
December, interrupted only by short trips by bus and train to make
speeches for FOR in Madison, Milwaukee, Cleveland, and Indianapolis,
and by meetings with other religious pacifists and socialists like Bernice
Fisher.

Bernice combined a fiery hatred of racism with a violent rejection of
war. Both evils made her fighting mad. I often called her "the most warlike pacifist I ever knew." When I did, her clenched teeth would open in
an easy, crackling laugh, and she would say, "That, Jim, was the most
unkindest cut of all." When I corrected her grammar, she blamed it on
Shakespeare. The bombs that fell on Pearl Harbor caused the intensity of
her feelings on both race and war to become even more explosive.

Wiry and impulsive, her clothes were sometimes ill-matched, her red-
dish-blond hair often in disarray, and her hose frequently had crooked
seams and runs, which she failed to notice. Bernice was completing her
master's thesis in religious education. I think there was nothing on earth
that she did not feel strongly about. An avid reader of such modern
theologians as Kierkegaard, Buber, and Niebuhr, she always knew precisely how many angels could dance on the point of every needle.

She and I quickly became pals and beer-drinking cohorts—when one of
us had the money—and we reveled in our private debates. Bernice was
intrigued to learn that I was preparing a plan for a Gandhi-type movement of nonviolent direct action against segregation and race discrimination. "Thank God! At last, maybe we can turn this nation around," she
said. "It's the most exciting idea I've ever heard!"

But she was chagrined to hear of my fascination with Winnie, with

*Excerpted from my memorandum to A. J. Muste, "Provisional Plans for Brotherhood
Mobilization," February 19 and March 9, 1942. (See Appendix A.) These concepts began
taking form during the early months of my tenure with FOR.

whom I had never even talked, and to hear my dreamlike description of her.

"Don't be a fool, Jim. What does she know about nonviolence? Or the race problem? You'd be bored to tears in a week."

How little Bernice knew of my needs. I did not need another *me,* an alter ego; one was enough. I needed a partner who would complement me, a foil for my own uncomfortable intensity, someone with whom I could have a respite from the wars on which I was now embarking.

"Why don't you just cut out a paper doll?" Bernice would say. "That would be cheaper and a hell of a lot less trouble. It must be just a superficial sexual attraction." She spat the words out with considerable annoyance.

I denied that. The truth is, I had never even thought of Winnie in sexual terms; it was something less tangible—you might even say more spiritual. I did not know if Winnie was married; the thought had never occurred to me. I only knew that she had to be mine.

Pearl Harbor strengthened my friendship with Bernice. We needed each other in a way. I was a kind of link for her, joining the lofty world of her egalitarian theories to the possibility of achieving equality in this nation—a bridge across the chasm between the races.

Bernice, were she still alive, would strenuously object to that formulation. She prided herself in color blindness, and I must admit, I have never seen anyone who better fit that term than she.

One of her favorite stories was of the small boy who returned home from first grade one day, excitedly telling his mother about the wonderful new friend he had in school, who lived in another neighborhood.

"Freddie," the mother asked tentatively, "is this new child colored?"

"I don't know," the boy replied. "I didn't notice. I'll look tomorrow."

That was the way we should all be, Bernice thought, and I agreed. And she passionately believed that was the way *she* was. But I was, indeed, a bridge for her between what was and what should be. After all, there were not many blacks—Negroes, as we were called then—who were pacifists and socialists and interested in direct action of a nonviolent nature against racism.

But if I was useful to her, she was also helpful to me. Her very enthusiasm was contagious, and she constantly voiced encouragement for me to continue working on the plan.

Not only did the onslaught of World War II weld that friendship, it also triggered two other war-related events in my life.

The mail one morning brought two messages: one was a 1-A card from my draft board in Washington, D.C., forwarded from my parents' home in that city. The other was a letter from my boss, A. J. Muste, executive secretary of FOR, calling me to an emergency staff conference in New York to consider the implications of war on our work.

Immediately, I fired off a letter to the chairman of the draft board, air mail special delivery, informing him that I was appealing the classification and requesting a personal appearance to argue my appeal before the board. I was coming to Washington in a week and would call for an appointment and would bring with me a Form 47, the form for conscientious objectors, and a personal statement of my views.

That done, my mind turned to the trip east. It would be Washington first, to visit my parents; then to New York for the staff conference; followed by a return to D.C. for the holidays. The bus trip back to Chicago after New Year's would be punctuated by stops for speeches at meetings in Pittsburgh, Detroit, and Ann Arbor.

Walking to the drugstore, my overcoat was unbuttoned and flying open, and though striding through the wintry cold, I was unaware of it. Mind had deserted the senses, for it nursed an idea. There would be no prosaic "How about lunch or dinner one day soon?" No crass "What're you doing after work tonight?" I would spin a web of enchantment and drama and she would find the lure irresistible. I would not risk being just one of the crowd, or chance an embarrassing turndown by asking face-to-face for a date. Instead, I would write a letter asking her to have dinner with me and mail it from my parents' home in Washington, D.C., sending with it an attractive Christmas card. I would ask that her reply be sent to me at 2929 Broadway, New York City—the intriguing address of FOR headquarters. I would gild the lily by phoning her from my "lecture tour" stop in Pittsburgh to nail down date, time, and place for the rendezvous.

Having made the decision, I entered the store boldly, with intentionally furrowed brow, and ordered not one, but six packs of cigarettes and four cigars. Winnie's eyes stretched at the quantity of the purchase, which told her that I was going away. That added to the suspense. She gazed beyond me, into some misty dream as if I were not there, and the tune she hummed this time was "Thanks for the Memories." When I turned to go, my words were "I'll be in touch, Winnie." She watched, without a word.

Ben Segal's unpretentious Southside flat was transformed magically into a castle as I prepared to embark on this journey, which was to me of monumental dimensions. Bare floors took on Oriental carpets. Painted woodwork became carved oak and marble. Ceiling light bulbs turned into crystal chandeliers.

Packing my large new Samsonite bag, which my father had bought for me, I perceived upcoming events to be a tryst with the future. In New York, there would be consultations with Muste, prior to sending him the memorandum, to feel him out on the plan to adapt Gandhianism to the American racial scene. I saw that meeting as pregnant with historical importance, a preliminary discussion before launching a "revolution."

The coming face-to-face with the draft board gave me a very positive feeling. It offered me a chance to take an iron stand, *against* the symbols of power, *for* something about which I felt very deeply. I hoped, however, that the board would accept my appeal for conscientious objector status; I did not relish prison at that point, for there was the plan to implement.

And, of course, there was also Winnie.

Bernice dropped by to join me in the taxi ride to the railroad station and to wish me the best. Before going through the iron gates to board the train, I kissed her lightly on the cheek and was conscious of eyes all around us—some curious, some shocked, some hostile.

CHAPTER 8

FOR CONSCIENCE:
OBJECTION AND A PROJECTION

UNION STATION IN WASHINGTON always was a beehive in the forties; and especially so on this day, December 17, 1941—ten days after Pearl Harbor. MP's and military brass standing around seemed strangely out of place against a backdrop of post-Renaissance Classic architecture.

Troops in motion moved with dispatch. Civilians eyed them with a mixture of pride and gratitude. It was a popular war. The faces on some of the troops, of course, were clouded by resignation, but others glowed with a grim sense of mission.

I, too, had a sense of mission, but of a different kind. Mine was twofold: designing a movement that I honestly believed transcended war, and embarking on the first romantic adventure of my life. And, also, confronting the draft board.

The crowd seeking cabs outside was formidable, so I returned to the station to wait a while. Luckily, a seat was available on one of the massive wooden benches lining the station in symmetric rows. It was an end seat next to the heating vent, and the hot air streaming up forced me to shed my heavy gray wool overcoat. I shoved the large suitcase against the seat behind my legs and lighted a cigarette, inhaling deeply. Suddenly my attention was riveted on an approaching figure.

He was a small man in his early seventies, enormously impressive. He clearly was not a part of the crowd and doubtless wished it would go away. Beneath the bald, egg-shaped head, furrowed brows framed piercing black eyes, which, despite his slight stature, peered over the heads of the masses around him in a private world of his own thoughts.

I leaped from my seat into his path, forcing the crowd to divide and go around us. Beaming, I looked down at him and greeted him: "Dr. DuBois!"

Small eyes impaled me. He placed a pince-nez on his nose and dropped his lower lip in a motion that caused his neatly trimmed Vandyke to quiver.

"Let me see," he said icily, "do I know you?"

Crestfallen, I shook my head and sat back down. When he reached the end of the row and made a right-angle turn, he slowed his pace and swiveled his head to look back at me and, meeting my glance, looked away and quickened his steps through a doorway going to the train gates.

Embarrassed by the rebuff, I vowed that we would meet again someday soon, and the next time he would know who I was, for a nonviolent "war" would be rocking the nation. Our next encounter would be as equals, I swore. Train and bus stations would be crowded on that day, too, as uniformed, unarmed, and peaceful troops hastened to distant "battlefields" in *this* land. We would not meet on those battlefields, for that fabled scholar and relentless warrior against crimes of racism, that born aristocrat, was not of the battlefield, but of the tent. Perhaps that was where we'd meet, I mused, in the "tent" of the coming struggle, poring over maps and debating strategies.

The thought so intrigued me that I forgot momentarily what I was waiting for. Soon, the bustling traffic in and out of the doors had largely ceased, though all seats were taken and soldiers, sailors, and marines stood around in droves, their duffle bags cluttering the floor.

Most of the GI's were white. A few black soldiers from a segregated unit stood in one corner, talking in subdued voices. The labor battalions were not moving yet, it seemed. Jim Crow in 1941 was bedecked and ribboned in the uniform of his country.

Leaving Union Station, I got a taxi with comparative ease. The ride home took twice as long as it normally did. Troop carriers, weapons carriers, and convoys of jeeps clogged the arteries. Khaki-clad GI's hugged and kissed sweethearts and wives at intersections. But in forty minutes I sat in my parents' modest living room in the ghetto at 1027 Euclid Street, Northwest.

Office hours were over when I arrived, so the call to the draft board had to wait till morning. That evening was for my father.

"Junior, what is this new plan you say you're working on?" he asked after greeting me with a man-to-man handshake. (We never embraced.) He seated himself in an inexpensive, overstuffed chair in the oppressively small room in the red brick row house.

For over three years he had been teaching at the School of Religion at Howard University as professor of New Testament and Greek, instead of his specialty, Old Testament and Hebrew. He was even thinner than when I saw him last in August. Diabetes does that to its victims. Otherwise, he looked well.

I explained in some detail that it was a movement of Gandhian nonviolent resistance against segregation. They could not segregate us, I reasoned, if we and our allies chose jail en masse rather than accepting it. If we had to, we would fill up the jails.

The middle-aged biblical scholar fixed his gaze on a spot on the opposite wall and frowned a hole through it as he plucked hairs from his nearly bald head. Suddenly, he jerked his head upward and looked at me.

"Junior," he said with the air of the academic, not the preacher, "the differences between India and the United States are far greater than the similarities. The British are a tiny minority and the Indians a huge majority. The philosophy of nonviolence is deeply rooted in the Hindu culture; in Hinduism, death is a happy release from this life. In our culture, only women and sissies back away from a fight, and the big fist wins. Furthermore, Junior, don't forget, the British are the epitome of civilization, while our bigots are murderous savages."

Without a moment's hesitation, I made my rebuttal: "Of course, we're a minority, but we'll cut into the numerical advantage of our adversaries. The majority of white Americans—Christians and Jews—think that they believe in democracy, freedom, and equality. We will exhort them and, if necessary, shame them into putting their bodies where their mouths are. Our new alliance will be the new majority.

"And, if there is nonviolence in Hinduism, so also is there in Christianity. 'Turn the other cheek.' Jesus putting the severed ear back on the head of the soldier. 'He who lives by the sword, by the sword shall perish.' 'Love thine enemy.' The Christians and the lions. And on and on.

"And if Klansmen are worse than the imperialists of Britain, then we'll just have to surpass Gandhi in our training and practice of nonviolence."

Daddy rose and said, "One question: are you Gandhi? The British threw him in jail. The 'Bamians and Mississippians would shoot him. Dead."

"No, I'm not Gandhi," I replied. "Nehru, maybe, but not Gandhi." (And that, literally, was how I viewed myself. Not the saintly, ascetic Gandhi, but the urbane, intellectual Nehru. I admired the incredible little man in his loin cloth, but had no desire to emulate him.)

"And for the time being, we'll sharpen our nonviolent swords in northern settings. When we go south, we'll be ready to face their bullets. If they have the guns, we'll have the inner shields. If they have the jails, we have the bodies. No doubt, some of us will die. If we have to, we'll be ready."

My father wore a baffling smile, as he said, "I'm going to bed, Junior. See you in the morning."

The next morning, first thing, I called the draft board. My appointment was set for three o'clock. That gave me time to write a letter to Winnie.

Would she have dinner with me, I asked, after identifying myself as the fellow who came almost daily for a cigar or cigarettes. I suggested the first Saturday after my return to Chicago, around the middle of January. She should reply to "my New York office," giving me a time and place. After receiving her eagerly awaited reply, before returning to her city, I would call to confirm the arrangements.

The Christmas card enclosed was a whimsical one showing Santa with a bag of toys over his shoulder, dancing through a mine field, dodging explosions, over the caption: "PEACE ON EARTH TO MEN OF GOODWILL."

The letter mailed in the corner box, I sat at the kitchen table and my thoughts turned again to the impending draft board confrontation. I had already filled out DSS Form 47, the official form required to claim conscientious objector status. I claimed it on both religious and humanitarian grounds. In other words, I believed that opposition to all war and all killing was not only mandated by a Supreme Being, but also by my conscience, which to me was equally compelling.

I was a pacifist, but since I was not a member of one of the historical "peace" churches, such as the Quakers, Brethren, or Mennonites, it was by no means certain that the draft board, in 1941, would accept that claim. I knew very well, though, that I would go to jail rather than violate my own conscience. But the prospect of a long incarceration was not alluring: there was the nonviolent movement to start and that could not wait.

Nor could Winnie.

I hoped that this draft board, undoubtedly all black due to the residentially segregated character of D.C. in those days, and dealing with only black draftees—almost none of whom were pacifist—would be sufficiently cognizant of the issues to deal with my petition fairly.

In addition to the official form, I also had prepared a lengthy statement elaborating on my views that war was mass murder and that I would have no part of it. I argued that even were I not opposed to all war on principle, there was simply no way I could, in conscience, enter the United States' racially segregated armed forces to fight for freedom, liberty, and equality on other parts of the globe.

So, on two counts, I would not fight—one, unalterable opposition to war, and two, refusal to be part of an instrument that gave the lie to the principles for which it fought.

It was two-thirty. Dressed in my one good suit, a gray tweed, freshly shined black shoes, white shirt, and black knit tie, I boarded the streetcar on nearby Eleventh Street and rode downtown to U Street and the draft board office. I expected to see a room full of somber faces awaiting the inquisition. But there was only one face, and it was not exactly somber; it looked bored.

The chairman of the draft board sat in shirt sleeves, leaning back in a bare swivel chair, one hand behind his head and the other removing an enormous black cigar from his lips. His legs were crossed at the ankles, feet on the desk top, which was bare, except for a telephone and a glass ashtray.

"Come in, Mr. Farmer. Sit down. Have a cigar." He blew the words through heavy smoke in a brusque, but tired, manner.

I thanked him and took the cigar. It was an imported Havana, much unlike the cheap panatelas with which I'd feigned sophistication in Chicago. I shoved it into my outside breast pocket for future enjoyment, sat down in an unpainted oak chair facing his desk, and looked about the room.

It was sparsely furnished—no luxuries, no frills. No drapes, just venetian blinds; the floor was uncarpeted. A few wooden chairs stood around the walls of the twenty-by-fifteen-foot room with floor-standing ashtrays between some of them. An eight- or ten-foot-long unpolished table with chairs around it occupied one side of the room. (Where the board met, no doubt.) A twelve-by-fourteen-inch photograph of Roosevelt hung on a wall. FDR's signature was plainly visible. It was autographed to someone, but I could not make out to whom.

The chairman, whose name I have since forgotten, was a well-known black lawyer in Washington. A large man with graying hair, and tall, to judge from the length of his legs as they extended across the desk, his bronze skin stretched tightly over hard-set jaws, which relaxed only to receive or to release the cigar.

He studied me through narrowed eyes. Both hands were behind his head and the Havana in his mouth was sending a thin stream of smoke upward. He smiled and, without removing the cigar, began chatting about the weather, observing that it was unseasonably warm for Washington. Suddenly, he became serious and swung his feet down from the desk and placed the cigar in the ashtray.

He said calmly, "Do those papers in your hand have something to do with the Selective Service? What are they?"

"They are Form 47 and a personal statement of my position."

"Form 47! Let me see. What the hell is that?"

"That," I said, "is the form for conscientious objectors."

"Let me see it."

He read it quickly, without a change of expression. He smoothed out the dog-eared edges of the form against the desk top and without looking up, said, "And now your personal statement."

I handed it to him.

When he had finished reading, he looked up quickly, piercing my eyes with his, and thundered in his most intimidating lawyer fashion, "This statement is entirely irrelevant." But I was not going to be intimidated. "In what way is it irrelevant?" I asked.

"You're a minister of the gospel," he fairly shouted. "You can't be a conscientious objector."

I found that assertion to be slightly amusing. A minister could not be a CO. Why? No conscience? Or no guts to object? But I was not going to be argumentative.

"You're mistaken," I countered. "I'm neither an ordained nor a practicing minister and have no intention of becoming either."

"Well, what the hell. You're a theological student. That's the same thing."

"You're wrong again," I replied. "I'm not a theological student; I graduated last June."

"Oh, what the hell!" he bellowed. Then he spoke in measured tones: "As far as we're concerned, you're a minister of the gospel. You're deferred."

For a few moments, I sat quiet and still, but my mind churned furiously. Would it be an easy out, accepting ministerial deferment? Some of my pacifist friends would think so. But even if I wanted to, how could I do otherwise? By returning the card? Or publicly burning it? Nonsense!

Selective Service records would still show me as deferred. I could formally reject it and go through the appeals machinery, demanding a formal hearing before the full board, but if I lost the appeal, then what? I would still be deferred, unless they accepted my rejection of ministerial classification and still refused me CO status. Then what? Jail? No freedom to do the things I had to do at this crucial time. Even CO classification would hamper that freedom, for it would mean going to a civilian public service camp, cutting down trees, or planting trees, or making little rocks out of big ones, or being sent on detached service as an orderly in a mental institution. My conscience would be clear then, but I would not be free.

I looked up to face the chairman's steady stare.

"But, I *am* a conscientious objector to war," I protested.

Massive shoulders lifted in a shrug. "As far as we're concerned," he repeated, "you're a minister. You're deferred."

"Will you place my statement on file?" I asked.

"If you wish," the chairman nodded.

I rose to go and he stood for the first time during the meeting. We shook hands and I left.

As I was closing the door behind me, his resonant voice called me back. "Oh, Mr. Farmer."

I stepped into the room.

"I want you to understand, Mr. Farmer," he said, "that we have nothing against CO's. We just don't want you fellows to use the Selective Service Agency for propaganda purposes."

"What do you mean by that?"

"I mean simply that we want to have as few as possible on our lists. So, if you can be deferred on any other basis, that will be done. Good-bye and good luck."

I nodded and left. On the way home on the streetcar, I felt twinges of guilt, of course, but the overwhelming feeling was a sense of joy at my own good fortune at being free to do what I wanted to do at this point in my life and at this time in the nation's history. There was, indeed, a God!

My father had arrived home minutes before I did. I shared with him my good news, giving him a blow-by-blow account of the encounter with the draft board chairman.

The old scholar smiled and said, "I have a feeling, Junior, that the chairman and some members of his board thought that you could fight better at home than abroad."

Two days later, I left on the second leg of my journey to New York and my meeting with A. J. Muste.

Manhattan had never ceased to thrill me. From my first visit in August 1938 till now, December 1941, I'd always known that New York was my home. I'd never lived there, but I knew that one day I would. I would stop other places here and there, now and then, but I would live in New York and someday there I would die.

Now I was excited not only because of New York, but because of the circumstances. Things were going well. Winnie was almost a certainty; the meeting with the draft board chairman had been a success. And now there was A. J. Muste. Gamblers say, or so I'd been told, that when you're hot, you're hot. So, I had to roll the dice boldly now.

I wanted Times Square. That was New York. So, with the suitcase I'd borrowed from mother, I walked from the bus terminal to Times Square before going to the apartment of John Swomley, another staff member of the Fellowship of Reconciliation, in the Columbia University area.

The flashing and blinking neon lights of Times Square mocked each other, transforming the streets and sidewalks into a Disney-like fantasyland. The honking horns of New York cabs were music.

As I stood looking at the news briefs circling the top of the New York Times building, an overpainted woman tugged at my sleeve. I moved away from her and she did not pursue.

The tiny white lights forming the words of the news items high above me screamed of war:

HIROHITO TELLS JAPANESE STAR OF THE U.S. SETTING IN ASIA . . . NIPPON'S STAR RISING . . . HITLER'S PLANES RAIN HELL ON BRITAIN . . . CHURCHILL GALVANIZES ENGLAND . . . FDR SAYS TOTAL MOBILIZATION OF THE U.S. AND TOTAL WAR WILL BRING TOTAL DEFEAT TO OUR ENEMIES.

Pangs of guilt bit at my heart, for if any war was just this was it. I quickly banished the thought; my course was set.

The next day was cold and the sky was gray and I was sleepy. John Swomley's living room couch was comfortable, but we had stayed up till the wee hours as he brought me up to date on the internal politics of the FOR. The organization was not large, less than twelve thousand members, and the staff was correspondingly smaller and underpaid. But the infighting was fierce. (When the players are few, the stakes seem bigger.)

The meeting at FOR headquarters at 2929 Broadway seemed designed to boost the morale of this cadre of pacifists in a time of crisis. There were also reports from each member of the field staff (some of whom I'd never met before) on the mood of the people in the area he or she covered.

A. J. Muste, the executive director, told us of the evolving regulations regarding conscientious objectors and of the latest intelligence from government sources indicating a much tougher attitude toward CO's now that war was a reality. We were given the information we needed to counsel aspiring CO's we encountered in our work.

Muste observed that this was the historic moment for religious pacifism to make its big push. The number of CO's, he assured us, would confound the nation. Some of us would live to see the day, we were told, when they would call a war and no one would come. The international pacifist movement would bring that about. (I didn't believe that, but as I looked around the room, most heads were nodding in agreement.)

The executive director concluded by stressing the importance of numbers. Each CO recorded on the books of Selective Service would proclaim to the world that the ranks of conscience were swelling.

Was that a reprimand to me for accepting a deferment without a fight? I searched his eyes for a clue, but found none.

A.J., as we called him, was a gaunt man in his fifties—just skin and bones, so thin as to look tubercular, with a face furrowed with the trenches of many political battles. His eyes spat bullets but twinkled and wrinkled at the corners when something amused him. He was a chain smoker, and his long skinny fingers trembled as he lighted each Pall Mall. The hair on the back of his fingers grew long and tangled like the eyebrows that hovered over a birdlike countenance with lean, sharp features, and arched upward when the wheels in the brain were turning. He was about six feet tall, though being so thin, he appeared considerably taller. Like most extremely thin men, he walked slightly bent over, as though the muscles were not strong enough to hold the torso upright.

A. J. Muste was an old Marxist-Leninist warhorse, now a dedicated Christian pacifist, born again. In the twenties and early thirties, he was the leader of one of the communist groups in America. There were the Stalinites and the Trotskyites, as everyone knows, but there also were the Oehlerites, the Lovestonites,* and, yes, the Musteites, who were among the toughest and most dynamic of American revolutionaries.

But Muste had grown disillusioned with the communist movement and returned to the church, resuming his role as a minister. Now he headed the FOR. He still wanted to revolutionize America, and I think he viewed Christian pacifism as a vehicle toward that revolution. That is not to say that it was only a vehicle. For him, it was also a deep commitment.

I walked into his spartan office where the desk groaned under mountains of paper, all piled in neat stacks. Two opened books also fought for space on the desk. The partitions were frosted glass, so there were no built-in bookshelves, but crowded bookcases lined the walls.

He looked up as I entered and said, "Come in, Jim. Sit down."

Then he got up and took a seat in a chair beside me, turning it so that we partially faced each other.

"I've been getting excellent comments about your speeches before FOR groups around the country. But I do wish you'd do more organizing—more setting up new FOR groups, more signing up new members. However, we can talk about that later. What's on your mind now?"

I took a deep breath and began outlining my proposal for the FOR to start a nationwide, interracial Gandhian movement using nonviolent direct action, including noncooperation and civil disobedience, in the struggle to end segregation. I saw it beginning with FOR members, then broadening its base and becoming a mass movement, filling up the jails if necessary.

*The followers of Hugo Oehler and the followers of Jay Lovestone

A.J.'s long, trembling fingers took the cigarette to thin lips and he inhaled deeply, blowing smoke out with a hissing sound.

"Do you have the plan down in writing?"

"I'm preparing the document now, in the form of a memorandum to you," I replied.

"Well, when will it be finished?" he asked with, I thought, a touch of irritation.

"Late January or early February. I'm thinking it through."

"Well, hurry it along, and send it to me airmail, and I'll send you my reaction without delay," he said as he stood.

I stood, too, and we shook hands.

"It's an interesting idea, Jim, but I have to see it in writing so I can study it," he said as he walked back behind his desk.

"By the way," he added, "remember what I said about signing up new members, starting groups, and organizing. Have a good Christmas."

I nodded and left, feeling a bit disappointed. But what did I expect? That A. J. Muste would jump for joy as I'd been doing inwardly for several weeks? After all, we clearly had different priorities. Peace was number one for him, whereas for me the top priority was racial equality. Furthermore, Muste had heard many pipe dreams and had seen most of them remain just that. And of those few that found their way onto the written page, most languished forever in some ego file.

How was he to know that my plan would be any different? He knew very little about me. I'd been hired on the recommendation of John Swomley, whom I'd known for several years in Methodist youth work. And I knew no more about Muste than he knew about me. But he would learn more about me as the nonviolent movement got under way. And I was destined to learn much more about him.

Yet, on the bus to Washington early Christmas Eve, to spend the holidays with my family, I was subdued. The euphoria was somewhat dampened. I had dreamed and thought so hard about the Muste meeting, and now it seemed like the mouse that came forth when the mountain labored.

Christmas at home was Christmas at home. There was the tree and the presents and the laughter and the carols on the record player. There was the turkey dinner and the eggnog. There were the family friends dropping by to bring and to receive gifts.

Yet my thoughts were elsewhere. They were on the memo to Muste and on a drugstore cashier in Chicago. Mother sensed my distraction: "A penny for your thoughts, Junior."

"Oh," I said, as if suddenly awakened from a sound sleep, "I'm sorry. I was just thinking about my work."

She smiled and patted my cheek. How I hated that gesture; I was not a child.

I made more of an effort to get into the spirit of the festivities, and also became somewhat better acquainted with sister and my brother, Nathaniel.

Sister, home for the holiday too, was working on her master of science degree at Cornell. After taking a premed course in college, she had switched to nutrition. She was doing well at the university; but, always the plodder, she had to work hard at it and, even during the holiday season, spent most of the time in her room poring over school books, memorizing charts, digesting data. She would no doubt succeed as a teacher of nutrition.

Naturally, she was concerned about my lack of conventional pursuits. She was horrified to learn of my salary, $15 a week, and mortified to know that I had chosen a life that promised to lead me to jail and that I looked forward to it.

Her advice to me was simple and direct: "Why don't you become ordained? You'd make a very good minister and the bishop knows daddy. I'm sure he would give you a big church right off the bat."

Nathaniel, tall and rangy, had just turned fourteen. He was a fair student and a far better athlete than I'd ever been. Well coordinated, he could run and jump and was great at baseball—the star second baseman of the Euclid Street Fungoes.

He had a pair of boxing gloves around the house, and we put them on in the basement. He had great legs and was quick and elusive; I surpassed him only in upper-body strength. Most of the time, he danced circles around me, but once when I caught him with a left, he leaped in and held onto me and yelled, "Time."

"I just let you do that," he said, untying his gloves, "to see if you could hit."

There was no more boxing. Ping-Pong, yes, where he easily outclassed me, but not boxing.

It was December thirtieth when the letter came. I retired to the small upstairs sleeping porch that was my room and closed the door.

All along, I'd been bubbling over with confidence, but now that the moment had arrived, I was filled with doubts. I sat for minutes, looking at the envelope and at the handwriting with its artistic flourish. Never before had the J and the F in my name looked so powerful. And the W and C in the name of the upper left corner seemed to have come from a new alphabet, majestic and intriguing.

I opened the envelope. If a man on trial could open the jury's verdict to read for himself his fate, his palpitations would be no greater than were mine at that instant. My finger was the letter opener and I took pains to slit the creased edge neatly. The faintest perfume teased my nostrils.

Dear Jim:

I was surprised to receive your wonderful letter and the Christmas card.

Of course, I remember you, and I will be glad to have dinner with you on the Saturday after you return to Chicago.

Let's meet at the Palm Tavern on 47th Street. It's a nice place, and I know you'll like it. There are palm trees around, artificial, of course, (smiles). I know the owner and I would like to introduce you to him.

I will wait for your call, letting me know which Saturday it will be, and what time . . .

Sincerely yours,
Winnie

She gave me both her home and work numbers. I felt tired, and warm, and relaxed.

On January third, I left for the speaking tour arranged by John Swomley. I would hit Pittsburgh, Cleveland, Detroit, Madison, and Milwaukee.

In each city, the FOR group would hold a public meeting at which one hundred to three hundred pacifists and pacifist sympathizers would be in attendance. I would give an interpretive analysis of the race problem, always stressing the imperative of nonviolent action. At each meeting, a collection would be taken up to help defray my expenses.

The trip went smoothly, though a heavy snowstorm in Milwaukee cut the attendance down to about fifty. Only the pure in heart. I had counseled over a dozen CO's and signed up five new FOR members. A.J. would be pleased. The collections not only reimbursed the national organization for the expenses of my trip east; they also more than covered my salary for the time that I was away from Chicago.

From Milwaukee, I called Winnie and told her that I would be back in town on Thursday, around my birthday, January 12. We agreed that we would meet on the following Saturday at 6:00 P.M.

The artificial palm trees seemed weirdly incongruous, with the snow reaching blizzard proportions outside. At 5:55, I sat in a booth where I could see the door, but far enough away to avoid a draft whenever it opened.

I ordered a glass of sherry and wondered if I would be stood up. I smoked a pipe this time, newly purchased for the occasion. The seconds hammered on my wristwatch and the blood pounded in my temples. I closed my eyes and leaned against the top of the backrest.

"Hello. Are you sleeping?"

I think that I stood before my eyes had popped open. The voice was unmistakably hers. How on earth had I missed the entrance?

"Not sleeping, but dreaming," I said, as I removed her cloth coat and hung it on the hook at the outer corner of the booth.

"Are you surprised that I came?"

I answered simply, "No."

"You're very sure of yourself, aren't you?"

"I felt the electricity when our eyes met in the drugstore," I said. "It was real."

She looked away, at nothing in particular, and replied in a voice hardly audible, "I guess I felt it, too. And I guess it was real."

She ordered sauterne. And we ate. I don't know what. And we talked. I don't know what about. All that I know is that it was perfect and complete, and that nothing else mattered.

Oh, I do remember a few bits of our conversation. I learned, for instance, that she had studied at the Art Institute of Chicago, but her West Indian father, recently deceased, was dead set against an art career for her. She also told me, in answer to a question, that, indeed, she was married, but separated and getting a divorce from Herb Jeffries, a singer with Duke Ellington's band.

My response to that was, "It's still snowing outside, isn't it?"

We sat in the Palm Tavern booth from 6:15 to 10:45. I felt somehow that we'd sat there forever. There was more sauterne and more sherry. But the drinks were quite irrelevant.

I took her home and we kissed a lingering good-night and agreed to meet again the next day for lunch and the afternoon.

And that was the emergence of a close bond, which, like a ring, had no beginning.

And would not end.

CHAPTER 9

MEMO MEMORIES

THE MEMORANDUM TO A.J. took final shape in the early days of February. Delivery was late, but never one for modesty, even at twenty-two, I considered the result worth waiting for.

The interminable debates with Bernice may have delayed completion, but did not interfere with the process.

The exquisite hours with Winnie—in Southside Chicken Shacks and cafés, and occasionally more private settings—may have been a diversion, but the boost they gave my morale more than compensated for any distraction.

With two fingers, hunt-and-peck fashion, I typed the memo from my hand-written draft and mailed it airmail special delivery from the post office, not a mailbox, to ensure its speedy arrival to the hands of Muste. I slammed the envelope down on the counter in front of the clerk as if I were, by that act, driving the first nail into the coffin of racism in America.

The contents of the envelope asked for a nonviolent confrontation with American racism. This movement should be comprised of a pacifist nucleus: black, white, Jewish and Gentile, all mobilized into a Gandhian approach to integration.

The next two weeks were filled with exhilaration as I awaited A.J.'s certain response. (How could it be other than positive?)

Things were moving fast. Bernice had become my advocate, my trumpeteer, telling everyone she knew that I had a plan. She always carried with her a carbon copy of the memo to shove under their noses as proof.

One of those so encountered was a sandy-haired graduate student at the University of Chicago, Jimmy Robinson. Robinson and several friends had just secured a lease on a large house on South Kenwood Avenue in the then lily-white Hyde Park–Kenwood section near the university.

Jimmy called me, saying that he thought the Muste memo superb, and explained that what he had in mind was to start an interracial living cooperative in the house in an attempt to break the residential color line. He invited me to come by and see the house and meet the fellows—and, he hoped, to move in. What they were trying to do was right in line with my memorandum, he said, and they wanted to link up with the projected organization.

I was delighted. Muste *had* to come through now.

It was a great stone house, and well maintained. But now, occupied by students, it was sparsely furnished. About fifteen blocks east of Cottage Grove Avenue, which was the dividing line between black and white, the house was owned by Mrs. Edgar Lee Masters, wife of the poet who wrote *Spoon River Anthology.*

Robinson, a master's candidate in English, wondered whether the poet's wife would sympathize with us when the community became aware that Negroes were living in the housing in violation of restrictive covenants that excluded them from the area. As he speculated aloud, a rueful smile came over his face.

That face was a slightly freckled one beneath crew-cut hair. He was a small man, no more than five foot six, with a sardonic smile and lips so thin that they seemed to curve inward when he spoke.

He offered me coffee and then discovered that the glass percolator had been dropped and broken.

"Let's go to the Jack Spratt Coffee House," Robinson said.

He put on a heavy mohair coat, a plaid woolen scarf, lined leather gloves, and earmuffs.

The brim of my hat was turned up in the back, like the collar of my coat, and down in the front. I had lost one glove, so I wore none, keeping my hands clenched into fists to frustrate the bitter wind. The pipe in my teeth was turned down to keep the sleet and snowflakes from extinguishing the fire.

Jimmy walked along with mincing pigeon-toed steps that seemed to accentuate his small size. Frosty breath blew from his nose and mouth as he told me that, though religious, he was not a member of FOR, but belonged to the Catholic Worker, a pacifist, philosophical, anarchist group led by the great Dorothy Day. He was also active in the War Resisters League, a nonreligious, pacifist group.

As we sat at the counter, I asked what led him, a Catholic radical, into involvement in the racial struggle.

"That is the heart of the matter in this country," he said. "If the nation cannot deal with this issue, all else is academic and absurd."

When I looked up at the manager of the Jack Spratt Coffee House, he was standing right over me, looking meanly into my face: "You'll have to get out of here. We can't serve you here."

All of my upbringing, my education, my training, my brooding, my planning had told me that those words would be spoken. But when they came, I had no defense, no response that would blow them out of the language. I had intellectualized a thousand answers that would destroy dragons and reduce that little man to ashes, but all that came out, above a churning anger was, "Why can't you?"

Jimmy Robinson's face was blood red. He spoke more intelligently than I: "I suppose you realize that there is a civil rights law in this state forbidding this kind of practice. Now, if you don't serve us, I promise that you're going to pay the stiffest penalty that the law allows."

I thought those words were very un-Gandhian but, nevertheless, effective.

"All right, what d'ya want?" said the manager, looking at neither of us. "I'll take your order."

Jimmy ordered black coffee. I asked for coffee and two doughnuts.

"Well, the doughnuts will be a dollar apiece," said the manager, turning his back to us.

"That," I ventured, "is rather steep for doughnuts, don't you think?"

"That's my price," he replied.

"Well, I know better," said Robinson. "I've gotten doughnuts here at two for a nickel and that's the price we're going to pay."

We were served and we ate.

I reached for my wallet, but Jimmy waved me aside. He paid with a one-dollar bill and was given the correct change. The doughnuts were five cents.

As we walked back to Boys' Fellowship House (there was also a women's interracial co-op called Girls' Fellowship House), Robinson said that he thought we owed it to that man's religion to return to his place of business sometime.

And return we did, two days later, and in larger numbers.

Winnie reluctantly joined us. Going where she "was not wanted" definitely was not her style, and the fierce-eyed young activist radicals around me were not at all her element. She came because I had asked her and I'd asked her because I thought she should at least glimpse the world in which I had chosen to roam. Perhaps, too, she would sense some of the euphoria I felt at starting something that was bound to explode into the nation's consciousness someday.

In the group there was also Joe Guinn, a black youth whose high forehead seemed about to burst with intelligence. He brought his girl friend, too.

And, there was Bernice, of course, and Jimmy, and two or three other white students.

We all met at Boys' House, where I was now living. Bernice and Jimmy assisted me in the briefing, since both shared some familiarity with Gandhian basics. The instructions were simple. We were to be peaceful and orderly. No loud talking or abusive language or otherwise unruly behavior. Keep calm at all times, with friendly smiles where possible.

We were to take available seats at the counter, with each white sitting beside at least one black. If there were not enough counter seats, then also use one booth, with at least one black and one white sitting there.

Whites were either to decline to order until all had been served, or to order and pass the food to a black friend beside them. If we were served, each person was to leave an appropriate tip and give enough money to Jimmy Robinson to cover the bill. He would pay the bill for all of us and give us an accounting afterward. In the event we were not served, we would sit there for the approximately three and a half hours till closing.

I noticed that Bernice did not appear to be listening to the briefing after her part of it was over. Instead, she was staring at Winnie, who sat on the couch beside me, aloof and uncomfortable.

As for me, I was consumed by an incredibly delicious tension, like the feeling that must burn in a young actor at a dress rehearsal before opening night of his Broadway lead. Every fiber of my mind and body strained.

On the way to the Jack Spratt, Jimmy walked with Winnie. (She thought he was "cute.") I walked with Bernice and said to her, "Unclench your fists and ungrit your teeth. If you slug this man, you'll blow the whole thing."

She laughed and did not reply.

Inside, we took seats, all at the counter. The manager looked first at me, then glowered at Robinson. For fully five minutes, he stood motionless, arms folded on his chest. The waitresses had disappeared from behind the counter.

Bernice could not resist. "May we have some service, please?" she said, with artificial sweetness, trying heroically to turn her scowl into a smile.

A couple of minutes later, a hand signal from the manager summoned the waitresses back and they took everyone's order.

I must confess, I tasted my sandwich and my soup with a bit of caution. They passed the test. I was no longer hungry, but now that I had it, I had to eat.

If food was anticlimactic, where had been the climax? Where indeed was the drama, except in the anticipation? All our planning was unnecessary. This fellow, it seemed, was not going to put up a fight.

Jimmy Robinson did some rapid calculations on a napkin and placed the proper amount on the counter atop our neatly stacked individual checks.

Scarcely had the door closed behind the rest of us than it opened again, violently this time. The manager ran onto the sidewalk, hurling our money into the street, screaming, "Take your money and get out! We don't want it!"

Dollar bills fluttered and coins rolled. One person started to pick it up, but I said, "No. Don't touch it; leave it there so he can't possibly say that we left without paying our bill."

Jimmy and Bernice agreed, and we wondered out loud whether the manager would come back and pick the money up when we were out of sight.

We headed for Boys' House to plan the next steps. Winnie said that she wanted to go home, so I told them that I would rejoin them later.

Saying good-night at her door, her eyes had a faraway expression and her kiss seemed perfunctory.

The discussion was hot and heavy when I arrived at Boys' house. Jimmy was chairing and several other residents of the house had joined the meeting. Someone had pointed out that there was a civil rights law in Illinois, dating back to Reconstruction days, and it was still in force. He argued that we should go to court and sue.

Bernice had disagreed, stating that that was "legal action," the NAACP's job, and that ours was nonviolent direct action, which nobody else was doing.

"Then why don't we call the NAACP and have them sue the bastards?" he countered.

"Why don't we just close the joint down?" someone else asked. "We can't let him get away with this stuff. Why don't we fill the place up every day from opening to closing? If they throw our money out, how long do you think they could survive that?"

Jimmy smiled. "We don't have enough Negroes with us to make it work."

One person suggested that we boycott and throw a picket line around the place.

Joe Guinn broke the tension with a little solemn-faced levity: "You fellows are making a simple problem far too complicated. All we have to do is pass out leaflets in the black belt Southside saying, 'Eat at Jack Spratt! Jack Spratt serves Negroes free of charge.' Problem solved."

After the guffaws, I picked up a book from a table in the room. It was *War without Violence*, by Krishnalal Shridharani, a disciple of Gandhi who had been with Gandhi on his famed salt march. The book was an analysis and outline of Gandhi's method of nonviolent direct action. It presented the three basic and essential steps as: investigation (to get the facts), negotiation (to try to solve the problem in face-to-face discussions), and direct action.

According to Gandhi's steps, I pointed out, we should now attempt to negotiate before using direct action at Jack Spratt. Although we were not slaves to Gandhi's steps, and Shridharani had not written the Bible, I urged that we make a serious and honest effort at negotiation before we clobbered our opponent—nonviolently, of course.

Jimmy and Bernice agreed, and so did Guinn. The others followed. I was asked to try to make contact with the coffee shop's manager to set up a meeting at which Bernice, Jimmy, and I would try to persuade him to change his policy.

The meeting adjourned, and only Bernice, Jimmy, and I remained in the living room of Boys' House. Jimmy and I shed jackets and ties. He left the room, returning in a minute clutching to his breast a fifth of Irish whiskey, three-fourths full. What a miraculous hiding place he must have found to protect that possession from a houseful of thirsty young throats. He brought three glasses and we raised a toast to the Jack Spratt campaign and to the memorandum plan.

We reviewed the events of the evening and found that we saw everything in the same light. The three of us agreed that a crying need at that stage was for more blacks to participate in our efforts. There was no shortage of whites with an awareness of Gandhi and an interest in nonviolence, but where were the blacks? This could not be a white movement.

I observed that Negroes who came in would be ends-oriented rather than means-oriented. They would join the movement because the program worked, produced results; not because of an ideological commitment to nonviolence.

That out of the way, Jimmy refilled the glasses, and I asked, "Well, what did you think of Winnie?"

Jimmy smiled and said, "Oh, I think she's fine. Very pretty, very feminine, and very sensitive," said Jimmy, "and I like her."

Bernice grimaced. "Maybe I shouldn't tell you this, since you seem to be enamored of her, but you asked, so here goes. For you, I think she's a disaster; she's decorative, but that's all. I talked to her for two or three minutes. I told her that I was setting up three action committees to fit in with your plan, so we can hit the ground running when the program is approved by Muste. And it will be approved, I told her, because A.J. knows that if he turns it down, we'll do it anyway and he'll have no part of it. I told her that each committee will coordinate the action projects in its field. There will be a public places action committee to coordinate projects like the one at Jack Spratt, a housing action committee to coordinate housing projects like what we're doing at Boys' House and Girls' House to break the color line, and an employment action committee to coordinate the employment projects we're going to develop.

"I asked her which action committee she would be most interested in. Do you know what she said?" Bernice asked rhetorically. "She said maybe housing because she has two friends who live in a housing project. Can you believe that?"

I tried to conceal my fury at her for having done that to Winnie.

"Of course, I can, Bernice," I said. "What does the word *project* mean to a person who has grown up in the ghetto and has had no contact with action organizations that have action projects? It means public housing, and if you put the word *housing* before it, it can have no other meaning. Isn't there more to life than social activism, Bernice?"

Jimmy Robinson said that he was tired, so Bernice said her good-nights and departed. On her way out she tossed back a cheery "See you guys later, probably tomorrow. Call me if you get the appointment set up with that Jack Spratt SOB, Jim."

Jimmy and I went to our respective rooms. In mine, I brooded until I fell asleep.

The next morning, I arose with the sun and called the manager of Jack Spratt. When I identified myself, he slammed the receiver down.

I drafted a letter to the manager, requesting a meeting to discuss the matter, at a time and place convenient to him. I requested a reply by letter or phone within ten days from the date.

Before Robinson left for classes, I showed him the draft. He liked it, and said, "Today you're sending a letter, and today I received one—from Mrs. Masters' lawyer, ordering us to vacate these premises at once, and in no case later than thirty days or face legal action."

"Great," I shouted. "Now, maybe we'll have a good case to test the constitutionality of restrictive covenants. I know the NAACP will help on the appeal, so we can knock those covenants out once and for all."

"Yeah," replied Jimmy, "but I have a hunch that these people will be very wary of going to court; they don't want a test going up to the Supreme Court if they can avoid it. However, I'm going to send this guy a letter, refusing to vacate and standing on the lease. Unfortunately, it's only a six-month lease."

That evening, I typed and mailed my letter. Then I sat in the large living room with my pipe, enjoying its aromatic vapors, and rereading Shridharani's book.

I was interrupted by a phone call from Ben Segal. A letter had come to his apartment for me from the FOR in New York. It was from Muste, no doubt, mailed before he got my change of address. I would come right over to get it.

I wanted to take a taxi, but could not afford it. So I struck out walking, bundled up for the cold. In half an hour I sat in the warm, familiar surroundings of Ben's apartment with A.J.'s letter in my hand.

A.J. Muste had found my memorandum "most interesting" and the proposal "promising." He thought that I had done a "good deal of impressive thinking" on this "important matter" and he would like to "press my thoughts a little further." Specifically, he would like my comments on two questions: the source of financing for such a movement and the source of its membership.

On the way home to Boys' House that night, I decided that I would sleep on the Muste questions and begin writing the second memorandum in the morning.

But the morning had its own problems. There was a letter from Winnie. It was brief.

Dearest Jim,

I've told you many times that I love you, and I do. I will always love you. But I'm never going to see you again. Please don't write, or call or try to see me. Believe me, it's better this way.

Jim, darling, it breaks my heart to tell you, we live in different worlds. I don't understand your world and never will. You don't know or understand my world.

It would never work, Jim. It just can't work. I've known this ever since we had dinner at the Palm Tavern, but I couldn't tell you. I couldn't even tell myself. I love you so much that it hurts. I want to help you but I can't, and I would never want to hold you back.

Trust me, my darling; I'm doing the right thing. There is no other way. Jim Farmer I love and will always love, but can't have.

All my love,
Winnie

I had never been one for tears, but that time I cried, silently.

Robinson came into my room. He started to say something, but looked at my face and saw the letter in my hand and turned and walked out, closing the door quietly.

That evening, I called Winnie's home. The phone was answered by her mother, a sweet and charming little lady, a mulatto from the Northside, who had a fondness for me, and I for her.

"No, Jim, Winnie is not at home. She has gone to visit her good friend Lucille. When she comes home, I will certainly tell her you called."

"Thank you, Mrs. Christie," I said and hung up.

I'm sure that the only antidote to a heart that hurts, aside from the unconsciousness of sleep, is to submerge oneself in work.

I took a yellow pad and began writing the second memo to A. J. Muste.

The paper was finished in record time for me, two days, and mailed on March 9, 1942.

I shared the second memo with Bernice and Jimmy before mailing it to Muste. Their enthusiastic reaction was infectious; Bernice assured me that Muste would be equally pleased.

"What we've got to do," said Bernice, "is get this group going now and bring others on board."

We agreed, but it was not until several weeks later than an opportunity arose for an action project.

Following one of our many meetings at Boys' House, a towheaded undergrad with a bottle of beer in one hand and a hunk of cheese in the other, sat beside me.

"Hey, Jim" he said, in a husky voice, "did you ever hear of White City?"

"Of course," I replied, "this is it. We're living in it. Black City is on the other side of Cottage Grove."

"No, no. I mean the real White City—a roller skating rink on Sixty-third Street, on the other side of Cottage Grove in the black belt. It's a huge building painted white with a white wall around it. "Negroes," he said, "can't skate there. Whenever a Negro shows up, he's told there's a private skating party that night, or it's private club night, and you have to be a member of the club in order to skate."

I smiled, full of confidence. "We can handle that."

I gave Bernice and Jimmy the responsibility of organizing the demonstration because I expected another letter from Muste any day now, which would tie up my time. (Also, I wanted to be free to pursue my lost love, if I could think of a way of pursuit.)

White City was an enormous place, covering most of a city block. It looked like a huge Gothic castle. Its white paint was peeling off in places, revealing red bricks underneath. The eight-foot wall around it was forbidding. Its iron gate was open during working hours and locked at other times.

It did a roaring business; there was always a line, but it moved quickly. Our first contingent was a group of twelve whites, who moved up with the line, purchased tickets at the ticket window, proceeded to the entrance door, and surrendered a portion of each ticket to the ticket taker. They entered and minutes later were seen skating past the open doorway.

At that point, our second contingent, composed of two whites and one black, entered the line. Shortly, they were at the ticket window, the black standing to the side, out of the ticket seller's line of vision.

One of the whites purchased three tickets, which were readily sold to him. The two whites and one black walked to the doorway leading to the skating area. They were stopped by the ticket taker, who told them that there was a private club party in progress and one had to be a member of the private club in order to come in and skate. When asked what club was giving the party, he said he didn't know.

One of the three men gave me a hand signal, tugging at the lobe of his right ear. I then entered the line and made my way up to the ticket window. The woman who sold tickets said that I could not buy a ticket because it was a private club party night and I had to be a member of the club to get in.

I asked her, "What club?" She didn't know but said that I would have to show a club membership card to get in. I asked to see the manager, and she summoned him. He was an irritable-looking man of medium build.

"The woman selling tickets tells me that one has to be a member of some unnamed private club to skate tonight. Is that correct?" I asked.

"That is right," the manager replied, looking above me, around me, and everywhere except *at* me.

"What club is giving the party tonight?"

"I don't carry that information around in my head; it's in my office," he said.

His anger seemed to mount as we talked.

"Would you mind getting that information for me?"

"I most certainly would mind," he said. "I don't have time for this kind of stuff."

"Well, now," I began, taking a different tack, "am I to understand that no one can skate tonight without being a member of that private club?"

"*Absolutely no one,*" he said, emphasizing each word.

"And everyone in there skating has a membership card in the club?"

"Everyone," he replied, jerking his head.

"Then why is it," I asked, with a trace of a smile, "that twelve of my friends are in there skating and are not members of any private club and have no membership cards?"

Two of the twelve stopped by the doorway and waved. I pointed them out to the manager. He visibly reddened.

"Are you *sure* they have no membership cards?" he asked lamely.

"Positive," I said. "What are you going to do about it?"

The redness had left his face; he looked deathly pale, and he stared into my eyes and said nothing.

The three who were stopped by the ticket taker had walked over to join in the discussion. One of them suggested to the manager that he should go into the skating area and make an announcement that everyone skating without a private club membership must leave immediately and get his money refunded.

The manager dropped his head and walked away in the direction of his office. He was a beaten man. But we had no victory. The situation was an impasse. We had exposed his club party ruse, but no blacks were skating. The line was still moving, and people were still entering and leaving the skating area.

We all left and went to Boys' House to discuss strategy. My thoughts, expressed at various points in the discussion, took the following form: We did not have enough "troops" to clog their lines and bring their business to a halt. Nor were we likely to win much support from others in the line at White City. They were young people seeking an evening of fun and relaxation, not a cause to champion.

Our visit to the rink had produced the ingredients for a perfect legal case. We could prove without doubt that the "private club" was nothing more than a ruse to exclude blacks. Yet the law, although not violent, was not part of the arsenal of nonviolence. Indeed, there were those purists among the pacifists, like some members of the FOR National Council, who would consider legal action to be *violent* because it did not seek to be loving, and because it relied upon police action for its enforcement, and police action is based ultimately on violence.

But I am no ideologue. Nonviolence and legal action must be twin weapons—either one being used when it seems to be most applicable, with each bolstering the other.

In the morning, I swore out warrants for the arrest of three persons at White City Roller Skating Rink: the manager, the ticket seller, and the ticket taker. I called an emergency meeting and passed the hat to raise money, then went down to bail out the three as a gesture of goodwill as soon as they were arrested. The bailees were astonished.

The machinery of justice creaked and sputtered and spun its wheels in the White City case. The process made us wonder about the efficacy of the court system.

Still, we all were emboldened by the daring of our venture, and we cheered our sure success. Our first demonstration and our first victory.

We were also cheered by having heard nothing further from Mrs. Masters' lawyer, though his deadline had long since passed. Jimmy informed us the attorney, Ulysses Keys, the NAACP man, did not expect them to go to court for fear of a decision knocking out restrictive covenants. He thought they would simply not renew the lease.

With that in mind, Jimmy was already exploring the possibilities of a large apartment closer to Cottage Grove Avenue, the dividing line, where we would be more likely to get definitive action on residential segregation.

I had yet another cause for celebration. And I sprang it on Bernice and Jimmy. There was a letter from Muste. He liked the plan. In fact, he thought it so important that he was mimeographing the two memos and sending copies to all members of the FOR National Council, the governing body, for discussion and action at its meeting in Columbus in a few days. Since the plan would require support of FOR people around the country, he thought it would be better to get approval from the entire council rather than just from the executive director.

"Good Lord!" Bernice exclaimed. "That's great. You're going to the council meeting, aren't you?"

"Of course," I replied. "I'd already planned to go, and now Muste insists on it."

"You lucky dog," said Bernice. "It's in the bag now. If you have a chance to make a speech, you'll have that national council eating out of your hand. I want to go to Columbus; I can scrape up the money for a round-trip bus ticket."

"That won't be necessary," I smiled. "I have a car for the trip. Ashton Jones loaned me his."

Bernice's big smile twisted into a grimace.

"Oh, no! Not *that* car. Don't we have problems enough? Everyone'll think we're a bunch of kooks."

Ashton Jones was a monomaniacal, one-man crusader for world peace.

He did not work for a living but traveled around the country, staying with friends, preaching world peace to anyone who would listen. He would "borrow" money if necessary, to get to the next friend in the next city.

Either Ford or General Motors *gave* him the car when he walked into their offices in Detroit, proclaiming the need for wheels to carry the message of world peace. (I always believed that they must have given him the car in order to turn off the sermon and get him out of there.)

He never paid for bridge or highway tolls, but instead preached sermons on world peace to the toll taker while frantic motorists behind him honked madly. Finally, in desperation, the toll taker would tell him to move on and "get the hell out of here." That, they say, is the way he also got gasoline.

The car itself was garishly painted in loud colors: "WORLD PEACE CAR." One side of the vehicle was covered with a painting of a blazing inferno, with bodies arching upward over hot coals and bombs bursting in air as a horned Satan smiled malevolently. The caption read: "WAR IS SATAN'S WAY." On the other side was an idyllic scene, with winged creatures looking down from the clouds, with the caption: "PEACE IS GOD'S WAY."

"Well, can't we at least have a paint job done on the car?" Bernice asked with a frown. "Something we can wash off when we get back?"

I shook my head.

"Okay, okay," Bernice said. "As Gertrude Stein would put it, 'a car is a car is a car.' As long as it will run. And, speaking of running, I'd better get out of here and start working on lining up a couple of other passengers for that hideous car so we can cut expenses in half. I'll call you tomorrow, probably about 7:00 P.M., to let you know who we'll have riding with us."

Jimmy Robinson said that he would not be one of them. He was not going, because FOR people drove him to distraction. They were "too nice, too good, too righteous, too loving, too saccharine—like the Quakers." He preferred the War Resisters League types, who had "less pretense and less hypocrisy."

The next day was lazy and lethargic. I garaged the car, even though I couldn't afford it, so it wouldn't be on the street attracting attention. I washed my clothes and packed, and sat and waited. Bernice had said she would call around seven, so I sat close to the phone.

At 6:55, the phone rang. I lifted the receiver from the hook. The voice that spoke, however, was not Bernice's. It was Winnie's—that languorous voice I'd been trying to push from my consciousness, but that kept pushing back. Here it was again, and real.

"Jim, I tried to stay away but I couldn't. So here I am. I thought I could turn and walk away, but I can't. I must see you again—if you want to."

"I'll come over tonight, Winnie."

"No, not tonight. I promised mother I'd go someplace with her tonight. But tomorrow will be fine."

"Tomorrow," I said, "I'm going out of town, to Columbus, for an important meeting. Back in five days."

"Call me when you get back. We'll go out. Maybe the Palm Tavern; it would be like starting over again."

"Great, Winnie. And I love you."

"I love you, too, Jim. Very much."

Bernice called, of course. We had two other passengers and would leave from Boys' House at 6:00 A.M. Our conversation was brief; I did not want to talk to her or to anyone else. I wanted only to sit in my room and think, and dream, and smoke my pipe.

CHAPTER 10

CORE IS BORN

THE CAR WITH THE boisterous personality sped through the countryside toward Columbus. My foot was heavy on the accelerator. I hoped that speed would blur the images on the vehicle's side to passersby.

Time went swiftly, too, for conversation was ceaseless and animated.

There was George Houser, who shared the driving with me. George, a graduate of Union Theological Seminary in New York, was fresh out of Danbury, a federal penitentiary, where he had served two years as a non-registrant for the draft. A small man, there was about him an aura of confidence and authority that made size unimportant. George had eyes that matched his fine intelligence, though they were red-lidded and sleepy-looking. He asked questions more than he gave answers, and the answers he received, like those of Socrates, were stored away for future reference.

George was going to be enormously useful in the new organization and the new movement. His talents for administration, organization, and management of details were extraordinary. He would be a particularly valuable asset since he was now working for the FOR in Chicago and was directing a committee of pacifist students at the university who were studying nonviolence.

Also in the car was Dr. Homer Jack, who held a doctorate in biology, but had switched disciplines and was now studying at the Meadville School of Theology, a Unitarian school in Chicago. Prematurely gray, Homer had the zest and wide-eyed enthusiasm of the perpetually young. Having swapped the world of life, cells, and enzymes for the world of body politic and social struggle, Homer was loaded with intensities—intense seriousness, intense excitement, intense wonder.

In the car, too, was Bernice, who was, of course, always Bernice.

As we swept by the pregnant earth of Ohio farms on that spring day in 1942, there was heady talk about *our* giving birth that year to a revolution in race relations with a technique new to America that would change the face of this nation.

On the following day, the FOR National Council turned to the business at hand. My address was at two-thirty, and I was relaxed and confident. The agenda item was "The Brotherhood Mobilization Plan."

A. J. Muste opened the session by reading from Kierkegaard, after which, in Quaker fashion, all heads were bowed in meditation. Then, it was my turn.

In that room, of forty members of the council and about fifteen staff members and friends, there were two black faces. In addition to me, there was Bayard Rustin, a thirty-one-year-old Quaker with a clipped, British accent, an impressive, deliberate speaking style, and a beautiful, lyric tenor singing voice. Bayard, who was called Rusty, had just been brought on FOR staff as youth secretary by A.J. He obviously was very close to A.J. and there was a deep affection between them. John Swomley jokingly referred to them as Muste and Rusty.

Rustin sat impassively as I walked up front to make my presentation. There were a few other impassive faces in the audience, but most were smiling sweetly and nodding encouragement.

I put my words in a religious context because this was, after all, the FOR. In essence, what I said was: "The Blessed Community and the Family of Christ are rent asunder by the evil practice of apartheid in America, which will not end until the decent and the religious people of the land will it so. God willing, segregation will end when the *good* people withdraw their cooperation from it and stop, wittingly or unwittingly, giving it their support. What I am proposing is that the FOR, because of its thorough-going commitment to nonviolence and brotherhood, take the lead in setting up a vehicle through which that noncooperation with evil can be forged into a national movement."

I then summarized the memoranda, which they had already read, and related our experiences in Chicago with White City and with the ongoing struggle against restrictive covenants and residential segregation. I also told of the coming campaign at Jack Spratt, and I sat down.

A portly, gray-haired council member rose slowly, adjusted his rimless eyeglasses, and spoke: "Jim, you speak of being open and aboveboard. Now, when the young white men signed the lease on Mrs. Masters' house, did they tell the agent that there would be Negroes living there? Apparently, not. Do you consider that open and aboveboard? Or was it deception and concealment? And another thing. Do you really think that you changed the hearts of the White City management? Did you persuade them that what they were doing was wrong? Or did you merely try to *force* them—back them into a corner and *coerce* them into changing their policy? Now, I grant you, coercion is better than hitting them over the head; but is it nonviolence? I think not. I think it is violence. Also, you had the three people arrested. How loving an act was that?"

Bernice was gritting her teeth and pounding her thigh with her fist as he spoke. Houser was smiling and shaking his head. Homer Jack looked at the floor and I knew that the questions posed by the portly member would be the heart of the debate, not only in the council, but throughout the FOR. The lines would be drawn. I tried, therefore, to be conciliatory rather than argumentative.

"I respect the sincerity of those questions," I said, "and appreciate their being stated so forthrightly, because they need to be discussed very frankly. On the matter of Boys' House, there was nothing about race in the lease. Restrictive covenants pass from owner to owner with the deed. Nor was there any restriction on subleasing. In view of those facts, we felt that it should be no more necessary to talk about the color of prospective residents than it would be to talk about their height, or weight, or the color of their eyes. On the question of coercion vis-à-vis violence at White City, if our efforts to change the mind and heart through negotiation fail, we have only two alternatives: (1) to walk away and allow the objectionable policy to continue, or (2) to apply pressure. Only the latter option is acceptable to us. Frankly, we could think of no Gandhian-type pressure in that situation so, reluctantly, we resorted to the law. Pacifists do respect the law, though sometimes their consciences force them to violate it."

The debate went on for over two hours, chiefly around the same issue. Previously expressed thoughts were being repeated in different words. No new thoughts were being expressed. None, that is, until one woman blurted out: "But, James, your program causes conflict. We don't want conflict. We want peace and tranquility."

I could be conciliatory no longer. I rose in indignation and quoted a modern theologian, Gregory Vlastos: "He who preaches love in a society based upon injustice can purchase immunity from conflict only at the price of hypocrisy!"

That brought a wide grin to Bernice's face. A.J., who was sitting alone in the back of the room, arched his brows sharply and a smile slowly materialized under them.

One council member went back and consulted briefly with A.J. A few minutes later, he said, "Mr. Chairman, I have a motion."

The FOR chairman, who till then had had little to do (FOR people are orderly and do not all talk at once), recognized him.

"Mr. Chairman, I move that the FOR not sponsor this new organization. But that we authorize James Farmer, on FOR time, to start an organization along the lines he envisions in one city, Chicago, and after that, the FOR may decide how it will proceed from there."

The motion was seconded and overwhelmingly passed by voice vote. There were no dissenting votes, but several abstentions.

The session was adjourned for dinner and I sighed with relief. My triad and I went into town for a sandwich and beer, and we missed the evening session, which was largely in-house business and music.

The following two days were boring—music and prosaic business. The business was stuff I could read in memos from the national office. The music consisted of moving renditions of Negro spirituals by Bayard Rustin. I wanted to listen to the songs and then leave, but that would be to "eat and run," so I sat through all the sessions, longing to get back to Chicago to continue building a movement.

When the council meeting ended, Ashton Jones's car leaped onto the highway and raced for home.

At the Palm Tavern, Winnie and I had the joy of being together again, but that joy was clouded by a certain shared, though unspoken knowledge. She wanted to articulate it, but could not find the words; I did not even search for them. We were being pulled inexorably into a fierce tug-of-war between two loves that were hostile and antagonistic: our love for each other and my love for an unborn movement. Home/work tension is commonplace. But this was more than that. It would be a war between two hot and wholly incompatible passions. The bond that joined us would be wrenched and twisted. Would it break?

In those youthful days, I believed that I was master of my fate and that anything was possible if I willed it so.

Winnie was not so sure. She said, "Jim, tell me that I was wrong, and that it will work."

I whispered words of reassurance. The red rose seemed to have dew drops on its petals as she lifted it from her hair and placed it in my lapel. She leaned across the table and invited me to do the same. Our lips met and parted with a kiss.

We talked of marriage. We had spoken of it before, but that had been wistful, end-of-the-rainbow talk. This time, it was serious for both of us. Once again, I had misgivings about the course my life was taking. How could I get married on fifteen dollars a week? But the law's delay bought time for me. Her lawyer had told her, she said, that her divorce might take six more months. That would give me time to work things out.

If a soul at peace allows one to rest, mine must have been tormented, for sleep eluded me all night.

I faced the blustery, overcast spring morning with bleary eyes from lack of sleep. It was an eager, bright-eyed cadre of idealists, however, that awaited me in the Boys' House living room on that Saturday morning in April 1942.

An air of expectancy hung over the room, for they were there to accomplish something unheard of in this nation. They were about to form an organization that would seek to impale racism and segregation on the sword of nonviolent techniques.* In attendance were George Houser,

*Meier and Rudwick, in their book *CORE: A History of the Civil Rights Movement, 1942 to 1968*, offer a somewhat different version of the origin of CORE than that here presented. Their source was a pamphlet, "A Short History of CORE," written by George Houser in 1949. That pamphlet considered CORE to have sprung directly from the FOR cell (Committee on Nonviolence) that Houser shepherded at the University of Chicago. The Houser group did indeed play a significant role in the development of the new organization. The fact is, my memoranda to A. J. Muste and the FOR National Council decision to authorize me to establish in Chicago a pilot project along the lines described in these memos constituted the original "game plan," which the University of Chicago FOR cell accepted and helped make work. Thus there was, in a sense, a kind of dual parentage for CORE.

Bernice Fisher, Jimmy Robinson, Joe Guinn, Homer Jack, Bob Chino, Hugo Victoreen, and I.

We leaped upon the tasks at hand with a zest that soon pumped enough adrenaline into my system to banish fatigue. I was elected chairman of this unnamed organization that had no structure as yet and no program except that which was implicit in the two memos, the work we were doing in Hyde Park–Kenwood and the three action committees Bernice was putting together.

Bernice became secretary and Jimmy treasurer. The action committees were fleshed out, and two committees were set up, one to draw up the bylaws and another to draw up the action discipline for the organization.

But what was the organization to be called? There had to be a catchy name with an unforgettable acronym. Bob Chino, a university student who was half Chinese and half Caucasian, shouted, "I've got it! Let's call it CORE, because it will be the center of things, the heart of the action."

The enthusiasm was unanimous. But now that we had an acronym, what did it stand for? The RE was easy: Racial Equality. The C had to be either Committee or Council, and we opted for Committee, because Council sounded more like a discussion group than one for action. But what was the O? On or of? On that question, the debate was lengthy and high-spirited. The discussion was philosophical, not frivolous. We believed, after all, that we were starting an organization that would soon become nationwide and would shake America to its roots; what it was called would be of utmost importance. On signified the subject of our efforts; but of—and this is what I argued—implied that the organization, in its structure, its methods, and its very being, would reflect the objective it sought. Like a seed, a real core, it would germinate and radiate its equality in wider and wider circles until it encompassed the whole nation.

CORE became the Committee of Racial Equality.

That settled, we agreed to meet again in two days to hear progress reports from the committees and to organize our campaign at Jack Spratt. The deadline for Jack Spratt had long since passed, with no response from its manager to my letter requesting negotiations. We sent a team of two women students—one black, one white—to go there and try to talk with him on the spot. Perhaps he would be more receptive and civil to women.

They found a woman in charge instead of the usual manager. She agreed to talk to them and told them that the policy was dictated by the requirements of business. Their other customers would object if they served Negroes, she said, and they could not afford the loss of patronage. Our team expressed the conviction that they would not lose money. That close to the university, they assured her, most of her customers would approve a change of policy, and those who dissented would easily be offset by the new patrons a change would bring. The woman disagreed. Our negotiators then suggested that she ask her present customers, or permit them to do so. She refused. Then they proposed that the three of them agree on a third party, preferably a bookkeeper or CPA, to check her books after a month of serving all people, to determine whether Jack Spratt had lost income. If they had, our negotiators said they would guarantee in writing, if necessary, to make up the deficit for that month and not return again.

That sounded like an unwise proposition to me, when I later heard their report. It seemed to say that if racism is good business, we will allow it to continue. But no matter. The woman had turned the proposition down anyway, and saying she did not want to talk anymore, she had walked away.

That night, we met to hear the report and decide on further action. Before we got to the matter at hand, Jimmy Robinson told us of another letter received from Mrs. Masters' lawyer, ordering us to be out of the house in ten days or to suffer the consequences. The only question was whether to reject the order or ignore it. The consensus was to reject it, in writing. I also suggested that Jimmy contact the NAACP attorney, Ulysses S. Keys, to alert him to the situation in case a quick legal response was needed.

The Jack Spratt matter was handled with dispatch. The decision: a large-scale sit-in, occupying all available seats. The date: three days hence. The time, 4:30 P.M. We would meet at Boys' House an hour before for last-minute instructions.

On that day in May 1942, we began what I believe to be the first organized civil rights sit-in in American history. A group of twenty-eight persons entered Jack Spratt in parties of two, three, and four. In each party, there was one black man or woman. With the discipline of peacefulness strictly observed, we occupied all available seating spaces at the counter and in booths.

The small restaurant staff was thrown into confusion. The man who we believed to be the manager was not there. The woman with whom our negotiation team had talked was in charge. Waitresses looked at each other and shrugged. Then they looked at the woman in charge for a cue, but none was forthcoming. All the while, we sat smoking and quietly chatting.

Two whites, who were not obviously members of our group and were sitting some distance from each other at the counter, were served. One, a well-dressed middle-aged woman, thanked the waitress when her food arrived, but sitting with hands in her lap, did not touch it. The other, a man, also older, promptly passed his food to the black beside him, who proceeded to eat it.

The woman in charge went to the lady who had been served and asked, "Is your dinner all right, ma'am?"

"Oh, I'm sure it's just fine."

"But you aren't eating it."

"I know. You see, it wouldn't be very polite for me to begin eating before my friends also had been served."

An elderly couple dining in one booth inquired what was going on. When informed by one of our people in the next booth, they discussed it between themselves and then passed the word to us that they agreed with us and would eat no more of their food until all of us were served. And they would not leave until we left.

This evoked a silent applause from the neighboring booths. Other customers, not in our groups, had stopped eating, too, or were eating very slowly; they did not want to miss any of this drama. They had, in effect, joined the sit-in out of curiosity if nothing else.

After making a phone call, the woman in charge swept past me and spoke to Jimmy Robinson. "If the colored people in your group will go to the basement, I'll have them served there."

I responded; "No, ma'am. We will not eat in the basement."

"Well," she said, still speaking to Jimmy, not to me, "if you'll clear out the two rear booths, then all the colored people can sit there, and I will have them served."

"No, thank you," I said. "We're quite comfortable where we are."

"I'll call the police," she said, and now she was looking directly at me with a triumphant expression on her face.

I told her I thought that might be the appropriate thing for her to do. (I had phoned the police precinct just before the demonstration, telling them precisely what we were going to do and exactly how. I had explained the discipline of nonviolence and had refreshed their memory about the little-used state civil rights law in Illinois. This was in line with the Gandhian principle of being open and aboveboard with the authorities.)

Within minutes, two of Chicago's finest walked in. After casting their eyes around the restaurant, they walked to her and one of them asked, "What did you call us for, lady? I don't see anybody disturbing the peace. What do you want us to do?"

"I want you to throw these people out, of course," she replied.

"Lady, we can't do that. What're they doing wrong? You're open for business, aren't you? They're not trespassing."

"Well now, won't you throw them out," she asked, "on the grounds that we reserve the right to seat our patrons and would serve some of them in the basement?"

The policeman slapped his thigh in exasperation. He went into the phone booth and made a call. When he came out he said, "No, lady, there's nothing in the law that allows us to do that. You must either serve them or solve the problem yourself the best way you can."

The cops left, one winking at me as he passed by.

The woman in charge ordered the waitresses to serve everyone.

After dining and leaving good tips for the waitresses, to compensate them for the time we had occupied the seats, we paid our bills and left. The money was not thrown out this time.

Jimmy wrote Jack Spratt a letter thanking them for the service and congratulating them on their change in policy. Subsequent tests over the next fortnight by small mixed and all-black groups confirmed that the policy had, in fact, changed.

In the meantime, continuance followed continuance in the White City Roller Skating Rink case for more than six months. The ticket seller failed to show up at court for an unknown reason on one occasion, and that produced a thirty-day postponement. She failed to show again, and this time the court was told that she was ill. Another postponement was granted, and defense counsel was admonished that if any of them were ill on the next date, thirty days hence, they must bring a doctor's certificate.

They appeared next time, without the lady in question but with a statement dated the previous day and signed with the name of a local physician, certifying that she was undergoing treatment subsequent to a serious operation and could not possibly be in court on the day of the trial. The fact was, however, that we had a witness who had visited the rink the previous night and had seen her working and apparently in good health and humor. When this was related to the judge, he called a thirty-minute recess so that my attorney could call the doctor to get his version of the matter.

When Ulysses Keys, who was volunteering his services in this case, made his report to the court, the judge's mouth dropped open in disbelief. The doctor whose name was on the certificate, dated the previous day, had been on vacation for two weeks and would not return to the city for another two weeks. His Honor looked at the defense counsel for some explanation, but in reply he got only eyes averted in embarrassment.

Keys argued for a contempt-of-court citation, but the judge merely ordered another thirty-day continuance. On the next date, he said, he expected all of the defendants to be present.

On the designated date, all were present. The judge asked the White City defense if they were ready for trial and they said yes. He then asked if I was ready and my reply was affirmative, too, and I indicated that Keys was my lawyer.

At that point, a man I had never seen before entered the courtroom and came down the aisle, saying, "Just a minute, Your Honor, I'm the assistant state's attorney and I will be the prosecutor for this case."

I was stunned and said, "But, Your Honor, my lawyer is Mr. Keys. He knows the case from beginning to end."

The judge looked shocked, but said nothing.

The assistant state's attorney spoke again: "That makes no difference. I'm the prosecutor in this case. This is a state case and I'll handle it."

"But my lawyer—" I protested.

"Your lawyer can be adviser to the state's attorney, but I will prosecute," he said.

Throughout the trial, the assistant state's attorney seemed to be defending the defendants rather than prosecuting them. He appeared to be prosecuting my witnesses and me. Yet I felt the case was so strong and the witnesses so unimpeachable that the outcome could not be in doubt.

I was wrong.

After the prosecution and the defense had concluded their cases, the assistant state's attorney spoke again: "Your Honor, as assistant state's attorney, prosecutor for the state, let me say that we have tried to prove that White City Roller Skating Rink has discriminated against Negroes, and we have failed completely. We have failed to prove that they discriminate, and as prosecutor for the state, I can make but one recommendation, namely that you find these defendants from White City Roller Skating Rink not guilty. Any other decision would be a miscarriage of justice in this court."

I gasped. The defendants smiled. The judge buried his face in his hands. Finally, he looked up, appearing tired and much older. He spoke softly but could be heard throughout the hushed courtroom.

"These complainants are honest and intelligent people. They have a right to skate in anybody's roller skating rink at any time, and I sincerely hope that there is no discrimination against them at White City Roller Skating Rink. However, in view of the recommendation made by the assistant state's attorney, the prosecutor for the state, I have no alternative but to find these defendants not guilty."

We groaned, shook our heads, and turned to walk out. The judge spoke again: "Mr. Farmer, I want you to know that any time you want justice, you can always come to my court."

Despite our setback, CORE was beginning to make a name for itself in Chicago and was starting to go national. Not that *nonviolence* was becoming a household term. The concept that violence could be greeted with love generally evoked only contempt. A common reaction from black and white leaders alike was, "You mean that if someone hits you, you're not going to hit him back? What are you, some kind of a nut or something?" But the daring and tenacity of this band of rebels was winning the admiration of some leaders in the black community. An official of the Chicago Urban League, for instance, observed publicly that "the Urban League is the State Department of civil rights; the NAACP is the War Department; and CORE is the marines."

A local luminary in the black community who befriended CORE was the Reverend Archibald J. Carey, pastor of the Woodlawn African Methodist Episcopal Church, and also a Chicago alderman. A red-haired, freckled, dynamic man, "Arch" became CORE's patron saint. When CORE needed money above that which could be raised by passing a hat at membership meetings, Arch would take up a collection in his church. He also gave us office space in the basement of his church and use of a mimeograph machine.

It was in that church basement that Bernice and I replied to letters from FOR people around the country, who wrote requesting information about starting Committees of Racial Equality in their cities. They had read about the action of the national council, and I had continued my visits to FOR groups in many places, speaking always about CORE.

Also, Bayard Rustin was traveling for the FOR as field secretary. On his

trips, he spoke of nonviolence, though not of CORE. In *Fellowship* magazine, the journal of the FOR, he reported on many individual encounters
with discrimination in public places, which he resolved nonviolently—by
talking with the manager and appealing to his conscience and reason, thus
winning him over. *Fellowship*'s editors referred to Bayard as "the FOR's
one-man nonviolent army."

Though these were individual exploits, not organizational action, they
did spread the message of nonviolence, leading many FOR people to ask,
"If individual nonviolence works, how much more effective would it be if
employed in organized action?" The inquiries were numerous, and their
spirit bordered on the ecstatic. In fact, a correspondent in Seattle always
ended her letters: "Ecstatically yours," which led Bernice and me to refer
to her in fun as the Seattle Ecstasy.

And then there was Margaret Rohrer, the FOR staff person in Denver,
who was off and running right after the national council meeting, even
before she had written to us and received a reply. She asked me to come to
Denver and give them a boost in their actions, which were patterned after
Chicago. They would raise the money to pay my expenses. Naturally, I
agreed to go.

There were more, and we invited them to come to Chicago for a
weekend conference in the middle of June 1943 to set up a national
organization of CORE groups to coordinate their activities.

I wrote to A. J. Muste, informing him of my plans to hold the conference, and his response was lukewarm. He wrote that the work being done
by FOR people on behalf of CORE in Chicago and several other cities was
impressive, but that he had some questions about the way things were
developing and wanted to discuss them with me. He said that he would be
in Chicago in a couple of days, and wanted me to come to FOR's Midwest
office in the Loop and sit down with him at that time.

The meeting with Muste was cool and unfriendly: employer to employee.

"What do you intend to have come out of this conference you're holding, Jim?"

"A national CORE organization," I replied.

"I distinctly recall," he shot back, "that in your two memos you recommended that this organization you were founding be a part of the FOR
until such time as the FOR chose to spin it off."

"A.J., the national council turned that down, and since then I've come to
the conclusion that they were right and I was wrong. The two organizations are natural friends and allies and should continue close cooperation,
but I now think that it would be in the interest of neither organization for
CORE to be a part of the FOR."

"Why wouldn't it be in the interest of FOR?"

"Because there will be many times when CORE actions will be an embarrassment to FOR. For instance, I swore out warrants for the arrest of
our adversaries at White City. I don't think that would sit well with our
absolutist friends in FOR."

A.J.'s eyes were narrow slits and his brows joined in the middle as he asked, "How do you expect to maintain a pacifist emphasis in CORE if it's not under the umbrella of FOR?"

"I don't," I replied. "CORE should not be a pacifist organization, but rather, it should bring pacifists and nonpacifists together under a commitment to nonviolence as a tactic, a device for fighting racism."

"Jim," he said with anger, "you can't hide your pacifism!"

"I'm not trying to hide my pacifism, A.J. I want CORE to become a mass movement. The masses of Negroes will not become pacifists. Being Negroes for them is tough enough without being pacifist, too. Neither will the masses of whites. Some individuals, no doubt, will see the effectiveness of domestic nonviolence and will make the transfer to the international scene; that will be fine. Others will not, and that, too, will be acceptable."

"One final question," said A.J. "How are you going to raise the money? You had an elaborate plan in your second memo, but that would take years. Where will you get the money for a national organization in the interim?"

"I think maybe we'll do direct-mail fund raising," I replied.

A.J. shook his head as he spoke: "No, I cannot permit that. Your sources are FOR sources. You may *not* engage in any direct-mail fund raising for CORE. That would interfere with FOR fund raising."

A.J. stood, which was my signal to leave. He then said, "By the way, Bayard agrees with me completely on all these matters."

We shook hands, but he did not smile. I rushed to the nearest phone booth and called Bernice, asking her to meet me for a beer, if she could pay. She did.

The beer washed away some of my anxiety, and in its place I was able to see our predicament through less somber eyes. "What we have here," I said, "is a reversal of roles. We wanted to give it to them, but they didn't want it. Now they want it, but we don't want them to have it."

Bernice laughed aloud and ordered a refill of our mugs.

"To put it another way," I went on, "we were the panting suitor in hot pursuit as the maiden fled to save her honor; but the worm has turned. Now, she is pursuing us as we run like hell to protect our virtue."

She was laughing so loudly now that, over the tinkle of glasses and the chatter, people turned to look.

"What old virtue?" she said. "You don't have any left. I'm sure that bronze bombshell of yours has seen to that."

"Muste is not joking," I said, shifting gears abruptly. "He's dead serious. He'll have my hide."

"How can he? He'd be a fool to fire you. If he did, you'd be free to raise funds any way you want."

"No, he won't fire me, but he can make things damned uncomfortable for me, especially with Bayard siding with him on every issue that divides us."

"What a pity that you and Bayard have to be on opposite sides in this. What a team you'd make."

"It's an old game, Bernice. The Romans called it divide and conquer."

"But why would Bayard let himself be used in this manner?"

"Maybe he's not being used," I replied. "Maybe he happens to agree with A.J. on these issues."

"How could he?" she asked. "It's obvious that CORE couldn't go any-place as a pacifist organization." Bernice paused for a moment, and then continued: "By the way, we only have A.J.'s word that Bayard agrees with him. I understand he'll be coming to town a few days after the CORE conference. Why don't we ask him?"

"Good idea," I said, "and it might help swing him over to CORE's side if we got the conference to elect him to some position, contingent upon his acceptance, since he won't be present—perhaps as a field representative. He could be very helpful in that role since he does a lot of traveling for FOR."

"Well, now that we have all that settled," said Bernice, lifting her mug, "let's make sure I have the line straight. We back off direct-mail fund raising for the time being, but do *not* compromise on CORE's autonomy and its nonpacifist character. Right?"

"Right."

That conference was filled with the highest hopes of reshaping the social contours of America. Every posture taken shamed the Statue of Liberty; every word rang the Liberty Bell itself. That crew of about thirty from Seattle, Denver, New York, Philadelphia, Evanston, and Chicago, gathered in Archibald Carey's church on June 15, 1943, could not have been more consumed with fire had they been a band of abolitionists convening in the mid-nineteenth century.

They formed a national organization and christened it, at my sugges-tion, the National Federation of Committees of Racial Equality. (It would be hard to imagine a more unwieldy name.) I was elected national chair-man; Bernice, national secretary-treasurer; and Bayard, field representa-tive, pending acceptance. A constitution was adopted, as well as the CORE rules for action. There was no staff, no budget, no money. It was all volunteer.

The conference was graced with one guest speaker: Krishnalal Shridha-rani. I was startled when I saw him for the first time. I had expected a Gandhiesque figure—ascetic, bony, waiflike. Instead, there was a round-ish, well-fed, thirty-two-year-old Brahmin, meticulous in a three-piece Brooks Brothers suit, lavender silk shirt, and impeccably shined shoes. A finger on one hand sported a large ruby ring, and on the other hand there was a star sapphire. Thin lips in a fleshy face caressed a long cigar.

Although I found a worldly man instead of another Gandhi, I felt more comfortable with him than I would have with Gandhi. Yet, when Shrid, as I came to call him, spoke of Gandhiji, the respectful term for the beloved Mahatma, he took on almost an ascetic appearance.

He told us that we were on the right track, and that the essential Gan-dhian method would work in the American scene. But it could not be lifted bodily from his country; for America was not India, and the Hebraic-Christian culture was not identical to that of Hinduism. On those themes, he elaborated at length in scholarly fashion.

There was a party, of course, and there was an action dinner at Stoner's, which George Houser had taken a special interest in. A giant restaurant in Chicago's Loop district, Stoner's was crowded every day with hundreds of people, at lunch and dinner, with lines waiting for empty tables. Apparently, they served good food—but not to blacks.

George Houser had made several test visits to Stoner's and had found the attitude of the management to be extremely hostile. On one visit, after holding up the line for half an hour, Houser and his friends were seated, only to have a tray of hot food spilled over the head of one of the blacks in the party.

On another occasion, George and I and several others went there for lunch. After we were finally seated, Mr. Stoner himself, scowling, took our orders. A few minutes later, Stoner, still doubling as waiter, brought our sandwiches to the table. Scarcely had he walked away, when one of the black busboys rushed over and whispered, "Don't eat those sandwiches. Mr. Stoner made them himself; he made them out of garbage. I saw him." We examined the sandwiches and saw that the busboy was right. The lettuce was wet and wilted, and there were coffee grounds on it as well as on the tomatoes. We wrapped the sandwiches up, taking them with us for future reference, paid our bills, and left. Later, the busboys all quit their jobs in protest. Stoner then hired black busgirls.)

George Houser had organized the dinner visit for the June 1943 conference. He made it a masterpiece of nonviolent strategy.

Since the restaurant was so enormous and our numbers so few—sixty-eight, including local CORE members and friends and the thirty conferees—each person had to do the job of several. Our first eight or ten parties of four each, all white, moved up with the line and were seated promptly by the maitre d'. If one of our parties was about to be seated close to another, its spokesperson was to ask for a different table. Their instructions were to try to scatter themselves around the large restaurant, covering as much area as possible, in order to lobby among other patrons—seeking to make sympathizers of the majority of persons in the restaurant. We had to compensate for the limited size of our group.

Next in line was George Houser and a black friend.

"One for dinner, sir?" the maitre d' asked George.

"No, two," he replied.

The man said, "Wait here." Then he went and spoke to Stoner, who stood at a distance, eyeing the situation. Time passed and the line did not move. One of our group behind George and his friend beckoned Mr. Stoner, who then walked slowly toward him.

"Why aren't you seating us?" he asked Stoner. "You have vacant tables. What's the holdup? We're hungry."

"Well, if you just step around this way," said Stoner, seeking to bypass George's party, "I'll seat you."

"No, we can't do that," the man replied. "These people are ahead of us; you have to seat them first."

Others in the line told Stoner to start seating people. The owner's frustration was obvious. He motioned to George and his friend to follow him.

They had not walked many paces when Stoner stopped, turned around and gave Houser a swift kick in the shin.

"That's all right, Mr. Stoner," said George, "we know how you feel about it."

They were seated. The line then moved quickly. A couple dozen more whites were seated, many of them of our group. Suddenly, the seating stopped again. There were eight blacks, in two parties, and I was among them.

Our advance lobby groups had done their job well. What they found was that most of the people there were not aware that there were restaurants in Chicago that did not serve blacks. "Down South, maybe," they thought, "but not here." How could it be that they had lived there so many years without knowing it? Institutional practices, it seems, perpetuate themselves mostly by their invisibility.

The color line was indeed, invisible—to all but the few who looked for it. Folks breathed it in the air and did not smell it; ate it with each meal and never tasted it. What *is* tends to persist.

Now, as Stoner walked nervously through his restaurant, he must have thought that everyone there that day was part of our group. He was besieged from all sides by people everywhere in the restaurant. "Why don't you seat those people? They've been standing there fifteen minutes."

"We don't have any tables free," he would answer.

"Yes, you do," one person observed. "There are two vacant tables over there."

"They're reserved," Stoner said as he walked hastily away.

Finally, he succumbed to the pressure and seated the first four of the blacks at one of the tables he had said was reserved. Minutes later, as the last four of our group—three other blacks and I—walked across the restaurant behind Stoner, a tremendous and spontaneous applause split the air. The black busgirls beamed. An old gray-haired lady, eyes blazing, looked up into my face as we passed by and shouted, "Bravo!"

The two springs that fed my soul flowed on through the rest of the summer and fall of 1943, each in its own path—bubbling, swirling, tumbling over the rocks, neither interfering with the other's course.

Boys' House moved to a new home. The lease on the Masters place had expired, and as expected, they would not renew it, so we had moved to a large apartment at 6314 South Ellis Avenue, just south of Sixty-third Street and only a few blocks east of Cottage Grove. Jimmy and two others had signed the lease, and all of us moved in.

After a month, the inevitable letter came from McKey-Pogue Realty

Company. "We are advised that there are in residence in Apartment 1, 6314 South Ellis Avenue, persons other than those of you who signed the lease, and that among those other persons are non-Caucasians, constituting a source of great annoyance to the neighbors . . ."

We were ordered to vacate the premises immediately, which, of course, we declined to do. Instead, we rang every doorbell in the building, asking our neighbors whether they objected to our presence. The answer was unanimously no. Most said that we were good neighbors, didn't make a lot of noise, and created no disturbance. But some of the other tenants were disagreeable and may have complained. Many signed statements in our support. Others declined to sign, for fear of trouble with the landlord.

Armed with the signatures, we went to court when summoned. McKey-Pogue was surprised by our advance preparation and asked for a thirty-day continuance to further prepare their case. It was granted by the judge and thus began another long series of postponements. Unable to scare us out, this landlord was no more anxious than the previous one had been to risk a court test on housing bias. (Late in 1942, the suit against Boys' House was dropped.)

To accommodate the court schedule, I had to cut short endless speaking trips. I was still traveling and speaking for FOR and organizing new CORE groups. There had been no special correspondence from Muste since our difference of opinion; the only communication had been routine staff letters on conscientious objector matters.

I had, however, spoken with Rustin, who had agreed to the letterhead title of field representative for CORE. When I asked his views on the issue of CORE autonomy and nonviolence as a tactic, his response was, "Jim, you can't hide your pacifism." The words sounded familiar.

CORE was a large part of my world, but most of the world knew nothing about it. There was no television to catch the drama, and the press largely ignored it. If we were lucky, there might be a small paragraph on a back page of the *Chicago Tribune* saying, in effect, that a few nuts and crackpots sat in a restaurant until they were served, or thrown out, or the place closed—whichever came first. Period.

Winnie occasionally asked about CORE and wondered why she didn't see anything about it in the papers. I explained that we weren't big enough yet.

I saw Winnie frequently throughout the summer and early fall months. But in the late fall, she broke it off again, this time without a word. Just disappeared. I could not reach her by phone or letter.

Finally, in desperation, I called Lucille, her best friend.

"Jim, I know Winnie doesn't want me to tell you this," Lucille said, "but I'm going to tell you, anyway. Winnie went to Detroit and was married yesterday. A childhood playmate of hers, who now works in a Detroit auto factory, came to Chicago two weeks ago and asked her to marry him. She said yes, and left almost immediately for Detroit."

"Does she love him?"

"No. She loves you."

Lucille gave me Winnie's married name and her address. The earth stopped spinning, and for days I walked around like a zombie.

I was scheduled to go to Detroit to talk with FOR people about starting a CORE group. After taking care of that business, I matched a name and address with a number in the directory and dialed. I did not know what I would say or do, but I would say and do something.

She answered the phone. I said, "Pack your things, I'm coming over there to take you home."

Those words were out of character and they startled me. It would be an insane thing to do.

She spoke quickly: "No, don't. You don't have to. I'm coming back in two or three weeks. I'll write you tonight. But don't come here."

She wrote, as promised. The gist of her letter was that she was through running, would flee no more. How could she have done such a horrible thing? I must forgive her. She would make it up to me. Whatever was going to happen in our lives together would just have to happen.

"Oh, no, no," I inwardly screamed. "What we *want* to happen, we will *make* happen!"

When she returned, we agreed to be married in June 1943.

Not long after that agreement with Winnie, I received a letter from FOR—not from Muste, but from John Swomley, the associate executive secretary and my friend. He informed me that A.J. wanted me to work out of the national office in New York, rather than Chicago, starting in February. He had also decided that I was to work full-time for FOR, with a raise in salary from fifteen dollars a week to a hundred dollars a month. Swomley congratulated me on my "promotion."

I knew at once what it all meant—New York, where they could watch me closely, and full-time so I would have less time to freewheel for CORE. I was being given bigger wings, but they would be clipped wings. A. J. Muste was smart and tough—and experienced.

Yet my heart beat faster. New York was more than a place where deadly traps were going to be set. It was home, though I'd never lived there, the place where I had always dreamed of living. It was the birthplace of the Harlem Renaissance, the fountain of intellectual and cultural ferment. I thought that anyone who would cut wide, new swaths in the forest of American bigotry must hone his axe on the pavements of New York.

The sojourn in Chicago had been my birth as a man, when I left my father's home and struck out on my own. My intellectual coming of age had occurred several years before at Wiley College, an obscure school in east Texas, and at the Howard University School of Religion—each, in its unique way, pointing me irreversibly toward New York.

PART FOUR

Intellectual Coming of Age

CHAPTER 11

TOLSTOI AND TOLSON

"FARMER, WHAT ARE YOU reading these days?" It was the voice of Melvin B. Tolson yelling, without straining, across a hundred yards of the Wiley College campus in Marshall, Texas, in the fall of 1934.

"Tolstoi! *War and Peace*," I bellowed.

"All right," Tolson thundered. "I'm glad to know that at least you are drinking the broth of knowledge; why don't you eat the meat?"

The meat, the broth, the whole meal of the college experience for this fourteen-year-old freshman was not the ivy-covered walls, though we had those, too, at this small black college. It was not the sunken garden in center campus, with its fountain and goldfish, its daffodils and zinnias and bluebonnets—where dreamy-eyed teenagers looked into each other's eyes and vowed that their love was forever. It was not the dances—where I was a wallflower, since I was so young. Or the football games, won or lost, with celebration and weeping. Nor was it the fraternities and sororities, or the college pranks and practical jokes. The real meal was not even the classrooms and labs of chemistry, in which I majored; or biology, my minor; or history; or French; or economics. The banquet of my Wiley years was the tutelage of Tolson.

A scholar without credentials (he had only a bachelor's degree), a poet and dramatist who had not yet published, Tolson taught English, but that was the least of the things he taught. He stretched the minds of all whose minds would be stretched.

My mind was pure rubber. I was at Wiley because my father was teaching there. He was a professor of religion and philosophy. Once again, he was the only Ph.D. on the faculty. My tuition cost him nothing, for two years earlier I had won a four-year college scholarship in a series of high school oratorical contests sponsored by the black Elks (IBPOE OF W).* Entering college at an age when most youngsters are entering high school, I hungered to learn everything and thought that I was capable of knowing all. Yet I had never learned to study, for I had never had to.

One morning in midsemester of my first year, Tolson asked me to remain after class.

"Farmer," he said, after the others had left the room, "you're doing good work. In fact, you're doing A work, but if you don't do better, I'm going to flunk you."

As I reeled from the incongruity of his words, he went on: "You're blessed with a good mind, an analytical mind, but you don't dig. You're lazy. You're not using half your mind, and like most youths with a gift for self-expression, you try to conceal your ignorance with filibustering.

"Well, I'm not going to let you get away with it. Above and beyond the class assignments, you're going to read and study and dig. Finish *War and Peace* and then go on to his other works. Then I want you to tackle Darwin, Freud, and Marx. Don't just taste them; chew them and digest them. Then we'll get together and argue about them. I'll take a devil's advocate position, and you defend your views. That's the way you sharpen your tools—in the clash of opposing views.

"Speaking of opposing views, my varsity debaters [he was also Wiley's debate coach] come over to the house every Tuesday and Thursday evening to prepare for the intercollegiate debate season. You come over, too. Some of them, at least one, will try to make hamburger out of you—a young upstart, and Dr. Farmer's son—so fight back, my boy, fight back.

"All right, Farmer, I'll see you tonight."

I nodded and stood, speechless, staring at Tolson. His eyes seemed ready to jump out at you, so intense was their penetration. He had the mobile mouth of an orator, with lips that wrapped around words. He was not a large man, maybe five eight or nine, but was square-shouldered and trim, though absentmindedly dressed.

"By the way," he added, "I want you to try out for the debate team. You won't make the varsity this year, but next year you'll have a good shot at it if you work hard."

As I left the room, I wanted at least momentarily to soak up everything on the library shelves.

When I entered Tolson's living room that night, three debaters were in hot discussion of some aspect of the manufacture and sale of munitions, which was the intercollegiate debate topic for the year. Tolson was pacing

*Improved Benevolent and Protective Order of Elks of the World

the floor, puffing on the last two inches of a cheap, smelly stogie, asking questions, interjecting comments, shooting down arguments.

Professor Tolson spun around and said, "Oh, you fellows know Farmer, a promising freshman."

Hobart Jarrett, a polished, dignified, cultivated young man wearing rimless glasses, smiled and greeted me, extending his hand. Cleveland Gay, a blasé senior, nodded. Henry Height, who had been a student at Wiley on and off for a few years and was older than most of the others, laughed loudly and said, "Well, if it isn't Leetle Jug-Head." (I think the reference was to a child character in the Barney Google comic strip, but I saw no similarity; I was six feet tall, though skinny, and my head was not shaped like a jug.) I ignored the remark but Height was not finished.

"So, you want to be a debater. Well, let me ask you one question, Leetle Jug-Head: what irony do you see in the name of Bethlehem Steel Corporation?"

"The Prince of Peace was born in Bethlehem," I snapped back, "and Bethlehem Steel manufactures implements of war, Barney Google."

Jarrett and Gay laughed. Tolson smiled, but as always, it seemed a collision between a smile and a frown. As with most great teachers, even his amusement triggered thoughtfulness.

The evenings at Tolson's were feasts at the end of days of humdrum class work and the petty interpersonal games that college students play. If it was not the night of the debaters, one or two other presumptive intellectual students sharing an interest in things cultural would drop by. They usually lost interest after a few visits and stopped coming. There were only a few regulars.

Sometimes the professor would use us as a sounding board, reading the poetry he was writing, getting our reactions, and dashing back to the typewriter, changing a word here or there. One of the pieces he was working on was an epic poem, later published under the title *Rendezvous with America.* Another was a delightful collection of poetic vignettes showing the many different faces of Harlem. In it, he did for Harlem what Edgar Lee Masters had done for a graveyard at Spoon River. It was later published as *A Gallery of Harlem Portraits.* If Tolson put his skills into *Rendezvous,* he poured his soul into *Gallery.*

When he read to us of Harlem, he came fully alive. New York was mecca to him, and every summer he went there to kneel at its altar. In the off-season, he worked on his master's at Columbia, but, more important, he hobnobbed with literary giants of the world. Breathing the air of Langston Hughes and Countee Cullen and others of the Harlem Renaissance, he recharged his batteries. He engaged in argument those thinkers who could teach him as he taught us. He also peddled his poems to publishers and his folk operas to producers. Only thirty-four at the time, he spoke of New York in hushed tones, as of the promised land.

When the evenings were not spent at Tolson's, they were rapped away in various rooms in the boys' dormitory, where there were endless bull sessions, usually about girls and sex or about individual professors, but sometimes about issues.

One evening, after nightfall, I crossed the campus from my family's home on the dirt road that bordered it, passing the familiar after-dark scenes of the small college campus. Hand-holding couples smiled and said, "Hello, Jim," or "Hi, Farmer." Their greetings always seemed at once condescending and admiring—condescending because I was a "child," admiring because I outperformed most of them in classes. Lovers in the sunken garden were startled by my footsteps; I might have been the campus watchman making his rounds. A lone coed walking toward the Carnegie Library, turned at the gentle honk of an automobile horn, and darted down the sidewalk to a waiting car. Purple-and-white-sweatered athletes headed toward the gym for a training session with "Pops" Long, Wiley's great coach and director of athletics.

I went to the room of Hamilton Boswell, a big mulatto from Los Angeles, who was also an aspiring debater and a classmate. The bull session was noisy and animated. The subject was the horrible implication of racial segregation—that social institution that chiseled in stone the pernicious concept of the inferiority of black people. We castigated segregation. We hurled venomous words at it and killed it. We buried it and wrote its epitaph and danced on its grave. I went home with a sense of rhetorical achievement.

A few days later, when I recounted to Tolson the discussion in Boswell's room, that frown and smile collided on his face. He began with an apparent non sequitur. "I hear there was a good movie showing downtown Saturday, a Hollywood extravaganza. Did you see it?"

"Yes, I saw it."

"Did you enjoy it?"

"Yes. It was a great picture."

"Where did you sit?" He asked the question calmly and without emphasis. Its relevance began to dawn on me.

"In the balcony, of course," I replied tentatively, "where we always sit."

"The other night, you damned segregation to hell; then on Saturday, in the pitiless glare of the sun, you walked downtown to the Paramount Theater, went around to the side entrance, climbed the back stairs, sat in the buzzards' roost, and enjoyed the movie. You hate segregation; but you've paid your father's hard-earned money for the privilege of being segregated."

The message struck like a two-by-four. I had no reply. He referred me to Henry David Thoreau, the essay on civil disobedience. He took it down from a shelf and tossed it to me. I caught it in midair and was riveted to a passage where the book fell open: "What I have to do is to see, at any rate, that I do not lend myself to the evil which I condemn."

I put the book aside and got up to leave.

"Take it with you, if you want to," Tolson offered.

"No, dad has a copy in his library."

At the door, melancholy edged into Tolson's voice as he said, "My boy, it's customary for a professor to tell his students that the world is waiting for them with open arms. Well, that's a lie. There are men waiting for you, all right—with a big stick. Learn how to duck, and counterpunch."

I relished the walk home in the December night; the cold air helped me think. Lights in both dormitories and the library were still on. The rest was darkness, except for the timid floodlights that dotted the campus. Beyond the campus on all sides lay Marshall, Texas.

I had been born in that town nearly fifteen years earlier, and six months later, we had moved to Mississippi, only to return to Marshall, after several other moves, in 1933, when I was thirteen. It was a town of eighteen thousand souls. In fact, it was two towns—two worlds—one black, the other white. The two worlds occasionally touched or brushed each other, but they never met except at the top and in some of the subterranean labyrinths at the bottom.

At the top, on the black side, there was Wiley's president, Dr. Matthew Dogan, D.D., L.L.D., and Professor Pemberton, principal of Central High School. Both were respected by the white world. They knew the town's banker and top businessmen; and that gave them influence with the white world and power in the black. Dogan and Pemberton were buffers between the two worlds; they kept the black one from collision with the white one. In return, they were honored and privileged persons. Yet, they had to respect the etiquette of the caste system: they were called not "Mister," but "Doctor" and "Professor," and there was some grinning and bowing and scraping and foot shuffling. They treated whites like sacred cows in their presence; but behind their backs, they talked about them and laughed at them. It was a classic case of role playing.

Many students considered them "Uncle Toms," but that did not define them; they were not owned by the whites, just rented. They were fully conscious of the role they were playing. They served their wards as well as their masters. Pemberton got money from the white school board for the segregated black high school, and Dogan raised a $600,000 endowment for Wiley.

Blacks, on the average, exceeded whites in educational level in Marshall. There were two black colleges: Wiley, which was Methodist, and Bishop, which was Baptist. For whites, there was one small junior college. But education was not a factor in segregation. Houses of educated as well as uneducated blacks were on unpaved streets, unless they happened to be on the thoroughfares. Educated and uneducated alike were denied the privilege of trying on clothes in most downtown stores and eating in places where food was served.

Education merely made it harder for the brain to adapt to the demeaning things the system told it to do. But adapt it did, and that adaptation was the focus of the thoughts plaguing my mind as I walked home from Tolson's on that December night in 1934.

How do people, how do I, go on day after day doing things that de-humanize—without burning up inside? Eleven years ago a Coca-Cola that I did not drink cut my heart out; but now almost daily I walk by places with invisible "WHITE ONLY" signs without a thought, with no pain. I climb those back stairs and it doesn't hurt. Each time I do it, it comes more naturally. What keeps me from a constant state of fury? It should hurt more each time I do it—till I finally explode. How can I climb those stairs, laughing and joking with friends, unaware?

The nerves must become calloused to protect themselves from too much pain. It forces us to accept what is and become what they think we are—contented inferiors.

We've got to remove those callouses, rub the nerves raw till they hurt more each time, till we can stand it no longer. Then we will turn and rend the system.

If in my freshman year I dangled my feet in the Wiley waters, in the next three years, I dove in, floating with the academic tide, and swimming in the crosscurrents of extracurricular activities. Four out of five of my grades were A's and the other a B, but as Tolson observed, I studied only as much as I had to.

It was the extracurricular activities that made the adrenaline flow. In my sophomore year, I was an alternate on the varsity debate team and was captain of the varsity the next two years. I was chairman of the chemistry club, chairman of the dramatics league, and class president during my senior year.

Yet I was not the complete BMOC (big man on campus). Socially, I was a bust. I had no girl friends; they were too much older than me. Further-more, though I loved words, I could think of nothing to say to girls. Nor was I a star athlete. I did not play football or basketball and never ventured near the track. At tennis I was only reasonably good.

Since Greek letter organizations dominated life at Wiley College, I pledged and joined Omega Psi Phi, but with great misgivings. The phoniness and pretense of the fraternities and sororities troubled me, but not to be a member was to be outside of the campus world, looking in through a knothole in the fence. Everyone joined except those whose parents could not afford it. Conscience told me that I should make com-mon cause with the "outsiders." But conscience was no match for the desire to be a "member of the club."

As a senior, I was elected "basileus," or president of the Omegas, and this merely increased my discomfort at having succumbed to the elitism that ruled student life. My first proposal to the Omegas was they establish themselves as cultural leaders by doing something unique. I suggested that we set one day aside as a poetry day for Wiley. In the morning, there would be a breakfast dance at the Wildcat Inn, where students met for snacks and conversation, after which the few students on campus who wrote poetry would be invited to read their work that evening in the auditorium. We would invite the entire Wiley community to come hear M. B. Tolson read his poetry. Everyone knew that Tolson was a poet, but most of them had never heard or read anything he'd written. My frat brothers approved the idea but insisted that at Tolson's poetry reading all Omegas would have to wear tuxedos to set them apart from and above all others. Reluctantly, I agreed.

Tolson was delighted at the opportunity to hold center stage with his works, which heretofore had been appreciated only by a select few of the intelligentsia. His delight, however, was dampened by the thought that he would have to rent a tuxedo for the occasion. He insisted that he would feel like an organ grinder's monkey.

When the poetry evening arrived, the auditorium was packed. My brothers were concerned that Tolson might not show, so a committee had been appointed to go and fetch him at the appointed hour. The committee told Tolson that all the preliminaries on the program had been taken care of and that Farmer was on the stage killing time and filibustering until the master's arrival. Tolson sent the committee back to tell me to keep talking for about ten more minutes and he would be there to make an entrance fully attired in his disgusting monkey suit.

I was fast running out of things to say when the door to the stage opened and in strode Tolson with a big smile on his face, meticulously attired in his rented tuxedo. But as my eye moved from his head to his feet, I observed his tattered and torn bedroom slippers, which he always wore at home. In midsentence, I swung my right hand around in a gesture toward Tolson's feet, hoping to catch his attention. The gesture succeeded. Tolson looked down and then said in what was supposed to be a whisper but turned out to be audible to everyone in the hall, "Oh, my God. I forgot my shoes!"

I kept on talking and the audience roared. Tolson ran out the door and home. Five minutes later he was back, panting and still smiling broadly, but wearing shiny patent leather shoes. I bowed, shook his hand, and turned the podium over to him.

Tolson held the audience enthralled for an hour and a half, and when he walked from the platform a silence of nearly thirty seconds preceded the ear-splitting applause that followed.

In the fall of 1937, most of the students were in an uproar—not over the issue of segregation in town, but rather of bad food in the dining hall. Some talked of burning the chef in effigy until it was pointed out that he was doing the best he could with what he had to work with and they should not "shoot the piano player." Food was left on many tables untouched, meal after meal. Meetings were held to plan a boycott of the dining hall. Though I ate at home, where I lived, and not in the dining hall, I attended the meetings. Never before had I seen such unity among the students at Wiley.

Dr. Dogan saw that unity, too. He asked all students to come to a meeting in the auditorium. He had an important announcement to make. Everyone assumed that he was prepared to offer a solution to the problem of putrid food, so the hall was packed. The president spoke movingly about the Wiley spirit, which had made our college the brightest jewel in the crown of black higher education in the Southeast. He told us that he wanted to see that spirit continue and to grow and that, therefore, he had a proposal to make.

The greatest event of the school year, he told us, was the annual homecoming game. This year, the Wiley Wildcats would play the vaunted Tuskeegee football team, and "Pops" Long had promised him that Wiley would be victorious. That announcement drew scattered applause, but President Dogan had not finished. The way to improve the homecoming spirit, he declared, was to have the Greek letter organizations elect the homecoming queen this year. Rather than having an ordinary election as we had done in the past, this time the Alphas and their sister Greek letter organization, the AKA's, should put up a candidate and the Omegas and their sister group, the Deltas, put up a candidate, and the other fraternities and sororities either field candidates of their own or back one of those chosen by the two major groups. Such a procedure, our president assured us, would add a lot of class to the homecoming event.

The Alphas, Omegas, AKA's, and Deltas rocked the auditorium with applause. Rotten food in the dining hall was eclipsed by dreams of the banquet fêting the queen each fraternity was certain it would elect. Where there had been unity before, there was now bitter Greek letter rivalry that split the campus open. My frat brothers and I met with the Deltas and selected our nominee. The Alphas and AKA's did the same. The Kappas joined us. The Sigmas joined the other camp. There were Zetas and the non-Greeks to be courted. We were certain that we had the majority, as the campaign moved into high gear.

So intense was the rivalry, that very little else happened on the Wiley campus during those weeks. On election day, tempers were hot. There was at least one fight in the men's dormitory between an Alpha and an Omega.

When the votes were counted, we discovered that the Alphas had stuffed the ballot box. They had done it badly, for there were more ballots cast than there were people eligible to vote. Hence, a new election had to be held. Walking down the sidewalk in front of the administration building the next morning, I looked up to see Hamilton Boswell, my debate colleague, who was president of the Alphas, coming toward me.

"That dirty son of a bitch," I said to myself. "I'm not even going to speak to him."

As we passed, each of us looked away and said nothing. We had gone less than ten paces, when we both stopped, turned around, laughed, walked back, embraced, and said, "What kind of stupidity is this?" I don't know who said it first.

I said, "Ham, let's go to the Wildcat Inn and talk."

Together, we walked in silence to the shack. Boswell and I decided to resign from our respective fraternities and start an anti-Greek association on campus with the objective of removing fraternities and sororities from Wiley. How could blacks ever unite against the common enemy of racism when they were victims of such fratricidal insanity as that fostered by the fraternities and sororities at Wiley?

He and I promised each other that on the following day each of us would call an emergency meeting of his organization at 7:00 P.M. At those simultaneous meetings in different locations, both of us would turn in his fraternity pin and resign in writing from the presidency and from membership in the organization. At ten o'clock, he would come to my house, and there we would plan our joint attack on the Greek letter organizations, hoping to force them to come together to fight us.

At seven o'clock the next evening, the Wiley College chapter of Omega Psi Phi met for an emergency session. I read to my bewildered frat brothers my formal resignation from the office of president and membership, removed my pin, and gave it to the secretary. I informed them that Hamilton Boswell was at that very minute doing the same thing. Never in my life have I seen such a shocked group of young men. Mouths were wide open in the stony silence of disbelief. I asked the vice-basileus to take the chair and I sat on another one, which I pulled to the front of the room so as to answer any questions. There were no questions, only harangue.

"But, Farmer, you can't do this! Once an Omega, always an Omega."

"You can't leave us."

"Nothing like this has ever happened before to the Omegas."

"Boswell won't do it. Wait and see. He'll double-cross you."

The meeting broke up without having officially adjourned. At home I waited anxiously for ten o'clock, wondering if indeed Boswell had kept the covenant. He arrived at ten-fifteen.

Our plan was simple. We would announce in a mimeographed leaflet the action that each of us had taken and would herald the formation of the Anti-Greek Association. The leaflet would invite members of the Greek organizations and non-Greeks to join us in this struggle for black unity. The leaflet would also challenge the Greek letter organizations to select two of their members to meet us in a public debate on campus on the topic "Resolved that Greek letter organizations are an asset to the black struggle for equality." (Needless to say, they did not accept because Boswell and I were the varsity debate team. It would be like the first-string football players inviting the Greeks to select eleven from their ranks to fight it out with them on the gridiron. It was a cheapshot offer.)

Each day, the Anti-Greek Association announced a new proposition, which would be boldly printed on the bulletin board in front of the administration building in the center of campus. The first proposition was:

"Greek letter organizations are uneconomical for minorities." Other propositions were: "Greek letter organizations are divisive, rather than unifying"; "Greek letter organizations are elitist"; "Greek letter organizations show contempt for the masses."

The campus was in an uproar. Boswell and I were drawn closer together, for in the perception of most, we had suddenly grown horns and forked tails. Only the non-Greeks sympathized with us and congratulated us on our actions.

The more despised we became, the greater was my exhilaration. This was my first experience at tilting at windmills of social fashion, and I loved it. The acrimonious words hurled in my direction sounded good to me, for I knew I was right.

Everyone assumed that Tolson, the campus radical, was behind all this, so he meticulously stayed out of it and withheld all comment. When harangued by other faculty members or students about the stand Boswell and I had taken, he merely said, "I don't think my debaters need any help from me in defending their position," and turned and walked away.

My father said he thought we were courageous and right, but we should have called it the Non-Greek Association instead of the Anti-Greek Association.

Dr. Dogan summoned Boswell and me to his office. He sat behind a large, ornate mahogany desk in what was easily the most luxurious room on campus. There were sculptures and paintings, velvet drapes, an oriental rug, and artifacts from all over the world.

His jaws were clenched as we entered. He removed his glasses, revealing eyes serene with authority. The sun coming through the window behind him bounced off his bald head and danced with rainbow colors on the large diamond ring on his left hand.

"Mr. Farmer, Mr. Boswell, what is this I hear about some so-called Anti-Greek Association on the Wiley Campus?" His mouth hardly opened.

We sank deeply into two overstuffed leather chairs and explained the rationale and purpose of our actions.

"Kick the Greeks off campus?" His mouth was opening now, and his slight lisp was less noticeable. "You can't kick the Greeks off campus. Greek letter organizations add a lot of class to Wiley College. If anybody is thrown off this campus, it'll be you."

He whirled in his swivel chair and looked out the window, showing us his back and the gray hairs that, unable to grow on his head, had retreated to the soft brown flesh at the back of his neck. When he turned back to us a minute later, his face had softened.

"Forget what I just said about throwing you off the campus. I didn't mean that. You're both good students and fine young men, and we're all proud of you. I'm sure this whole thing's going to be worked out somehow."

The somehow proved to be the most astonishing sequence of events imaginable. The executive committees of the Omegas, Deltas, Alphas, and

AKA's met together and agreed on a plan that was subsequently approved by their respective memberships. The plan was simple and precise. I wondered if Dr. Dogan had suggested it. There would be not one reigning monarch, but two: a homecoming queen and a May Day queen. There would be no loser; each candidate would win. The ballots asked students to vote for one of the two candidates for one queenship, and the second for the other; or, if preferred, write in a candidate for each royal throne.

For the rest of the year, the fraternities and sororities met together frequently, and the Anti-Greek Association, having served its purpose, faded away. It was rumored, though never confirmed, that Boswell had revoked his resignation from his frat, but I never rejoined mine.

What I learned from all of this was that the way to bring adversaries together is to confront them with a common enemy, which poses a greater threat to both than either does to the other. They suddenly discover much in common.

To what use would I put all of my newfound knowledge? Thoreau and Tolstoi and Tolson? In short, what would I do with my life? Coasting through a premed course, I'd thought of being a doctor, but a minor explosion in the chemistry lab had scuttled those plans. A classmate's arm had been gashed; and I'd panicked and become ill at the sight of the blood. Clearly, I would have to explore a different occupation. But what?

My ambition was to wage war on racism, but how would I earn a living in a manner consistent with the fighting of that war? (It did not occur to me that in the civil rights struggle I would see more blood than I ever would have seen in a doctor's office or a hospital operating room.)

The answers that I found led me toward the social gospel ministry. In that volatile environment I would feel at home.

The youth organization of the black Methodist Episcopal churches in the area sent me as a delegate to the National Conference of Methodist Youth at Miami University in Oxford, Ohio. In that setting, my eyes, ears, and brain were stretched wide. Rather than a big fish in the Wiley pond, I was a small black fish in an ocean of larger, more secure white fish. The only thing about which I knew more than they was how it felt to be black in a white world. That knowledge gave me a distinction that, though rare, was not unique in Oxford. There were a handful of other black youths there, and among them were two whose names were legendary in Methodist circles: Karl Downs, a frail, charismatic man just out of theological seminary; and Juanita Jackson, a brilliant, gifted woman from a prominent Baltimore civil rights family.* Both Karl and Juanita were

---

*A few years later, Karl Downs became president of Samuel Houston College in Austin, Texas. Shortly afterward, in his early thirties, he died following routine surgery. Juanita Jackson became a community leader and Baltimore attorney and married Clarence Mitchell, Jr., Washington bureau chief of the NAACP.

extraordinary personalities, spoken of with awe by all at Oxford who knew them.

Those idealistic white youths were all friendly, even going out of their way to be so, for did Scripture not say that God hath made all races of one blood? Yet, I was uncomfortable; being in a white world, even though an idealized one, was wholly beyond any experience I had known. They tried to be color-blind, to view me as simply another human being; and I tried also, but I was constantly aware of my color and knew that they, coming from a color-conscious society, were too.

I found to my satisfaction, that I could hold my own in discussions, even arguments, with them, and that discovery deepened my own self-confidence. If some of the plenary session debates bewildered me, when an issue arose in which I was keenly interested the juices began to flow and I rose to the occasion. One such occasion was the fierce controversy sparked by a motion to call on Congress to pass a federal antilynching bill.

I was astonished and shocked to see those dedicated Christian youths split along sectional lines. The speakers from southern states did not wave Confederate flags or shout rebel yells, but they passionately argued the states' rights doctrine. No one liked lynching, but it was up to the southern states to punish the crime and bring it to an end. The federal government must not invade the prerogatives of the states. Washington must stop abusing the South and tarring southerners with the same brush. They didn't need help, they said; they could deal with their own problems. The arguments sounded confused, but, after all, every southern speaker revealed an amalgam of feelings—conscience, guilt, idealism, and a depth of patriotism for his region that only the defeated can know.

Nevertheless, indignation rose in me and I had to speak—or explode. Opportunities to enter the fray came and went. Verbal bombs were bursting all over the place. My hand was up, tentatively, several times, and I must confess to a certain relief when another was given the floor; and the next speaker always seemed to say what I had thought of saying. But I had to say something. How could I endure a battle like this without getting into it? How could I explain to Tolson that in a floor fight on lynching, I had said nothing?

My hand began to wave in the air, not tentatively, but like a cowboy lassoing a running bull. The chairman recognized someone else, who stood quickly and said, "Mr. Chairman, I yield the floor to Jim Farmer of East Texas."

Those words hit me like a thunderbolt. I'd been asking frantically for the floor, and now that I had it I didn't know what I was going to say. Heads swiveled and eyes were riveted upon me as I rose. Maybe I had thought that if I opened my mouth, the Lord would fill it. Apparently, He did.

I do not remember all that I said, but I do recall having a slight tremor in my voice as I spoke. And I recall the peroration: "Everyone here wants to stop lynching. The only question is how long do we have to wait? How long, oh, Lord, how long? The purpose of this motion is not to damn the South and the many decent people who live there. It is not to open up old wounds, but to heal those that have scabbed over while still festering underneath. The motion seeks not to whip the South or hurt its people. The purpose of this motion is to *stop lynching now!*"

Applause broke out and the audience rose to its feet. When quiet resumed, a blond with a thick southern drawl moved the previous question. The voice vote was overwhelming.

This was my first taste of the heady wine of public acclaim, one that I was destined to savor many times in the reliving of it. My star ascended in young Methodism to join those of Karl Downs and Juanita Jackson. The National Conference of Methodist Youth elected me a vice-chairman of its select governance group, the National Council of Methodist Youth. That body sent me as a delegate to the Christian Youth Council of North America, which also elected me its vice-chairman.

Back home at Wiley, my mentor was overjoyed that I'd had an opportunity to "rub shoulders with some of the brightest young men and women in America."

"That will stand you in good stead, my boy," Tolson said. "We can't live in a black vacuum in this country.

"By the way, speaking of rubbing shoulders with those on the other side of the nation's tracks, there'll be another opportunity in a couple of weeks if you're interested. I have a letter from a graduate student in sociology at the University of Texas—Cy Record—inquiring whether any Wiley students were going to the meeting of the National Negro Congress and the Southern Negro Youth Conference in Richmond next week. If so, he wanted to go along with them. I told him you and Boswell were going. He'll be coming here in a couple of days to join you for the trip."

When Cy Record arrived, he, Boswell, and I met at Tolson's to plan the trip. We were going to drive: my father had loaned me his car. Boswell had a road map and had drawn a line northeast to St. Louis, across to Washington, D.C., and down to Richmond, thus avoiding the worst part of the South. Record interrupted to propose a different route. He suggested that we shoot straight across Louisiana, Mississippi, Alabama, and Georgia, and then up to Richmond, and on that journey through the deep South he wanted to be "a Negro."

Boswell laughed mirthlessly. "Cy, how can you be a Negro? You don't look black."

Record was brunette, and somewhat tanned.

"On your campus today," he said, "I saw a couple of students who looked whiter than I. In fact, Hamilton, *you* look almost as white as I."

"Uh-huh," replied Boswell, with a wry smile. "We *have* had a good deal of nighttime integration in these parts."

Record reddened, but made no comment. The route decided on, we parted.

On departure day, my mother prepared an early-morning breakfast for us at our house. Then we headed out in the two-year-old Dodge sedan.

The highways, if they could be called such in 1938, were battered black-tops or gravel roads through much of Louisiana. The drive was wearing and the opened windows let dust into our throats and lungs, and thirst came soon. I'd planned to bring a thermos jug, but had forgotten it.

"Hm," said Boswell, "there's a railroad station; maybe we can get a drink of water there."

The station, being in a small town, had a single waiting room. On one side were several wooden benches, with a sign over them: "WHITES ONLY." On the opposite wall was a bench with a sign over it: "FOR COLORED." Similar signs hung over the water fountains and the doors to the rest-rooms. Several people were seated on both sides of the room, reading newspapers and comic books. The air hung heavy with tobacco smoke.

When we entered, a few people looked up, and then back to the enter-tainment in their hands. Cy Record walked unhesitatingly across the wait-ing room to the white water fountain, bent over to drink, and froze in that position, sensing, no doubt, that Boswell and I were not with him and were standing across the room, watching. He slowly straightened up, turned, and walked back to us, shamefacedly, and said, "Sorry, I forgot."

Boswell laughed. I felt more compassion than amusement at Cy Rec-ord's predicament. It occurred to me that this trip might teach him, and perhaps us, more sociology than would several years at the university.

Record followed us in drinking at the "colored fountain" and in using the restroom for "colored men." We three then returned to the car, re-suming the journey. Cy sat in silence for the next couple of hours, looking out the window at the passing scenery, but probably not seeing it.

"It's lunchtime," said Boswell. "What say we get a bite?"

"Good idea," Record agreed. "Where can we eat?"

"Noplace," Boswell chuckled.

"There's a restaurant down on the corner," I said. "Let's try that one. Are you game?"

"I am," said Record.

"Well, you two fools go on in there," retorted Boswell. "I'll sit out in the car and keep the motor running so we can make a fast getaway when you come high-tailing it out of there."

No sooner had Cy and I entered the small restaurant than the proprie-tor, in shirt sleeves and sweating, confronted us.

"We don't serve niggers here," he said matter-of-factly to me. Then, looking at Cy, "Wha' y'all want?"

Record spoke: "Three of us are traveling to Richmond, and we're hun-gry. Isn't there someplace in town where we can eat?"

"Well, I c'n serve *you*, but I cain't serve yo' colored boy. Y'all will have to take a sandwich out to them."

Cy flushed. "He's not my boy, and I'm a Negro, too," he said.

"You are? Well, ah'll be darned. I never woulda thought it. Well, in that case, I cain't serve none of y'all here. There is a nigger woman who lives out on the edge of town who sometimes serves niggers passin' through at her little house. Maybe she'll cook up somethin' for y'all. But, come to think of it, she ain't there now, 'cause she works daytimes now. So I cain't suggest nuthin' to ya' except I could serve y'all in the kitchen. My colored cook can fix up sumpthin' for y'all at the table where she eats back there, if y'all wanta do that."

I finally spoke: "Well, Cy, do you want to do it?"

"Who, me?" he asked, the blood rising in his face. "I'm not eating in anybody's kitchen."

We left the restaurant and the Dodge's clutch shuddered as Boswell pulled away from the curb while I recounted the conversation to him.

"Next stop, a grocery store," he said grimly. He did the shopping, and came out with bologna, bread, mustard, potato chips, milk, and soft drinks—enough for lunch and dinner.

Since leaving the restaurant, Cy Record had sat absolutely silent and still. His eyes mirrored a torment raging inside. Sociology textbooks had not prepared him for this. We did not talk to him, for clearly he did not want to talk. Once my eyes met his and what looked back at me was a mixture of shame, guilt, and terrible fury. For one dreadful moment, I thought that he was going to beg my forgiveness; but then his eyes moved slowly away.

When we pulled off the road, outside of the town, Cy's hunger seemed to have vanished. He nibbled at a sandwich, but threw most of it back into the paper bag and went back to entertaining his private agony.

Dinner was no more tantalizing than lunch had been. A few hours after the evening meal, and after pit stops in the bushes to relieve ourselves, we looked in vain for a Negro hotel, before resigning ourselves to the inevitable: our hotel room for the night would be, as our restaurant had been, the car off the side of the road.

Boswell and I slept, though I suspect Record did not. We were awakened by a powerful flashlight beam bathing our faces and a rough drawl that said, "Hey, wake up! Whut y' boys doing out heah?"

"Sleeping," I said. "We have a long drive ahead of us. We're going to Richmond."

The flashlight moved again to Record's face and stopped, and the sheriff's deputy said, "Hey, wait a minute. Are you white? Whut y' doin' in here with these niggers?"

"I'm a Negro," said Cy.

"Well, I'll be damned," the cop said. "Ah b'lieve you are. We got a lotta niggers in this state who look white, too, but didn' know they had any in Texas. But I'm not s'prised. When a white man gets really hard up, even a nigger woman looks look good t' him."

He laughed, then went on: "There ain't nuthin' wrong with that, just 's long as y' take a good bath when y' gets through." He laughed again.

The sheriff's deputy puckered his eyebrows and said, "Are you sho' yo ain't white? Lemme see yo' hands. Y' can always tell by lookin' at the fingernails."

Cy held his right hand out to him palm up.

"Turn it over," the deputy ordered and Cy complied.

The man examined his fingernails carefully with his flashlight.

"Yep," he said. "Yo're a nigger, all right. Fingernails don't lie. Jus' like fingerprints. Tell me somethin', boy. I bet yo' mama's a good-lookin' wench, ain't she?"

He laughed long and loud and then said, "All right, you boys get y'selves a good sleep, an' then drive on t' Richmon'. Don' have no accident with this here boy in heah whose daddy's a white man."

His laugh faded in the distance as he walked to his car, made a fast U-turn, and sped away.

"Hey, Cy!" called Boswell. "Are you sure there was no colored gentleman in your family's woodpile? You know, fingernails don't lie."

Record tried to laugh, but what came forth was a kind of asthmatic wheeze.

Sleep gone, we pulled back onto the road with me at the wheel and headed for Richmond. The second day was as the first, and we reached Richmond overcome with fatigue. A room was reserved for us at a Negro hotel, two single beds and a cot. I wanted to take the cot, but Cy insisted that that was his, and so it became.

In Richmond there were constant sessions to attend. We heard Angelo Herndon, head of the Southern Negro Youth Conference, whom I quickly discerned to be the black "fair-haired boy" of the communist youth movement. We saw Max Yergan, executive director of the National Negro Congress, deftly manipulating the plenary sessions of the Congress.

I was enthralled and humbled by one of the greatest orators I've ever heard—the incomparable Mordecai Johnson, then president of Howard University. After winning a series of high school contests, after two years of touring with the Wiley debate team, and after a triumph at the National Conference of Methodist Youth, I thought that I could make a speech; but Mordecai Johnson showed me that I had not even begun to learn the elemental art of the platform. He had me weeping and laughing, and laughing and weeping, and determined to go out and slay whatever dragons remained alive when this overwhelming experience had ended.

And I saw, met, and heard the fabled A. Philip Randolph. The founder and president of the Brotherhood of Sleeping Car Porters took the platform to deliver his address as chairman of the National Negro Congress. Tolson had told us of this giant and invited us to read more. He was the most feared and the greatest black leader of the thirties, and perhaps of the twentieth century. He had been called by his enemies "the most dangerous Negro in America."

A majestic figure of a man, Randolph began quietly in his Oxford accent and stentorian voice and moved quickly into a devastating denunciation of the National Negro Congress, its leadership, and its executive director. The officers and leaders of the organization, he charged, had constantly bypassed him, making decisions without consulting with him, and announcing without his knowledge positions on issues with which he had basic disagreement.

This attack caught the NNC leaders unaware and sent them scurrying about on the platform. Murmurs swept the audience in waves.

Randolph climaxed his assault by resigning from the organization and its chairmanship. The conference was in an uproar, and the session was quickly adjourned.

Outside, on the steps, Dr. Ralph Bunche, then professor of political science at Howard University, was explaining the background and implications of Randolph's action to a group of puzzled delegates. I moved into the group and listened attentively. The NNC, Bunche told us, had needed a prestigious and nationally respected black man as its titular head, so it had invited Phil Randolph to be chairman. It was surprising, he said, that Randolph, a socialist, had accepted, since the NNC was controlled by the communists, who hated the socialists, and vice versa.

But the leaders of the NNC did not know Randolph; he was not a man to be trifled with. A man of great courage and integrity, he would never be a figurehead for the communists or anyone else. The break was inevitable, Dr. Bunche said, and Randolph's departure probably would sound the death knell of the National Negro Congress.

Back at Tolson's house at Wiley, the professor was drawing generalizations from the experiences of the trip, which we had related in detail.

Cy Record was virtually in tears. The trip for him had at been at once a revelation and a crucifixion. "I'm not blind and I'm not insensitive. How could I possibly have grown up and lived in the South all these years without seeing, without knowing, the hell that we put you through every day of your lives? How do you live with it? How do you take it? How do you stand it? Why don't you commit suicide?"

"Well, Cy," said Boswell, "we have to work so hard trying to keep you white folks from killing us that we don't have time to think about killing ourselves."

Final exams were a snap, and graduation was anticlimactic. The cap and gown was a steambath, and "Pomp and Circumstance" bored me. The speaker was an antidote for insomnia, the intoning of classmates' names a dreary ritual, and I could not wait to face another small part of the world that loomed ahead of me.

That other part of the world was Washington, D.C. My father had accepted a post at the Howard University School of Religion, teaching New Testament and Greek, and there I would study for the ministry.

More alluring was the knowledge that Washington, unlike Marshall, was at the heart of events, and it was also closer to New York.

CHAPTER 12

GOD AND GODDAMN

IN 1938 WASHINGTON WAS a far cry from the thriving, black-dominated metropolis of today. No one dreamed then of a black mayor, or any mayor at all. It was truly a federal colony and totally segregated. The only places where a black could eat outside the ghetto were in the Senate cafeteria and the railroad station.

I thought I'd never left the South; and, in fact, I hadn't. My parents had a hard time finding a suitable house to rent. Since my father had spent his postdoctoral years working in southern church academia, we were upper middle class in social status, but lower middle class in capital assets. Most of the available houses were either out of our price range or in the slums. While daddy and mother searched, we were guests in the home of Doctor Benjamin E. Mays, dean of the School of Religion at Howard, who had invited daddy to take the position that brought us to Washington. While sister, Nathaniel, Carl, and I awaited their daily reports, what sprang to my mind were the words and melody of that gravelly voiced twelve-string guitarist and folk singer without parallel—Leadbelly:

> Come all you cullud people,
> And listen to me.
> Don't never try ta get a home
> In Washington, D.C.
> 'Cause it's a bourgeois town.
> *Lawd*, it's a bourgeois town.
> I'm go'n' take this message,
> And spread it al-l-l aroun'.

Success in the search finally came with the aid of Dorothy Height, the brilliant young executive director of the Phyllis Wheatley branch of the YWCA. Mother's appraisal of Miss Height was instant and categorical. "She is a *great* young lady." Two decades later, I came to respect, with enthusiasm, my mother's judgment of Dorothy Height.*

That the nation's capital was a Jim Crow town spoke something of national policy, which gnawed at my insides each day like a Promethean vulture. Equally discomforting to me in the Washington of 1938 were the cold gray buildings with cold gray men at desks inside. To a young, black southerner whose experience with officialdom, though mostly vicarious, had been emasculating, the faceless bureaucrats with their ominous forms and interrogations had power to punish and destroy. There was no reason in those days for me to perceive the federal government as anything different.

---

*Dorothy Height later succeeded Mary McLeod Bethune as president of the National Council of Negro Women and became a stalwart of the civil rights movement.

Washington was that, but it was much more. It was, at Howard University, the black Athens. Walking across the campus daily were luminaries and scholars of whom I'd heard and read at Wiley. There was Sterling Brown, a towering figure in the explosion of black literature in the twenties. Also figuring in that revival was the philosopher Alain Locke, and he, too, was at Howard, as was E. Franklin Frazier, the prolific sociologist. There was Ralph Bunche in political science, Abram Harris in economics, and William Hastie, dean of the law school. And in history there were Carter G. Woodson, Rayford Logan, and Charles H. Wesley. This was long before integration in academia led the nation's major universities to seek the greatest of the black scholars.

It was also before religion occupied a central role in the black struggle, and before religious thinkers became intellectually respectable among the austere ranks of black scholars. Reflecting that perception of religion's role was the facility in which the school was housed: a dilapidated old frame house, in need of paint, across the street from the main campus.

Its faculty members, however, were not inferior and would hold their own with those of any theological seminary in the country. My father, of course, would have been a star anyplace. Benjamin E. Mays, the dean who also taught church history, was a fine scholar, administrator, speaker, and writer. There was also Paul T. Lutov, a White Russian from the Russian Orthodox church, who taught Old Testament and Hebrew and was more at home with the language he taught than with the English in which he taught it. (Sometimes he would strain so hard in silent search for the right English word or phrase that we thought he was going to burst a blood vessel; even his neatly trimmed beard seemed to turn red. Then, he would shrug and speak Hebrew words, which sent us to our Hebrew-English dictionaries.)

And there was the incomparable Howard Thurman. Mystic, poet, philosopher, preacher, he was professor of social ethics and dean of the chapel. When Thurman occupied the university pulpit, Rankin Memorial Chapel was packed. Though few but theologians and philosophers comprehended what he was saying, everyone else thought if only they *had* understood it would have been wonderful, so mesmerizing was his resonant voice and so captivating was the artistry of his delivery. Those who did grasp the meaning of his sermons were even more ecstatic.

Howard Thurman, in the classroom, was no less splendid to some and enigmatic to others. He was not a handsome man; his beauty was inside. He was overweight and did not trouble to dress extravagantly. His front teeth were large, and one was prominently capped with gold. Although only about forty, his hairline prematurely receded almost to the middle of his skull. The whites of his enormous eyes, like his teeth, emphasized his satiny black skin. The voice was pure velvet, and it vibrated like the strings of a bass violin.

When this extraordinary man walked into social ethics class, a silence born of awe reigned. It always seemed as if we had dragged him away from private meditation. He would look over the heads of those in class, into space, for what seemed minutes. Then he would open up, in his slow, laborious manner, with a provocative thesis, such as "When you young preachers fulminate about what you should do in any given situation, remember one thing: we are what we do—in spite of reservations."

He would wait for a response. My hand usually was up first with a question: "Dr. Thurman, are you saying that if a soldier kills the enemy, he is a murderer, or at least a killer? Or if one accepts an assigned status of inferiority—let us say, sits in the balcony of a Jim Crow theater—he *is* inferior?"

Thurman would say, "Ah," and recognize one of the several hands now held aloft.

We would leave the class with no answers, but many intriguing questions that had not occurred to us before. It was Thurman's belief that answers must come from within, from the bit of God in each of us. Perhaps I partly agreed with him. I did not want answers. I wanted only questions. The answers I could find for myself, but not from God; from my own powers to reason. If those came from God, then so be it.

Only a handful of my classmates participated in those discussions in Thurman's class. Most of them were bewildered, but bewilderment was not unusual among first-year students in the Howard School of Religion in 1938.

Coming to the seminary with a devout and dogmatic Sunday school theology, many were far more than bewildered in my father's class when Scriptures were subjected to the scrutiny of biblical criticism. A few, for instance, were devastated to learn that there were other messiahs, contemporary with Jesus, who performed miracles and were hailed as sons of God; and were angered to be told that Paul either did not know of the virgin birth or did not think it important to mention, for the concept came later.

One first-year seminarian came to class one morning red-eyed and falling asleep; he'd been up all night crying and praying for his professors' souls. Two others packed up and went home within the first month.

The professors were critical scholars, but they were also very devout. From the very beginning, I had been ambivalent about the ministry. I loved the social gospel of Walter Rauschenbush and was enthralled with the study of Christian ethics, but I was not sure what I believed about God. I was troubled by the air of pious devotion that permeated the school—that leap beyond reason into faith—and hungered for something else to fill another, less esoteric side of my being. So I took a few days off from school to visit my mother's sisters in Harlem, in New York, the mecca of my dreams.

I had not seen Sadie, my youngest aunt, since she lived with us in Holly Springs, Mississippi, in 1923 and 1924. Aunt Helen, Uncle Fred, and my cousin Muriel I had last seen when they visited us in Austin in 1929. My middle aunt, Louise, I'd never met before. They all lived in the same large brick apartment building at 468 West 148th Street, Sadie and Louise on the ground floor and the rest three stories up. It wasn't Sugar Hill, but it was close. One might have called it Strivers Row.

The two-day visit with family was festive and fun. There was an abundance of exquisite food; there was also hilarity and whiskey, which was never served in my father's home. Yet, when the time came, I was ready to leave. The visit to relatives was nice, but it was an excuse, not the reason, for my trip to New York.

The real purpose of the trip was to see a man with one of the finest minds I had ever known: V. F. Calverton—literary critic, scholar, lecturer, writer, editor, hedonist, bon vivant. I had come into contact with him earlier when he had made a most unusual visit to Wiley College.

Around the first of the year in 1938, three Wiley students had written one-act plays. As chairman of the Drama League, I proposed that we hold a drama festival in the spring, inviting other black colleges in the South to bring their drama groups to Wiley and present their plays. On the final night, we would present plays written and produced by our students.

Tolson liked the idea and suggested that we invite a Broadway critic to give a lecture on opening night and to criticize the Wiley plays on closing night. He said that the person to try to get was Calverton, who wrote the monthly "Cultural Barometer" column for *Current History* magazine and edited a classic, *Anthology of American Negro Literature,* which had an introduction of brilliance and perception.

I wrote Calverton, asking if he would come and for what fee. The answer was immediate: yes, and for only one hundred dollars (which wouldn't even cover expenses), provided we would arrange lectures for him at two or three other black colleges in Texas. We did that, and the deal was set.

The arrangement was almost derailed when we were unable to find lodging for him on campus. President Dogan rejected the ideal solution, having him as a guest in his home: "What would the white folks downtown think? They'd think I believe in social equality." When I wrote Calverton that I was reserving a room for him in the downtown Marshall Hotel (for whites), the distinguished New Yorker exploded. "What kind of nonsense is this? I'm coming down to speak at your college, largely at my own expense, and I can't even stay on campus as I'm sure most other guest speakers do? Let's just forget the whole deal. Invite me at some future date when you find the guts to fight those barbaric customs."

We found, not the guts, but lodging on campus. A bachelor professor agreed to move out of his apartment and turn it over to Calverton when he came. The arrangements were back on track.

He arrived in a battered old Chevy. A young man was driving, and with Calverton was an attractive woman.

"You're Jim Farmer," he said, extending his hand casually. We shook firmly and he added, "This is Helen."

"How do you do, Mrs. Calverton," I said. (After all, this was a Bible belt

Methodist school. People broke the moral code every day, but they concealed it when they could.) The two of them looked at each other and she shrugged her shoulders.

Calverton was a roundish man of thirty-eight, with a large head in need of a haircut. His forehead was very broad and he had a bushy mustache that covered his upper lip and extended beyond the edges of his mouth. His clothes looked as though he had slept in them.

I took them to the apartment so they could freshen up. Then Calverton and I went to Tolson's, where a few of the brightest students were waiting to meet him. As we entered, he looked around and groaned. He was weary from the long ride, but was going to have to work. He took the easiest chair, tossed a foot across his knee, and leaned back.

"I'm thirsty as the Sahara. Son, would you please get me a drink?" He spoke to Wiley Tolson, one of our host's children.

"Yes sir."

In no time, the boy was back with a glass filled to the brim. Calverton thanked him and tinkled the ice against the glass for a moment, took a big gulp, and sputtered, "Pfew! What the hell is this? Water?"

"Yes sir."

"I asked for a drink, son. I wash my hands in this stuff; I don't drink it."

The boy looked confused and again said, "Yes sir." Within seconds, Mrs. Tolson was in the room with an unopened Haig and Haig Pinch bottle, which she doubtless had been saving for some special occasion. It was set on a table by Calverton's chair. A bowl of ice and another glass followed. He mixed his own, took two long gulps, made a grateful sound, then lighted a cigar. Now he was ready.

The students had done their homework. They knew that, despite his comparative youth (thirty-eight), he had written or edited fifteen books of solid scholarship, spanning many disciplines—sociology, anthropology, literature, psychology, history. The students came with questions that covered everything from foreign relations to domestic policies, Greek classics to contemporary black writing, party politics to Marxist-Leninist factionalism.

Calverton was in no mood to be serious; he began answering questions in a light vein. These students, however, were not prepared for levity from this savant, so they searched for serious meaning even in answers that were clearly meant in jest. Sensing that, he began giving detailed answers to even the most trivial questions.

Several other students came in. When there was a female among them, Calverton's mind may not have wandered but his eyes did. Finally, he yawned and Tolson mercifully brought the interrogation to an end.

The opening night was a smash hit. V. F. Calverton was no orator, but the organization of his thoughts was superb, and the language was precise, full of verve.

The lecture began with an exposition of the lost cities of Africa whose ruins, uncovered after the turn of the century, compared favorably with those of Athens and Rome, revealing ancient civilizations of great refinement, with judicial systems, libraries, and scholars who would put to shame most of our Ph.D.'s of today. Then followed a discussion of Afro-American art and literature, tracing its roots to two sources, Africa and the ordeal in America. That led to a critique of contemporary black creative writing, ending with the revelation that last night he had read the poetry of our own M. B. Tolson and considered it of superb quality. Upon his return to New York, he said, he would make every effort to secure publication of that poetry so that Tolson could take his rightful place as probably one of the major American poets of the twentieth century.

The applause was prolonged and deafening.

Calverton spent the next few days on campus watching the performance of our guest drama groups, playing tennis (badly, I thought), drinking, making passes at coeds, and answering endless questions from would-be intellectuals.

On the festival's closing night, we presented the three one-act plays written and performed by Wiley students. I had the lead role in the last of the three, a melodrama. Calverton sat in the back row of the auditorium, smoking a cigar, much to the annoyance of Dr. Dogan, for the auditorium was also the chapel.

We did our very best; after all, there was a Broadway critic in the audience. After the final curtain and the dutiful applause, the critic strolled up the aisle to the platform, with his inevitable cigar. We awaited words of approbation.

He spoke: "Jim Farmer has asked me to use the Broadway yardstick in judging these plays, and that is what I shall do. About the first two, I shall say very little, for there is very little to be said. They were positively lousy."

A young lady left her seat and hurried out of the auditorium in tears. She had written one of the plays. Calverton gave reasons for his harsh judgment: "Poorly conceived, plot unclear, characterizations inconsistent, hackneyed, no dramatic appeal, etc., etc."

He went on: "The third, however, was the best amateur play I've ever seen. This playwright should write more."

After giving his reasons for that appraisal, he turned to the individual performers. "The best actor of the evening was in the worst of the three plays: the young man who played the role of the drunk—Richard Virgil."

Someone in the audience corrected him: "Virgil Richardson!"

Calverton shouted back: "All right. Richard Virgil, Virgil Richardson. What's in a name?" Then he continued. "I've never seen a drunk played with more subtlety, more sensitivity, more depth of understanding than this man showed. I had great difficulty in believing that he was really sober and was acting. I think this young man, Richard Virgil, Virgil Richardson, has acting genius. If he is interested in pursuing an acting career and will come to New York, I will guarantee to get him a start in a Little Theater production. After that, he will be on his own."

After discussing a few of the other performers, he said, "There was another performer worth mentioning. Jim Farmer had a complex and difficult role and he conceptualized it with intelligence, analyzed it well, and executed it credibly, but without acting talent. He was never the character which he was playing: he was always Jim Farmer playing the character he was playing. I like Farmer, despite the fact that he refused to let me use his tennis racquet yesterday." (I had watched him miss a shot and let his racquet fly with a string of expletives. The profanity survived, but his racquet was smashed. I was not going to let that happen to mine.)

When the laughter subsided, he concluded: "He may become a good analytical and critical thinker, but he'll never be an actor."

He strode from the platform and down the aisle to the loudest ovation I'd ever heard in the Wiley auditorium. He'd given them none of the "You people this, and you people that," which they'd grown to expect and always found infuriating in white speakers. There had been no patronizing soft soap, no paternalistic big brotherism. It was straight talk—to equals—and let the chips fall where they may. And they loved it.

The next morning, Calverton and his "wife" tossed their baggage into the trunk of their old Chevy, climbed into the car, and shook hands all around. Then Calverton said, "When you come to New York, Jim, look me up."

Now, six months later, I looked him up. *Current History* magazine provided the number and I called it. Calverton answered.

"*Jim Farmer!* Goddamn! Sonofabitch! What the hell are you doing here?"

I explained my visit and he asked, "Well, you're coming over, aren't you?"

When I said yes, he put in, "Well, don't come early because I have a lecture this evening and won't be back till ten-thirty or eleven. Oh, what the hell, come over any time you want to, but I won't be here till late."

I told him that I would get there about eight and would wait for him, if that was okay.

He replied, "Fine, but Jim, there's something I must ask of you. . . . You remember Helen, the woman who was with me in Texas? Well, she was not my wife."

I laughed and said, "I know."

"Well, when you get to the apartment, you'll find another woman there—Nina, Nina Melville. Don't say anything to her about Helen, please."

It was in Greenwich Village, 16 St. Luke's Place. It was the ground-floor apartment in a large brownstone. A poised and beautiful woman answered the door. She invited me in to wait, though Calverton had forgotten to tell her I was coming.

"Jim Farmer." She repeated the name as I followed her into the apartment. "From Texas? George has spoken of you many times." (George Goetz was his real name. Calverton was a pen name. His friends called him George.)

Nina led me into a large studio apartment, tastefully decorated. Every available wall space was covered with bookshelves. The balcony, which hung over the dining area, was also filled with books in every conceivable place.

She motioned me to a comfortable couch, brought me a bourbon, and perched herself on a small, pink, leather-upholstered chair with her highball. Her large, fluid eyes studied me and made me comfortable. She wanted to hear about Calverton's visit to Wiley and I gave her a full rundown, careful not to mention Helen. Then she inquired about my family, what I was doing now, and my plans for the future.

At ten o'clock, the phone rang. It was Calverton. He was sorry he'd forgotten to tell her I was coming. He told her, "For Chrissake, give Jim a drink. Give him anything he wants." He would be home in half an hour. He said the lecture went okay, "but the crowd almost mobbed me in the Q-and-A period when I said Chamberlain was as bad as Hitler."

"Well, we're close to war now," Nina said. "You can't expect people to be rational."

When Calverton arrived, he greeted me like a long-absent friend—not a son, but a friend. He told me that he had gotten Virgil Richardson a decent role in a Little Theater play, as promised, and they were now in rehearsals. Soon we would find out if he had been right or wrong in his opinion. Also, Tolson was up for the summer, and a reputable publisher was now interested in his works. His first book, *Rendezvous with America,* was soon to be published.

"M.B.," he said, "is a great talent, but despite his erudition and sophistication, he's still a dear old goddamn Puritan. When he was here, I sicced a young woman on him and he ran like hell. He said, 'George, you know I can't do anything like that; I've got a wife and children.'" We shared a good laugh about that.

He asked Nina if he could have another drink. She said, "No, but I'll get one for Jim." He shrugged with a gesture of helplessness.

When I told George of my studying at the Howard University School of Religion, I expected a contemptuous sneer, for years before he had written a book entitled *The Passing of the Gods.* Instead, there was a long, pensive look, and a nod. Then came the astonishing comment: "I spent a short while in seminary in 1921, after college at Johns Hopkins. They threw me out for sleeping with the wrong woman."

Then, with an abrupt change of subject: "So, you're living in Washington. That's only a hop, skip, and a jump from Baltimore. I spend weekends at my place there. Every Saturday evening a bunch of friends come over. Most are just ordinary people who've read a lot and are interested in the worlds of ideas and letters. Usually I lecture on any topic of common interest to the group, but sometimes I'm lucky enough to get some celebrity to come over and relieve me of that chore. Then there's a verbal free-for-all, with no holds barred. We look upon it as a kind of intellectual and literary Rotary. There's booze, of course, and sometimes

sandwiches that Bessie [he lowered his voice], my, er, secretary in Baltimore puts together. Some famous people drop by occasionally. Thomas
Wolfe of *You Can't Go Home Again* and *Look Homeward Angel* was there
once. Katherine Hepburn's mother was there once. Ernest Sutherland
Bates of Columbia, Sidney Hook of NYU, and Ralph Bunche and Abram
Harris of Howard have dropped by. H. L. Mencken came once, and M. B.
Tolson was there last summer. But mostly, as I said, they're just plain
people. It's all strictly informal; no structure whatever. If you're interested, I'd like for you to come over on Saturdays if you can. I think you
may enjoy it."

I said that I would, and he told me that he would contact two of the
Washington regulars—Dick Paige, a taxi driver, and Doc Hollod, a chiro-
practor. One of them would always pick up the Washington group and
drive over.

V. F. "George" Calverton became one of my two mentors during seminary
years at Howard. He was a superlative foil for the other, Howard Thurman, and Thurman for him, though the two never met. One was a sensual, hedonistic, atheistic iconoclast; the other an icon—spiritual, theistic,
moralistic. One was dedicated to things of the mind, with the spirit thrown
in; the other was dominated by things of the soul, with the mind thrown
in. Neither would accept any dichotomy between mind and spirit.

Thurman, who introduced me to the study of Gandhi, believed the
Mahatma to be a great soul, a saint. Calverton, who led me through
Marxist revisionism to Fourier and Gene Debs and Democratic Socialism,
thought Gandhi a superb politician, strategist, and tactitian. Both were
cosmopolites with limitless compassion for mankind. Both, in those intellectually formative years, nurtured my growth. Each, in his own way, wove
intricate threads of truth, but I hungered to glimpse the whole fabric.

War clouds hovered over Europe and Asia. As the English bulldog
whimpered and then growled before the madman in Berlin, the little
brown man in India twisted the bulldog's tail, reminding it that his people
were still in chains. I was fascinated by Gandhi. Thurman was acquainted
with him from two visits to the Subcontinent, and he loaned me books on
the Mahatma's life and work.

I was a pacifist. Upon the recommendation of Thurman, a former
National Council of Methodist Youth colleague, John Swomley, engineered my appointment by FOR as a part-time student secretary in Washington. The salary was $40 a month. The job interested me hugely, for
younger members of FOR were beginning to explore nonviolence as a
technique for social change. One of the areas being drawn into focus was
race, and race was my chief concern. It was also one reason I was moving
farther away from the notion of being a minister.

My denomination, the Methodist Episcopal Church, North, was moving
into unification with the Methodist Episcopal Church, South, and the
Methodist Protestant Church, to heal the Civil War breach. The

unification was a segregated one. There were to be six jurisdictions in the united church—five of which were geographical, and the sixth, racial. A black church, whether in Portland, Oregon, or Chitterlingswitch, Georgia, would be in the euphemistically named Central Jurisdiction. That, it should be mentioned, was long before any ideas of black identity and cohesion surfaced as major currents of thought among black Americans.

How was I to preach Christ in a church whose structure gave him the lie? To switch denominations would have meant more of the same.

My brooding over these questions led to selection of a topic for my final thesis at Howard. I made the choice late in my first year. In the next two years, all my studies were pro forma, except those that contributed to the writing of my thesis.

The topic chosen was "A Critical Analysis of the Historical Interrelationship Between Religion and Racism." My plan was to expand the study, upon graduation, into a full-length book. Howard Thurman encouraged me in the ambitious undertaking, and I spent several evenings at his home discussing it.

In the meantime, Saturday evenings found me in Baltimore usually till daybreak Sunday. The house on East Pratt Street was a different kind of stimulation from that of delving into church history under Mays and discoursing on ethics under Thurman. The uniqueness of George Calverton lay not in the fact that he would have been at home clinking a mug with Ben Jonson at the Mermaid Tavern, nor that his vocabulary included the choicest of epithets, nor that he believed in and practiced "free love." It was instead that he embodied an eclecticism that placed less importance on the disciplines themselves than on the way they related to each other. What good is an economist who does not appreciate the psychology of the poker chip players in the game of finance, or a sociologist who does not understand the historical context of the phenomena he examines, or a historian blind to the economics and sociology of past events?

One evening there, I cornered him and told him of my planned thesis. We discussed several of the more hair-raising intrigues in medieval church history. Afterward he referred me not to further sources on ecclesiasticism, but to a couple of volumes on the economic and social history of the period, which he loaned me. Before I departed the next morning, he gave me a copy of his new book, an undoctrinaire Marxist history of America entitled *The Awakening of America*. The book was runner-up to one by Charles and Mary Beard for the Pulitzer Prize in history that year. It was inscribed: "To Jim Farmer, one of the finest, realest guys, and one of the swellest friends I've ever known."

In some discussions, Calverton found gaps in my education and moved to help me fill them. One night, for instance, after I had been in spirited argument with some others in the free-for-all following his lecture, we talked privately in his library. Though I had easily held my own in the argument, he told me what I was debating was not opinion, but fact, which is not debatable, just verifiable. And the facts were on the other side. I bamboozled my adversaries, he said, but they were right and I was wrong. He loaned me two more books.

Rabelaisian humor and sensuous living were never far below the surface. One Saturday, Dick Paige, an old friend of Calverton's, and one of the regulars from Washington, who usually drove us over, brought a girl friend with him. The woman took a fancy for the star of the gathering, and much to Paige's consternation, he returned the interest. Not long after the lecture, George and the woman disappeared down the steps and out the front door. Dick Paige was outraged and sought consolation from a fifth of Canadian; but it didn't help. Three hours later, when a sound at the front door indicated they had returned, Dick staggered hurriedly to the steps, met them halfway, and threw her back down the stairs. George, coming up behind her, broke her fall and yelled for me to come and restrain Dick. We went back to Washington without the girl friend. This time I drove, hoping that Dick would sleep it off, but he alternately dozed and awoke to curse "that sonofabitch, George Calverton."

In spite of that incident, Dick Paige continued to go to Baltimore every Saturday without fail, and without the girl friend. He wrote George a letter apologizing for his "irrational behavior" on that occasion, explaining that he'd "had too much to drink." He ended the letter by saying, "Actually, I didn't mean to throw her down the stairs; I meant to throw her into your arms to show my contempt for her."

On another Baltimore Saturday, in November 1940, there was a noticeable yellow tinge in George Calverton's skin, and I asked about it.

"Oh, just a slight case of jaundice," he said, his face for an instant becoming more sober. "Nothing serious."

Then he grinned, reaching for another drink, and added, "That's the way I show my sympathy for the struggling Chinese." He gave me a copy of his newest book, *Where Angels Dared to Tread*, a study of cooperative and communal religious communities in American history. He inscribed it: "To Jim, a very dear friend, and one of the 'angels' of the world."

Often in those months, if it must be told, I felt as though I were leading a double life—one of divinity on weekdays and ribaldry on weekends. The schism, however, was not destined to last long. I received a wire from Nina in New York, just a few days after my last Baltimore visit: "Share my grief. George died this morning. Memorial services . . ."

In my twenty years, it was the first time death had struck so close to me. In the emptiness that followed, I knew that from then on my search for myself would be lonelier and much less exciting.

I threw myself into Howard Thurman's classes, the thesis, FOR recruiting. I had already ventured onto the periphery of American politics.

Franklin Roosevelt was going for an unprecedented third term to make the nation the "arsenal of democracy." War industries were flourishing, but underemployment among blacks remained high. A. Philip Randolph was talking about a mass march on Washington to protest discrimination in employment, particularly in war-related industries. Randolph's mass meetings were drawing huge crowds of blacks around the country.

Roosevelt's Republican opponent was a political newcomer, Wendell Willkie, whom Norman Thomas, the socialist leader, called "the barefoot boy from Wall Street."

Thomas, the candidate of the small Socialist Party, crisscrossed the country, demanding that we keep America out of war in order to halt the drift toward totalitarianism here. Persistently, though unsuccessfully, he challenged the majority party candidates to debate with him the issues of the world crisis, the nation's economy, and discrimination against minorities.

It was Norman Thomas I supported and campaigned for, though I was too young to cast a vote. Once, at a campaign rally in Washington, I spoke on the platform with Norman and his running mate, Maynard Krueger, a University of Chicago economist. My speech stressed the point that competition for jobs in a capitalist economy set race against race, fanning the flames of hate. Many corporations, I argued, used the Roman rule of divide and conquer to keep the workers from getting together in united strength.

Roosevelt, of course, was reelected, but my contact with young Democratic Socialists continued after November.

Inexorably, work on the thesis progressed. Its main theme derived from the Weber/Tawney thesis and was a bit involved.* It was, first, that the functional role of religion regarding race has been to preserve the secular racial values of the dominant among its members at any given time in history. It then argued that certain parts of Protestant and especially Calvinist thought and ethics provided the rationalization that its partner, the robust young capitalism, needed at the beginning of the modern age to morally justify what was done through economic compulsion: the colonization, exploitation, and enslavement of distant lands peopled by strange folk of darker hue.

The resulting set of theories formed the basis of racist doctrines that subtly inculcated Anglo-Saxon cultures in the early modern age.

On the American scene, a study of writings and speeches of early New England theocrats revealed a clear distortion of Calvin's views on the "elect" and the "unelect" and predestination, to fit them into a moral justification for participation in the slave trade. Without the rationalization, such participation, though economically impelled, would have been repugnant to the sensitive Puritan conscience. Those theories of God-

*Max Weber wrote *The Protestant Ethic and the Spirit of Capitalism* and R. H. Tawney, *Religion and the Rise of Capitalism.*

ordained inferiority of blacks and superiority of whites with all the trappings that accrued, went wherever slavery went, and where slavery survived longest, they persisted longest.

In slavery, blacks were forced to conform to those theories. After slavery, the thesis contended, the segregation system continued the enforcement of those racist beliefs. The beliefs, then, became father to the fact and will outlive it by far.

When the thesis was finished, Howard Thurman was enormously pleased, gave it and me an A, and urged that I expand it and find a publisher. That I intended to do. I wished that Calverton were alive; finding a publisher for a serious work by an unknown and uncredentialed author would have been much easier and more probable with his help.*

Graduation was at hand and thoughts turned inevitably to the future. One day, in May 1941, as my father and I walked the half mile or so home from the School of Religion, out of the clear blue, he asked, "Junior, shall I notify the bishop and the district superintendent that you'll be available for ordination after graduation?"

"No," I said matter-of-factly, without looking at him, "I've decided not to be ordained."

After a long silence, he said, "I'm not surprised. I know how you feel about the unification plan. After reading your excellent thesis, I understand. I know that whatever you do you'll do well, but what *are* you going to do?"

"Destroy segregation," I replied.

"How?"

"I'm not sure yet, but it'll have something to do with mass mobilization in the use of the Gandhi technique. I don't know just how; I've got to work on it. But what I'd really like to do now is to go to New York, get a basement flat and a part-time job, develop the thesis into a book, and at the same time work out the overview and details for a movement of nonviolence against segregation in this country, and maybe get it started. And above all, to think, think, think."

"How long will that take?" my father asked.

"Who knows? Maybe six months. Maybe two or three years."

The old biblical scholar looked aloft, almost as if summoning divine assistance.

"Well," he said, "if that's what you want to do with this period of your life, I can lend you about three hundred dollars. That won't last long without income, so I advise that you find a job before getting the apartment. I'm sure you can stay with your mother's relatives in Harlem in the meantime."

I thanked him, but I did not want to stay with relatives. Incredibly, John

---

*In the following three years, I expanded the thesis into a book-length manuscript. It received many enthusiastic and glowing letters of rejection, but no publisher.

Swomley called from New York that evening and asked if I would be interested in staying on with FOR in some part-time capacity after graduation, and, if so, in what capacity? I said of course I wanted to stay on and told him I would like something in the field of race, and in New York, if possible.

John said that he would take it up with the FOR's executive director, A. J. Muste, and get back to me by mail. He added that he was not sure about New York, because A.J. was all for decentralization and felt they were already a little top-heavy at headquarters.

What was offered was a job in Chicago, and I jumped at it. When, two years later, I was rerouted to New York by Muste, nothing could have deterred me.

PART FIVE

Looking for a Place to Stand

CHAPTER 13

BIG APPLE BLUES

THE HARLEM ASHRAM on Fifth Avenue, one house below 125th Street, was as incongruous in Harlem as the Bucket of Blood Bar, which faced it, would have been on a street in Bombay.

When the several women—permanent residents, disciples of the leader, and all white—drifted in and out, some people thought a new whorehouse had moved into the neighborhood. When these women gave friendly smiles to passersby or stood at the large windows overlooking the street, observing the passing scene, this only served to heighten such suspicions. In fact, the women had to contend with frequent midnight knocks at their door. But their callers soon learned that, though this was indeed a house of love, the love was religious and not erotic, and what the women were selling was not flesh but the spirit.

In 1943, while the leaves were still on the trees in Morningside Park, a half block to the south, I moved into the ashram. It was nonviolence oriented, and also the cheapest place to stay. At first, some on the street thought a new pimp had taken over, but the inconspicuous nature of my attire soon persuaded them otherwise.

The leader of the Harlem Ashram was an ex-missionary to India, Jay Holmes Smith. He and another missionary, Ralph Templin, had been expelled from India by the British for refusing to take a loyalty oath: a pledge to do nothing contrary to the interests of the British Empire. Being men of conscience, they wore their expulsion as a badge of honor. Upon their return, Ralph Templin chose a life of speaking, writing, and teaching. Jay Holmes Smith took a different course. He started the Harlem Ashram, a place of "voluntary poverty" and of devout Gandhian meditation and social action.

Not one for asceticism, I would not have gone to the ashram had there been a realistic alternative. Nor did I accept the credo of voluntary poverty—the doctrine that the best way to make common cause with those one seeks to help is to adopt their afflictions and become one with them. My poverty was wholly involuntary: an unfortunate necessity in pursuing the things I wanted to accomplish in life. If there had been a financial "angel" or a remunerative job allowing me to do the same thing, I would have been delighted.

But there I was, in the ashram, making the best of it. The walls were dark and dingy, and the furnishings old, cheap, and tasteless. There was, however, a roof over my head, and food—all for ten dollars a week. The meals, unfortunately, were an inducement to fasting. Breakfast was a bowl of lumpy oatmeal. Dinner was a pot of tasteless, watery soup, and another dish, either potatoes or beans. The salad was wilted lettuce, and the bread was "day old," though it had seen more days than one. The food supplement was "grass"—large green tablets containing chlorophyll and, presumably, some minerals.

One day, there was a guest for dinner and the soup had more body than usual. A part of that body, was a large cockroach that had wandered into the pot and given up the struggle. It produced a major crisis, for there was no more soup in the kitchen. Having witnessed the insect's debacle, I caught Jay's eyes and, with a motion of my head, directed them to the soup. With a quick finger to the lips, he implored me to silence. After saying grace, he reached for the pot, bringing it beside his bowl. In violation of rules of etiquette, he ladled his bowlful first, including the inert beast. He took a spoonful of the concoction, as though tasting it for quality, smacked his lips, and nodded his head. The cockroach was no longer in his bowl. Jay then moved the pot around the table, starting with me. I passed, and sent it on its way.

This was not the New York I had longed for. Somewhere out there was the Alice in Wonderland place of my dreams, but I had no access, no entrée. On weekday mornings, when I walked from the ashram to the FOR office at Broadway and 116th Street, I saw a bit of Harlem, but not the Harlem of romance and scintillating movement that I had read about. What I saw was ugliness and filth, wretchedness and pain.

My office was a glass-partitioned cubicle, but it was adequate. More than adequate was the young lady assigned to me from the secretarial pool, a Japanese-American, Shizu Asahi, with superb stenographic skills. Her shorthand was as rapid as I could talk; her manual typewriter, a symphony of sound. In fact, she was so good that I lost her. My boss, A. J. Muste reassigned her to his office, which, as chief executive officer, he had a right to do. Yet, from that point, I began to feel put upon, and by experts. With a vastly inferior secretary, my output slowed down. I was kept traveling, and to uncharming and out-of-the-way places, which made it very difficult to keep in touch with what the CORE groups were doing and to organize others. A race relations institute was conducted by FOR in one upstate New York city; I was there, but as a decoration more than anything else. Though my title was race relations secretary, I was not allowed to speak. Clearly, I was out of favor.

There was no one to talk to; I wished for Bernice, but she was not there. I dreamed of Winnie to balm my wounds, but she appeared only in my dreams. Most other women seemed insipid, except for an occasional venture into the ecstasy of youth.

I was outmaneuvered and outgunned. Should I resign? Down in the mouth, I walked home one evening, if the Harlem Ashram could be called home. Walking up the stairs, shaking my head in disgust, I looked up. At the top of the staircase stood a young man, a long-term resident, beaming down at me with his pale face and bovine eyes overflowing with warmth and compassion. I was in no mood for such saccharinity; I looked down again and continued trudging upward. Reaching the top, I saw that he was still there.

He said, "Cihu."

"What did you say?" I asked with reluctance.

He repeated: "Cihu."

"Uh-huh," I mumbled, "that's what I thought you said."

I brushed past him and went into the shabby living room and sat in an overstuffed chair.

He followed and stood in front of me, the sympathetic smile still on his face.

"Cihu," he said again.

"Cihu," I repeated under my breath and sighed. "What is that?"

The smile on his face erupted into a cackle. "You see," he spouted excitely, "it's working." He spoke rapidly, almost deliriously, each word forming before the previous one had ended. "I've aroused your curiosity. I've made contact. We're communicating. I'm going to make *Cihu* the most important word in any language. More powerful than 'Heil Hitler.' And it'll be worldwide. It'll stop wars. In every country people'll be saying, 'Cihu! Cihu! Cihu!' It'll—it'll—it'll—"

"Yes, yes, yes," I groaned, "but what does it mean?"

"Can I help you?" he said excitedly. "C-I-H-U—Cihu! Everybody, every country, feels hurt and lonely and wants to hit back. Cihu will sweep the world and stop hate and stop war." His full lips grew red, but his face remained pale and his eyes opened wider.

"We'll go over to Berlin and place our hands under Hitler and raise him up, up, up to the heavens—Cihu! Then we'll come back to 1600 Pennsylvania Avenue and lift Roosevelt up, up, up to the heavens—Cihu! Then we'll go to Number 10 Downing Street and raise Churchill up, up, up—Cihu! Then we'll go to the Kremlin and—"

"I think you'd better lift Uncle Joe twice," I said, as I brushed past him to go out and walk along 125th Street. I decided to skip the ashram fare and have a bowl of chili, a hamburger with everything on it, and a glass of milk at the Texas Tavern and Restaurant down the street. Then I would sit with a beer and a ten-cent cigar in blessed solitude.

The Harlem Ashram was not all idiocy. Jay Holmes Smith, Ruth Reynolds, Maude Pickett, Jean Wiley, Abe Zwickel, and one or two of the other permanent residents were intelligent folk with a firm grip on the real and its twin, the absurd. They knew the difference; and having chosen a life-style for themselves, they knew, too, that life itself was more than a matter of style. Yet, I was not close enough to any of them to share my private feelings. So the dreary walls of the ashram merged with my private gloom.

There were interludes, however. On Friday evenings, the ashram's living room sprang to life. That was when the New York CORE met. It was a vibrant, earthy group. The chairperson was Dottie Sullivan, a quick-witted young white woman from Georgia and a former circus aerial artist, who had as tenacious a grasp on the battle against bias as she once had on the flying trapeze. There was Ina Sugihara, a Japanese-American with fierce commitment, a lively intelligence, and laughter that disarmed even the worst racist. If a court jester was needed, he was there in the person of a blind black youth, Vincent Baker, whose disability seemed to sharpen his mind and enhance his Churchillian rhetoric. Jim Peck was always there, though he hated meetings as much as he loved action on a dozen fronts for social justice. Then there were a beautiful ebony-skinned model named Melba Stewart and Anabelle Henry, a tall girl whose spirit in every crisis matched her height. There were others, and I attended when my travel schedule permitted.

CORE groups always compensated for their few numbers with frenetic activity that put older organizations to shame. Nonviolent direct action felled some offending giants and dwarfs in the New York area. One of these was Palisades Amusement Park, across the Hudson in New Jersey, which excluded blacks from its swimming pool. "Afraid," said Vincent Baker, "that the charcoal hue will come off in the water and deposit its residue on the milk-white skins of *Herrenvolk.*" Some barbershop policies fell, too, beneath the peaceful bludgeoning. Nowhere was there greater courage than with the black who sat in the chair of an angry barber in the shadow of his open razor, asking for a shave, while white CORE members occupied all other seats and refused to be served out of turn.

Several apartments were secured for blacks, long before fair housing laws were enacted, through the simple device of having whites sign the lease and then sublet when the lease did not bar such a practice. Volunteer lawyers stood ready to back us up.

Scores of jobs were found for blacks in banks, downtown department stores, and airline ticket offices. Picket lines, a rarity for civil rights objectives in those years, coupled with negotiations, did the trick.

With all the vinegar and guts being churned up by CORE groups in a dozen cities, I still had the sensation that we were a flea gnawing on the ear of an elephant, trying to bring the animal down. If we irritated the beast that we sought to make prey, it showed no signs of annoyance.

We knew what we were doing, but no one else did. Except for the *Amsterdam News,* a Harlem weekly, the media ignored us. It took more than enthusiasm, and more than a paper plan, to stand the nation on its head.

We had our second annual convention in Detroit in the summer of 1944 and changed the name of the national organization to the *Congress* of Racial Equality. I was reelected national chairman, and Bernice was again elected secretary-treasurer. One overriding organizational question inevitably erupted early in the convention. That was the issue of the authority of the national office vis-à-vis the local chapters, and its counterpart, the autonomy of the chapters. The national office was dispersed and, therefore, ineffective. Headquarters officially was still in Chicago at Archibald Carey's church, but I was in New York, working full-time. Bernice was still in Chicago, in school part-time. We remained in constant communication by mail, but that was not enough to run a tight ship. George Houser was now working out of the Cleveland FOR office, where he had started, and was leading an active CORE chapter. No one was being paid by CORE—it was all volunteer—for there was no money, and I had a pact with my employer not to embark on a direct-mail fund-raising campaign.

These problems raised two questions on which CORE's survival hung. First, functional—how to nurture an infant national movement without a central hand in one location to hold the bottle. The answer agreed upon was to let the child hold its own bottle, with the parents monitoring and coordinating its progress. In other words, chapter autonomy. The second question was financial—how to buy the milk to fill the bottle.

The Vanguard League, of Columbus, our newest and largest affiliate, volunteered to hold a fund-raising dinner where I would speak, and they would split the proceeds with the national office. CORE, they said, could expect between $750 and $1,000. The other chapters also agreed to hold fund raisers, but since they were smaller and less experienced in money gathering, they anticipated netting only $100 or $200 each.

In addition, Bernice was certain that Archibald Carey would take up a collection that would bring in $200 or $300 if I spoke in his church one Sunday morning on my next trip to Chicago. "I'm sure you still have strong personal attractions in Chicago that will bring you there again soon," she said with a smile that widened her face but did not unclench her teeth.

Another issue brought hot passions to the fore. That was the matter of communist infiltration and how to prevent it. Those were the days when U.S. communists, acting under party discipline, frequently entered organizations, especially in the area of civil rights, with the express purpose of molding the organizations' policies into conformity with the goal of world revolution as seen by Stalin and, if possible, to capture control of the organization themselves. Sometimes, for all their seriousness, their machinations provided a touch of humor. They had to invent a dialectic to support each of the many flip-flops of the party line, necessitated by sudden shifts in Soviet foreign policy. Nevertheless, it remained an aggravating problem.

CORE had a constitutional provision barring membership to communists. Obviously, it was not easily enforceable except in the case of well-known persons: How could you prove party membership? The debate, however, was over whether such a policy should be constitutionally stated, or should be removed.

There were cries of "red baiting" and "witch-hunt." Many other dedicated CORE members viewed it as a basic civil liberties question: how could we fight for freedom and deny to those of different political views the freedom to participate in our efforts?

I argued that CORE's loose structure and relaxed rules made it particularly vulnerable to infiltration, and that without vigilance, the organization indeed could be taken over by a disciplined political group with only secondary interest in the race problem. I went on to state that I did not want to see CORE become a tail to anybody's political kite, even one that I myself might be helping to fly. I was a pacifist, but was fighting to prevent pacifist control. I was a Democratic Socialist, but would not yield to socialist control of the organization. The communists, I insisted, would take control only "over my dead body." There would be no loyalty oaths, no witch-hunts; but give us a policy to stand on, I urged.

The provision was kept in the constitution, barring membership to those whose loyalty was to a foreign government, and who were subject to an external discipline antagonistic to the mission of CORE.

If the greatest heat was generated by that constitutional issue, the most searching discussion was reserved for another question: where were the wings to enable the organization to take to the sky? A motion was introduced to "invade" the South, a step that certainly would have brought national attention to nonviolence, if not national acclaim. After vigorous debate, the motion, at my urging, was tabled on the grounds that it would have been suicidal at that point in history.

As an alternative, I was mandated to talk with A. Philip Randolph—the towering civil rights figure of the period, who had been toying with the idea of nonviolent direct action for six months—to ascertain whether his enormous prestige could be used to make nonviolence come alive on the national scene and catapult CORE into the limelight.

Randolph's threatened march on Washington in 1941 had been called off when Roosevelt capitulated to his demand to outlaw racial discrimination in employment. He had roared through the country holding "monster mass meetings," telling the crowds about the outrage of booming war industries in America, the arsenal of the fight for freedom, which still discriminated against blacks. Inspired by the crowds, he went on to say in his polished Oxford accent, "This is the age of mass pressure, masses on the march. Discrimination against Negroes in employment will not cease until the president and the Congress of the United States see five thousand, ten thousand, twenty-five thousand Negroes standing on the lawn of the White House in protest."

Then Randolph posed, with chin jutted out, and the crowds were delirious.

The NAACP's Walter White and the Urban League's Lester Granger had joined in the call for a march, but Walter White later said that Phil wouldn't have had five hundred people in Washington. There was no organizing behind it. Roosevelt, however, did not know that. He was terrified that the march would embarrass him in the world community at a time when he was trying to put a great and clean face forward.

Randolph, master of the tactical bluff, hung tough and went eyeball to eyeball with the president. He did not blink when Eleanor Roosevelt went to New York to talk with him and Granger and White. He demanded a meeting with the president, and she arranged it. At that meeting, according to Randolph, FDR asked them to call the march off.

"Mr. President," said Phil, "what will you do about discrimination in employment to persuade us to call it off?"

"What," asked the president, "do you wish me to do?"

Said Randolph, "We want an executive order outlawing discrimination in employment on grounds of race, color, creed, or national origin."

"You shall have it," the president replied.

When Roosevelt issued Executive Order 8802 in June 1941, outlawing discrimination in employment and setting up the Fair Employment Practices Commission (FEPC) to enforce it, Randolph called off the march. But he kept what he called the MOW (March on Washington) movement going.

In December 1942, A. Philip Randolph had another call. This time, it was something for the MOW movement to do. Bernice and I had talked with Phil several times in Chicago about the Gandhi technique and about what CORE was doing, and he was impressed.

On December 30, 1942, Randolph had announced in a press release that the May conference of his March on Washington movement would consider launching a broad program based on nonviolent civil disobedience and noncooperation, patterned after the campaigns of Mohandas K. Gandhi in India. Such a program, it was stated, would call on all Negroes, except those on duty in the armed forces or at work, to disobey all laws that violated their basic citizenship rights, such as Jim Crow cars and all forms of discrimination. They would be asked to exercise their civil rights and eat in all places in every city where citizens normally dine, to boycott Jim Crow cars in the South and ride in the cars provided for citizens generally, and to refuse to go into Jim Crow waiting rooms, but to enter those rooms provided for everybody. If ejected, it was stated, they should not fight back, but should continue the program in an orderly, peaceful, and quiet manner.

That startling announcement had created not a furor, but at least a few ripples in the black press. Muste and Rustin had been elated. I had had my misgivings. Someone suggested that I was simply piqued because it was going to be the MOW and not CORE.

Actually, my concerns lay elsewhere. Nonviolence for the masses could not be maintained merely by asking that it be so; there had to be training and discipline, both of which were lacking. Further, the MOW movement was not a functioning organization. Phil had appointed old friends—those who had helped him and given him a platform a decade earlier, when he was organizing his union, the Brotherhood of Sleeping Car Porters—though some of them were despised in the communities they were assigned to serve. Such fierce loyalty to old friends spoke well of personal character traits, but not of organizational acumen.

I thought MOW could not do it, and if it tried, there would be shoot-outs in the South and bloody massacres. I feared a fiasco that would set back a nonviolent movement in the United States for decades.

I sought the views of others. Upon arriving in New York in January 1943, I had started and begun editing a monthly news bulletin on nonviolent direct action at FOR. It chiefly reported on activities of CORE chapters. The March and April issues were combined in a symposium on the Randolph announcement. I asked a broad range of thinkers and doers for their opinions on this startling proposal from a man whose words found receptive ears in America's black world. Among those responding were such luminaries as Reinhold Niebuhr; Howard Thurman; Norman Thomas; Roger Baldwin, founder and head of the American Civil Liberties Union; Haridas T. Muzumdar, author of *Gandhi Triumphant* and *Gandhi vs. the Empire;* Lillian E. Smith, editor of *The South Today,* and author of the best-selling novel *Strange Fruit;* Richard B. Gregg, author of *The Power of Nonviolence;* Oswald Garrison Villard, former editor of *The Nation* and grandson of the abolitionist William Lloyd Garrison; and over a dozen others.

The consensus was that such a program should not be attempted without extensive training and rigorous schooling in the principles and practices of nonviolence. I was pleased with the document and sent a copy to Randolph prior to his May MOW conference.

As I sat before that magnificent man on a sunny September day in 1943, basking in his benevolent smile, which lent radiance to the somber simplicity of his office on 125th Street, an elusive likeness haunted me. He reminded me of something, but I couldn't put my finger on it, so I made small talk while I searched for the similarity that was bugging me. A. Philip Randolph was a Great Dane—the majesty, the gentleness, the noble head, the supreme dignity, the grace of movement. Years later, when I owned a Dane, I told Phil that I had named the animal after him, calling him Randy for short. Randolph laughed with his regulated, patrician "haw haw haw" and said, "Jim, I don't know whether to be flattered or insulted. I don't know whether you're saying that I'm regal and majestic, or whether you're calling me a dog!"

He had more than his share of affectations, with the posturing and posing and the exaggerated Oxford accent. After all, he was, as he often said, a frustrated Shakespearean actor. No less theatrical was his tendency toward grandiose ideas and visionary schemes.

It could be said that something in Randolph mirrored a part of myself, but that is not why I admired him so. He was and remained one of the three heroes of my life. The other two were Eleanor Roosevelt and Norman Thomas. The three shared two rare qualities—not their intelligence and their courage; those are common commodities and can be used for good or evil. Hitler possessed both. It was, instead, their compassion and integrity, which each possessed in abundance.

"Jim," said Randolph, "I want to express my appreciation for the splendid symposium you edited regarding my tentative proposal for a civil disobedience campaign. That pamphlet helped to clarify my own thinking on the matter. That's the chief reason I did not ask the MOW movement to launch the program at this time. It may be that you saved us from committing a grievous error, and I thank you for it."

I thanked him "for raising the issue so we can get some thinking going in this country along those lines" and explained to him that the CORE convention had asked me to talk with him to seek some way in which his great stature and our activism and experience with the techniques could combine to get a nonviolence movement of major proportions off the ground.

He pondered the matter just a moment and then responded, "Well, I think we can accomplish that very simply. I will instruct the MOW chapters to work with CORE wherever CORE groups exist. In addition, whenever I am going to a city where there is a CORE, I will have the MOW people alert CORE and invite it to participate in all the proceedings. If you happen to be in town at the same time, I will want you to speak on the program with me at major functions. Another way we can help each other would be for you to let either my assistant, Ben McLaurin, or me know when you're going to a city where we're organized. We will ask our people to bend every effort to make your visit productive and enjoyable."

It was not the electric spark I wanted, but it was something. The MOW movement had no sinews, but it had Phil Randolph and that was a great deal.

The months dragged wearily on in that city where the dreams for which I had reached had eluded my grasp. Travel continued to such places as Augusta, Maine; Oshkosh, Wisconsin; Bemidji, Minnesota; and Boise,

Idaho—all places with dedicated pacifists who arranged good meetings. But none were productive for CORE.

More productive was a trip to Chicago. A collection at Arch Carey's church raised over $250 for national CORE, which would allow Bernice to have new stationery printed and pay for a good deal of postage and phone calls.

I also saw Winnie for the first time in a year. Our fortnightly letters had kept the embers burning, and the magic was still there, undiminished. It was with a mixture of relief and disappointment that I learned her divorce was still months away. How could I get married on a puny income from a job that was precarious? And where would we live; the ashram? I could imagine no greater absurdity. Yet, I did not want to lose her. But how long would she wait? When, as we parted, she told me that though Chicago had her roots, it held no charm for her any longer, and that she was going to move to New York, I felt she was buying time for me to prepare for our future.

From Chicago, I headed west. At Big Flats, Arkansas, there was a Civilian Public Service camp, one of the "concentration camps" where conscientious objectors who did not go to prison served their time. The most striking thing about it was the waste of human resources. Ph.D.'s, instead of dissecting ideas, were making little rocks out of big ones. Rather than lifting the burden of poverty from the backs of the poor, frail young intellectuals were making like steam shovels, hoisting dirt from the earth with hand tools. Sensitive hands, which could have been wielding artist's brushes or surgeon's scalpels, were swinging axes into the trunks of mighty trees.

I also visited another kind of concentration camp, one of the relocation centers into which Japanese-Americans, uprooted from the West Coast after Pearl Harbor, had been thrown. In one of the ugliest pages in the American saga, a great and industrious people—thriving farmers and businessmen—had been shorn of their possessions and herded together behind barbed wire, bewildered and hurt.

With the insensitivity of those of single-minded purpose, I spoke to that audience about the problems of black Americans and our efforts to develop nonviolent solutions to them. They listened attentively and appreciatively and applauded warmly.

As I walked to my room after the meeting, I heard footsteps behind me. I turned and waited. It was a jeans-clad teenager, as American as a milkshake at a soda fountain on a Sunday afternoon. Her oriental eyes were full of fears and tears.

"B-b-but," she stammered, "what's going to happen to *us* kids, Mr. Farmer?"

She buried her face in my chest and sobbed. I assured her that this country was big enough and great enough to recognize its terrible mistake and correct it. They would be all right and everything would be fine as soon as this nightmare was over and we could all go back to living again.

She brushed her tears away with a finger and stood on tiptoes and kissed my cheek lightly. She seemed reassured. But I was not.

The real struggle was being waged out of Randolph's office at 125th Street. Sprinting back and forth across the country, he thundered at mass rallies that this was a day of mass pressure, and that the powers in this nation forget that you exist if you do not come together with shouting voices and marching feet. Phil drew his greatest applause when he spat fire at the terrible spectacle of our fighting for democracy and freedom in a Jim Crow army, navy, and marine corps.

It was all talk, but talk with a threatening potential. Randolph still dreamed of leading the minions on a march to the nation's capital, but felt that it might be counterproductive in wartime. Some pacifists urged civil disobedience against the draft, but he thought that might be treason when America's sons were dying abroad.

Things changed, however. Roosevelt had died and Truman was president. The little haberdasher from Independence, Missouri, took charge with something approaching greatness. In 1947, Truman's Committee on Civil Rights issued its report, "To Secure These Rights," in which it urged, among other things, that the nation eliminate all forms of racial discrimination from all of the armed forces of the United States.

The stage was set for a vintage Randolph drama. Testifying before a congressional committee on the armed services in March 1948, Randolph vowed that he would "rot in jail" before he would countenance the continuation of segregation and discrimination in the armed forces of the United States. He then returned to New York and announced to the press that at an upcoming outdoor rally at 125th Street and Lenox Avenue in Harlem, he was going to urge black youth to refuse to be drafted. Much of the nation held its breath. That was long before going to jail became commonplace for leaders and other civil rights activists. Would handcuffs be put on the revered Randolph? If so, how would blacks react? What would the world think?

On that fateful Saturday afternoon, expectant crowds swarmed through the streets, clogging the intersecting arteries, pushing and shoving to get close enough to hear Phil's thunder and to see if the government's lightning would strike.

Federal agents and plainclothes policemen were easily identifiable by their set jaws and icy eyes searching Randoph's immobile face for some clue as to his intentions. Photographers held their cameras aloft, snapping furiously, each trying to get the definitive picture of the leader. The press dotted the audience with pads ready and pencils poised, as the electric moment approached.

Phil spotted me near the front of the crowd and smiled and nodded. He rose to speak and the murmuring of the crowd halted abruptly. In his inimitable fashion, he chronicled the crimes of the military against the rights of black Americans. Then he paused as more cameras clicked. The pencils of newsmen moved closer to their pads and hovered there.

"And so, brothers, I say to you: *if they try to draft you, don't let them do it!*"

Having dropped his promised bombshell, the man of the hour paused and awaited the reaction. The crowd withheld its applause for a few seconds and then thundered its approval. Cameras clicked again, and there was some movement in the audience as a few newsmen rushed to phones to call in the story: A. Philip Randolph had deliberately violated the Selective Service and Training Act by counseling blacks to disobey the draft law!

Most of the reporters waited, however, to see if handcuffs would be put on the premier leader of black Americans at that time. Wisely, the feds and local police made no move to arrest him. He had no movement yet, but had they taken him in custody, that act would have created for him an instant movement of major proportions.

Randolph continued. He told the young men in the audience that if they took his advice they would go to jail, and their families would suffer hardships. But freedom would never come without suffering. He told them that they should call his office for assistance. I learned that Muste had assigned Bayard Rustin to work for Randolph on FOR time, helping to coordinate the fight against "Jim Crow in Uniform." He was a capable organizer and it appeared that the campaign would get off the ground.

Truman responded in July 1948 by issuing Executive Order 9981, banning racial discrimination in all of its forms throughout the U.S. armed forces and setting up a committee to assure its prompt implementation.

His demands met, Randolph called off the campaign. Rustin publicly opposed that move and stated that the draft resistance campaign should continue. A. J. Muste also argued that since militarism, like Jim Crow, was evil, draft resistance by blacks should go on. Randolph disagreed and closed down the anti–Jim Crow in Uniform office, and Bayard returned to the FOR.

I agreed with Randolph. But A.J. sent a letter to Phil strongly condemning his action and stating that the two of them should sit down and talk about the matter someday soon. Phil's reply, which A.J. showed me, was curt and brief: "I agree that we should sit down and talk someday. Fraternally, A. Philip Randolph."

Prior to Randolph's historic campaign, the FOR and I had gone our separate ways and my life's journey had taken a detour.

One day during the spring of 1945, Muste called me into his office and told me that I was still not organizing, not signing up new members for FOR. I was not asked to resign, but it was clear that Muste wanted me to do so, so I obliged him.

I set an early effective date for the resignation in the late spring of 1945, and it met with A.J.'s approval. The effective date was just before I was scheduled to make a one-month speaking tour through the South at the invitation of Constance Rumbaugh, the FOR southern secretary. I told A.J. I would let Constance know that I would no longer be on payroll at the time of the trip, so it would be necessary for the colleges, churches, and FOR groups to provide honoraria for all speeches. A.J. thought that would be fine and said he would write Constance, too, confirming the agreement. He asked me what I was going to do for a living, and I told him that I honestly did not know.

It seemed that I was losing touch with my child, CORE. Bernice had left Chicago and gone to St. Louis to work for Harold Gibbons of the Teamsters Union—Jimmy Hoffa's intellectual. George Houser had offered to assume the burden of executive secretary of CORE, without pay, while performing his FOR duties, and the 1944 convention had approved it. A.J. had then transferred George to FOR headquarters in New York.

Winnie also came to New York, as promised, and my mother, knowing that I was in love and in trouble, came too. She and Winnie hit it off at once, and Winnie went to Washington with her to wait with my family while I got myself together.

On the way to the southern tour, I stopped in Washington for a nice but brief visit with Winnie and my family. When I returned a month later, I had $250 in a bank in New York, $600 in checks in my pocket, and did not know from where or when my next check would come. With my father officiating, we said our vows.

CHAPTER 14

HEARTBREAK

A LONG AND ENTHUSIASTIC letter had come from Robert O. Ballou, an editor at Harper Brothers, rejecting my book, *Religion and Racism*. He said that he had recommended it as strongly as he knew how, but the profit-and-loss people had turned it down. Ballou offered to help in finding a publisher.

Kissing Winnie good-bye for a while, I returned to New York to pursue the publication leads Bob Ballou had given me and to look for a job so that I could bring my bride to our home in our dream town.

Glowing letters but no acceptances were the result of my efforts regarding the manuscript; and I found no job in New York. A job almost came through as director of religious education at the prestigious Community Church of New York, a Unitarian establishment, but the minister, Donald Harrington, talked with Muste and changed his mind.

I did not stay at the ashram during those awful weeks, but at the apartment of friends. Ina Sugihara, of New York CORE, and her boyfriend, Bill Greiner, had an apartment on East Thirty-fourth Street in Manhattan—a fourth-floor walk-up. They both had jobs and I didn't, so they insisted I stay there rent and board free. I was reluctant to accept such generosity, but they pooh-poohed my reluctance.

Another friend found me a job. Morris Milgram, the brilliant and energetic young head of the Workers' Defense League, told me that the Upholsterers' International Union of North America (UIU-AFL) was looking for an organizer for their campaign in the furniture industry of Virginia and North Carolina. I jumped at it, and Milgram informed the union's director of organization, Arthur G. McDowell, of my interest and availability. McDowell was a Democratic Socialist and knew me through my association with the Young People's Socialist League (Yipsels). I went to UIU headquarters in Philadelphia immediately and McDowell hired me. In one week, I was to be in Martinsville, Virginia, to join the organizing drive at American Furniture Company.

I was glad to have a job, of course, and the pay would be good—$175 a week plus living expenses. I was not happy, though, to have to be away from Winnie almost constantly in order to earn a living for us. Also, the job would be tough; it was a jurisdictional war against the United Furniture Workers–CIO, which was allegedly communist led. They had some of the factories organized, and we would be trying to take them away from them. It was bound to get nasty. Yet, it would be bearable because it would be only temporary. Something would surely come through in New York, and my wife and I would have a home together, with enough money saved up to give us a start. I rushed to Washington to tell her the good news.

She seemed a bit taciturn, as though this was not at all the way she had expected marriage with me to be. Nor was it the way I had thought it would be, but I told her that we would fight it through and come out all right.

"Yes," she said with the confidence I had grown to expect from her when the chips were down. "I know we will. We always have." She managed a smile.

Suddenly, my eyes were glued to the dresser. She caught my gaze and her face was awash with smiles.

"Yes," she said, "I've started knitting booties. I'm pregnant."

My lips worked but no words came. She laughed a most delicious laugh and said, "You see, the yarn is pink. It's going to be a girl."

"How do you know?" I managed to ask.

"Oh, I just know. In fact, I already have a name for her if you don't mind: Francesca—it goes so well with Farmer. *Francesca Farmer.* Doesn't that sound nice? We will call her Fran for short. She's going to be a great child and a great lady—half you and half me."

The next day we walked and talked and cried and dreamed about Francesca. Growing within Winnie was life—me and her, joined—

irrevocably. We were not two persons then, but one. Our minds, souls, and bodies were in perfect tune.

We began preparing for my trip to Martinsville. Shirts had to be washed and ironed, and suits dry-cleaned. She emptied the pockets of my suits and then erupted like Mount Saint Helens. She had found and read a letter in a pocket of a suit hanging in the closet.

My darling,

I hear that you are getting married. If that event is carved in stone, I want, once more, to hold your beautiful, brown, sylph-like body in my arms, close to me. Then I will be able to bear the unbearable. Please call me.

The languorous lady instantly became a witch on the warpath. She read the letter over and over with rising volume and intensity, crumpled it and threw it down and picked it up before I could retrieve it. She read the second sentence again, and this time, it was a hysterical scream. I almost failed to duck in time as a heavy glass ashtray flew through the air and gashed a hole in the dry-plaster wall behind me.

"I don't want this child," she shrieked. "I never want to have a child by you. If you want a child, go have one by one of those bitches! *Damn* you!"

The words cut right through me, and she ran into the hall and down the stairs with the crumpled letter in her hand, to show it to my sister and maybe my mother, too.

I sat on the bed in a daze. That night, Winnie did not speak to me, and in the morning I left for Martinsville, Virginia, with scarcely a good-bye.

The Negro "hotel" in Martinsville was an old three-story brick building in which the landlady had rooms on the second floor. My room also was on the second floor. Most of the other rooms were vacant until no-luggage couples came in for a two-hour occupancy. On Saturday nights, when there was a dance downstairs, the hotel did a land-office business. Springs were noisy and walls were thin, so on those nights, sleep for me was a phantom.

The organizing staff briefed me, and I went to work preparing leaflets and passing them out at the crack of dawn and in the afternoon as workers were changing shifts. I spoke on soapboxes at plant gates and in the evenings visited black workers at their homes.

Our hopes were dim. The UFW (United Furniture Workers) had a firm grip on most of its members. Our gains there were limited. We were cutting more deeply, but not enough to give us a good shot at victory in an election.

A major problem was the negative image of the AFL among the black workers. Most had unskilled jobs, even those who possessed skills, and they knew only too well the reputation of the hated AFL craft unions in excluding or segregating blacks. The Upholsterers' International Union had shaken off its craft label and was now an industrial union and had a staunch commitment to racial equality, but convincing blacks that that was possible for an AFL union was not easy.

Anticipating defeat at the American Furniture Company, we had already begun an organizing drive at the Stanley Furniture Company, part of the great Bassett chain of furniture factories, in neighboring Stanleytown, Virginia. Stanleytown, as its name indicated, was a classic company town in 1945.

Thomas Bahnson Stanley, a former furniture worker, had married one of Bassett's daughters and received a furniture factory. The town was named after him and he was elected to Congress in 1946. His workers lived in company-owned houses and made their purchases at a company-owned store, buying things on credit. That tied them to the jobs as effectively as if they had balls and chains around their ankles. No union had been able to make headway before.

The plant was now rife with grievances and anger. In two weeks' time, we had received eighty-one mailed-in authorization cards. The workers had been reluctant to sign anything, for they thought their boss would find out. We had assured them, however, that there was no way Stanley could find out. The U.S. Post Office would not be amenable to his surveillance, and once in our hands, the cards would be put into a locked safe where no one could get to them.

Three days later, eighty-five workers at the Stanley Furniture Company were fired and evicted from their homes, including seventy-eight who had signed our authorization cards.

We immediately filed unfair labor practice charges against the company with the National Labor Relations Board.

No sooner had I gotten to my room after that shattering day than the following telegram arrived from my sister:

COME HOME AT ONCE. WINNIE MISCARRIED. NOW IN SERIOUS CONDITION IN FREEDMEN'S HOSPITAL.

Within minutes, I was packed, and in an hour and a half was on a train for Washington.

She was on the critical list. The dead fetus had been removed in pieces. It had been a boy. The afterbirth inadvertently was left in the uterus. Fever had raged between 104 and 105 degrees.

I called her mother in Chicago and explained the dangerous situation to her. She asked if she should come, and I said no, but I would let her know immediately if that became necessary. Did I need money? No, I was earning a good living and would be able to pay all the bills. Winnie would get whatever she needed.

The fever broke and began declining slowly. My mother, father, sister, brother, and I, whose lives had stood still, began breathing again. In two more weeks, she came home. The hurt in her soul showed through. She threw herself across the bed, face down, and shook convulsively.

Still wounded from her earlier disavowal of any desire to have my child, I struck back with cruelty, exploding with my own grief and doubts: "I guess you're satisfied now."

The sobbing stopped. "What do you mean?" she mumbled hoarsely.

"You said you never wanted to have my child. Now you won't have it." I felt relief in saying it, but no sooner were the words out than I wished they had remained unsaid.

Winnie turned over and sat to face me. She stared into my face expressionlessly and spoke slowly, without emphasis: "You don't really think I meant that; I was hurt and angry and wanted to hurt you. You don't really think I did something to kill my baby."

Our marriage was dead from that moment, six months after it had begun; we both knew it, but neither spoke of it.

In the union wars in Virginia, fighting as hard as we might, we suffered defeat after defeat. I was moved to High Point, North Carolina, to join in the drive on the Globe Parlor Furniture Company. It was at High Point in the spring of 1946 that a letter was forwarded to me from George Houser. The U.S. Supreme Court had just ruled in the Irene Morgan case that racially segregated seating on interstate buses was unconstitutional.* FOR and CORE were jointly sponsoring a most imaginative project to be called the Journey of Reconciliation, testing the enforcement of that decision. A small group of whites and blacks were going to ride regularly scheduled buses through the upper South—Virginia, North Carolina, West Virginia, and Kentucky—blacks sitting in the front and whites in the back, refusing to move when ordered and responding to violence and arrest with nonviolence. Would I go along?

The plan was exciting and intriguing, but my answer had to be no. I had a job that I needed, I wrote George in reply, and I had been away from it for too long already, due to my wife's miscarriage and illness. Regrettably, I could not quit the job, for we needed the money for survival.

I brooded about it for many hours as I passed out leaflets and talked with workers at the Globe Parlor plant gate. Was I in the trap that killed dreams as cages killed once-free minds? Was marriage, I asked myself, the enemy of the movement?

Winnie was back in the hospital; the infection had recurred with moderate fever. She would not hear of my returning home. I had been away from work too long the other time. This time, it was not serious, and she would be back home in a few days, as soon as the fever was knocked out. A few days later, a note from her told me that she was returning to Chicago to complete the recuperation. She would write a long letter from there.

I called Arthur McDowell, the director of organization, to explain my personal plight. He said that after the Globe Parlor election in North

*Morgan v. Virginia, 66 S.C. 1050, June 1946.

Carolina, which we expected to lose, and a smaller one in South Carolina, which we expected to win, I would be transferred to Cincinnati, where I would be closer to my wife. The elections went as anticipated and I got my transfer, making a detour to Chicago en route to Cincinnati.

Winnie was living in the home of her brother-in-law, Doctor Charles Thompson, a prominent dentist, and her older sister, Violet. I had been sending her money to pay rent and board, so she would not feel uncomfortable, and to take care of her other needs. She had been in the hospital again briefly, but was back home now.

We talked at length and went out to dinner and back to Charles and Vi's house for the night. Things were not the same. I still loved her; that I knew. I thought she still loved me; but of that I could not be sure. There were momentary flashes of the old fire, but it flickered and went out, like the flame of a damp match.

The Cincinnati assignment was easier than the southeastern one had been. There was a strong and established UIU local with a competent business agent. In short order, I organized and won the election handily in a small mattress and bedding factory.

Walking the streets of Cincinnati's west end, I came to be known as the "union man." Several workers from a large scrap metal junk yard stopped me on the street one day and asked me if I could help them; their pay was a pittance and working conditions were hell. I told them that upholsterers didn't organize scrap metal places, but I would organize them and find out what union in town could do the best job for them.

I called a meeting the next day and 90 percent of the junkyard workers showed up and signed authorization cards. In one more day, I had signed up eight of the absent ten. I then called UIU headquarters for advice. Their president, Sal Hoffman, suggested I try the Teamsters, because they insisted that if trucks were used or if the materials or workers got there on wheels, the jurisdiction belonged to them. The Teamsters grabbed the workers hungrily and gratefully.

While in Cincinnati, I learned that some members of the Journey of Reconciliation had been arrested in North Carolina and sentenced to thirty days on the state chain gang. Among those arrested was Bayard Rustin. Once again, I felt pangs of guilt for not having been there.

Winnie and I wrote regularly. I asked her to come down some weekends; the trip was not long. She had agreed to come down the next Friday evening, but missed the train. The following weekend, she had a bad cold. On the weekend after that, she missed the train again. The excuses were endless.

The distance was so short and months had passed and she had not come. I sent her a letter suggesting a divorce. Two days later, I had a letter from her asking for a divorce. Our letters, of one mind, had crossed in the mail.

In a phone call, I suggested that she consult a lawyer and initiate divorce proceedings on any feasible grounds. I would sign anything, consent to anything, and pay her lawyer's fee.

When he heard what was in the works, McDowell granted me a transfer to Chicago, where I could be close to the action. In mid-1946, back in the city where it had all begun, I set about the task of tidily closing out one of the dreams that, for five years, had motivated me.

I moved into the men's cooperative apartment at 6314 South Ellis Avenue. They were still there; McKey-Pogue Realty had failed to get them out.

I saw Winnie frequently. She had a job in a photographic studio— retouching, photo coloring, and air brushing. We had lunch now and then, and I gave her checks for the lawyer and signed the necessary papers, consenting to the divorce and waiving the right of appearing in court. The grounds were desertion. I had gagged at that one and she said, "But you said you would—"

"I know. I know," I interrupted. "I'll sign it."

Her sister and brother-in-law invited me to their home for dinner on occasion. One time, the guest of the evening was Duke Ellington. Dr. Thompson knew everyone, and his gracious home was perfect for entertaining. He was fond of me and considered me a promising young man and could not understand why Winnie and I were going our separate ways.

After the gourmet dinner at Dr. Thompson's table, the Duke and I engaged in conversation. I told him of my interests and this elegant gentleman nodded with sympathetic understanding and appreciation.

Then I said to him, "Duke, I know where your heart is, but how can you continue to play before segregated audiences in the South?"

Duke Ellington did not take offense, nor did he smile. He merely said in a calm voice and level tone, "Jim, you are a crusader, and I honor you for it. I'm not a crusader; I'm an entertainer. I make my living by making music. Would you have me turn down half of my engagements because I don't approve of the social views and practices of the people who pay to hear me play?"

"I guess not," I said, "not yet; but the time will come, Duke."

"When the time comes, Jim," he said, "I'll come with it."

"Some people make music," Charles interjected, "and others make movements. Someday the music will be a part of the movement, and the movement a part of the music."

(That was long before a civil rights movement made such demands of commitment upon the people's artists. When such demands were made, the Duke, like many others, was not found wanting.)

Winnie unobtrusively stood and left the room. I excused myself and followed her to her room.

"Winnie, it's not too late. We can still call off the divorce and try it again."

She shook her head slowly but emphatically. "No," she said.

"Then delay it for a few weeks so we can talk and think."

She looked unwaveringly into my eyes and said, "I don't want to delay this divorce a single day."

The wheels of the law moved rapidly this time, and in short order the divorce was final from a Chicago Heights court. I requested and got from UIU a transfer back east. I would organize the mattress and bedding industry in Baltimore while living in Washington.

I knew quite well that was the end of the line with the Upholsterers' International Union. Arthur McDowell had been moved to another job, assistant to the international president. The southern drive had ended, and the organizing staff was being cut back. It was no surprise, therefore, when two weeks after arriving in Washington and one week before Christmas, 1946, the letter of termination came, effective January first.

My family made the holidays nice, but I knew I could not stay. I could not stand the eyes revealing all the sorrow they felt for me. I had lost Winnie. I had lost CORE. And once again, I was unemployed.

I headed for New York to lick my wounds.

CHAPTER 15

LULA

INA SUGIHARA AND BILL Greiner received me with open arms. They had "killed the fatted calf"—a roast duck in orange sauce. The rice was wild, and so was Beethoven's Fifth on the phonograph.

There was a dinner guest who had invited herself and dared them to say no. She was Lula Peterson, who had moved to New York in 1945, fresh out of Northwestern University with a Phi Beta Kappa key in economics. It was she who had written the letter Winnie had found.

As we finished the snapper turtle soup, the record hit a crack and absurdly repeated one of its dramatic moments. Bill rose to correct it, but the dinner guest was already there; she gently lifted the needle over the obstruction and returned to the table.

"Jim," she said, "I can hardly believe you're back in New York. I'm so glad. This town hasn't been the same since you left."

I had met Lula Peterson two and a half years earlier, on my visit to Chicago to raise funds for CORE. There was a party and dance at a ballroom in a downtown Chicago hotel. On the dance floor, two hundred people of all colors were making motions that defied definition. It was still the jitterbug era, and the gyrations exhausted me to merely watch them. I kept my distance.

During the intermission, the band, made up of CORE members performing without pay, gave an introduction of rolling drums exploding into silence. Bernice Fisher reviewed recent and current CORE activities. Then I spoke, giving an overview—the plans for CORE, the vision of the future. I left the microphone to an accompaniment of more drums rising to a crescendo of clanging cymbals.

I rushed to the cash bar. Edging up beside me was an attractive young lady with a face pure and fresh as the wheat fields of southern Illinois after a late summer rain.

"That was a good speech, Jim."

"Thanks."

"I'm a member of Evanston CORE. I'm sure you've heard of our activities."

"Yes, of course," I lied. "I see you prefer cones to dishes for your ice cream," I said, looking at the double-dip affair precariously held in her hand.

"Oh, yes," she laughed. "Though I'm a senior at Northwestern now, I still like ice cream cones. I can lick them better. I have a long tongue," she said with full innocence. Before my raised eyebrows could settle back into place, her tongue shot out and curled upward and touched the tip of her button nose.

I gasped with astonishment. Then she discovered that she had tipped the cone and the chocolate dessert had fallen down the front of her pretty white dress. With a mass of paper napkins and a glass of water, I cleaned the mess off her dress as best I could. She thanked me and walked away.

Upon graduation in the spring of 1945, she moved to New York and came to live for a while at the Harlem Ashram, of all places. After the usual Spartan dinner, I took her out and bought her chocolate ice cream—in a dish.

Although she was a whiz at mathematics, statistics, economics, and something called econometrics, her real love was the theater. Like many ivory-scrubbed young ladies who came to New York, she dreamed of being an actress.

A year later, while I was in High Point, North Carolina, I received a telegram from her, telling me she was doing summer stock theater in New Jersey (or was it Delaware?), and was out of money and would I please send her $75 so she could eat again. Immediately, I wired her $100.

After dinner at Ina and Bill's apartment, we talked about the past eighteen months. I did not want to talk about mine; they were too painful. So we talked about Lula—her summer stock, and now her studies in the theater with Herbert Berghof and Uta Hagen. Among the other hopeful thespians in her class was Maureen Stapleton. For a living, Lula was now working for Consumers Union as a typist for their publication *Consumer Reports*. She was earning $45 a week. She had tried the telephone company, but was told that she was overqualified.

She now had what could charitably be called an apartment—a two-bedroom cold-water flat (no central heat), a sixth-floor walk-up in the lower Manhattan warehouse district at 27 Desbrosses Street. It was January. I wondered what she did for heat. There was a gas cooking stove in the kitchen and a wood-burning fireplace in the living room, she told me. She also had a small electric heater in her bedroom. If that was roughing it, so what? The rent was only $18 a month.

There was one problem though: keeping wood in the fireplace, which was the major source of heat. A 120-pound girl could bring only so many of those crates and boxes upstairs, and the stuff burned so fast. Now, if she only had a big strong man to help her, things would be easier. Also, she was a little worried about going down to hunt for wood late at night. It was, after all, a tough and unlit area. However, she could run fast and she always took her little dog, Wendy, with her at night. He had a fierce bark and would bite anyone, including her.

Since I was unattached, she thought she might be able to talk me into moving in and helping her. All her problems would be solved and she could go on studying for the theater.

Three pairs of eyes bored holes in me as she talked. Ina passed the bottle of Grand Marnier around for refills.

"Okay, I'll be over in the morning. Maybe I can help out for a while."

"Great," Lula said, "1947 is going to be a good year."

Since she was half German (and half Swedish) and loved Wagner, Bill Greiner put the *Der Ring des Nibelungen* on the record player, and we all relaxed with another drink.

The next morning, I climbed the five flights of stairs with both shoulders piled with dismantled shipping crates. I entered the flat and Wendy bit me. He was sternly reprimanded with a "shame, shame, shame," which impressed neither him nor me. I went down for more wood, and this time when I returned the dog sniffed my ankles and eyed me suspiciously, but did not bite. It was Saturday, and Lula did not have to go to work, so we watched the roaring fire, read poetry aloud, drank coffee, and talked about her career and aspirations, and about CORE.

For over two years, 27 Desbrosses Street was home. When anyone asked either of us where we lived, we would say, "Number Twenty-seven Day-Brossay Street in Manhattan." That sounded as though we were doing well in the big town.

Actually, the opposite was the case. Her take-home pay was miniscule, and I gave only occasional lectures for small fees. We did not keep the wolf away from the door, but between us, we always managed to slam the door in his face. Lula was a genius at making the most inexpensive meals nourishing and tasty.

The next winter, Lula's mother, a hard-working but poor widow living in Chicago, suffered a massive stroke, which left her partially paralyzed and speech impaired. Lula, the only child, brought her to live with us.

I was more needed than ever. In the living room where Mrs. Peterson slept, the fireplace had to be kept blazing. Someone had to be at home when Lula was at work. I was the only one who could carry the ninety-pound invalid up and down the stairs on occasions when it was necessary.

Having to care for her mother had scuttled Lula's dreams of a career in the theater. She did not talk about it, but I knew the heaviness of heart was there. I mentioned it once on a February day, thinking that perhaps it would help for her to talk about it. She smiled, looked out the window at the swirling blizzard, and said, "That's the way the snowflakes fall."

Despite the heaviness that hung over our lives, we did not let ourselves be robbed of all joy. She saved a dollar here and a dollar there so we could buy the cheapest of tickets for the theater. From lousy seats we exulted in fine art: Tennessee Williams's *Streetcar Named Desire,* Paul Robeson, Jose Ferrer, and Uta Hagen in *Othello.*

On most weekends, we joined up with Bill Greiner and Ina and some of their friends. We drove to Montauk Point, Long Island, for the weekend in those days when it was still isolated. We pitched tents, cooked out, and skinny-dipped in the surf.

Before long, the inevitable came to pass. In early March, 1949, we sent to our friends a mimeographed announcement of our marriage, to be held in May at a mid-Manhattan ballet studio. Among the many notes and calls of congratulations was a letter from Dr. Katherine Breydert of the New York Infirmary for Women and Children. She wrote that she had received the announcement and that it was most urgent she talk with me before the wedding. I should please call immediately for an early appointment.

Lula's face was shrouded with a pall of apprehension. "Dr. Breydert is my doctor," she said. "I told you shortly before you returned to New York that I had a swelling removed from my neck. She's had me coming back in periodically for checkups, to see if other swellings occur, she said. Each time, she says I seem to be in good shape. Do you think it could be something serious, Jim?"

"We'll know very soon, Lula," I said, and I kissed her.

Two or three days later, I sat in the New York Infirmary office of Dr. Breydert. The sanitized odor of hospital walls entered my nostrils and, as usual, increased my tension.

Dr. Breydert picked her words carefully: "Mr. Farmer, when I learned that you and Lula were planning to be married, I felt it my duty to tell you that she has Hodgkin's Disease."

"What is Hodgkin's Disease?"

"It's a malignancy of the lymph glands," she replied, "incurable and fatal."

We sat in silence for a few minutes.

"Why," I asked, "hasn't Lula been told this?"

"We thought the knowledge of impending death might shorten her life, or at least make it less pleasant."

"Shorten her life? How much time does she have?"

"Who knows? But not much," she said as she gazed steadily into my face. "We usually say eighteen months in Hodgkins cases. It has been over two years now, and that is most unusual. Any time now this disease will erupt into its terminal phase, and the end will come quickly.

"Can't anything be done?" I asked.

"Yes," she said. "We can use X-ray treatments when the recurrence appears, and that may prolong things for weeks or even a few months."

The doctor paused for a moment and then went on: "If you do go through with the marriage, by the way, Lula *must* avoid pregnancy, at all cost. Pregnancy will trigger the final stage of the disease. I would urge that you use not one, but two birth control methods simultaneously."

We sat in silence, and I sipped at a cup of coffee. I got up and left, but at the door I turned and looked back to thank her. I could not find the words, so I simply nodded. She said, "I'm sorry."

Half an hour later, I entered a Chock-Full-o'Nuts to meet Lula. I sat at the counter beside her. There was terror in her face when she whispered, "What did she say?"

I relayed my conversation with Breydert as faithfully as I could; I told her the truth. She stared down at the remaining half of her sandwich.

"Jim," she said, "you don't have to marry me. I'll understand if you don't want to."

"What kind of nonsense is this?" I asked. "Of course we're going to get married. I'm not a quitter, and neither are you. We're going to fight this thing through together and lick it."

She squeezed my hand hard and her nails dug into my flesh. "But, Jim, do you mind not having a child?" I heard her voice break.

"Of course not. After a few years, we can adopt one if we want to."

Lula said, "Darling, I have another errand to run. You go on home, but don't tell mother. I'll be home in a couple of hours."

"Are you sure you don't want me to go along with you?" I asked.

"Yes, I'm sure, but don't worry. I'll be there in about two hours."

Her errand was a trip to the public library to read up on Hodgkin's Disease.

The next weeks moved swiftly, and we did not talk much about her illness, but concentrated on preparations for the wedding. Lula designed and made her own outfit. It was a black suit with a white blouse. There was no engagement ring; we could not afford it. The wedding band was a strip of gold with small rubies embedded in it.

We wrote our own marriage rites, and George Houser, who was ordained, agreed to perform the ceremony. There was to be no "love, honor, and obey," but "love, cherish, and respect." There would be no mention of God, but much mention of humanity, integrity, and individuality: both Lula and I were humanists.

There is never enough time for such preparations. Things that should be routine have a way of becoming crises. When the realization dawned that I needed my divorce papers in order to get the marriage license, the document could not be found. There was no choice but to write Winnie, asking her to lend me her copy of the decree. It was a terrible thing to have to do and was bound to hurt her. Yet I confess to a certain childish glee in writing the letter. It was saying to her, "See, I did not roll over and die; there is someone else."

Winnie complied promptly with my request, and with the document came a letter:

Dearest Jim,

Don't do it. Please don't marry her. I know you don't love her.

I'm so sorry about all that has happened. I wish there were some way that I could erase it, but I can't. All I can say is come back to me and let's try it over again. It will work this time.

Please let me know.

Much love,
Winnie

When I returned the papers, my note said, "I'm sorry, my darling, but it's too late now. I've made a commitment and I shall keep it. I love you, Jim."

The day before the wedding, Lula went into town to buy odds and ends needed for the next day. Since her arms were full, she took a taxi home. The cab collided with another cab at an intersection. Lula was rattled around and wound up bruised on the floor of the vehicle.

She came home in another cab and called from downstairs for me to help her with her bundles. Not long after she arrived, an insurance adjuster for the taxi company came with release papers and a check for Lula's inconvenience. She happily signed, for the check would pay for a honeymoon.

"What else can go wrong?" she laughed in her curious way of laughing while talking.

"Don't lose the ring, Jim," and she laughed again. Among the other last-minute chores, she ironed my shirt and pressed my suit, as I shined my shoes. I opened a bottle of wine a friend had brought us.

Something else did go wrong the next day. When we got to the ballet studio, there were a dozen early arrivals outside on the sidewalk. The door was locked.

They applauded when Lula, her invalid mother, and I got out of the cab. "So what?" someone said. "We can have the wedding out here on the street, New York style."

"There's always Central Park," another chimed in.

Among the lockouts were A. J. Muste, George Houser, Ina and Bill, and the lady of the late George Calverton, Nina Melville. She had married a well-to-do industrial chemist, Peter Berdeshevsky, and they had a baby daughter, Margot. Nina and Lula had never met, but Lula had heard me speak of George and Nina. The two women rushed to each other's arms. No words were spoken, but none were necessary.

A quarter of an hour passed before the studio person with the key came trotting toward us. "I overslept," he said. "Sorry."

It was not long before the studio filled up with more than a hundred friends of all colors, mostly socialists and pacifists, or members of New York CORE, in attire ranging from blue jeans and shorts to business suits and cocktail dresses.

Lula was radiant. She was thin, having lost weight in the past few years, probably due to the silent killer that lurked within her. She had been to no beauty parlor; we couldn't afford it. She had shampooed her hair several times and had combed and brushed it at length, with the help of her mother's one good arm. It hung below her shoulders, shining and glimmering like spun gold. Her dancing blue eyes and ecstatic face shamed the angels in heaven. Her lips, always turned up at the edges, were now a Cupid's bow.

Her mother's eyes never left her, and the smile that dominated her twisted, half-paralyzed face made her seem even beautiful.

Also there were my mother; her three sisters; my cousin Muriel; my sister; and my brother, Nathaniel, who was my best man. Dad was in Texas and could not come.

There was a small band made up of CORE members who had instruments and knew how to use them. I don't think they had ever worked together before, but you never would have known it.

There was also a ballerina. Two or three years earlier, she had told me that when I got married she would dance at my wedding. I had called her and told her that the time was now. True to her word, she had come with black leotards underneath her long skirt. When the music began, she ripped off the skirt and blouse and walked to the platform with the measured, arrogant steps of the ballerina. It was sensual, modern interpretive dancing with which she favored the crowd, to their total delight.

I turned to look at the stage. The music had revved up to a jazz beat, and the dancer had moved into a mad boogie-woogie, index fingers on each hand jerking toward the ceiling with each twist. She ended with a pirouette and a low bow, with her head almost touching the floor.

The preliminaries over, Reverend Houser took charge. The ceremony, which Lula and I had written, went smoothly and raised no eyebrows. George read from *The Prophet* by Kahlil Gibran and we repeated our vows:

> I, Lula Peterson, take this man to be my lawfully wedded husband, and promise to love, cherish, and respect, to stand with him even when I must stand alone, through sickness and in health, through times pleasant and times unpleasant—forever.

I, James Farmer, take this woman to be my lawfully wedded wife, and promise to love, cherish, and respect, to stand with her even when I must stand alone, through sickness and in health, through times pleasant and unpleasant—forever.

And so we were joined.

Everyone had to kiss the bride. My cousin Muriel took the piano seat and played a Chopin polonaise that became a popular song known as "Till the End of Time."

The honeymoon was a drive around the Gaspé Peninsula in Canada with a borrowed car. At least that was our intention, but a quarter of the way around the peninsula the road was blocked without prior warning. The sign said: "STOP. GO BACK. BRIDGE OUT."

Nevertheless, we enjoyed the time in Canada. Before crossing the George Washington Bridge on the way home, the fuel gauge registered empty, and we also needed two quarts of oil. Between us, we had enough money for one gallon of gas and one quart of oil. We arrived home happily exhausted and broke.

The fates began to smile. A friend who was moving to the suburbs with his growing family offered to sell us his coop apartment at Bedford and Barrow Streets in Greenwich Village. It was not luxurious—a fifth-floor walk-up—but it had central heating and two fireplaces, three small bedrooms, a living room, dining room, kitchen, and bath. It was across the street from Chumley's Restaurant, the famous basement rendezvous whose walls were papered with book jackets. The price was reasonable, and we bought it. Lula's mother had almost enough in U.S. savings bonds to pay for it. We scrounged up the rest.

Lula got a better job: director of program budget for the Institute of International Education, a foundation that administered the Fulbright program and student exchange programs for the U.S. State Department.

I, too, got a job. Norman Thomas called to inform me that the League for Industrial Democracy (LID), a Democratic Socialist educational organization, a kind of American Fabian Society, was looking for a student field secretary. The job would require a good deal of speaking on college campuses and organizing the Student LID. The SLID, as it was called, would always be teeming with the factional in-fighting so common among youth who were left of center and right of the communists. I would have to "mother hen" the operation. Was I interested? If so, I should call the LID executive director, Dr. Harry W. Laidler, and make an appointment to see him, taking a resumé with me. Norman had already spoken with Laidler about it.

The salary wasn't great, only $50 a week, but that seemed like a fortune compared to the sporadic and low fees I earned from speaking engagements. My pay was a good deal less than Lula's, but neither of us had an ego problem with that; we were just glad to pay the bills and live a little for a change.

There had been another development of immense importance to me. George Houser, who had done a first-rate job of keeping CORE's house in order during those years between 1944 and 1950, when CORE appeared to be going nowhere, had resigned from his post at FOR and from the executive secretaryship of CORE. With consummate skill and with extraordinary administrative gifts, George had walked the tightrope between FOR and CORE without compromising either. Now he had resigned to launch and lead the American Committee on Africa.

Jimmy Robinson, the non-FOR pacifist who was also a veteran of the Chicago days of CORE's genesis, had taken over. Though a proofreader by trade, Jimmy had developed knowledge and fund-raising skills. Now that CORE had slipped from under the FOR saddle, funds could be raised by mail, and if this meant competition with FOR, so be it.

Jimmy finally got the appeal letters to more than pay for themselves. Lula, who had gotten accountancy training at Price Waterhouse in Chicago as she worked her way through college, kept the books and receipted each contribution. Jim Peck, who could write, edited the organization's paper, *The CORElator*. At the outset, no one was paid, and the three of them—the transition triad—kept the organization alive through the lean years of the first half of the fifties.

It was not long before Jimmy was raising enough money to pay his own salary as executive secretary and that of a typist. Lula and Jim Peck continued as volunteers. CORE had a tiny office at 38 Park Row, near City Hall.

Both Lula and I resumed activity in New York CORE and those meetings also were held in our Village flat. Lula attended the national conventions each year, and I attended when I could. Everything seemed to be moving as if prearranged.

Between her full-time job and her volunteer CORE activities, Lula worked her head off. In my spare time, I cleaned house, and we shared the cooking. Her spirits were joyous, despite the ordeal of caring for her mother. There were no signs of a recurrence of Hodgkins. I told her over and over, to convince myself as much as her, that the diagnosis was in error. Yet every headache, every pain, darkened her face with fear.

Only momentarily, however, did the fears erase her smiles. She saw humor in the little disasters that plague everyday living and drove me up the wall.

Once, for instance, we came home from a meeting late, and her mother was asleep. Gretchen, the little dachshund I had bought to replace Wendy, whom we had given away to a woman who loved neurotic dogs, had gone on a tear. One table lamp was on the floor in pieces. A garbage container had been opened and its contents scattered about the kitchen floor. Gretchen had also unwound a full roll of toilet paper and trailed it throughout the apartment, wrapping it around chairs and table legs.

Down the hall the tissue had rolled and then back again and over and around a couch and a coffee table. With a final triumphant gesture, she had tossed the nearly empty roll into the air and it had landed on the mantelpiece, where it stayed.

"Oh, my God!" I exclaimed when we walked into the apartment. Lula laughed so long and hard that tears rolled down her cheeks and she was too weak to stand; she sat down and swept the little dog into her arms and hugged and kissed her as she laughed.

"Oh, Jim," she said as words found their way out between paroxysms of laughter, "did she have fun while we were gone!"

One great thing about the League for Industrial Democracy was that it enabled me to bask in the elements on which I always thrived. Nowhere was I more at home than in the forensic atmosphere of critical and idealistic young minds.

Among the bright youths honing each others' brains in SLID were Michael Harrington, now chairman of the Democratic Socialists of America, author of *The Other America,* and professor of economics at Queens College in New York; Gabriel Kolko, who subsequently became an economist and the nation's leading authority on distribution of income; Elaine Gellis, now professor of history at Morgan State University; Gabriel Gersch, a professor of English in a New York university; André Shiffrin, now president of Pantheon Books; Jay Sorenson, now a specialist in Russian language, politics, and culture; Bogdan Denitch, now chairman of the sociology department of the Graduate School, City University of New York; Susan Gyarmati, free-lance editor; and Earl Mittleman, an editor with the U.S. Information Agency.

Public speaking, which was my forte, was a major part of the job. I always died of nervousness before mounting every platform, but when I stood to face those before me new life was pumped into my body.

If my last two years with FOR had been a slow shriveling of the soul, the five years with SLID stretched it again and allowed dreams to soar. The currents on which they flew, however, were not smooth.

After I spoke for five minutes at the annual luncheon of LID in 1952, Walter Reuther, president of the liberal United Automobile Workers Union (UAW), who was the main speaker, asked me to have breakfast with him the next morning.

At breakfast in his hotel, he offered me an influential job with the UAW. It would require that I be a member of the union for at least a year, so he proposed that they arrange for me to get an assembly-line job at the Ford Motor Company for a year, after which I would be pulled out and moved into a key job at union headquarters.

Knowing that Lula would approve, I agreed to the plan. Reuther said that he would have it all worked out and okayed by the necessary members of his executive board and would be back to me with the final details within a month.

When two months went by with no word from Detroit, I called Reuther's top representative in New York, the regional director, Martin Gerber, and asked where the matter stood. Gerber informed me that the deal had fallen through, because one of the union's vice-presidents had strenuously objected on grounds that I had a white wife. I was disappointed and shocked, but not really surprised.

When I told Lula, she closed her eyes and whispered, "I'm sorry, Jim. Are you sorry you did it?"

I tapped her jaw with a mock left hook and said, "Don't you *ever* ask anything like that again."

Not long after that, a letter came from Roy Wilkins, inviting me to apply for the position of director of the youth department of the NAACP. He urged me to send him a brief resumé and an outline of a suggested program for the NAACP youth chapters. He had signed the letter as acting executive secretary of the organization. (Walter White was on leave from the organization for an indefinite period, and apparently it was not known whether he would return.)

I did so. The program I suggested was for nonviolent direct action. It was for sit-ins by the association's youth and student chapters at lunch counters and restaurants, stand-ins in cafeteria lines, wait-ins at hotel registration desks, ride-ins in non-Jim-Crow coaches on trains and in front seats of buses, and wade-ins in public beaches and swimming pools. It proposed a training program in nonviolence to precede this drastic action.

Roy Wilkins called shortly afterward to inform me that Walter White had returned as executive secretary and wished to talk to me, and that I should call and make an appointment with Walter, which I did.

Walter White shook my hand firmly, but greeted me coolly. He spoke at length on the theme that he and he alone was charged with the responsibility for hiring and firing of personnel in the association. After half an hour of one-sided conversation, he rose from the chair behind his desk. Taking the cue, I also stood. We shook hands, and upon parting, he said that he would review my resumé and program suggestions as well as those of other applicants and would be in touch with me shortly.

I did not hear from Walter White, but later learned from another source that another individual had been hired for the job. I sighed with regret, for the vast network of chapters the NAACP had could have provided the impetus needed to spark a movement of unprecedented proportions.

In 1955, the irascible and lovable labor leader and Democratic Socialist Jerry Wurf offered me a job organizing for District Council 37 of the American Federation of State, County, and Municipal Employees (AFSCME) in New York, which he headed. I took it, for I felt I was beginning to stagnate at LID.

Jerry and I had spoken on soapboxes together at rallies in Norman Thomas's presidential campaigns in 1944 and 1948. He was the meanest, orneriest, cussingest, toughest, softest, kindest, lovingest, most compassionate sonofabitch in the world. To understand Jerry Wurf, one had to know what it was like to be an undersize, polio-crippled Jewish boy growing up on the Lower East Side, fighting to survive. He had to be the toughest, loudest kid in the neighborhood, or he would get beaten up every day. Sitting in a wheelchair watching other kids play, he also became the smartest, for he read everything, including Eugene Victor Debs. Those who loved Jerry also hated him, and those who hated him also loved him. I took the job believing that we would clash and fight, and I would quit or be fired.

After giving LID two weeks' notice, I sat in Wurf's office on a Monday morning.

"Okay, Jerry," I said, "where am I going to organize, Harlem or Bedford-Stuyvesant?"

"Neither," he replied. "Staten Island."

"*Staten Island?*" I erupted. "Nobody lives there but lower-middle-class Italians."

"So what? What've you got against Italians? And what've you got against the lower middle class?"

"Nothing," I said.

"Well, in a week I'm striking the city's Parks Department and Robert Moses, the parks czar. I want you to turn the Staten Island park employees out for the strike. Lennie will take you around on the Island and introduce you to the leaders among the parks workers."

Lennie Selig was young, tall, slim, and slightly bent over at the shoulders. He had been a parks employee in Queens himself and was now an organizer for the union.

In a fleet rental car, which each organizer got as a fringe benefit, Lennie and I toured the Staten Island parks, talking with employees. At each location, the shop steward called the men together and introduced me. I spoke, explaining the reason for the strike action and exhorting them to join the fight against Bob Moses's tyranny by walking off the job on the designated day. After listening with expressionless faces, they broke into applause.

The shop steward said, "Jim is our brother and we're all going to be with him on that picket line. Right?"

They echoed, "Right! We'll be there."

The Staten Island workers all thanked me warmly, many shaking my hand in both of theirs.

The turnout for the strike was overwhelming, from all boroughs. Wurf was delighted. Unlike the lackluster affairs we had grown accustomed to in labor disputes in the fifties, with dispirited placard bearers grudgingly doing their time on the picket line, this one had thousands of uniformed parks employees sprightly stepping in time with their lively chant: "Bob Moses must go."

On her lunch hour, Lula skipped lunch and came from her job at IIE to join the picket line. The scowling face of Wurf beamed like the sun when he saw her. There was a long embrace and a kiss.

At the front of the line was a truck carrying a large animal cage, inside of which were several parks employees in their uniforms, jumping up and down at passersby, acting like gorillas or lions. A sign on the top of the cage read: "BOB MOSES' ZOO." That gimmick was the brainchild of Mildred Kiefer, a union staffer who later became Mrs. Jerry Wurf.

Needless to say, the whole event was a media picnic. Bob Moses, who was famous for *never* capitulating, capitulated and met with Jerry Wurf. We had no legal right to collectively bargain, but Wurf bargained from the barrel of a strike. A good agreement was reached.

After the strike, I was assigned to organizing blue-collar workers in city hospitals, where the majority of workers were black or Puerto Rican. They were the most dumped upon workers in New York City and the poorest paid—earning in a good week, when they were not docked for time, maybe $40 gross. Organizing those workers, hungrier for dignity than for money, was easy, but AFSCME Local 420 had a rival: Teamsters Local 237. The stakes were high: a potential bargaining unit of thirty thousand, and the organizing became a nasty, back-alley type of union warfare.

I was threatened with blinding, and a Teamster goon on numerous occasions brandished a blade and said to me, "I'm gon' cut yo' fuckin' throat." The threat had to be taken with some seriousness, for he was known in Harlem as a proficient knife man who would not hesitate to use his weapon.

The organizing was fun, for I thrive on competition, and the workers, by and large, were among the most sincere, loyal, and decent people I've ever met. But the threats were not fun; if I had to die violently, I wanted it to be on the front lines of the fight for racial equality, not in the dark alleys of a union jurisdictional scuffle.

The Teamsters were ahead. They had about six thousand members and we had four thousand, but we were slowly gaining. We knew that one day there would be an election for exclusive representation, so we could not let up.*

Nine years had now passed and Lula's killer disease had not recurred. Lula and I both wondered if its existence had not been an illusion and the diagnosis mistaken. I wrote to Dr. Evan Thomas, Norman's younger brother, who was highly respected in the medical profession. He was in Albany, heading up the State Health Service. I told Evan that I wanted to talk with him on a private matter next time he was in New York. He replied that he would be in the city the following week and stated a time and place we could meet.

*That election was held in 1962 and though Local 420 was still behind before the election, it won by a narrow margin.

James Farmer at eight months in September 1920. Serious already.
Source: J. Farmer

James Farmer at about three years in Holly Springs, MS, 1923.
Source: J. Farmer

James Farmer with his mother, Pearl Farmer, and his sister, Helen, in summer of 1924.
Source: J. Farmer

James and Helen Farmer with their father, James Leonard Maximillian Farmer in Holly Springs, MS, about 1925.
Source: J. Farmer

James at thirteen, in 1933, after winning high school oratorical contest. The prize was a four-year college scholarship of $250 per year. *Source: J. Farmer*

Studio photo of James, and Lula just married; 1950. *Source J. Farmer*

Farmer on a picket line with daughter Tami, inside the 1964 World's Fairgrounds, Queens, New York. *Source J. Farmer (CORE photo)*

President Johnson talks with civil rights leaders in his White House office. From left: Roy Wilkins, executive secretary of the NAACP; James Farmer, national director of the Committee on Racial Equality; Dr. Martin Luther King, Jr., head of the Southern Christian Leadership Conference; and Whitney Young, executive director of the Urban League. *Source: World Wide Photos*

A young demonstrator;
Jonesboro, LA, 1965.
Credit: Edward Hollander

A Life photographer is assaulted by an onlooker during a civil rights march in Bogalusa, LA. *Credit: Edward Hollander*

Farmer addresses CORE national convention in Durham, NC, August 1965.
Source: J. Farmer (CORE photo)

Jerome Smith, CORE field secretary, talking to a group about voter-registration procedures. *Credit: Edward Hollander*

March 9, 1965. Second abortive march from Selma, AL, to Montgomery. The marchers were able to cross the Edmund Pettus Bridge but were turned back by U.S. marshals. From left: Fred Shuttlesworth, Martin Luther King, Jr., James Farmer, and James Foreman (SNCC). In the foreground: Andrew Young. *Credit: Edward Hollander*

June 21, 1965. Memorial march to Mt. Zion Methodist Church. *Credit: Edward Hollander*

On the hustings; 1968
campaign photo.
Source: James Farmer

Campaigning in the Bronx,
1968. *Source: J. Farmer*

Farmer with Richard Nixon. *Source: J. Farmer*

Farmer with Jimmy Carter. *Source: J. Farmer*

Norman was six-three, but Evan was even two inches taller, and so thin he looked like a walking skeleton. They both had the clearest, most honest eyes I'd ever seen, bluer than Sinatra's. Both had voices that seemed to be painfully scraped from their throats.

Evan Thomas had been a conscientious objector in World War I. When Norman had visited him in federal prison, he had found his brother hanging by his wrists from the ceiling with his toes barely touching the floor. Norman, then a young Presbyterian minister, with that righteous anger he reserved for great crimes of social injustice, had raced into Washington and pounded official desks, demanding that Evan be cut down from that ceiling.

Evan was cut down. It was only after he had been released from prison that he had entered medical school, and he was then over thirty. He became a great doctor, discovering a cure for syphilis long before the "wonder drugs" rewrote medical textbooks.

As I walked into his New York City office, I thought that he must have suspected I was coming in to talk to him about the specialty that had earned him his reputation. He soon found out that it was another dread disease.

"Jim, I know very little about Hodgkin's. I've treated only three cases of it, and all three patients died within eighteen months. But if Lula has gone nine years without a recurrence, I would say that either it was wrong diagnosis, or they got it. After they removed the node for a biopsy, what did they do, use radiology?"

"Yes."

"Well, maybe they cured it. When they say a disease is incurable, that doesn't mean that no cases are ever treated successfully. It simply means that there is no treatment known to be successful in a significant number of cases."

"There must be some test that can be given to determine whether she actually has Hodgkin's or not," I said.

Evan shook his head. "Not unless there's a recurrence, a swollen lymph node. Do you know whether the lab report on the node nine years ago was *probably* Hodgkin's or *definitely* Hodgkin's?"

I didn't know.

"That's something we'll have to find out," Evan said. "In either case, I want you to talk to someone who is more knowledgeable about this thing than I. I know two men who've made a kind of specialty of Hodgkin's. One is in New York, Dr. James Ewing, Jr. He's a good guy, but he doesn't ordinarily take private patients. He teaches at Columbia University Medical School and conducts research. But I'll twist his arm and get him to see you and Lula, and I hope he'll take her on as a patient."

"One more question," I said. "What about pregnancy? We're told that we must avoid it at all costs, for it would trigger the final stage of the disease."

"I don't know." He spread his hands in a gesture of helplessness. "There must be literature on the subject of Hodgkin's and pregnancy. When I get back to Albany, I'll read up on it at the state medical library and send you a letter with my opinion."

As we shook hands in parting, that beanstalk of a man towered over me and his Lincolnesque face told me that if it was possible for him to make things all right, it would be done.

Scarcely a week had passed before a handwritten letter arrived from Thomas, telling me that he had read the literature and he found no evidence of any relationship whatever between Hodgkin's and pregnancy. It was his opinion that we should go ahead and have a child if we wished. However, he wanted us to check that with Ewing before acting on it. If Jim Ewing disagreed, he wanted to discuss it with him and hear the rationale for Jim's opinion.

Thomas had spoken with Ewing and Ewing had agreed to see us and to take Lula as a patient. James Ewing, Jr., after whose father a city hospital was named, was a hearty man who would have been at home on the deck of a sailboat, casting a line into the deep, matching wits with a game fish just right for the wall over his fireplace. But with us, he was authoritatively scientific.

He rolled in a blackboard and drew diagrams of Hodgkin's cells, explaining what they did to themselves and to each other. He told us that it was now known that there was a chronic Hodgkin's, which could remain dormant for a long time, as well as the acute type, which rushed to its conclusion. Undoubtedly, Lula had the chronic type. In the event of recurrence, they would attack it with radiology.

One the question of pregnancy, he agreed partly with Evan Thomas, and thought that we should go ahead and try to have a child. However, if there should be a recurrence within the first four months, he would terminate the pregnancy. If one occurred after that, he would have to weigh the respective risks to the mother and child and act upon the conclusions of those deliberations. Dr. Ewing said that he would want a ob-gyn doctor who was knowledgeable on Hodgkin's, and gave us the name of Dr. Hugh Barber.

Several months later, Lula was pregnant. Dr. Barber, a trim, energetic, ex-football player, was elated. He watched over Lula as if he were the mother and she and the fetus were the baby.

It was soon determined that there were twins. At seven months, Lula went into labor. One of the twins had died. Dr. Barber had to remove the living one first in order to get at the one who had died, but it was far too small to survive. The tiny boy and girl were buried together.

The physician was even more distraught than either parent. "I'm sorry. Try again," were the words he forced out.

Six months later, efforts bore fruit again. This time, caution was even greater, if that were possible. At four months, a swollen lymph node appeared on Lula's neck.

Dr. Ewing was called in. The node was removed and sent down to the laboratory. The word came back: "definitely Hodgkin's."

Dr. Ewing whirled to face me. "You understand, of course, that we'll have to terminate the pregnancy."

Dr. Barber, standing several paces from us, said in a loud voice, "No, you won't."

"What?" said Ewing.

"You will *not* terminate this pregnancy," said Barber.

"We will *have* to terminate it in order to treat the disease." The two doctors were facing each other now, hardly more than a foot apart.

"If you terminate this pregnancy," said Barber, "it will border on the unethical. I will take full responsibility for the safety of both mother and child."

Ewing faced him in silence for quite a while, then turned and slowly walked to me.

"Obviously, we cannot terminate the pregnancy," he said softly. "In order to do so, I would have to go to court and get a court order. I won't get that order if the ob-gyn man comes into court and says that it's not necessary. I'll chart the treatments," he said as he sat down at a little table with some graph paper. Here was a fine medical mind, straining to prove itself wrong.

Dr. James Ewing, Jr., shook hands with me, looked at Dr. Hugh Barber, and walked out.

The instructions from Ewing had called for a certain radiologist who Ewing had said would follow his charting to the finest calibration. Lula was seated in a chair in the center of a large room. She was covered with a lead gown from her head to the floor. There was a small hole in the gown at the point of the incision in her neck where the node had been removed.

The radiologist was with her machine in a room enclosed with thick glass. The machine was aimed at the hole in the lead gown. More adjustment took place before she was ready to begin firing X-rays.

The treatments continued at intervals over several weeks. On February 14, 1959, Tami Lynn Farmer, six pounds eight ounces, was born. Hugh Barber had come down the stairs, four steps at a time, with the message. Athletic as he was, he ran up to me blowing and heaving, as if he had just taken the pigskin across the goal line for the winning touchdown with only seconds to go.

"It's a fine little girl. She's strong and healthy. You may go up and see her now. She's with Lula. Mother and daughter are fine."

I sat in a chair at bedside, with a sterile mask over my nose, held Tami in my arms, and counted her fingers and toes as Lula smiled. Her beach-sand-colored face, framed by a full head of black hair, was heart-shaped, as it should have been, for this was St. Valentine's Day.

It had been a "natural" childbirth, as Lula had wanted. She was fully conscious, watching in mirrors.

Lula had challenged an unseen foe and knowingly risked her life to give me a child, for she knew that, despite my protestations to the contrary, I dearly wanted one. I was inspired by her courage and loved her for her love. Those private events of courage and love enriched our life together.

Just a few years earlier, in 1956, there occurred a public event of immense importance that startled the nation and etched nonviolence into its consciousness. It was an idea whose time had come at last.

PART SIX

Spreading of the Wings

CHAPTER 16

KING AND THE GREENING OF THE MOVEMENT

THE FIRST CAPITAL OF the Confederacy had become the mecca of the civil rights movement in America, and an eloquent Baptist preacher sat as its high priest and stood as its prophet.

A tiny schoolteacher named Rosa Parks prepared the ground in December 1955, by preferring a seat in the city jail to a seat in the back of a city bus. A Montgomery Pullman porter, E. D. Nixon, designed the edifice when he conceived the plan to "pull the people off the buses," a boycott of the city transportation system. But it was Martin Luther King, Jr., who established the shrine of Gandhian nonviolence in a southern city in the United States of America, drawing to him, as a magnet, pilgrims and press from all over the world.

There was none of the strident rhetoric that had characterized the struggle for so long. It was now a seductive gentleness: "Though you hate us . . . yet we will love you; and we will wear you down with our capacity to suffer."

The action, however, was sinewy and tough. Tens of thousands of weary blacks walked miles to work and back home, refusing to ride segregated buses. Despite sore feet and aching muscles, they sang:

> Ain't gonna let nobody
> Turn me roun', turn me roun',
> Turn me roun'.
> Gon' keep on a walkin',
> Keep on a talkin'
> Walkin' to the Promised Land.

Here was a movement of black Americans flying in the face of the American cult of "the big fist wins." Here was a movement dedicated to the proposition that one could win without using any fists at all, except those pounding within the soul.

King's Montgomery protest not only repudiated the violent machismo of America; it also stirred to awakening another America—the America of Emerson and Thoreau, of the Quakers, of the abolitionists, the America of principle and compassion. A part of America was born again, one might say, and the rebirth lasted through the decade of the sixties.

On the first day of the Montgomery bus boycott, I sat in Jerry Wurf's office, and together we listened to the news from Montgomery. I went home early. After dinner, Lula and I sat down with a glass of wine. Gretchen was in my lap, licking my face.

"Jim, I know you have mixed feelings about the developments in Montgomery, but—"

"What do you mean, mixed feelings?" I said. "I think it's the greatest thing that's—"

"Jim, this is me, Lula. I know you have mixed feelings, you're human. But don't. Please don't. This is precisely the spark that you've been working and hoping for, for years. The nonviolent moment now has the nation's attention, and it's off and running. But you tilled the field, Jim. I know you'll share in the harvest. I *know* you will."

With unerring perception, Lula had read my thoughts. The great day has come at last. The nonviolent movement in America is airborne. Why am I not more exuberant? Is it because it is not I who leads it? Is there a green-eyed monster peering through my eyes? I had labored a decade and a half in the vineyards of nonviolence. Now, out of nowhere, someone comes and harvests the grapes and drinks the wine.

I am only human. What I have hated most in people is pettiness. Am I now consumed by that which I hate? I must kill the green beast inside if I am to battle the dragons outside and keep faith with that child in Holly Springs and that teenager in Marshall, Texas. But can I? Am I enough of a person to see the spotlight on another while I do my dance in the low lights and shadows?

Shortly after the bus boycott had begun, A. Philip Randolph phoned to ask me to come to a small meeting at his office to discuss Montgomery. Also invited were Bayard Rustin and William Worthy, Jr., a young black activist and writer.

Phil told us of his delight at what was happening at last in a larger southern city, and under inspired charismatic leadership. He had not heard of Dr. King before, but after all, he was very young—under thirty. The Reverend Dr. King clearly had the ability to speak effectively, not only to his constituency, Randolph observed, but also to the nation. Indeed, he added, his constituency was the nation.

"And so, I was thinking," Phil said, "that we have a responsibility to give Dr. King and his campaign all the help we can. I think we should send someone down there to work with the boycott and help him to keep it going. You and I know very well that the enemies of freedom will use every trick in the books to break the boycott, just as they break strikes."

"Whoever we send," I interjected, "must go there not to take over or control or to project himself, but to be supportive of Dr. King. It is, and must remain, his show."

"Absolutely," responded Randolph. "That is precisely what I told Dr. King when I called him yesterday, and he would welcome such a supportive person. Whom should we send?"

I suggested that Bayard go, since he was a good organizer as well as an excellent singer and particularly skilled in leading group singing. Further, he knew the gospel songs, spirituals, and folk songs and could be very helpful in bolstering morale, which tends to sag after a couple of weeks. Phil said he was about to make the same suggestion. He asked Bayard if he would go.

Not many days went by however, before Randolph requested me to contact Rustin and ask him to leave Montgomery and come home. The Montgomery daily press and city officials were beginning to zero in on him as a possible source of embarrassment to the boycott leaders. The press quoted Rustin as having said he was a reporter for *Le Figaro,* and a check with that paper had exposed the claim as false. Who is the ubiquitous Negro who speaks with a British accent? Who sent him and what is he doing here?

City officials were beginning to look for derogatory information with which to smear the bus boycott. Bayard complied with Phil's request and returned to New York.

As the Montgomery bus boycott went on, Jimmy Robinson's fund-raising expertise continued to grow. More and larger contributions came in response to his photo-offset letters, enclosed with the *CORElator,* which detailed CORE projects and successes. The letters were signed by such notables as Eleanor Roosevelt; Norman Thomas; A. Philip Randolph; Roger Baldwin, head of the American Civil Liberties Union; and Lillian Smith, southern writer and editor.

A roving field secretary was hired and a skeletal support staff came to the national office. Lula continued at the nerve center of the organization on a volunteer basis, keeping the books and guarding the budget.

New chapters were organized across the north and in South Carolina, Louisiana, and Kentucky. I attended CORE conventions and was, in my mid to late thirties, prematurely an "elder statesman."

Spirits were high in CORE throughout the late fifties. Activity was jumping and the soil was fertile. The boost had come. We were on the threshold of the fulfillment of aspirations: a movement rooted in Gandhi and Thoreau. If we had plowed the ground for a decade and a half, the

Montgomery movement had fertilized it and put the seed in, and now the plants were growing and spreading. No longer did we have to explain nonviolence to people. Thanks to Martin Luther King, it was a household word. CORE was a beneficiary of the emergence of King.

Since I was known in certain limited circles as one of the authorities on the Gandhian movement in America, I was not surprised when, in early 1959, I received a call from Roy Wilkins, again inviting me to come to the staff of the National Association for the Advancement of Colored People. Wilkins was head of the organization now. He wanted me to help devise program activities. Wurf's AFSCME was a growing empire on the New York labor and political scene, but that was not where I wanted to make my career.

Compared with the dinky little CORE office in a walk-up in an old building at 38 Park Row, the NAACP headquarters at 20 West Fortieth Street were on a different planet.

Wilkins was fully aware of my other work, but CORE at that time posed no threat to the NAACP. Hence, no conflict of interest was perceived.

Roy Wilkins was warm and friendly. With his arm around my shoulders literally and figuratively, he introduced me to his professional staff, most of whom I already knew slightly. With a few notable exceptions, they greeted me with snake-eyes and forced smiles. They seemed to be asking themselves if I was being brought in as the heir apparent.

The exceptions, who were genuinely friendly, were Mildred Bond,* in charge of life memberships; Herbert Hill, labor secretary; Jack Wood, housing secretary; and James Ivy, editor of *The Crisis*. They frequently visited my office, and I theirs, and I often lunched with one or another of them. They tried to be helpful, describing the terrain, charting the mine fields, identifying the concealed traps.

The friendly ones shared with me the in-house jokes, the scuttlebutt, the anecdotes. One anecdote, apocryphal of course, had me in stitches.

It seems that crank calls were common at the NAACP switchboard, but one stood out. A man with a thick southern accent demanded, "Let me talk to the head nigger."

The operator hung up on him, but he called back: "Ah said, Ah wanna talk to the head nigger."

"Sir," said the switchboard operator in her most cultivated voice, "we're very busy here. Please don't call again."

Not to be denied, there he was again. "Look, lady, who do you think you are? Ah gotta talk to the head nigger."

This time, the operator put the call through to Dr. John Morsell, assistant to the executive director.

"Hi, are you the head nigger?" the caller asked.

"Now, look here, fellow," Morsell growled, "we're about serious business

*Now Mildred Bond Roxborough

here. We don't have time for your kind of foolishness. If you have to make crank calls, kindly make them elsewhere. Don't bother us with them."

The irrepressible voice came again. This time, he was connected to Wilkins's private line.

"Are you the head nigger?" the man asked.

"Now see here," said Wilkins. "This association has spent a half century fighting against your kind of bigotry. We'll keep on fighting until we've wiped your racism out of the consciousness of this nation. I don't know who you are, but if you keep on calling, we'll trace your calls and find out where you're calling from. Then it should be a fairly easy matter to discover who you are, and I assure you that you will be prosecuted to the full extent of the law."

"Well, Ah'm sorry," the caller responded. "Mah mother jus' died, an' she always loved the niggers. In her will, she said she wanted one 'n a half million dollars of her money to go to help the poor niggers. An' so I jus' thought that if I cud talk to the head nigger there, Ah cud work out an arrangement to transfer that money to help the niggers."

Wilkins cleared his throat loudly. "Head nigger speaking!"

The unfriendly staff members viewed me as an interloper and dealt with me as bureaucracies always deal with interlopers: they boxed me in.

My title was "activities coordinator," which I considered a nontitle, and titles are all-important in bureaucracies. Wilkins told me that the title was purely temporary, and that it would be "program director" as soon as he could work it out.

Gloster Current, the director of branches who presided over the functioning of the association's more than fourteen hundred local groups, which raised perhaps 80 percent of the budget, told me bluntly once, "I coordinate the activities of our branches, and *I* am the director of their programs."

His words carried much weight. I had the feeling that Wilkins was not in control of his organizational house, but was in a way prisoner of his own bureaucracy. He tried to break me out of the box I was in. Whenever he called a meeting of his top staff, the department heads, the "cabinet," I was always called in, too. The others looked at me strangely, resenting my presence.

Many of those sessions were about King—how to respond to him and how to deal with him.

"Some bright reporter," said Morsell, "is sure to examine the facts someday and discover that it was not the hullabaloo of the boycott that desegregated Montgomery city buses, but a court case won by the NAACP."

The real question, however, was money. King's mass meetings in churches across the South were draining away dollars that otherwise would have come to the association. Furthermore, many influential Baptist ministers in the South who had been NAACP leaders were defecting to SCLC (Southern Christian Leadership Conference) and holding fund-raising rallies for King. NAACP and SCLC were joined in a war against the common enemy, but they were divided by intramural skirmishes over the wherewithall to wage that war.

King was sensitive to the problem and moved to head off conflict. One morning, Wilkins called his "cabinet" to a meeting in the conference room. Seated at the conference table were Dr. King and the SCLC vice-president, Ralph Abernathy. King and I shook hands warmly. We had met before, during the bus boycott, in a New York hotel room with Muste and Rustin. King had come up for a rest from the battlefield. He seemed surprised to see me. Apparently, he had not heard that I was on the NAACP staff. I had seen Abernathy only in photographs with King.

Wilkins sat at the head of the table. He puffed on his expensive cigar, smiled, and began the meeting with tongue in cheek.

"Dr. King and Dr. Abernathy, we are honored to have the leaders of the Negro struggle visiting the house of W.E.B. DuBois and James Weldon Johnson and Walter White. What can we do for you?"

King also smiled and responded without hesitation: "Well, Mr. Wilkins, Ralph and I are flattered to be here and to have the greats from the dark past looking down upon us from these hallowed walls. What we came for is to try to work out a modus operandi through which both the NAACP and the SCLC can thrive and prosper."

Wilkins chuckled. "From what I hear, Dr. King, you and the SCLC seem to be prospering pretty well."

"We're not doing all that well," Martin said. "We have to spend a lot to make a little. We're not a big organization. We don't have the great network of branches that you have."

Gloster Current laughed and said, "Martin, you don't really mean that." The sparring over, they got down to business.

"What do you suggest, Martin?" Wilkins asked.

"Well, as I understand it, the NAACP's lifeline is its branches and its membership drives. Our lifeline is church rallies and the collections taken up there. I propose that the SCLC refrain from becoming a membership organization and concentrate on church rallies as its financial base, urging people who attend those rallies to join the NAACP. As a quid pro quo, I suggest that NAACP not concentrate on rallies, but urge its members to attend our rallies and support our work."

Gloster laughed again. "We can't agree to anything like that," he said. "We hold rallies, too; that's a basic part of our operation."

Wilkins nodded agreement.

"We're not saying you can't *hold* church rallies," Ralph Abernathy said. "It's a question of areas of concentration. You concentrate on one thing; we concentrate on another."

Current shook his head vigorously. There was considerable back and forth on this point before King showed signs of irritation.

"All right, all right! We can't reach an understanding, so SCLC will go ahead and become a membership organization, and we'll have all-out competition for members and funds all across the country."

"No, no," said Wilkins quickly. "We don't want that. Let's discuss it some more."

The discussion went on for some time and concluded in cordiality, but without agreement.

In the ensuing months, I basically twiddled my thumbs. I wrote memoranda to Wilkins seeking approval for program activities and they gathered dust on his desk. The association's more than fourteen hundred branches were all too often mere collection agencies, signing up members once a year, collecting dues, and holding annual freedom fund banquets under the slogan "Completely Free by Sixty-three."

In a lengthy memorandum to Wilkins, I suggested that to approach the goal of freedom a good deal more needed to be done. What I proposed was that we identify the problem areas affecting black Americans, define the objectives in each area, designate the methods likely to be most effective in each, and indicate who should do it and establish a timetable. In short, for each problem, there should be answers to the questions: what, how, who, where, and when. I outlined several problem areas and suggested that the program be worked out in much more detail and the branches be asked to launch activities in selected areas simultaneously. The national office would coordinate the program, monitoring and evaluating as it proceeded.

Upon reading the memo, Wilkins called to say that he thought it very interesting, and he wanted to discuss it with one or two people and he would get back to me. The "getting back to" never occurred. The document languished on his desk, along with the others I had sent.

I busied myself speaking at branch rallies and freedom fund dinners around the country and conducting a leadership training institute for branches on Long Island.

Meanwhile, my wife's mother had died. It was a sad time for Lula, but death for Mrs. Peterson was merciful; life is not much fun for invalids.

Winnie had come to town to visit her brother, who lived in New York. It was her second trip to the city since I had remarried. She had also remarried, and raising and loving a family of four stepchildren gave real meaning to her life. She and I had dinner together on both occasions, and hours of warm conversation. The years had eased the hurt. The bond between us was not yet broken, but of course there was Lula.

Out of the blue, a thunderbolt struck NAACP headquarters. On February 1, 1960, four black freshmen students in Greensboro, North Carolina, had conducted a sit-in at a Woolworth lunch counter, asking for hot dogs and coffee. Four well-mannered collegians seeking a traditional snack and declining to leave when refused service had an electric effect on the nation.

At closing time, they left their seats at the counter and visited the Greensboro NAACP chairman, Dr. George Simkins, a dentist. They planned to return to the Woolworth counter the next day, and the next, and they wanted help. Simkins, though an NAACP official, called CORE—an action that, when it became known, did not endear him to the association. He had been familiar with CORE's sit-ins since the early forties and thought they would have the expertise to be of greatest help to those youngsters.

CORE had two field persons at the time—James T. McCain, who was black, and Gordon Carey, white. McCain was on jury duty in his home town of Sumter, South Carolina. So Jimmy Robinson sent Carey in response to the call for assistance. Zipping into town, Gordon set up a nonviolence training institute. The number of students participating in sit-ins in Greensboro grew, and television cameras were there to flash the story to the nation.

Students in black colleges across the South saw on the tube the events in Greensboro. They then went out and did likewise. Carey and McCain moved from campus to campus, conducting training institutes.

Thus, a mass movement among black students of unprecedented proportions was born. There were sit-ins and there were marches and there was singing. There were arrests and bail-outs and rearrests. In living rooms throughout the land, America sat on the edge of its seat, watching the unfolding drama.

One conservative editor, James J. Kilpatrick, of the *Richmond News-Leader*, saw in the scenes being enacted a reversal of images. Sitting peacefully at lunch counters were well-dressed black college students, courteous and polite, textbooks under arms, quietly asking for service. Coming in to taunt them were whites—rowdy, dirty, uncouth, violent. "Gad," Kilpatrick concluded, "it gives one pause."

This new image presented by black youth did not immediately erase the stereotypes in the minds of their adversaries. In Orangeburg, South Carolina, for instance, when several hundred marching students, led by Tom Gaither, a local CORE chairman, were arrested, their personal belongings were taken from them as they were being processed. Among the things taken from them were school books, notebooks, and slide rules. One of the city cops was fascinated by the slide rule. He pulled the sliding part out one side, then out the other, turned it over, squinted his eyes, and scrutinized it carefully. Then he shook his head and held the contraption before his partner and said, "Damndest switchblade I ever saw."

There were no switchblades and all the violence was on the other side. This new surge of nonviolent activity was without question inspired by the example of Martin Luther King, Jr., in Montgomery. Nonviolence was now a "respectable" tactic, the mightiest weapon for the weaponless.

Southern black college youth were transfigured. Rejecting inequality and acting as equals, they were now indeed the equals of anyone. A whole people shared joyously in that sunburst of equality. Crime figures dropped where action commenced; hope had been reborn.

They were not a part of the SCLC; most of them had never even met King. They were not in CORE; their only contact with that organization had been through Gordon Carey and his training institutes. Some were, or had been, members of youth chapters of the NAACP, but they were not acting under the banner of the NAACP. They were acting as themselves, free, autonomous.

In most cases, college administrators searched their souls and finally backed up their bold students for doing what they wanted to do themselves. There were, however, exceptions such as Dr. Felton Clark, president of Southern University in Baton Rouge, Louisiana, who suspended and expelled demonstrating students.

If the first spark had been in Montgomery, the second spark, the student movement, was nationwide. Northern blacks and white allies joined in the fray by boycotting the variety chain stores whose southern lunch counters were segregated.

The nonviolent movement had seemed to flounder after Montgomery. Other boycotts had been conducted by Dr. King and SCLC, but none had fired the imagination of the country as the first one had. Now, however, the imagination was flaming bright and hot.

When the summer of 1960 came, the southern students gathered in Atlanta to coordinate their efforts. They organized the Student Non-Violent Coordinating Committee (SNCC), with Marion Barry as its first chairman.* The ideological leader of SNCC, its spiritual father, was a young Methodist minister from Nashville, the Reverend James Lawson. Jim Lawson was an exceedingly impressive man—intelligent, courageous, and statesmanlike. He had a thorough grasp and a deep feel for the principles of nonviolence, having come out of FOR about a decade after I did.

Thoughts of retooling to meet the new challenge engulfed CORE. The dream that had made our hearts beat since 1942 was in 1960 a reality.

Jimmy Robinson was skilled at fund raising, a tiger on details, and as fiercely dedicated as any person alive. But he was unprepossessing and could not lead Gideon's army, nor sound the call for battle. Furthermore, he was white. If CORE was to be at the center of the struggle, its leader and spokesperson had to be black. That was the conclusion of the staff and the National Action Council, most of the members of which were white. The decision was unanimous, and it precipitated a palace rebellion that removed Jimmy as executive secretary while he was out of the country on a Mediterranean cruise with his new wife.

I was made aware of the rebellion from the beginning by one of its

*Marion Barry is now mayor of Washington, D.C.

194   LAY BARE THE HEART

leaders, the treasurer—my wife, Lula. I thought of Jimmy Robinson at
Jack Spratt Coffee Shop, eighteen and a half years earlier. And of Boys'
Fellowship House and Mrs. Edgar Lee Masters, and of the apartment on
South Ellis Avenue. I thought of the lonely years between 1949 and 1960
when Robinson, Jim Peck, and Lula kept the organization going when it
seemed to be going nowhere. My heart sorrowed for Jimmy Robinson,
but I did nothing to stop the coup I knew had to be staged.

The National Action Council and its steering committee were unanimous on the ouster action, but the search committee could not agree on a
successor. As CORE's founder and a participant in its councils most of the
time since its beginning, I had the inside track. A black woman on the
committee opposed my selection on the grounds that I had a white wife.
She suggested, instead, that the post be offered to Dr. Martin Luther
King, Jr. The other members of the search committee were of a mind that
the only conceivable way that would be possible would be through a merger of CORE and SCLC. They felt certain that such a notion would not
prove feasible. Nevertheless, the committee's chairman, Val Coleman, was
dispatched to Atlanta to broach the idea to King. King's response, as
expected, was that he could not possibly merge SCLC, a religious organization, with CORE, a secular organization.

Orchestrating the whole process was CORE's national chairman,
Charles Oldham, a young white St. Louis attorney. Oldham phoned to
tell me that he had received a letter from A. J. Muste, indicating an urgent
desire to talk with him before a decision was made on a successor to
Robinson. Oldham chose to ignore the letter and take before the National
Action Council the majority recommendation of the search committee:
that I be offered the job as national director of CORE. The offer and
acceptance after New Year's 1961 were merely formalities.

What was not routine was talking with Wilkins. After the torrential
events of 1960, he might now consider CORE a rival organization, and
with me at its head, it could become a dangerous competitor. There would
be, too, inevitable staff eyes hurling unspoken charges of turncoat and
traitor. I delayed as long as possible, and then in the middle of January
went to speak to him in his office.

Wilkins sat in his "judge's seat," eyes narrowed to fend off the smoke
from the elegant cigar he held in his long fingers.

"Jim, I wondered when you were going to come in to talk," he said
casually.

"What?" I asked, shocked.

"Oh, I've known for two weeks that you're going to leave us and head
up CORE. I debated whether I should call you in or wait for you to call. I
decided to wait."

"How did you know?"

He smiled. "CORE's general counsel had a couple of drinks at a cocktail
party over the weekend and spilled the beans."

"I founded CORE, you know."

"Yes, I know. In 1942," Wilkins said. "Mind you, I can't say that I blame you for leaving, after what you've been through in this can of worms we have here.

"There are only two things I want to say to you, aside from wishing you luck. First, I should have listened to Minnie.* She said, 'Roy, clean house. They're all Walter White's people, loyal to him.** Get them out and put your own people in, who'll be loyal to you. If you don't do it, you won't be able to do anything.' I should have followed her advice then, in the honeymoon period with my board. I can't do it now; it's too late. If I'd done it, things would have been different for you during your almost two years here. Or maybe you'd have been among those I would have brought in at the outset."

Wilkins looked out the window and a wistful smile slyly edged into his face.

"The second thing is this: you're going to be riding a mustang pony—while I'm riding a dinosaur."

CHAPTER 17

THE FREEDOM RIDE BEGINS

THANKS TO MARTIN LUTHER King, Jr., and the student sit-in movement that had roared across the South, nonviolence was now a popular concept. When one said one would use the nonviolence tactic, no one asked, "What are you—some kind of nut or something?" The nationwide movement of which we had dreamed since 1942 was now under way—in its infancy, it is true, but nevertheless under way.

Hundreds of college students had gone to jail, but they all had been bailed out right away. There was no "filling up the jail" yet. The action was still regional and sporadic, though well covered in the media. To some extent, CORE was already identified with the movement; field secretaries Gordon Carey and Jim McCain had moved about the South in timely fashion, conducting institutes on nonviolence in cities where action was taking place. CORE had spearheaded the highly successful nationwide picketing and boycotts of the variety chain stores, which refused to serve blacks at their lunch counters in southern states.

My small staff—Marvin Rich, community relations director; Jimmy Robinson, fund raiser; McCain and Carey, field secretaries—and I sat down in the tiny CORE office at 38 Park Row, New York City, to ponder the next step. It was February 1, 1961, my first day at my desk as national director of CORE. Several letters were already before me from blacks in

*Mrs. Roy Wilkins
**Walter White was Wilkins's predecessor as executive secretary of the NAACP.

the South, complaining that despite the Irene Morgan Supreme Court decision in 1946 and the Boynton decision in 1960, when they sat on a front seat of an interstate bus or tried to use waiting room facilities other than those consigned to blacks, they were beaten, ejected, or arrested. "What do decisions of the United States Supreme Court mean?" they asked.

Gordon Carey proposed a second Journey of Reconciliation patterned after the first one conducted in 1947, with a small interracial group riding interstate buses through the South with the blacks sitting on front seats and the whites on back seats, refusing to move when ordered. Carey suggested that at every rest stop the whites go into the waiting room "for colored" and blacks into the waiting room "for white." Unlike the 1947 Journey of Reconciliation, the target would be segregated bus terminal facilities as well as segregated seating on the buses. Also, unlike the previous project, he suggested that we go into the deep South, including Georgia, Alabama, Mississippi, and Louisiana.

I thought it a capital idea, a superb answer to the question "What next?" But it should not be called a Journey of Reconciliation. Such a name would be out of touch with the scrappy nonviolent movement that had emerged. The cry, I said, was not for "reconciliation" but for "*freedom.*" It would be called the "Freedom Ride."

Marvin Rich, Gordon Carey, and Jim McCain instantly got their heads together to work out the plans for the Freedom Rides of 1961. Jimmy Robinson did not participate in the excitement of this planning. I understood that, for I knew what torment must have been tearing at his soul. An executive secretary of an organization cannot be demoted to simple fund raiser working under the supervision of his successor and then be expected to function joyously. When deposed, a person has to be fired, not demoted. It was clear that he had accepted the fund-raising job only until he found some position outside of CORE. In the meantime, almost anyone in his situation would drag his feet at best, and at worst, try sabotage. I viewed the anguish of Robinson's plight with an overwhelming sadness.

In a way, we were still thinking in the small terms of the CORE of past years, the premovement days. The perception of my staff was not of a mass movement, but of a small, tightly disciplined cadre of well-trained individuals. Nor was their thinking at this point in terms of something that would galvanize the entire black community and drive it into action. For instance, when a young Harlem intellectual who had heard of the Freedom Ride plan came into my office to meet with my staff and me and suggested that we hold a kick-off rally at Harlem's Abyssinian Baptist Church, where Adam Clayton Powell was the minister, some staff reactions were negative. Marvin Rich said he was unalterably opposed to holding any meeting in Harlem. (This was an era, it must be remembered, when most civil rights activists sought not to improve conditions in the ghetto but to wipe out the ghetto itself. The demand was not for better schools in the ghetto, but for getting black children into schools outside the ghetto; not for wiping out slum housing in Harlem, but for allowing blacks to get housing elsewhere.) I said to Marvin that a meeting at Abyssinian Baptist Church would help to get the black community in on the ground floor of this burgeoning new nonviolent movement.

Marvin Rich replied, "We are not interested in the black community. We are interested only in the *activists* in the black community."

I studied Marvin's face for a while and decided to defer this critical battle within CORE until a later date, after the Freedom Ride.

The detailed plans for the Freedom Ride evolved quickly. We would recruit from twelve to fourteen persons, call them to Washington, D.C., for a week of intensive training and preparation, and then embark on the Ride. Half would go by Greyhound and half by Trailways. We would leave Washington, D.C., on May 4, 1961, and follow an itinerary that would take us through Virginia, the Carolinas, Georgia, Alabama, and Mississippi. We hoped we would arrive in New Orleans on May 17, the anniversary of the Supreme Court's desegregation decision.

In March, I wrote to the president of the United States, the attorney general, the director of the Federal Bureau of Investigation, the chairman of the Interstate Commerce Commission, and the presidents of the Greyhound and Trailways corporations, informing them of our plans and enclosing copies of our itinerary. This was in line with the Ghandian principle of being open and aboveboard, informing officials—even those unfriendly to the cause—of what we intended to do, how, and when. No replies came. (Later, however, when the Freedom Rides exploded into the national conscience in Alabama, Robert F. Kennedy also exploded, but to his staff, angrily shouting, "How could something like this come about without our knowing about it in advance?" Presumably, my letter had never reached his desk. Presumably, too, this led Bobby to direct stricter FBI surveillance of civil rights organizations.)

The band of thirteen recruits gathered in Washington, DC., in the latter part of April for the training sessions. The group included, in addition to myself, Dr. Walter Bergman, a sixty-year-old white professor of education at the University of Michigan, and his wife, Frances; James Peck, a pacifist and CORE activist from the early days, and a veteran of the 1947 Journey of Reconciliation; the Reverend B. Elton Cox, an eloquent young black minister; Charlotte DeVries, a white writer from New York; Albert Bigelow, a navy captain during World War II; Hank Thomas, a Howard University senior from St. Augustine, Florida; Jimmy McDonald, a folk singer and part-time CORE staff member from New York; John Lewis, a black student from Tennessee Bible Institute in Nashville; Genevieve Hughes, a young field secretary recently hired by CORE; Joe Perkins, a CORE staff member; and Ed Blankenheim, a young white CORE activist.

I conducted an orientation session to explain the rationale for this adventure and provided an overview of what we were going to do, how we were going to do it, and the most optimistic and pessimistic outcomes possible. Then an attorney took the podium. He provided a succinct statement of the federal and state laws covering interstate transportation. He detailed the Supreme Court's rulings on the issues and summarized the current situation. From his viewpoint, he told us what we should do if and when we were arrested and discussed our legal rights. Next came a social scientist, who elaborated on the mores and folkways of the areas through which we would be riding and described the lengths to which the local populace probably would go to force compliance with their sacrosanct racial customs. The scholar was followed by a social activist who described what really was going to happen to us, including clobberings and possibly death.

Extensive discussions followed each presentation. The discussions were neither academic nor undisciplined rapping; each person, after all, was offering to put his or her life on the line. The air was filled with electricity, not frivolity.

There were intense role-playing sessions—sociodramas—with some of the group playing the part of Freedom Riders sitting at simulated lunch counters or sitting on the front seats of a make-believe bus. Others acted out the roles of functionaries, adversaries, or observers. Several played the role of white hoodlums coming in to beat up the Freedom Riders on the buses or at lunch counters in the terminals. Since the dramas were for survival, not entertainment, the action was all too realistic. People were thrown out of bus seats and clubbed, knocked off lunch counter stools and stomped. Realism was imperative so that we could learn how to reduce the probability of serious and permanent damage in the real-life situation facing us.

After each scene, there was vigorous discussion about what the Freedom Riders could have done better to enhance their protest or to protect their persons from injury. Then roles were reversed and the scenes played over again. After a week of such arduous preparation, I felt that everyone in the group was prepared for anything that might happen, including the ultimate. On the night of May 3, 1961, the eve of our departure, I took the whole group to a downtown Chinese restaurant for dinner. Someone referred to the meal as the "last supper."

Over dessert and coffee, I spoke briefly from my chair at the head of the table. There were no theatrics, no melodrama; the situation itself was too frought with emotion for embellishment. I told the group, which had become like a family, that no one was obligated to go on this trip except possibly me. There was still time for any person to decide not to go. Everyone should ask himself or herself at that point whether or not he or she really wanted to go. If the decision was negative, there would be no recrimination, no blame, and CORE would pay transportation back home. Reverend Cox suggested a moment of prayer. I countered with a suggestion for a moment of silence, since some were agnostics or atheists. After about five minutes, during which the only sound at the table was an occasional sipping from a cup of coffee, I stated that no one had to announce a decision right then. He or she could tell me later that night or just not show up at the bus terminal in the morning, whichever was easiest.

The next morning, everyone was there. About half of the group was at the Greyhound terminal and the rest across the street at Trailways. With us on one of the buses was a brilliant and courageous young black journalist, Simeon Booker, representing Johnson Publishing Company (publishers of *Jet* and *Ebony* magazines).

The ride through Virginia was routine. The "for colored" and "for white" signs had been taken down the previous day. There were no arrests and no violence. "They knew we were coming and they baked a cake," one of the riders observed.

In North Carolina, the signs were still up but were not enforced. At the last stop in the Tarheel State, Jim Peck bought a bottle of fine imported brandy to sustain him and possibly me through the coming crises. At the first stop in South Carolina, Jim was arrested for illegally transporting a bottle of alcoholic beverage across the state line. That delayed one bus for a while. After the arrest, I bailed Jim out, and though knowing my lawyer would have conniptions, I urged him to jump bail so the Freedom Ride could continue on schedule.

At another stop in South Carolina, we began to taste southern hate. At Rock Hill, John Lewis approached the waiting room "for whites." Leaning against the doorjamb were two tough-looking white youths with leather jackets and ducktail haircuts.

"Get to the other side, boy," ordered one of the young men as he jerked his thumb in the direction of the "for colored" waiting room entrance, "where the niggers go."

"I have a right to go in here," said John with ministerial dignity, "on grounds of the Supreme Court decision in the Boynton case."

Those thugs did not know what Boynton was. They probably did not know what the Supreme Court was. John attempted to walk through the door between them and was struck and knocked down. They began to kick and stomp him as he covered up in the manner learned in our role playing.

A city policeman stood by, watching but not interfering. Albert Bigelow, the ex-navy captain, tried to intervene by stepping between John and his attackers. The two youths slugged him, but they had to hit him several times before he dropped to one knee.

Bigelow, like John Lewis, did not strike back. Only after Bigelow fell to the ground did the policeman show any interest in the proceedings.

He walked up and said to the two hoodlums, "All right, boys. Y'all've done about enough now, why don'cha y'all go on home now."

The Ride went on, with Band-Aids sealing two cuts over John Lewis's eyebrows.

At every overnight stop on the Ride, CORE had arranged rallies in the black community in support of the Freedom Ride. In churches and colleges, each Freedom Rider was introduced to the capacity audience amidst thunderous applause. The Reverend Elton B. Cox and I spoke. Elton B. Cox was an eloquent preacher-orator who brought the "amens" rising to a crescendo throughout his talks. On the early part of the Freedom Ride, he earned the nickname derived from a contraction of his name: "Beltin' Elton." His was a tough act to follow.

In Georgia, as in North Carolina, the segregation signs were not enforced on the day of our trip. We encountered neither arrest nor violence. They, too, knew we were coming and made appropriate preparations.

To insure that all was quiet on the southern front in Atlanta, I called Dr. Martin Luther King, Jr., to inform him that we had arrived on schedule, and that our advance CORE organizers had made the arrangements for us to stay overnight in the dormitories at Atlanta University. We would have two nights and a full day in Atlanta and hoped that we could meet with him during that time.

Dr. King invited the entire group to have dinner with him the next evening. He asked us to meet him at an excellent black-owned restaurant in Atlanta. Everyone was delighted at the invitation.

At the dinner, the Freedom Riders recounted in graphic detail their experiences thus far on the trip. Dr. King listened in a very relaxed and interested fashion and observed that this was nonviolent direct action at its very best. He said that he was proud of it and pleased to be a member of the CORE National Advisory Board. He wished us well on the rest of the trip and invited us to call him if there was any way that he could help further.

The waiter left a large bill, for the restaurant was not inexpensive. After waiting a reasonable period of time for our host to pick up the check, I finally reached slowly for it, certain King would beat me to the punch. He made no move, so to my surprise I found myself picking up the tab.

King shook hands warmly with each Freedom Rider and we returned to Atlanta University, heartened by this contact with the man who had become, without question, the symbol of the civil rights movement in America.

That evening, we met for a final briefing and the division of responsibilities for the most ominous leg of the journey, the ride through Alabama. As the leader of the Ride, I announced to the group that at each rest stop through Alabama I myself would lead the testings at the bus terminals for the riders on the first bus—the Trailways. I assigned Jim Peck, also experienced in nonviolence, to lead the testing on the other. Discipline had to be tight, and decisions had to be made on the spot. Where feasible, we would consult in making those decisions; where that was not possible, we would make the decisions ourselves and request strict compliance. Everyone agreed. The meeting adjourned after we all embraced in a huddle, singing, "We Shall Overcome."

That night I was awakened with the news that I had a long-distance phone call from my mother, and that she was on the line at the telephone in the office on the first floor. I threw on trousers, shirt, and shoes and went downstairs, my head whirling with the certain knowledge of the nature of the call awaiting me.

Ten days earlier, during the training session in Washington, D.C., my father lay in a bed at Freedman's Hospital, in serious condition with medical complications following surgery to remove a cancerous growth on the tongue. In addition to that acute illness, he also suffered from diabetes. He thought long and hard, probably recalling his own childhood and youth growing up in South Carolina and Georgia, sixty and seventy years ago. Finally, he looked up at me through eyes dulled by strong pain killers and dimmed by the knowledge of his own terminal illness. He said, "Well, son, I think you will be all right through Virginia, North Carolina, South Carolina, and maybe even Georgia. But in 'Bama, they will doubtless take a potshot at you. With all my heart, I hope they miss. Can you leave me a copy of your itinerary?"

I complied.

"Son," he said, "I wish you wouldn't go. But at the same time, I am more proud than I have ever been in my life, because you are going. Please try to survive."

I took the receiver to hear from my mother's lips that which I already knew in my heart—my father had just died and I must return immediately to help bury him.

I cannot really explain the confusion of emotions that took me over at that moment. There was, of course, the incomparable sorrow and pain. But, frankly, there was also a sense of reprieve, for which I hated myself. Like everyone else, I was afraid of what lay in store for us in Alabama, and now that I was to be spared participation in it, I was relieved, which embarrassed me to tears.

All Freedom Riders rose early so we could meet together at breakfast prior to boarding the buses. I informed them that just a few minutes before they boarded a bus to Alabama I would be boarding a flight back to Washington, D.C., to bury my father, but that I would rejoin them as soon as the funeral was over. In the meantime, I wanted them to keep in touch with me by telephone at my parents' home in Washington.

As usual, when a deceased person has suffered so much, the family's bereavement was softened by a relief that the pain was over. Mother emphatically stated that daddy had willed the timing of his death, which he knew to be inevitable, in order to bring me back before the trip through Alabama. Each day, he would unfold my itinerary and squint at it, saying, "Well, let me see where Junior is today."

Mother said he nodded with satisfaction until the fatal day and hung tenaciously to life and consciousness. When the itinerary told him that the next morning I would head into Alabama, he said, "Oh!" Then he released his grip on life, she said, and slipped away. She believed until her death that dad had consciously done that in an effort to save my life.

From all sources—my staff, the Freedom Riders themselves, and the press—word came to me of a carnage in Alabama. When the first bus had crossed the Alabama state line, a half dozen young white toughs had boarded with their weapons in sight—pieces of chain, brass knuckles, blackjacks, and pistols. Shortly thereafter, the driver pulled the vehicle off the road and brought it to a stop.

"I ain't movin' this bus another foot," he said, "until the niggers get into the back of the bus where they belong."

No one moved.

The thugs then got up and began beating the black Freedom Riders who were seated in the front.

Doctor Bergman and Jim Peck tried to intervene.

"Here, you stop that!" one of them said. "These men haven't done anything to you."

"They have a right to sit where they want to," the other said. "You leave them alone."

Peck was hit with an uppercut that lifted him off the floor and deposited him unconscious in the aisle. Bergman was knocked down and repeatedly kicked in the head. As his wife, who was also on the bus, described it, "They used my husband's head for a football." Dr. Bergman later suffered a cerebral hemorrhage, which put him in a wheelchair permanently. His doctors agreed that the stroke was a direct result of the beating he had suffered.

The blacks were then thrown bodily into the back of the bus. The driver moved the blood-splattered vehicle on. One woman passenger, not a Freedom Rider, exclaimed, "Doggone, it looks like there has been a hog killing on this bus!"

At Birmingham, the Freedom Riders entered the terminal to test its facilities in prearranged fashion. Jim Peck, who led the testing, was accosted by a mob of whites, who beat him and left him unconscious, lying in a pool of his own blood. They probably thought him dead. It required fifty-six stitches and prolonged hospitalization to close the cuts on his head. The Reverend Fred Shuttlesworth, an associate of Dr. King, came to the terminal, got Peck to the hospital, and saw him through the terrible ordeal.

At Anniston, Alabama, the bus carrying Freedom Riders stopped at the terminal. A mob of angry whites was waiting with lethal weapons in hand. Quite properly deciding that discretion was the better part of valor, the Freedom Riders informed the driver that they were not leaving the bus at Anniston. The driver started his motor, preparing to move on. Members of the mob, with knives and ice picks, slashed and punctured the tires on the bus. Mingling with that mob were several uniformed policemen, laughing and chatting with its members and not interfering. The bus moved on, but just outside of town its tires blew out and it came to a halt. The mob had followed the bus in cars and now surrounded it and held its doors shut. They broke one of the windows and hurled a firebomb into the vehicle. It filled with smoke and burst into flames.

One of the Freedom Riders on that bus was Albert Bigelow, the former navy captain and combat veteran from World War II. Cool and schooled in making decisions under fire, he took charge. No doubt, he saved lives. Bigelow got the emergency door of the bus open and began evacuating its passengers in orderly fashion, deciding that it was better to face the mob outside than certain incineration inside.

One of the policemen who was among the mob then fired his revolver into the air. As if upon signal, the mob pulled away from the bus, allowing the front door to open. Freedom Riders stumbled out, choking and coughing, and fell on the ground, writhing and gasping for air. Fred Shuttlesworth and several men from his church arrived on the scene and got the Freedom Riders to the hospital for treatment for severe smoke inhalation.

The Greyhound bus burned to the ground. Some enterprising photographer got the picture of that coach in flames. I think that photograph was on the front page of every newspaper in the world.

When I saw the photograph of the burning bus on the front page of the *Washington Post,* I called my staff in New York and directed them to superimpose that photograph on the flame on the torch of the Statue of Liberty immediately and to use that composite picture as the symbol of the Freedom Ride. And so it was.

I got a call at home from Diane Nash, a leader of the Student Non-Violent Coordinating Committee (SNCC) in Nashville, Tennessee. In line with the unwritten pact between CORE and SNCC that neither organization would move in on the other's project without permission, Diane said to me, "Your group of Freedom Riders are so badly chewed up that they cannot go on now. Would you have any objections to members of the Nashville Student Movement, which is SNCC, going in and taking up the Ride where CORE left off?"

"You realize it may be suicide," I replied.

"We fully realize that," she said, with a touch of irritation in her voice, "but we can't let them stop us with violence. If we do, the movement is dead. Whenever we start a drive, all they will have to do is roll in the violence and we will turn over and play dead. Your group has been badly battered; let me send in fresh nonviolent troops to carry the Ride on. Let me bring in Nashville students to pick up the baton and run with it."

"All right, Diane, do it. After the funeral day after tomorrow, I'll fly down and join you wherever you are. Keep in touch with me by phone so I'll know where to come. If you can't reach me, call my office; I'll be in constant touch with them."

The young SNCC men and women were beaten and chased in Alabama, but they persisted with all the courage and determination characteristic of their young organization. The Department of Justice tried to help. Assistant Attorney General John Seigenthaler was down there on the spot, showing personal courage beyond the call of duty. He physically stopped some beatings and rescued a fleeing woman student from a pursuing white mob.

I called my office in New York and instructed my staff to get in touch with the New Orleans CORE chapter leaders and ask them to quickly recruit, train, and send to Montgomery a contingent of young CORE members from New Orleans. Quite frankly, although I welcomed the intervention of SNCC, a concern burned within me. I could not let CORE's great new program slip from its grasp and be taken over by others.

After my father's funeral, I flew to Montgomery to join the SNCC and CORE youth. Martin Luther King, Jr., had flown in from Atlanta to speak at a rally at the First Baptist Church in support of the Freedom Ride. Ralph Abernathy was also there. Shuttlesworth, with two men from his church, met me at the airport in Montgomery. He told me that there was a riot going on, with large bands of frenzied white men roaming the streets and now closing in on the First Baptist Church where King, Abernathy, Wyatt Walker (executive director of the SCLC), Diane Nash, and the young SNCC and CORE Freedom Riders were being held under siege.

"Can you get me into that church, Fred?" I asked.

"Wrong question, Jim," replied Fred Shuttlesworth. "The only question to ask is: how will I get you in?"

When the courageous band of thirteen had met in Washington, D.C., at the end of April, I had not dreamed that in a few short weeks a new kind of civil war would rock the nation—a war not "without violence," but with violence on only one side. We had not dreamed that Jim Crow would so quickly be stood on its head and its supporters driven into trenches in a do-or-die battle to save it. But so it was.

CHAPTER 18

SIEGE IN MONTGOMERY

ON THAT MAY MORNING in 1961, Fred Shuttlesworth revved the engine on his large car and nosed it toward the First Baptist Church. The streets of Montgomery were empty except for roving bands of shirt-sleeved white men who shouted obscenities as they raced by.

Several blocks before the church, the streets were clogged with crowds of men waving small Confederate flags and shouting rebel yells. We were forced to stop and the mob rocked the car back and forth, their intentions clear. Fred shoved the automatic gear shift into reverse, heavy-footed the accelerator, and we zoomed backward. Screeching to a halt, he made a U-turn on two wheels with tires whining and tried another approach to the church.

There was no more success this time. Another U-turn headed us to a black-owned taxi stand several blocks away.

"I have Jim Farmer," said Shuttlesworth. "He has got to get to that church. How can I outflank the mob and get him there?" We were directed on a circuitous route and instructed to park the car, walk through a graveyard, and approach the back of the church from that direction. The mob might not have covered that entrance yet.

Exiting from the cemetery, we found we were too late. The mob was already there, blocking even that entrance to the church.

"Jim, we've got no choice. We have got to go right through them," said Fred. Without waiting for a response, he proceeded to walk right into the mob. Fred Shuttlesworth was a small man, short and thin, but never before in my life had I seen such physical courage.

He walked right into the mob, elbowing the hysterical white men aside, saying, "Out of the way. Let me through. Step aside."

Incredibly, the members of the mob obeyed. I walked behind Fred, trying to hide in his shadow. Looking back on it now, I can only guess that this was an example of the "crazy nigger" syndrome—"man, that nigger is crazy; leave him alone; don't mess with him."

When we entered the church, Martin Luther King, Jr., Ralph Abernathy, and Diane Nash were huddled in a corner. They greeted me and King said, "I have just been on the telephone with Bobby Kennedy. He has sent a group of U.S. marshals into town and is now trying to get Governor Patterson to declare martial law and bring in the National Guard."

Seconds later, the phone rang, and Martin went into the office to answer. Some time later, King emerged from the office looking very weary. He called me to him and said, "The attorney general asks that you halt the Freedom Rides and have a cooling-off period to give him time to try to work things out."

"No, Martin," I replied. "I won't stop it now. If I do, we'll just get words and promises."

"But, Jim," King said in his slow southern drawl, "don't you think that maybe the Freedom Ride has already made its point and now should be called off, as the attorney general suggests?"

"Just a minute" I said. "Let me check with Diane."

I walked a few steps away, called Diane Nash over, told her the substance of the attorney general's request, and of my conversation with Dr. King.

Diane shook her head. "No," she said. "The Nashville Student Movement wants to go on. We can't stop it now, right after we've been clobbered."

I walked back to King and said, "My objective is not just to make a *point*, but to bring about a real change in the situation. We will continue the Ride until people can sit wherever they wish on buses and use the facilities in any waiting room available to the public. Please tell the attorney general that we have been cooling off for 350 years. If we cool off any more, we will be in a deep freeze. The Freedom Ride will go on."

King said, "I understand" and returned to the office, closing the door behind him. A few minutes later, he came out and said, "Well, I guess it's about time for the rally to start. The people are all here. Let's go upstairs."

Upstairs in the church sanctuary, the Freedom Riders had the entire congregation singing freedom songs, clapping their hands, and stomping their feet. The sounds of the mob outside could be heard clearly. The singing inside went through the whole freedom repertoire, ending with, "Ain't Gon' Let Nobody Turn Me 'Round" and "We Shall Overcome."

Wyatt Tee Walker, executive secretary of the SCLC, spoke first. Abernathy followed him. Both had the audience talking back to them, shouting "amen." I followed them, and King was the finale. After he finished, there were more freedom songs. I felt the entire audience was ready at that moment to board buses and ride into the Promised Land.

During the rest of that night we were under siege in the church. The mob was still screaming outside. At one point, they pounded on the basement door. Some of the men in the church had propped a chair against the door handle and backed chairs up to the door to impede the progress of would-be intruders. It was not long before the door was kicked open and the barriers knocked away. Angry white faces surged inside.

As if materializing out of empty space, U.S. marshals were there, blocking their path. No doubt, they had been waiting in one of the basement rooms and had stormed into action when the occasion demanded. Shoulder-to-shoulder, with clubs in hand, they forced the members of the mob back out the door, across the street, and dispersed them.

By morning, there was quiet outside. Martial law had been declared and steel-helmeted Alabama National Guardsmen patrolled the streets in Jeeps, with rifles in hand. Occasional gunfire could be heard. A curfew was enforced, and we proceeded, with permission and under guard, to the various homes to which we had been assigned to freshen up.

The next evening, we all met at the YMCA to take stock of the situation and plan our next steps. The SNCC and CORE youngsters were of one mind: the Freedom Ride would go on to Jackson and New Orleans. They asked King if he would go with them to Jackson.

"No, I can't go. You see, I'm on probation from my arrest in Atlanta."

The answer was not satisfactory to the youngsters. They scoffed at the matter of probation.

"I'm on probation too," said one.

"So am I," shouted another.

"Me, too," someone else yelled.

"We're all on probation," said someone else. "That doesn't stop us. We're in a war. Probation can't keep us from doing what we have to do."

No one had asked me whether I was going. They simply assumed that I was. After all, it was my show. Yet, I had other thoughts about it. I did not want to go and did not intend to, but hoped that I would be spared informing them of that until departure time the next day.

They continued to pressure King.

"What's your real reason? Why can't you go? You're the leader of this nonviolent movement. How can you stay home?"

"Well, now," said King, "I think I should choose the time and place of my Golgotha."

That statement evoked loud laughter and derisive comments. The meeting broke up as many of the youngsters got up from the floor where they were sitting and stormed out of the room, scornfully referring to King as "de Lawd." The CORE kids looked at me for a cue. I motioned them to silence and they said nothing.

I don't know what was going through Martin's mind at that time, but I know what was in mine. I was frankly terrified with the knowledge that the trip to Jackson might be the last trip any of us would ever take. I was not ready for that. Who, indeed, ever is?

I was not about to be critical of my distinguished colleague for declining to go when, unknown to the youngsters, I, too, had decided not to make the trip. It was only the pleading eyes and words of the teenage Doris Castle that persuaded me to get on that bus at the last minute.

In the morning, the courageous kids from Nashville and New Orleans, with a few who had come in from other cities, were prepared for departure. The tension was so heavy, it must have been greater than that felt by troops being dispatched to a battlefront where bombs were bursting and comrades were dying. These young men and women had no guns with which to defend themselves—no weapons at all, except those of the indomitable human spirit.

<hr>

CHAPTER 19

THE CUTTING EDGE

THE TWO YEARS FOLLOWING my release from Parchman State Penitentiary in Mississippi, in July 1961, were a crucible of the incredible. I lived lifetimes in those months. Eternity squeezed into days and hours stretched beyond all endurance. Those around me grew old and young simultaneously.

Sudden fame was an Alice-in-Wonderland world. Stepping off the Electra turbojet at LaGuardia Airport in New York, I was blinded by flashbulbs. Microphones were shoved in my face as newspersons jockeyed for position. Television cameras recorded my walk to the terminal as if each step were a stride into history. It was dizzying.

Inside the terminal, I was greeted by a deafening chorus of "We Shall Overcome," then the verse "Black and White Together" coming from more than a hundred lusty throats. Everyone wore a big button: "FREE-DOM NOW—CORE." A hoarse male voice began another song, based on a spiritual:

> Farmer is our leader,
> We shall not be moved,
> Farmer is our leader,
> We shall not be moved.
> Just like a tree that's
>   planted by the waters,
> We shall not be moved.

My eyes watered. I think all the passengers rushing to boarding gates stopped and gaped, and all the planes stopped flying.

A huge banner was unfurled: WELCOME HOME, BIG JIM. Lula, six months pregnant, was there and she picked Tami up so that our two-and-a-half-year-old child could see. Someone shouldered a path for them through the crowd. As they approached, a camera caught Tami, eyes stretched, pointing a finger as she asked, "Is that daddy?" I'd been away for three months. I hugged the two of them and kissed both as more flashbulbs exploded.

Amidst it all, Val Coleman strode around like a proud maestro, positioning electronic media persons here and there, promising individual interviews, and alerting everyone about a news conference at CORE headquarters the next morning. The skinny, blond Irishman who had been a member of the National Action Council since 1960, had quit a plush job as assistant director publicity manager at United Artists to work for CORE at less than half the salary. Volatile Val, now where the action was, assisted Marvin Rich in handling press relations for CORE.

Lula, Tami, and I were sitting in the back seat of a car being driven home. I thought of Winnie. Would she be proud of me now? Or embarrassed? Or ashamed? Struck by guilt at my thoughts, I squeezed Lula's hand. She squeezed back and snuggled closer, with Tami sitting on both our laps. We stopped to put in an appearance at a CORE demonstration. We were picketing someplace in midtown Manhattan about something—I don't remember where or what. The "freedom now" chants became louder as we joined the line. Picket signs were brought to us and Tami held hers with both hands. Marv and Val had notified the press, and they were there with their cameras.

The CORE office was the inside of an anthill—not chaos but purposeful haste and teeming industriousness. Everyone trotted, no one walked—no one, that is, except Jimmy Robinson, who walked but mostly sat at his desk brooding and poring over a draft of the next direct-mail appeal letter. He should not have been humiliated by being there, but the sky had fallen so suddenly that there had been no place for him to run.

The debris from the fall-out and the bus ride it propelled had so magically fertilized the soil that the organization was mushrooming in growth. Twenty chapters had become sixty, and every mail delivery brought requests for permission to start new ones.

By 1963, Jim McCain, whom I had made director of organization, had hired additional field staff to consolidate and absorb this new growth. Gordon Carey was made assistant to the national director, to help bear the administrative burdens since I was going to be away from my desk so much of the time. Marvin Rich would become community relations director, and Val Coleman his assistant.

Festering in my mind was a certain impossible situation. I had, in effect, been hired by my staff. If Jimmy Robinson had problems, so did I. In the tiny organization that CORE was prior to the coup, staff was on the National Action Council—the board of directors—and dominated it, for they had the information others lacked. If chairman Oldham had orchestrated the process of the overthrow, Marvin Rich and Gordon Carey had conceived it. How could I *direct* when those to be directed had been responsible for my employment? I had to seize control of my organization before it seized control of me, on top of everything else I now had to do.

The mail was stacked in neat piles on my desk, all opened and acknowledged by Clora Coleman, the superb secretary I had brought with me from NAACP. That which required handling had been dealt with by staff. My schedule was jam-packed with speaking engagements. I was going to be as busy as a one-armed paper hanger with the hives, but I didn't want to cancel a thing. There were requests for me to appear on radio and TV talk shows and panel discussions. On top of the list of engagements was a wire from Wilkins inviting me to address the NAACP convention then in session in Philadelphia. I put through a call to let him know that I would be there on the following morning to deliver the address as scheduled.

The Freedom Ride was not over. In line with my directive to Gordon Carey from the Mississippi jail, we were still pouring riders into the southern arena to face the lions. We were winning. The score was now: Christians (and Jews), 355—Lions, 0. And we were still coming.

There was a constant flow of applicants into the office, coming in for screening. Among them was a young, black middleweight boxer. The young pug walked into my office with just a hint of bobbing of head and shoulder, as if feinting for an opening, which revealed his profession. I would have guessed his occupation, even had he not been introduced.

"I want to be a Freedom Rider, Mr. Farmer," he said.

"Now look, killer," I ventured, "this is a nonviolent movement, you know."

"Yeah, I know. Nonviolent—like Martin Luther King. That's all right. I can do it."

"You're a fighter," I said. "Your fists are deadly weapons. What's going to happen if somebody throws a punch at you?"

The trim young man studied his fists for a minute and, with his head bobbing and weaving to punctuate his words, said "It's okay if they throw a punch at me, Mr. Farmer, but just tell 'em—don't ring a bell!"

I let him be a Rider, cautioning him that if the time came when he thought he might lose control, he should check with whoever was in charge for CORE and leave the project. We would pay his way home.

As he left, my mind swung to another athlete, bigger, stronger, and tougher than he: Jim Brown, the professional football player. It was said that Jim had taken a private Freedom Ride, flying to Alabama, boarding a bus, and sitting on a front seat.

The driver said, "Boy, get up out of that seat and get into the back of the bus where you belong."

Jim Brown neither moved nor spoke in reply.

"Boy, didn't you hear me?" the driver asked. "I said get up out of that seat and get in the back of this bus."

There was still no response from Brown.

"Boy, I ain't gon' to tell you no mo'. If you don' get up out of that seat, I'm gon' come over there and throw you into the back of this bus."

Jim Brown got to his feet, walked to the driver, grabbed him by his collar and tie, and jerked him up off the driver's seat.

"Look man," he said, "you made two mistakes. First, I ain't no boy. Second, I ain't one of Dr. King's nonviolent niggers. Now move this damn bus!"

The driver obeyed.

The phone kept jumping off the hook. Chapters were calling in from all over to announce new recruits for the Ride and to give detailed information for CORE records.

The Mississippi "lions" were losing, but they were just beginning to fight. The city officials of Jackson had agreed to the customary procedure in mass arrests, requiring only one or two typical cases to show for arraignment and trial and applying the findings in those cases to all the others.

Two weeks before the arraignment, though, the officials notified us through our lawyer, Jack Young, that they had changed their minds and were now demanding that all three hundred plus of the bailed-out Freedom Riders must be back in Jackson on the designated date on pain of forfeiting the $500 bond CORE had put up on each.

The Jackson city attorney was very frank; they were trying to bankrupt us. "We figure that if we can knock CORE out of the box," he told Jack Young, "we've broken the back of the so-called civil rights movement in the state of Mississippi; and that's what we intend to do."

Immediately, I put the organization on an emergency basis, canceling all leave and ordering that staff, including myself, be on call for duty around the clock and reachable by phone. Many of the Riders were mobile persons of tenuous roots, otherwise they might not have been able to volunteer to spend forty days in jail even for so compelling a cause as ours. Tracking them down would be no small task.

Yet, locating the scattered army was perhaps the least of our problems. There was also the matter of getting them to central checkpoints, onto chartered buses to Jackson, where we would have to feed and house them for an indeterminate stay, and then get them back to their homes. The cost of that operation would be staggering and as open-ended as Mississippi chose to make it. The need for funds was so immediate and large that direct-mail appeals were no answer.

Marvin Rich worked miracles on the phone. Calling trade unions, corporations, and our top contributors, he brought in enough emergency money to give us a fighting chance to survive this first slash of the lion's claws. The creditors for goods and services, however, were still knocking at the door.

I called Roy Wilkins. He came to the CORE office to join me for lunch. Over a second cup of coffee, I explained our plight. Roy seemed to be engrossed in the floral design on his coffee cup. Finally, without looking up, he said, uncharacteristically, "Man, Mississippi is a *bitch!*"

"We may be facing bankruptcy, Roy," I said.

"I'll send you a check for $1,000 today. That's the maximum I can send without board action, and you can't wait for that."

The check came by messenger the next morning.

We found all but one Freedom Rider. On two others, we deliberately forfeited—one being in northern Saskatchewan, Canada, and the other in Istanbul, Turkey.

Thanks to Tougaloo College, a black institution just north of Jackson, board and lodging was economical. Our stay was brief, only two days. Jack Young argued hopelessly, but it took only seconds for the appeal of each defendant to be denied and the previous conviction upheld. Young informed the officials that we were appealing to the U.S. Supreme Court.

Then came the second swipe of the lion's paw. Bond was tripled for each defendant. We had an additional third of a million dollars to raise. How many times could one go to the well and not find it dry?

I thought we had found a bail-bond company in Connecticut that would provide bond for the Riders. Our celebration was premature. They called me back the next day to cancel the commitment; they had been informed by Mississippi that if they wrote bond for even one Freedom Rider they would lose their license to operate in the state.

Marv was on the phone again, and I was too. This time, it was not for gifts, but for interest-free loans, repayable in two or three years. We got some, but not nearly enough.

At a cocktail party, during those days of staring into the face of financial disaster, I chatted with Thurgood Marshall, then head of the NAACP Legal Defence and Education Fund, Inc. (the "Ink Fund").

"Jim, boy," Thurgood said in his booming voice, "I hear Mississippi's really socking it to you."

"That's the understatement of the year," I replied.

"What's the problem, bail-bond money?"

"Right, They tripled the bond on us. Fifteen hundred dollars per person!"

"What the hell!" boomed the great advocate. "The Ink Fund has about $300,000 in bail-bond money. It's not doing anything but sitting there. You might as well use it as long as it lasts."

If he'd been a woman, I would have kissed him. I could hardly wait for my staff meeting the next morning to let them know that one part of our problem was solved. But my announcement at the meeting was met with less enthusiasm than anticipated.

Marv had grave misgivings about the idea. He feared that other organizations would share the credit for the Freedom Ride. Some organizations were already raising money on the basis of the Ride, but the money was not being used to pay any Freedom Ride expenses. In addition, someone from either NAACP or the Ink Fund had said publicly in an off moment, "CORE gets people in jail and we have to get them out." It was not true and it rankled.

Yet, I would not let organizational rivalry force us down the drain. It was not going to be said that when our backs were against the wall, we refused to accept proffered help from a sister organization. I told Marv that we were going to accept it, and he must call Jack Greenberg, Thurgood Marshall's assistant director, and work out the details of the bookkeeping, accounting, and reporting procedures they required, and clue Lula in, because she would be handling the financial record keeping. The call was made and the wheels were turning.

The maelstrom of activity had no respite. Vintage CORE activity was erupting all over the country, and especially in Mississippi. Many SNCC and CORE members, released from Parchman prison, decided to remain in the state and work on voting rights, employment, and public accommodations. SNCC had not yet developed its fund-raising capacity, so they came to us and asked only nominal living expenses and a stipend for spending money. We scraped the bottom of the barrel for the wherewithall to keep them going.

The greatest tactical oversight of my life was that I did not at that time move for a merger between CORE and SNCC. Such a step was possible in the wake of the Freedom Ride and would have unified the action wing of the movement as nothing else would.

Our conceptualization of the problem inherent in the federal government's failure to enforce federal law in interstate transportation, and my decision to continue the Ride beyond the point when self-preservation demanded a folding of the tents and stealing away, was correct. The federal government acted in our behalf.

As brave souls, white and black, continued to fill up Mississippi jails, and no end was in sight, Attorney General Robert Kennedy called on the Interstate Commerce Commission to issue an order with teeth in it, so he could enforce it, bringing an end once and for all to the travesty of racial segregation in interstate transportation.

In response to Bobby's request, in September 1961 the ICC ordered that all "for colored" and "for white" signs come down from the buses and terminal facilities used by interstate passengers. They were to be replaced by notices, prominently posted, stating that segregation by race, color, creed, or national origin was unconstitutional and was an offense punishable by fine and/or imprisonment.

The order was to take effect on November 1, 1961. I informed the attorney general that as of the date of the issuance of the ICC order, I was halting the Freedom Ride. No additional riders would be recruited and sent to Mississippi, but those already in jail would continue serving their forty days. On November 1, the effective date of the order, I advised him, I would send out interracial teams to crisscross the South and test the enforcement of the order. If it was not enforced, the Freedom Ride would resume immediately.

On November 1, the ICC order was enforced.

In the CORE office, my staff held a party to celebrate. I was too tired to celebrate, too drained by the constant pressure. My sensation was that of tilting not at windmills, but at buzz saws.

But there was another saw in motion, I was aware, moving up from my rear, which I would have to turn and face.

Gladys Harrington and New York CORE were planning a move to seek my ouster at the upcoming convention. Jimmy Robinson had become active in New York CORE and joined forces with Gladys. I should have fired him then, but quite enough had been done to him already. I preferred to wait until he left of his own accord, when the counterrevolution had failed and he had found other employment.

The annual convention of 1961 had been postponed from its usual time, summer, to fall, because of the Freedom Ride.

The attack would be on Lula; they would try to get at me through her. Jimmy did not attend the convention. Though he desired the same outcome, there was no way that he could involve himself in a whispering campaign about a "black leader" with a white wife. Revenge can drive a person to do many things, but it could not drive him to do that. Furthermore, since he himself was white, it could have backfired.

Lula offered not to attend, but I told her, "I'm not going to hide you."

A replacement for me had already been selected: the Reverend Fred Shuttlesworth. But it never came to that. The plan to remove me was killed in the halls and side rooms and never came to the convention floor.

Following the convention, Jimmy handed me his resignation. He had found a new job. We shook hands. I do not think he and I have seen each other since. Thus ended a painful episode in my life.

Gladys Harrington was an able and compassionate woman. We became friendly after that and never spoke of the past. The only reference to it that I can recall was a remark she once made: "Jim, I thought you were going to be just a black face, but you fooled me."

CHAPTER 20

THE BIG SIX

"My brother has a blond, blue-eyed daughter."

Dick Gregory slowly paced the flood-lit stage. In his hand was the microphone, which he had removed from its stand. He ran his fingers down his dusky cheek and went on: "Well, you just gotta take some things on faith."

The CORE audience roared. Gregory's performance was a marvelous respite from the arduous labors of the 1962 convention in Miami. The harmony was almost eerie. Flushed with its victory in interstate bus travel, and savoring its new status as the cutting edge of the civil rights movement, CORE was a family once again—a big family now, but a family.

Hours before his show, Gregory had been in Lula's and my room, bouncing my second daughter, Abbey Lee, on his knee. Abbey was less than eight months old and she took after Lula.* She had fair skin and blue eyes and her hair was blond and straight. (It later curled and tangled and she had a blond afro.)

After Gregory's show, when I was relaxing in the hotel's bar, a delegate rushed in to tell me that Martin Luther King had arrived. I went out to greet him and show him to his room and chat for a few minutes, and then I left to give him time to rest and prepare for the banquet, where he was the featured speaker.

*Curiously, by a quirk of New York state laws, my first daughter's birth certificate lists her as a Negro and the second one is classified as white. When Tami was born, a child of mixed marriage was Negro, and when Abbey was born, a child took its race from the mother.

The delegates gave King a rousing ovation, and he wowed them with his rhetoric, drawing prolonged applause when he praised CORE for pioneering the use of nonviolent techniques since the early forties. Applause was equally sustained when he credited our organization with giving the current nonviolent movement a significant boost with its successful Freedom Rides through the South.

I had not expected Martin to accept when I invited him to speak at our convention; I had not yet become accustomed to the status I then had in the civil rights community. He not only spoke; he reciprocated by inviting me to address the SCLC convention later that year. I was now accepted as one of that select group, a top general of the movement. I soon discovered, however, that civil rights generalship was one-fourth leadership, one-fourth showmanship, one fourth one-upsmanship, and one-fourth partnership.

The partnership part was crystallized by Stephen Currier, a young New York multimillionaire philanthropist. Beginning in 1963, Currier's Taconic Foundation called together and hosted meetings of the "Big Six."* The press frequently referred to the group as the "Big Four," ignoring Dorothy Height, president of the National Council of Negro Women, and John Lewis, national chairman of SNCC. Age bias and sexism were even more rampant then than now.

The other members of the group were Wilkins, Whitney Young, and King. At the first meeting of the elite sextet, we decided to call ourselves the Council on United Civil Rights Leadership (CUCRL); to meet regularly, monthly if possible; to limit participation to the heads of those six civil rights organizations; and to have a rotating chairmanship.

Others could attend only by invitation. The sending of surrogates was not to be permitted; the leaders had to attend for themselves. The only exception to that rule was in the case of SNCC, which had dual leadership, a national chairman and an executive secretary, who shared power. Either of the two, John Lewis or James Forman, but not both, could attend.

The United in CUCRL's name was more a posture than a reality. These were no joint chiefs of staff poring over maps to determine where and when the final assault was to be launched and by which branch of the forces. There was, instead, a jockeying for position to determine who would be first to march victoriously into the nation's heartland, and for whom the flags would be waved and the bugles sounded.

Martin Luther King, Jr., was far and away in the lead. In a sense, it was a battle for media coverage, for along with headlines in print and on the tube came money to fuel more dramatic thrusts for the media to cover. Ever since the Montgomery bus boycott, King had been a magnet to the press. Envy of Dr. King's visibility was inevitable.

---

*Many of the meetings were held at the Carlyle, a small, exclusive hotel on Manhattan's West Side.

At one CUCRL meeting, Wilkins leaned across the table and said to King, "One of these days, Martin, some bright reporter is going to take a good hard look at Montgomery and discover that despite all the hoopla, your boycott didn't desegregate a single city bus. It was the quiet NAACP-type legal action that did it."

"We're fully aware of that, Roy," Martin replied, with simple poise, in his slow southern drawl. "And we in the SCLC believe that it's going to have to be a partnership between nonviolent direct action and legal action if we're going to get the job done."

Roy appeared to ignore the reply and pressed his point.

"In fact, Martin, if you have desegregated *anything* by your efforts, kindly enlighten me."

"Well," said Martin, "I guess about the only thing I've desegrated so far is a few human hearts."

Roy conceded that one and nodded.

"Yes, I'm sure you have done that, and that's important. So, keep on doing it; I'm sure it will help the cause in the long run."

Another time, when Wilkins, King, and I were in the elevator together, rising to the Taconic Foundation suite, Wilkins turned to King and said with no malice, "Martin, I'm going to catch up with you yet."

King merely smiled.

Once, after a plethora of profiles on Dr. King had appeared in the press, stressing his jailings for the cause, Whitney Young of the National Urban League, who was chairing the CUCRL's meeting, said, "The meeting will come to order, and I want to begin the discussion by saying, *boy*, it's sure tough these days trying to be a civil rights leader without going to jail."

Everyone laughed, including Dr. King.

We were the knights of the round table, but there was no King Arthur. Each one there was a leader and no one *had* a leader.

Whitney Young was a sort of "chairman of the board," for that was his style. A large man, six feet tall and two hundred twenty pounds, he was about two years younger than I and had assumed the helm of the Urban League very shortly after I became leader of CORE. We felt a kinship there, for we both were relative newcomers, but there the similarity ended. By virtue of my CORE role, I was an activist and a fighter.

The Urban League was not an activist group; it negotiated, bargained, and even cajoled—all with the finest professional skills. Whitney was at home in that element, and he was also comfortable and effective in corporation board rooms. Not that he was unaware of the value of the iron fist of the militants. He *used* it as a threatened right cross when his negotiations' left jab failed to produce the desired results.

"If you don't do what I'm asking you to do," he would say to corporation heads, "Jim Farmer and CORE will be coming after you." The threat usually worked, he said.

At CUCRL meetings, Whitney's role was that of moderator, compromiser, mediator. As, for example, when Wilkins and Forman were at daggers' points over SNCC's moving into one southern community, according to Wilkins, "and starting its so-called movement without troubling to contact the NAACP branch that had been alive and active for many years."

James Forman had countered that the "live and active" NAACP branch was doing nothing and did not have the respect of the youth in the community. Whitney intervened to smooth ruffled feathers. Sometimes, action was done quietly to avoid telegraphing our punches, Whitney observed. But our young people sometimes mistook the quiet for inaction, he went on, and we can understand their impatience.

"We may have a generation gap here," he said, "but we've got to remember that we all agree on objectives, and usually agree on strategy; it's on the tactics of the moment where we disagree. That's why CUCRL is so important. It's where we can hash out those differences."

By the time he had finished with the bromides, tempers had calmed. Whitney Young was an asset in the search for unity.

Forman was volatile and uncompromising, an angry young man. His head had been clubbed many times on the front lines in Dixie. He was impatient with Urban League and NAACP types; he was nervous and perhaps a trifle battle-fatigued. When he sat in for John Lewis, everyone expected fireworks.

Lewis, on the other hand, was the soul of decorum and gentlemanliness. Small in stature, he was huge in dignity, and that dignity was matched by a quiet courage and flawless integrity. John was not very talkative at CUCRL meetings. He did not speak to "get things off his chest." He kept those things inside. Only when he believed that his intervention would be of genuine usefulness to the entire group did he share his thoughts with the rest of us.

Also quiet through most of the meetings was King. Like many great orators, he preferred the podium to the conference table. Not that this group intimidated King in the least, for he knew that his presence gave added significance to the meetings. His name was a household word in every part of the nation. He would rather rally the masses than rail at his counterparts.

Dorothy Height was a worthy successor to the legendary Mary McLeod Bethune as president of the National Council of Negro Women. Fresh in my memory was the day two dozen years earlier when Dorothy had helped my parents find a home in Washington. Now she was a celebrated leader of black women and respected in women's circles nationwide. A statuesque woman in the mold of Eleanor Roosevelt, she also had the great first lady's immense dignity of person.

Civil rights leadership in the early sixties, like most leadership in the nation, was a man's world. Dorothy Height moved with grace and assurance in that world as the spokesperson for women. In meetings of the Big

Six, she spoke sparingly, but effectively, and with clarity and conviction.

The National Council of Negro Women is not an activist organization, in the usual sense of the word. It was not in the foxholes and trenches, but women were everywhere in the movement. Yet most of the bows were taken by men. Dorothy Height's presence at CUCRL helped to change that.

Wilkins, of course, was Wilkins. He was the senior person in the group and represented one of the two senior organizations; the rest of us were newcomers. Smart, witty, and secure, he was confident in the belief that whatever was being done had been done before by someone, somewhere, at some time in his association's rich past. In so many words, Roy said so, using the phrase "reinventing the wheel," and no one would gainsay him.

Despite his usual propensity for the diplomatic, Roy Wilkins sometimes was acerbic and caustic at CUCRL meetings, lashing out to protect the honor and prerogatives of the association. But, after all, that is what, among many other things, we were there for: to air any gripes we had with each other. That was a prescription for unity. Or greater disunity.

There were a couple of grievances that I aired.

I complained to Roy that, according to my chapter officers, NAACP people, both national and local, were still saying that "we get 'em in jail, and they have to get 'em out." That, I insisted, was unfair and untrue. "We bail our own people out," I said, "and the only exception to that was the Freedom Ride appeal bond, when Mississippi was trying to put us out of business, and then it was not the NAACP, but the NAACP Legal Defense and Education Fund, a separate corporation, that offered us bail assistance."

"You're right," he replied, "and I want you to know that it's not I who is making such statements. I'll look into it, and if it's any member of my staff, I'll put a stop to it. If it's some of our branch people, all I can do is tell them that they're wrong, and ask them to stop it. They may or may not comply with my request. You should appreciate that, Jim, because your chapters are even more autonomous than our branches."

I had another complaint, this one directed at the SCLC. They had raised money on the basis of the Freedom Ride, I asserted, although CORE paid all the expenses of that project, and the bills resulting from it. The only exceptions of which I was aware, I stated, were the thousand dollars Wilkins had sent us from the NAACP and the bail-bond money put at my disposal by the Legal Defense and Education Fund.

Martin did not remember such fund-raising by SCLC, but conceded that if it did occur, it was wrong and should not be repeated. However, he said, he thought he did recall CORE appeal letters in 1956 referring to the Montgomery bus boycott, and in 1960 mentioning the southern student sit-in movement. He was saying that not in criticism of CORE, but just to suggest that anything any of us did that was constructive helped all of us, because we were all in this fight together.

Basically, the Big Six was not a squabbling squad. It was much grander than that. We discussed many things of importance, including the possibility of joint fund raising.

It was Steven Currier who broached that subject. His suggestion sent Roy's eyes to the ceiling, Whitney's to the yellow pad on the table in front of him, and Martin's to Currier's face. The discussion that followed showed interest, but it was wary, hard-nosed, businesslike. Each had stewardship of an organization to maintain, and that consciousness pervaded the room.

The substance of the dialogue was that it must be new money, not money that any of the organizations might have gotten anyway. There must be no public appeals, for those might divert funds from individual organizations. There would be no sharing of lists of contributors. That pretty much narrowed the sources down to foundations, and the funds would have to be earmarked for a tax-exempt program not yet in operation, such as voter registration.

Currier agreed to attempt to raise the funds for a massive voter education and voter registration drive to be jointly conducted by the CUCRL member organizations. His Taconic Foundation would prime the pump with a grant of its own, and he would call some of the other foundations, asking them to match it. The funds raised would be divided according to a formula based on the organizations' budgets for the previous year, 1961.

I frowned at the formula because the NAACP and Urban League were practically standing still, whereas CORE was burgeoning that year (1962) in chapters, membership, and budget, and its peak was not yet in sight. In 1961, the year of the Freedom Ride, we had only six months of rapidly expanding budget, but in 1962 it promised to expand for a whole year. SNCC would draw the shortest straw of all, for 1961 had been the first year of its tooling up to raise funds. I voiced the concern but yielded, since the formula devised seemed to be the only feasible one.

I had another concern, which I kept to myself. There lingered in my mind a feeling that one motivation was to get CORE and SNCC off the streets with their highly visible demonstrations. I knew that the Kennedys were anxious to halt the demonstrations, even though we were nonviolent, and were doing only that which federal law gave us the right to do.

On one occasion, while I was in Parchman State Prison, a committee of CORE and SNCC members had met with Robert Kennedy. The attorney general had said to them, according to one of the CORE persons there, "If you'll cut out this Freedom Riding and sitting-in stuff, and concentrate on voter registration, I'll get you a tax exemption."

The young activists gasped at the statement and considered the suggested tradeoff to border on bribery. They also thought that it revealed a lack of sensitivity to the indignities imposed by segregation, which had to be addressed *now* and could not wait until free access to the ballot box could bring about change.

One of the SNCC persons jumped to his feet and he and Bobby went chest to chest, shouting at each other. A CORE person stepped between them and gently helped the SNCC man back away and resume his seat.

I was aware, also, that Stephen Currier was friendly with the Kennedys, and I suspected that the joint fund-raising plan was a more sophisticated Kennedy ploy to achieve the same results as the cruder Bobby Kennedy proposal had intended to accomplish.

But no matter, voter registration was of great importance; it could change the face of the South in a decade. CORE could do both—the short range and the long range. I had the staff and the volunteers and the energy, and with joint fund raising, we might have the money to take on voter registration with the fervor that was our trademark.

And so I smiled and agreed to the plan. Currier looked relieved.

Although Wilkins, King, Young, and Currier were close to the Kennedys, I was not. I was considered uncontrollable, since I would not halt the Freedom Ride when asked to.

John F. Kennedy decided to meet with each civil rights leader. My meeting with the president in 1962 turned out to be the most insulting session I've ever had with a government official. I was ushered into the Oval Office on schedule. The president came in five minutes later with a sheaf of papers in his hand. He shook my hand limply without looking at me, and took a seat. He proceeded to look through the papers before him, making notations on some, initialing others. Still, he did not look at me; I might as well not have been there. I began talking, trying to break through the seemingly impenetrable barrier. I did not succeed. Occasionally, he would nod in agreement; otherwise, there was no acknowledgement of the fact that I was speaking.

Suddenly, I stopped talking, and there still was no change in the president's demeanor as he worked on his papers. Finally, I said, "Mr. President, if you're too busy for this meeting, I'm sure it can be rescheduled for a time more convenient to you."

"No, no," he said, looking up for a second or two, "go right ahead." Then, he resumed work on the papers before him.

When the allotted time of half an hour had passed, I said, "Mr. President, I see that my time is up,. I won't impose further on your schedule. Thank you for seeing me."

JFK nodded, stood, shook my hand, and without a word went back to his work.

I asked Wilkins, Young, and King if they had a similar experience of insolence with Kennedy, and they had not. They had found him warm and friendly and most attentive.

A short while later, an experience with the attorney general confirmed my suspicion about the Kennedys' attitude toward me. In the summer of 1962, I moderated a two-week seminar for corporation executives at the Aspen Institute for Humanistic Studies in Colorado. Upon completion of the seminar, Joe Slater, director of the Aspen Institute, asked me if I would remain in Aspen for another two weeks to help Bobby Kennedy answer questions from a group of foreign students about America, since surely many of the queries would deal with the racial scene and the civil rights movement. After checking with my office to clear the calendar, I agreed to do it.

The next day, Slater informed me that he was embarrassed because he would have to withdraw his invitation to me. The attorney general had said that he would not come "if that sonofabitch Farmer is there." Bobby Kennedy further stated that if Slater would cancel me, he would bring Thurgood Marshall, by then a federal judge, to help field questions.

I was embarrassed and hurt, but Lula, who loved Aspen, was more disappointed than I that our working vacation in the Colorado mountains could not be extended.

Though the Kennedys despised me in those days, I found the vice-president, Lyndon Johnson, more than cordial. But then, vice-presidents need friends; presidents have them.

LBJ greeted me with his Texas rancher's hand shake that nearly jerked my arm out of its socket. He leaned toward me as we talked, gripping my eyes with his.

As vice-president, he was chairman of the President's Commission on Equal Employment Opportunity. It was that capacity of his that led me to request a meeting.

Statistics showed that the median average income of blacks was stalled at less than 60 percent that of whites. Worse, the gap was widening. I was convinced that the simple color blindness of antidiscrimination codes had taken us about as far as it could. The Fair Employment Practices (FEP) laws triggered by the executive order that Randolph had extracted from Roosevelt in 1941 had become obsolete. Something more advanced was now needed.

Johnson closed his jaws tightly, knotted his brows, and continued boring into my eyes. Then he spoke: "What d'you suggest? What could be more advanced than antidiscrimination?"

"What I'm proposing," I replied, "is that as a matter of policy in employment we replace color blindness with color consciousness aimed at eliminating inequities based on color."

The vice-president's eyes narrowed more, and his lower lip pushed harder against the upper one.

I continued: "What I am suggesting is that we no longer tell employers to be oblivious to the color of applicants, but to look at their color to see if the minority applicants are too few or nonexistent. They should then consider the possibility that they are not advertising in and recruiting from the right places. I'm proposing further that if two applicants are equally qualified, the fact that there are too few minority persons employed there should weigh in favor of the minority applicant. In a word, what I'm proposing is a policy of 'compensatory preferential treatment' similar to that used with veterans."

Johnson considered what I had said for several seconds and reacted with enthusiasm. "I think you're right. I agree with you. We have to give minorities an extra push to help them catch up. It's not fair to ask a man to run a race when the other fellow is halfway around the track. But don't call it compensatory—what was that?"

I repeated the phrase.

"Oh, that's a terrible name. We can't call it that. Let's see, what can we call it? We have to move the nation forward, act positively, affirmatively. That's it: affirmative action."

When I related that conversation to the Big Six at a CUCRL meeting in the spring of 1963, Whitney Young remarked that he'd been talking about the same thing. Wilkins, however, expressed misgivings about the idea.

"I have a problem with that whole concept," he said. "What you're asking for there is not equal treatment, but special treatment to make up for the unequal treatment of the past. I think that's outside the American tradition and the country won't buy it. I don't feel at all comfortable asking for any special treatment; I just want to be treated like everyone else."

Wilkins saw that I was about to reply, so he continued: "I understand and sympathize with the motivation and rationale, of course, but I need to give the question more thought. I don't want to debate it yet."

Whitney leaped at the opening: "Speaking of debating, I read in the paper that Jim is going to debate Malcolm X on network television. I think that would be a mistake. I don't think we ought to appear with that guy; we can't win. All we do is give him a platform and an audience."

Roy nodded, "Yes, I agree."

"It's not a debate. It's a panel. There'll be two other persons on it," I said.

Roy smiled. "With Malcolm X, if there's a microphone, it's a debate."

Whitney nodded and chuckled.

Martin joined the discussion: "I was asked to be on that panel with Malcolm X, but I declined and told them that Wyatt Walker, the executive secretary of SCLC, would be there instead of me."

"A good decision, Martin," said Whitney. "I think all of us should agree here in CUCRL that none of the top leaders will appear on a platform, radio, or TV with Malcolm X because we just give him an audience. The only person I've ever seen hold his own with Malcolm was George Schuyler."*

---

*Schuyler, now dead, was a black journalist and writer who in his later years had become a John Birch–type conservative.

Roy interrupted: "Yes, Schuyler kept saying, 'Man, why don't you answer the question?'"

"I guess maybe you have to be a reactionary to handle Malcolm X," said Whitney.

I'd had enough. "No," I said, "I'm not going to agree to anything like that. In the first place, Malcolm does very well getting platforms and audiences by himself; he doesn't need our help on that. Second, I'm not afraid of him. I've debated Malcolm before, once up at Cornell. I can handle him. I have every confidence that I'll do all right on that panel."

All looked at me without a word, as though condolences soon would be in order.

CHAPTER 21

"IF ANY MAN MOLEST YOU . . ."

OF ALL THE PERSONALITIES springing from the black struggle in America, none was more exciting and controversial than Malcolm X. In some ways, his appeal to the black consciousness was as strong as King's; in other ways, stronger. As the huge throngs of religious folk in churches across the land became an extension of the powerful personality of Martin Luther King, Jr., when he mounted the podium, so the angry militant masses in urban black America blended with Malcolm X as his long arm shot out in a forceful gesture.

Malcolm was the antithesis of King in almost every conceivable way. King was short with a slight tendency toward obesity. Malcolm was tall, lean, and hard. King's slightly Asian eyes were dreamy; Malcolm's burned holes. King preached turning the other cheek; Malcolm thundered with clenched fists, "Attack no man, but if any man molest you, may Allah bless you!" King spoke to the conscience of America, reminding her of the professions of democracy and equality. Malcolm condemned the hypocrisy that denied equality to blacks. King believed America could change; Malcolm did not. King promised, "Though you spit on us, yet we will love you." Malcolm demanded black hate for the white haters. King was a Ph.D.; Malcolm had a grade-school education. King dreamed that a man be judged "not by the color of his skin, but by the content of his character." Malcolm, who had reddish-tan skin and reddish hair (and was called "Big Red" in his vice-lord days), when charged in debate with talking "so black" when he obviously had white blood, would thunder back, "My grandmother was raped by a white man! Should I recognize a single drop of that white blood?" His audiences shouted back, "No, no no!"

It is incomprehensible to most white Americans that deep in the heart of every black adult lives some of Malcolm and some of King, side by side. The black experience has not been monolithic and the black response is seldom without ambivalence. The same audience that showered Martin with "amens" could punctuate Malcolm's rhetoric with emphatic shouts of "right!"

Malcolm X was one of the most feared debaters on the American platform, capable of demolishing an opponent with a one-liner. In one debate, for example, his opponent, also black, kept insisting, "I am an *American.*" Malcolm demanded that blacks call themselves black men and women and not Americans. His opponent persisted, and this led Malcolm to ask, "Why do you call yourself an American, brother?"

"Because I was *born* in this country," shouted his irrepressible adversary.

Malcolm smiled and spoke softly: "Now, brother, if a cat has kittens in the oven, does that make them biscuits?"

Despite his lack of formal education, I found Malcolm X to be a well read and brilliant man with a sharp and exceptionally quick mind. He came to wide public notice in 1959 when he, along with his chief, Elijah Muhammed, were featured in a documentary film done by Mike Wallace and Louie Lomax entitled *The Hate That Hate Produced.* He came across as a towering and intimidating man with a great gift for phrase making.

In my first encounter with Malcolm, I had underestimated him. It was a one-hour radio dialogue on the "Barry Gray Show" in New York in 1961. I was saved, perhaps, by a booming voice and speed of delivery as we fought for the microphone, but I must confess to being surprised by his quickness and sharpness of repartee. On that occasion, we developed a mutual respect.

About a year later, I was invited to debate Malcolm on a public platform at Cornell University. The letter from the student council stated that Malcolm had agreed to the debate and asked if I would accept the challenge. My answer was yes, but I wanted to speak last. I had no intention of being destroyed by a "kittens in the oven" bombshell in his final rebuttal. Malcolm agreed to that order of proceedings, and the debate was arranged.

One week before the debate, however, I got a frantic call from the chairman of the student council at Cornell. Malcolm had sent them a wire saying, "The Honorable Elijah Muhammed teaches us to attack only when attacked; therefore, I must speak last or no debate." Would I agree to have the first speech and the first rebuttal.

I pondered that until a plan evolved and then I answered, "Yes, I would be glad to on one condition: that after Malcolm's rebuttal, there be an open-ended one-on-one cross discussion between him and me with the moderator not interfering." This was, of course, another safeguard against being blown out of the water by a final bomb.

Malcolm was at his most awesome when on the attack—when blasting the crimes committed by the white man and the white world against black people for centuries and at present. Any black opponent was in an untenable position trying to defend the white world against Malcolm's valid criticisms. He had to come across as either an imbecile or a "Tom." Malcolm was at his weakest when discussing his program for a solution to the problem. Programmatically, he was stuck with Elijah Muhammed's dogmas calling for a separate black state or land that someone would give us somewhere on the globe. For all but the most naive audiences, such a solution was subject to endless ridicule.

Since I was to make the opening speech, my plan was to give Malcolm's speech. In other words, to catalogue the crimes committed against blacks throughout history. I knew the speech well enough almost to give it word-for-word, softening the language here and there, of course. Then I would go into my solution, the CORE solution, the nonviolent direct action solution for a new America and a new world, finally turning the platform over to Malcolm, demanding not a restatement of the diagnosis, but instead his prescription for a cure.

Also, I had a trump card. In my pocket, there would be a document about the Nation of Islam that I felt confident would win the debate. It was a shocking piece of paper, and I would use its contents only if it became necessary.

And that is the way the debate proceeded. After I had catalogued the abuses, diagnosed the disease, and prescribed my treatment, I ostentatiously looked at my watch and shook it. I announced to the audience that I had three minutes remaining of my allotted time, but instead of using them, I would turn them over to Malcolm so that he would not run short of time in telling us his solution. I then turned to Malcolm, smiled, and said, "Brother Malcolm, don't tell us any more about the disease—that is clear in our minds. Now, tell us, physician, what is thy cure?"

Never before had I seen Malcolm slow to rise and take the microphone. He began in quiet tones, offering flattering words to his opponent: "I am pleased and honored to share the platform with James Farmer. Brother James is the only one of the top leaders of the so-called Negroes who has the guts to face me on a public platform in debate. I respect him for that."

Then he floundered around for a few minutes with some unaccustomed inarticulateness, obviously searching for a speech. Then he spoke briefly about all the money that the nation owes us for the centuries of slave labor and exploitation. It was only right, he argued, for this nation to give us land or buy land for us someplace so we could build our black nation and have a homeland. Without much elaboration, he then moved smoothly into high gear and roared into an attack on nonviolence and the indignity of begging the white man to let us into his places of business, when with all the money we spend on booze, tobacco, Freedom Rides, sit-ins, bail bonds, and lawyers, we could build our own restaurants and hotels and lunch counters.

The refutations were a toe-to-toe slugfest. And I thought I had slightly the better of it. The one-on-one cross discussion that followed lasted over a half hour. When the moderator finally called a halt, the audience roared its approval of the debate as soon as Malcolm and I both stood and bowed. He and I shook hands as his bodyguard stood by watching.

Afterward, the three of us went out for coffee. It was then that I showed him the document I had held in reserve. He read it carefully, and reread it, looking up to say, "Brother James, I want to thank you for not bringing this up in the debate."

It was a photocopy of a letter from George Lincoln Rockwell of the American Nazi Party. I had had a CORE member get on Rockwell's mailing list so we could keep abreast of what the American Nazis were saying and doing. It read, in part, as follows:

> I have just had a meeting with the most extraordinary black man in America: The Honorable Elijah Muhammed, leader of the Nation of Islam. I was amazed to learn how much they and I agree on things; they think that blacks should get out of this country and go back to Africa or to some other place and so do we. They want to get black men to leave white women alone, and white men to leave black women alone; and so do we.

> The Honorable Elijah Muhammed and I have worked out an agreement of mutual assistance in which they will help us on some things and we will help them on others.

> Can you imagine a rally of the American Nazis in Union Square protected from Jewish hecklers by a solid phalanx of Elijah Muhammed's stalwart black stormtroopers. Oi, oi, oi!

"I give you my word, Brother James, that I knew nothing of any such meeting, but I will check into it," Malcolm said. "If such a meeting did take place, I promise you that there will be hell to pay within the Nation of Islam."

I don't know whether he checked into the matter or, if so, the results of his checking. I do know that a few weeks later Malcolm called to inform me that on the next Thursday afternoon a group of young American Nazis were going to picket the CORE office. I asked him how he knew. He replied that someone had called him, saying that since he wanted to make black men leave white women alone, and so did they, and Farmer was married to a white woman, they wanted him to join them in picketing CORE on Thursday.

I asked Malcolm if he were going to be out there picketing us. He said, "No, I am not. I told those creeps that I am not picketing any black brother who is fighting for freedom."

That Thursday, a small band of seven or eight grinning Nazi youths marched up and down in front of the CORE office carrying signs calling CORE a communist organization and a den of race mixers. As I crossed the line, one sign forced me to laugh. I did not know the Nazis had such imagination. The sign read simply "LITTLE RED RIDING HOODS."

There was another forensic encounter with Malcolm X. This time on network television in mid-1963. That was the debate which the Big Six had urged me to cancel. It was a panel, really, including in addition to Malcolm and me, Wyatt Tee Walker, executive director of the Southern Christian Leadership Conference, and Alan Morrison, New York editor of *Jet* and *Ebony* magazines.

The fireworks began after the first fifteen minutes. Malcolm had the mike, and in the course of his remarks he referred to President Kennedy as "that Ku Klux Klan president." Among the civil rights leaders, I was by no means the greatest admirer of the president, nor he of me. But such a characterization was much more than I could bear.

"Now, wait a minute!" I shouted over Malcolm into the microphone. "Let's give the president his due. He does not do as much as I want him to do, or as fast as I want him to do it, and I have made that clear ever since he has been in Washington. But the speech that he made after James Meredith had failed a second time to get into 'Ole Miss' happens to have been the strongest civil rights statement made by any American president in history, barring none. To call Jack Kennedy a Ku Klux Klan president is the sheerest kind of nonsense."

I must say that the TV camera work was superb. I am told that it looked as though Malcolm and I were wrestling, grappling for holds as he struggled for the mike, and gesturing toward each other. Finally, after five or more minutes of voice-over-voice shouting into the mike by Malcolm and me, the Muslim minister leaned back in his chair, grinned, and was silent for a while. Wyatt and Alan merely watched the battle, smiling.

It was many weeks later when I met Malcolm on 125th Street in Harlem. He shook hands and walked together to the Shabazz Restaurant, a Muslim establishment, for coffee.

"Brother James, I think we should stop debating each other," he said. "I'm not going to change your mind, and you're not going to change my mind. I know what you're going to say, and you know what I'm going to say. I could make your speech for you and you could make mine for me." And with that he broke into a wide grin. "All we're doing is conducting a circus with two black guys belting each other's brains out verbally for the amusement of a largely white audience. I suggest that when you have something to say to me, you call me up and come by my house and say it, and I'll do the same."

I agreed, and we shook hands and parted with a verbal nonaggression pact.

I did not see Malcolm for some time after coffee at the Shabazz, but Lula did at the time of the march on Washington, when I was in jail in Plaquemine, Louisiana. Lula, of course, went to the march. In the hotel lobby, the previous evening, she saw a crowd of people gathered around Malcolm as he harangued them, spitting verbal bullets at the concept of the march, the "absurdity" of nonviolence, the "weak-kneed behavior of the so-called civil rights leaders," and the trickery of the Kennedys.

Lula worked her way through the crowd and stepped up to Malcolm, extending her hand and saying, "Hello, Malcolm. I'm Lula Farmer, Jim's wife."

He shook her hand and turned back to the crowd, gesturing with his pointing index finger: "See, it's just like I was telling you. There is Jim Farmer, one of our great so-called Negro leaders—" Then he looked at Lula, obviously intending to make reference to her race. Changing his mind in midsentence, however, he went on: "And where is he? In jail. And what are the Kennedys doing about it? Nothing."

In spite of the image he carefully projected, Malcolm was basically a civilized gentleman who would have hated himself had he insulted Lula before that crowd of people.

On Christmas Eve, 1964, when rumors were rife and newspaper reports abundant about threats and attempts on Malcolm's life, he visited me in my apartment in lower Manhattan. He had heard on radio station WINS, New York's round-the-clock news station, that I was about to make a tour of Africa to counteract the impact of Malcolm X on his trips to Africa. Malcolm had called to ask if the report was true. I told him that it was half true and half false. True that I was going to Africa, false that I was going to counteract him. I would be making a tour of Africa at the request of the American Negro Leadership Conference on Africa, composed of Randolph, Wilkins, Whitney Young, King, John Lewis, Dorothy Height, and me. The purpose of my trip would be to develop a liaison between the new nations of Africa and the civil rights movement in America. He asked if he could drop by and give me names and phone numbers of some people whom he had met on that continent, people I might enjoy talking with.

"By all means, come right over," I said.

He walked into my apartment with his bodyguard. Taking their hats and coats and showing them to seats in the living room, I asked, "Malcolm, why did you bring your bodyguard with you? Do you think I'm going to try to kill you?"

"No, Brother James," he replied. "You're not going to kill me, but there are a lot of people after me and I am convinced they're going to get me."

"Who are these people?" I asked. "The Black Muslims?"

The most feared black man in America shot a look at his bodyguard, who was impassive, and then met my eyes. "Brother James, I honestly think the so-called Black Muslims are the only black people in this country at this point in history who are capable of political murder and assassination. I know what they will do because I taught them everything they know."*

---

*It should be pointed out that at this time Malcolm had broken with the Nation of Islam, having been suspended by Elijah Muhammed for his comment after the assassination of President Kennedy, to the effect that "the chickens have come home to roost." The suspension had been made permanent, and Malcolm now had his own group of followers, Muslims, but not members of the Nation of Islam.

We were quiet for a minute or two. During the lull in the conversation, Gretchen climbed up on the couch and into Malcolm's lap and proceeded to lick his face as he patted her head.

"Would you like coffee, Malcolm?" Lula asked.

"Yes, please," he replied.

"How do you take it?"

"Plenty of cream and sugar, please."

I chuckled and said, "Malcolm, I'm disappointed in you, the leader of black nationalism in the United States, integrating your coffee like that. And even sweetening it. As for me, I take my coffee like my women— *strong, hot,* and *black!*

Malcolm, glanced at Lula, who was frail, weak, and white. Both he and his bodyguard erupted into loud and prolonged laughter. Gretchen fell to the floor, and I thought Malcolm was going to follow her. Minutes later, while he was giving me names and phone numbers of people in Africa, he would suddenly think of the coffee jest and would break up in laughter again.

"By the way, Malcolm," I asked, "did those two postcards you sent me from Mecca indicate a change in thinking?"

"Refresh my memory, Brother James. What did I say in the postcards?"

"The first postcard said, 'Dear Brother James, I am now in Mecca where I have seen pilgrims *of all colors* worshipping Allah in perfect peace and harmony and brotherhood, such as I have never seen in the States.' And you signed it, 'Your Brother, Malcolm.' The second card, which came weeks later, said something like, 'Here I am in Mecca again. I am still traveling, trying to broaden my mind. I have seen so much of the damage that narrow-mindedness can make of things. When I return to the States, I shall direct what energies I have to repairing that damage.'"

"Yes, I remember them, now. They did indeed indicate a change in my thinking. I was not lucky as you were, Brother James. I had little formal education—only grade school. Consequently, I believed everything the Honorable Elijah Muhammed told us. He told us that Islam was a black man's religion, and that the blue-eyed devils couldn't get close to Mecca; they would be killed if they tried to come in. I had believed that, but in Mecca, there were blond, blue-eyed Muslims kneeling beside me, worshipping Allah, just as I was. Obviously, the Honorable Elijah Muhammed had lied, so I had to do some rethinking.

"Then later in Ghana I was meeting with the Algerian ambassador. He asked me what my plans were, what my program was for my brothers. I proceeded to tell him in elaborate detail of my program for my black brothers in the United States. He said, 'That kind of leaves me out, doesn't it, Malcolm?'

"'What do you mean?' I asked.

"'I'm your Muslim brother, but I am not black. I am Caucasian.'

"Well, that floored me. I was forced to search my soul."

"Where has the soul-searching led you, Malcolm?"

Without hesitation, he replied, "I have concluded that anyone who will fight along with us—I said *with* us, not *for* us—is my brother."

"Well, why didn't you say that Saturday at your rally in Harlem Square? At that meeting, you spouted the same old line. Why didn't you tell the faithful that you had changed your mind?"

"Brother James," he said slowly, "you're enough of a politician to know that if a leader makes a sudden, right-angle turn, he turns alone."

Our business concluded, Malcolm and his bodyguard rose to leave. He walked over to the kitchen door and spoke to Lula, thanking her for her hospitality and coffee—a perfect gentleman. Lula shook his hand and said, "It's a pleasure to see you again, Malcolm."

"I guess I might as well tell you," I said. "Lula is a Malcolm X fan. She thinks you won our debates, but I tell her that she is out of her mind."

He smiled broadly and said, "True confession is good for the soul, or so they say. My wife, Betty Shabazz, is a staunch James Farmer fan. She told me that I had better stop debating you because you keep on winning and I keep on losing."

Malcolm's bodyguard smiled benignly at the mutual admiration society, and the two men departed.

After a whirlwind tour of sub-Sahara Africa in January 1965, during which I had been given letters from Emperor Haile Selassie of Ethiopia and Presidents Julius Nyerere of Tanzania, Kenneth Kaunda of Zambia, and Benjamin Azikiwe of Nigeria, expressing in glowing terms their solidarity with the struggle of their black brothers in the United States, I arrived in Accra, Ghana.

I got to my room and placed a call to Flagstaff House to seek an audience with President Kwame Nkrumah. Immediately afterward I received a call from a young black American woman I had known in the States. She had read in the papers of my coming visit and had called the leading hotels to find where I was registered. I invited her to come by and have dinner with me that evening so we could renew our acquaintance.

In the hotel dining room, we shared a bottle of Ghanaian beer before dinner, as I brought her up to date on the movement back in our country.

"Malcolm was here a couple of months ago, and I had dinner with him, too," she said, abruptly becoming serious.

"I know, he told me."

"He is going to be killed, you know." She dropped that remark in a matter-of-fact way.

I shrugged my shoulders and said, "Malcolm says that; everybody else says it; and now you are saying it. I think it's just a rumor, but okay, if he's going to be killed, when is it going to happen?"

She put her glass of beer down and with a napkin dabbed at the moisture the glass had deposited on the tablecloth. Then she studied the ceiling.

"Now, let's see," she said, "this is February 1. He will be killed sometime between now and April 1."

I almost jumped from my seat. "That's only two months. That's calling it pretty close, isn't it?"

She nodded.

"You must know something," I said.

Again she nodded.

"Then who's going to kill him? The Black Muslims?"

"Oh, no, no, no." She was now talking in a whisper, and I leaned closer to hear. "The Muslims are after him, but I think they just want to beat him up to teach him a lesson. One of them might shoot him, but it would be sort of a spur-of-the-moment thing; not on orders of Elijah Muhammed. There is another group far more dangerous than the Muslims that's going to get him, and it will be blamed on the Nation of Islam."

"Who is this other group?" I demanded.

"I have nothing more to say on the subject," she said with finality. "And if you quote me, I'll deny that I ever saw you."

When I continued to press her on the identity of the group that, according to her, was going to murder Malcolm she became almost hysterical, glancing furtively about the room. I dropped the subject.

Back home, three weeks later, I drove to a friend's home in upstate New York to put the finishing touches on my book *Freedom When?* A call came from Lula. The message was curt and solemn: "Malcolm was just shot and killed at the Audubon Ballroom in Harlem."

"I'll be right home. Call Val Coleman and Marvin Rich and have them set up a press conference for me for tomorrow morning."

At the news conference in the CORE office, with unconcealed emotion I expressed my sorrow at the loss of a good friend and a great man. He was a man with whom I disagreed on many things, sometimes sharply, but whom I had learned to respect deeply for his integrity, his keen mind, and his talents. We would miss Malcolm, I said, and I, personally, would miss him an awful lot.

"The Black Muslims did not kill him," I said, trying to head off a blood bath between Malcolm's followers, who were already heading for Chicago to seek vengeance, and those of Elijah Muhammed, who would be their target. The reporters almost dropped their pencils and stared up at me in disbelief. My statement flew in the face of the conclusions drawn by all the media, and practically everyone else. I continued: "Malcolm's murder was a political killing with international implications."

I declined to elaborate or to answer any questions and the news conference was adjourned.

Following it, a young white Quaker friend called to tell me that he had witnessed Malcolm's murder. He had gone to the Audubon Ballroom that night, with a tape recorder in his hand. At the entrance, he found security extremely lax. There was only one uniformed policeman standing there, and he seemed totally unconcerned. One of Malcolm's men guarding the entrance looked at the tape recorder and asked the young Quaker, "What are you, a reporter?"

The young man lied, and said yes.

"Well, no reporters admitted," the guard announced sharply and went about the business, somewhat lackadaisically, of checking others coming into the hall. The Quaker youth stood aside for a few minutes and then walked in and neither the policeman nor the guard at the entrance made any effort to stop him. He took a seat front row, center.

My young friend considered it extraordinary that security at the place was not tighter, particularly in view of the fact that Malcolm had said, unwisely, in an interview published in the *New York Times* a few days earlier that he was going to be killed, and that he was going to be killed because he knew too much, and at the Audubon Ballroom meeting he was going to tell what he knew and who was going to kill him for knowing it. He had also said that he placed his information in a sealed letter on the desk in his office, another indiscreet revelation.

My friend may have been the only white face in the ballroom as he sat up front with his tape recorder. He related to me that as Malcolm stood to speak and began with his customary preparatory words, "Brothers and sister, ladies and gentlemen, friends, enemies, FBI, and CIA," two young men in the back of the hall stood and began scuffling.

One shouted, "Get your hands out of my pocket. What you got your hands in my pocket for?"

They began exchanging punches and one chased the other to the aisle, down the aisle, and in front of the platform. Then both men turned, crouched, drew pistols, and fired at Malcolm in the area of the heart. At the same time, he was being blasted with a sawed-off shotgun from a wing of the stage.

The two men with pistols then pocketed their weapons and ran out, unobstructed. The shotgun assailant was wounded in the legs by one of Malcolm's bodyguards and taken to the prison ward at Bellevue. Malcolm lay prone with blood coming from his mouth and the left side of his chest, probably dead.

The Quaker said that it was more than ten minutes before any official came in to investigate the incident. Meanwhile, Malcolm lay on the floor, unattended.

A police official sauntered down the aisle to the platform and said, "Now, let's see, what was the name of the man who was shot?"

My Quaker friend asked me what he should do, and I asked him if he could identify the gunmen.

"Of course, I was close enough to touch them. It seemed that everyone else ducked down behind their seats when the shooting started, but for some crazy reason, I just sat there looking."

I urged him to go to the police station and offer his services in identifying the suspects.

He reported that at the police station two stalwart black men were brought in for him to identify. He informed the police officers that those two were definitely *not* the gunmen. They were at least a head taller than the gunmen and bore no resemblance to them whatsoever.* Leaving the police station, he saw on the bulletin board an "important notice" that said simply, "Narcotics arrests needed."

The day after my news conference, there was some press speculation as to what I had meant by "political killing with international implications." The *Daily News* editorialized that I might have meant that the Chinese reds got him. The *New York Times* was more discerning, saying that what I had implied may have been that Malcolm's assassination related to the rackets in Harlem, especially those dealing in the drug market, with its ties to organized crime downtown and the international drug trade.

The *New York Times* was correct. That was precisely what I meant to imply. I was not more explicit because I was not in a position to prove my allegations.

Days later, at a banquet in New York, Percy Sutton, who had been Malcolm's lawyer, came over to me on the dais and said, "Jim, I don't know whether you realize how right you were in what you said about Malcolm's murder."

Percy walked away and then came back and said, "Furthermore, I understand the smart boys in Harlem are wondering how you could know so much from the outside."

It almost goes without saying that right after Malcolm's assassination his office was ransacked. The intruders no doubt were looking for the letter Malcolm had allegedly left there sealed. Percy Sutton's office was ransacked also.

Crank phone calls and death threats were commonplace in the lives of civil rights leaders in those days, but following my news conference about Malcolm X, those calls coming into *my* home were more persistent and more ominous than ever before. The calls would come at night, and usually while I was out of town, which was frequently. The caller, with no southern accent, would ask Lula, "Your husband's not home yet, is he?"

"No, he isn't," she would reply.

"That's right," the caller would continue. "He is going to be a little delayed. In fact, he won't get home. He has been called away to a funeral—his own."

Another call would come from the same voice an hour or so later, saying, "I forgot to ask you. What kind of funeral do you want for him, and what kind of flowers do you want us to send?"

Lula, spiritually and intellectually prepared for such harassment, and

---

*Those two men, however, both Muslims, were tried and convicted for Malcolm's murder, along with a third person—the wounded assailant with the sawed-off shotgun. Toward the end of the trial, the wounded man confessed, admitting that he'd killed Malcolm and been paid to kill him. He said further that he had three accomplices, but the two Muslims on trial with him were not among them. They had nothing to do with it and he had never seen them before the trial began. He refused to say who paid him to assassinate Malcolm or why Malcolm was killed. He denied that he was a Muslim and refused to say what his religion was. All three suspects were convicted and sentenced to long prison terms.

fully aware of the risks of my occupation, was usually cool. On one occasion she said to the caller, "Oh, thank you very much."

"What?" the voice asked.

"You just reminded me to pay last month's installment on my husband's life insurance policy."

Yet, even she became alarmed on two occasions. On the first, I was giving an evening speech someplace in New York when the caller said to her, "I think your husband will be trying to come home in a couple of hours or so. If you look out the window, you will see that tall streetlight. In about two and a half hours, he is going to be hanging from the top of that. We are waiting for him. When we get him, we are coming over to that apartment to get you and the girls."

Lula called a friend of ours who lived in the same building and told him of the call. He came down and sat in our living room with his loaded gun until I returned safely to the house.

On another night, the persistent harasser insisted that "we are going to kill your two little girls." Lula called me in whatever city I was in. I phoned the commissioner of the New York City police, Michael J. Murphy, at his home.

Murphy said that he would immediately station police guards at the entrances to my building and would have a patrol car circling the block, keeping in touch with the guards by radio. He asked me to call the Bank Street College of Education in whose preschool and elementary school my daughters were enrolled, alerting them to the threats and instructing them not to release my daughters to anyone after school except my wife or me, even if some other person showed a letter presumably signed by Lula or me. He also asked that the school notify him whenever the children were to be taken on field trips to the beach, the zoo, the woods, or elsewhere, and he would have a plainclothes guard keeping watch on my children.

CORE did not feel entirely comfortable with "New York's finest," so three husky CORE members stood guard outside my apartment building, too. They were nonviolent on CORE demonstrations, but off demonstrations, they were on their own.

I was the only civil rights leader present at Malcolm's funeral in Harlem. Malcolm's bereaved followers went out of their way, even on this sorrowful occasion, to show me every courtesy and recognition. They were fully aware of my friendship with their murdered leader during the last year of his life.

Unsuccessfully, I sought to locate the lady in Ghana who had forecast Malcolm's death and called the timing of it so accurately. She was not to be found, having left Ghana two weeks earlier. The last line I got on her was that she was doing a striptease act in a Sicilian nightclub.

The threatening phone calls continued to come, and I was a little reluctant to leave home, but CORE work had to be done. One trip was to

Milwaukee for three days of speaking engagements arranged by the local chapter of CORE.

When I landed at the airport, there were Milwaukee city policemen standing around, armed with rifles. Such a sight would not have been unusual in a southern city, for the officials of many southern towns would have preferred that, if I were going to be killed, it be done elsewhere. I was astonished, though, to see it in Milwaukee.

I asked a police lieutenant if the armed guards were really necessary.

"We have been informed that something is going to happen while you are here," he said.

"To whom?" I asked.

With no trace of emotion, he said, "To you."

The drive to the hotel was with a police escort, sirens included. At the hotel, I was surprised to find that CORE had reserved a suite for me; I did not encourage such extravagance by our chapters. The chapter chairman informed me, however, that the police department had insisted they cancel the single room originally reserved and instead reserve a suite, for security purposes.

Two of the city's finest entered the suite first, with drawn revolvers, searching every conceivable hiding place, and then allowed me to enter. The two officers stayed in the living room of the suite all night, while two other policemen were in the room across the hall, and there was walkie-talkie communication between them. A police officer was also stationed at each end of the hall throughout the night. I was never told the specific reason for those precautionary steps, but presumed that it was related to Malcolm X assassination and my news conference following that event.

At each meeting where I spoke, the cops mounted the platform, first checking the doors, windows, and curtains, and flanked the platform throughout the meeting.

After the last meeting on the third day, the screaming sirens of police cars escorted my CORE chairman and me to the airport. After checking in and discovering that the flight was late, the chairman and I chatted about the chapter's plans for future activities. A few minutes later, another CORE member came dashing into the airport, and upon locating me, exclaimed, "Jeez, Jim, I was afraid we had missed you. We broke all speed limits getting here."

"What's the rush? Is something wrong?" I asked him.

"Just a few minutes after you left, a guy came up to the church and he had your bag. He wanted to give it to you."

"No, he does not have my bag. The bag I have here is the only one I brought to town, and as you can see, I have it."

"Well, he insisted that he had your bag and wanted to give it to you."

"Where is the fellow" I asked.

"I think he's at the ticket window, trying to find out if you've already checked in."

"Well, he made a mistake," said I. "Go and tell him that I said thanks, but I already have my bag."

A few minutes later, when the plane's departure was called, I bade good-bye to my chairman and proceeded through the gate toward the plane. Before I reached the aircraft, two persons—one a short, slight black fellow with a neatly trimmed beard and one of the early, moderate-length Afros; the other a tall white policeman—came running toward me, the small fellow shouting, "Wait, wait!"

I turned around and waited for the pair to reach me. The black man spoke.

"I got your bag, man. Here, take this bag."

In his hand was a medium-size tan leather suitcase, very similar to the one I had.

"That's not my bag," I said. "The bag I have with me is the only one I brought to town."

"No, no, no. Take this bag. You gotta take this bag, man," the man said. The policeman standing beside him nodded his head in agreement.

"What's in that bag?" I asked suspiciously.

"Everything. Everything you have been talking about is right here in this bag. Here, take this bag from me."

"Send it to me," I said. "I'll give you my address and you can mail it to me."

"No, I can't mail this bag to you, man, you gotta take it. Come on, come on. Take this bag."

"Do you know what I'm going to do?" I said. "I am going to turn my back on you and walk up the steps to that plane. See the stewardess standing there? The plane is late. She wants to roll those steps up and get it on its way. I am going to turn my back on you and walk right up those steps with the bag I have in my hand."

The little man turned to his tall companion and said, "Leave us alone for a minute. I've got to talk to the brother alone."

The policeman returned to the boarding gate and stood with his back to us. The black fellow walked even closer to me and said in a whisper, "Look man, I know this ain't your bag, but you *gotta* take it."

"Why do I gotta take it?" I asked.

He was standing practically against my stomach as he said, still in a whisper, "You don't know me, do you?"

When I said no, he said, "I'm the cat who impersonated Martin Luther King, Jr., in Philadelphia."

I didn't even know that King had been impersonated in Philadelphia.

I must say that I was tempted to take the bag, partly out of curiosity. Could it have contained proof of who killed Malcolm X or other priceless documents? I resisted the temptation. Instead, I said to him, "Do you remember what I told you a minute ago? I'm going to turn my back on you and get on that plane, and my own bag will be the only one that I'm going to be carrying."

"Well, what am I going to do with this bag, man?"

"That's your problem. Eat it."

I didn't look back until I had climbed the steps and was standing on the landing before entering the door to the aircraft. The little man with the beard was still standing there, staring at me. Still in his hand was the bag that looked so much like mine.

As we became airborne, I wondered what was in the other bag. Could it have been a bomb set to go off while I was in the air? Curiosity still haunted me after we landed in Chicago, and I walked toward the departure gate of the flight to New York.

Standing at that gate were four policemen in uniform. One said to the others in a stage whisper, "That's him. That's Farmer."

All their eyes moved swiftly from my face to my bag. Walking by them, I held the leather bag up so they could get a good look at it, turning it around as I passed. None of them made a move.

On the flight to New York, I had been troubled less about the contents of the other bag than about what would have happened in Chicago had I been in possession of it. My guess was, and is, that the bag no doubt had some marking that would identify it to the policemen at the boarding gate. They would have taken it from me, opened it, and no doubt found contraband in its lining—heroin probably. The judge would have died laughing when I explained to him that a little fellow came up to me and said, "Take this bag, man; you gotta take this bag." His laughter, I am sure, would have continued as he sentenced me to the maximum that one gets for possessing or transporting—or whatever the charge would have been—heroin or some other illegal drug.

That speculation confirmed my belief about Malcolm's murder.

On the following day, I relaxed on a one-coach commuter train to Poughkeepsie, New York, where I was going to speak at Vassar College. This was just a short train ride; there would be no bags thrust toward me, no frightening take-offs or landings; all was comfortable and serene.

Serene, that is, until the trainman came dashing out of his compartment in the front of the coach shouting, "Hang on to your seats."

He jerked the emergency brake cord and the train's wheels locked as it plowed into an automobile that was across the tracks. The train wobbled for a hundred yards or so before finally coming to a stop.

While we were awaiting repairs to the oil tank broken by the collision, we learned that two women had been driving the vehicle when it stalled on the tracks. They had left it and gone up the tracks to try to hail oncoming trains, but they had gone in the wrong direction.

Once more under way, I tried again to relax. The trainman came down the aisle and said to me, "Mr. Farmer, when you write your memoirs, you can say that you missed it by about that much." He was holding his index finger and thumb about one inch apart.

When I asked why, he said that the moment we hit that car, we were passing a speeding freight train going in the opposite direction. There was a very narrow clearance between the two trains, he told me, maybe no more than a foot. Upon impact, we wobbled and he estimated that had we wobbled another inch or so, we would have been clipped by the speeding freight and by now would be over in the field on our right, burning.

After the events of the past few weeks, I had to fight off paranoia. In all probability, the near disaster on the train ride to Poughkeepsie was pure coincidence, but one had to wonder.

I do not know who paid the gunmen to kill Malcolm X, but the belief that his assassination was related to drug traffic and the syndicate has remained with me. He was hurting their business with his weekly exhortations in Harlem rallies, urging his followers to "chase the pushers out of Harlem." Proving nothing, but bolstering my suspicions was the fact that when Malcolm was on his trip to Europe, the Middle East, and Africa, DeGaulle had refused to allow him to leave the plane at the Paris airport. He had said that he feared Malcolm would be killed in Paris.

I was aware, of course, that Marseilles, France, was an important station in the world traffic of heroin; much of the processing was done there before the finished product was shipped to other key points in the industrial world.

What was it that Malcolm knew that made him such a prime target for those who stalked and finally killed him?

There are those, especially young militants, who are more enamored of the CIA theory, which is possibly correct. Yet, it must be remembered that on occasions the CIA and the mob have worked together when their interests coincided or when there has been an acceptable quid pro quo for both.

CHAPTER 22

THE MARCH AND ITS GENESIS

IT SHOULD BE NO surprise to anyone that Malcolm X was not a member of the Big Six. He was not a civil rights leader; he was a black nationalist leader. His objective was the building of a black nation, not the integration of blacks into the American nation. The meetings would have been pure bedlam had he been there. The debates in those sessions at the Taconic Foundation would have been not over strategy and tactics, but over basic objectives. Nothing would have been accomplished.

There was another man of great stature who was not a part of that inner circle. The venerable A. Philip Randolph, who for years had been the top black leader in the country, and even in the early sixties probably was more widely respected than anyone except Martin Luther King, Jr., had no accepted civil rights organization. The Brotherhood of Sleeping Car Porters, which was Phil's base, was a labor union; when he spoke out on civil rights, he spoke as an individual.

In early 1963, Randolph phoned Wilkins, who was serving his stint as chairman of CUCRL, requesting permission to come before the Big Six to make a presentation. With the concurrence of the other members, Roy invited Phil to do so.

Ever since 1941, when FDR's issuance of Executive Order 8802 led Randolph to cancel his march on Washington, the dream of such a march had burned brightly in his mind. His proposal to the Big Six was that their organizations combine resources to have a gigantic march on Washington during the coming summer. He spoke, with a visionary gleam in his eyes, of more than a hundred thousand people congregated in the District of Columbia to speak with a mighty, unified voice for jobs and freedom. Randolph proposed further that Bayard Rustin serve as director of the march to coordinate the efforts in such an undertaking.

Phil turned to me and said, "I am sure you agree with these recommendations I am making, Jim, don't you?"

I nodded and said, "Yes, I do."

Roy Wilkins expressed lukewarm feelings about Randolph's idea, saying that he was not sure such an effort at such great expense would accomplish anything.

If the objective was to push for a civil rights bill, he thought that a great mass of people going to Washington would have far less effect than the professional lobbying of a person like Clarence Mitchell, who headed the Washington bureau of the NAACP. However, Roy added that he was not going to oppose the idea and, if others supported it, would certainly go along with it with the reservations he had expresed.

Wilkins expressed considerable misgivings, without saying why, about having Rustin as the director of the march. He suggested, instead, that Phil be the director, and that we hold Phil accountable for what happened during the planning and preparations for the march. Wilkins said that Phil Randolph could then select whomever he wished as his deputy. Whitney Young agreed with Roy's sentiments.

Thus, the work on the march on Washington began with Bayard Rustin doing most of the work in coordinating the massive venture. I had had my differences with Bayard in the past and was destined to have more differences with him in the future, but I must say that I have never seen such a difficult task of coordination performed with more skill and deftness. Though the staff of the various cooperating organizations—including the National Council of Churches, the National Conference of Christians and Jews, and various labor organizations and Jewish groups, as well as organizations headed by the Big Six—were at his disposal, it is Bayard to whom much of the credit must go for the successful fruition of Randolph's idea.

According to John Lewis of SNCC, three organizations with the strongest membership produced the bulk of the more than 250,000 persons who marched on Washington—the NAACP, the United Automobile Workers (UAW), and the International Union of Electrical Workers (IUE).

I was represented by staff members at some of the planning sessions for the march, since I was traveling a good bit of the time. It had been my pledge at the beginning of my CORE directorship that I would be no swivel-chair general, but would be in the foxholes and the trenches. I was trying to keep that pledge.

CORE and I were then Freedom Riding on the United States highways, attempting to do for automobile travelers what we had achieved for those journeying by interstate bus. African diplomats had been embarrassed in eating establishments on Route 40 between New York and Baltimore. Minor international incidents had resulted.

In dozens of automobiles, CORE members took to the road, sitting in at all restaurants that refused us service on Route 40. As our ranks were swelled with other CORE members coming in from different parts of the country, restaurant owners on Route 40 agreed to negotiate, and the segregation bars were lifted.

In spring 1963, we mapped plans to expand what we called the "free-dom highways" campaign, begun in 1962, to such major restaurant chains as Howard Johnson's and Holiday Inn up and down the southeastern states. In a press conference, I announced that we were going to start with Howard Johnson's in the state of Florida. In the negotiations that were to precede direct action, Howard Johnson's desegregated its Florida restaurants. We then shifted to North Carolina, where negotiations had no such success.

We went to the drawing board to prepare plans for a statewide freedom highways campaign in North Carolina. The fact that the Tarheel State had a liberal governor, Terry Sanford, and a liberal image nationwide was not going to make the task any easier. Our key statewide honcho was to be attorney Floyd McKissick, who, prior to becoming a CORE leader in the state, had been a prominent NAACP attorney. Gorden Carey from my staff made frequent visits to North Carolina for lengthy discussions with McKissick to coordinate plans.

In the meantime, the CORE national office, which thrived on bustling, nonstop activity, like our frenetic chapters around the country, was constantly sparking new programs in every part of the nation. Daily headlines and television news broadcasts were dominated by CORE action nationwide, SNCC action in southern states, and marches and speeches by Martin Luther King, Jr.

In that atmosphere, while putting the finishing touches on the freedom highways drive in North Carolina, I announced in a news conference that our research showed very few black professionals were employed by Sears, Roebuck, and that we were beginning a drive to make that company a bit more "colorful." I wrote to Sears, Roebuck, requesting a conference to seek to negotiate a solution to the problem so as to make CORE's nonviolent direct action unnecessary. A prompt reply from the management of Sears informed us that they had openings for some twenty-five top black professionals and would appreciate it if we would help them locate qualified persons to fill those openings. We helped them fill the openings.

Boycotts and sit-ins were held in similar firms—manufacturing, distributing, and retailing. There were countless arrests and, in most cases, the results were successful. The majority of our campaigns concluded favorably in the negotiation stage, without the necessity for action. Negotiations don't make headlines; only action does. We began to feel like the prizefighter whose awesome reputation made it impossible for him to find opponents. North Carolina, however, had a ring waiting for us. It also had some jail cells waiting.

In Greensboro, the student leader for CORE was a young senior at North Carolina A and T who was a big man on campus—on the dean's list, and the football quarterback. His name was Jesse Jackson. He and I led many marches through town, and there were countless sit-ins. At one point, there were three thousand persons in jail, mostly students from North Carolina A and T and Bennett College. Jesse and I called another mass meeting at the church. There were at least a thousand students in attendance; we had just about cleared out both campuses. In Jesse's opening speech to the assembled crowd, he shouted this question: "How many of you are willing to go to jail?"

The throng of students responded by waving their toothbrushes in the air. I think everyone there had a toothbrush for the occasion. A march and more sit-ins were scheduled for the following day, and everyone was told to come with a toothbrush. The meeting ended with a singing of "We Shall Overcome." It might have been heard as far away as the State House in Raleigh.

We were notified that the officials were dropping all bail requirements for those three thousand in jail. Everyone could get out on his or her own recognizance. The jailees refused to come out, saying, "You arrested us and put us here; now you keep us here and feed us."

Word then came to me that I should tell the jailed students that the governor said they have to come out of jail. Again, the students refused.

When the authorities came to remove them the students went limp, refusing to walk out on their own power. Authorities commandeered all available buses, and city police, sheriffs, deputies, and state police physically carried the students out of jail and into the buses, drove them to their respective campuses, and there deposited them on the grounds.

The removal complete, the jail doors were locked.

It was the first and only jail lock-out in the movement, following what I believe to have been the largest jail-in for civil rights activity in this country.

To my eternal puzzlement, hardly a word of those events in North Carolina got outside of the state, even though the media gave the freedom highways campaign full coverage and representatives of the wire services and networks were there. There was no other major civil rights story at the time, yet we were unable to get that story moved beyond what I came to call the "tobacco curtain." I do not pretend to know how the conspiracy of silence was accomplished, but I believe that it had something to do with what has been termed "management of the press," emanating from powers available to the State House. Governors of most southern states do not want adverse publicity about their states spread around the nation. That is particularly true when they are trying to get national industry to come in; nothing must be allowed to interfere with that goal.

My public relations persons in New York, Marvin Rich and Val Coleman, were not able to move the story from that vantage point, either. I was informed by a black writer for the *New York Post* that he had seen a memorandum being circulated, stating that if stories came in on the wire about CORE's freedom highways campaign, they were not to be printed, but to be sent up to the desk of the publisher.

Governor Terry Sanford of North Carolina, a fine and liberal gentleman, and highly competent, contacted me, inviting me to the State House for lunch to discuss solving the problems of discrimination in places of public accommodations in his state. Durham attorney Floyd McKissick and I went to the State House to hold these discussions with the governor.

The governor offered to set up a blue ribbon panel in the state to be administered by the North Carolina Human Relations Commission. It would negotiate with the franchise owners of the chain restaurants on North Carolina highways to get across-the-board desegregation. As a part of the deal, he asked that we have a cessation of demonstrations immediately, pending the results of the panel's efforts. Floyd and I requested a few minutes to consult privately. When we returned to the room, I told the governor that we agreed in principle to his plan, but the moratorium on freedom highways demonstrations would not begin immediately. We required a hiatus of two weeks. Terry Sanford accepted that modification of his plan.

As the governor's panel was being put together, we sought to build up a little more pressure on them with a huge march from Durham to a Howard Johnson's ten miles outside of town, and a rally on the spacious grounds in front of that restaurant. As a gesture of solidarity, I invited Roy Wilkins to come down from New York and participate in this demonstration after informing him that he would not be embarrassed by being confronted with an arrest situation. We had secured the necessary permits and, in the unlikely event we were ordered to disperse from the restaurant's grounds, we would try to negotiate a change in those orders. Failing in that, we would disperse peaceably and march back to Durham.

Roy Wilkins came down and joined me on the improvised platform. I introduced him as the leader of our sister organization—no, our mother organization—the National Association for the Advancement of Colored People, and urged the huge crowd to give him an appropriate welcome. The applause was deafening amid shouts of "freedom now."

Wilkins spoke without a written speech. Freed of slavish reliance on a written text, he was warm and inspired. Roy was at his best on that occasion. When he had finished we embraced and the crowd roared its approval.

Sanford's panel came through with a negotiated desegregation of the major chain eating establishments on North Carolina's highways. Like the Freedom Ride, freedom highways had been a success. But unlike the Ride, few persons outside the state ever heard of freedom highways.

My staff surrogates reported to me that plans for the march on Washington were going well under the guidance of Bayard Rustin. It now appeared that there would be well over the hundred thousand persons there that Randolph at first envisioned. Behind the scenes, much wheeling and dealing was going on.

The Kennedy administration, fearful that such throngs in Washington would produce rioting, had tried to get the march called off. Failing in that, they sought to ensure that the march's nature would not be inimical to the political interests of the administration. Working through Walter Reuther of the UAW, Roy Wilkins of the NAACP, and Whitney Young of the Urban League—who were on the planning committee—the White House naturally made every effort to shape the character of what promised to be a historic event. The leaders, including Randolph, King, Reuther, Wilkins, Young, and I, were invited to the White House to meet with the president and the attorney general. At that meeting, the Kennedys expressed their concern about possible violence and we assured them that the march would be peaceful and nonviolent. We would have sufficient trained marshals in the crowd to maintain order. We ourselves would assume responsibility for policing our march.

Meanwhile, in the planning council itself, a battle was raging between the older, more established groups on the one hand, and SNCC and CORE on the other. SNCC and CORE "troops" were still getting their heads broken by billy clubs, their eyes damaged by tear gas, their flesh and clothing torn by police dogs, while FBI agents stood by, taking notes. Our representatives wanted the march to be one of protest against the recalcitrance of bigotry and segregation, and the as yet relative inactivity of the federal government on our behalf. Others wanted it to be a testament of hope and faith and prayer.

At first SNCC, with some CORE backing, had called for civil disobedience in Washington, including sitting down on thoroughfares and blocking traffic, sit-ins in the offices of congressmen and senators from many southern states, and mass arrests. That proposal provoked anger from Wilkins and he, Reuther, and others beat it down, getting a vote from the planners that any organization participating in the march *must* abide by the accepted discipline of no civil disobedience, no disruption, and no arrests. The decision rankled many of the younger militants, yet the planning and organization of the march proceeded remarkably apace.

The Kennedys, who had opposed new civil rights legislation, reversed themselves and promised to introduce such a measure, prodded no doubt, by King's widely publicized Birmingham demonstrations and by the upcoming march on Washington.

In my office, I received an astonishing cablegram. It was from Mao Tse-tung. Chairman Mao, with whom I had had no prior contact, expressed his solidarity with the march of black Americans on Washington and offered to help in any way that he could. My staff and I thought at first it was a practical joke. Further consideration, however, persuaded us that there was no reason to doubt its authenticity. My reply to Mao by cable rejected his support and informed him that we were perfectly capable of dealing with our own problems.

A week or so before the march, I was in Plaquemine, Louisiana, at the request of local blacks, to speak at a rally and lead a march protesting police brutality. When the march reached downtown Plaquemine, I was arrested, as were the local leaders and over two hundred of the marchers. The town jail did not have space for all of us, so the local leaders and I were transferred to a jail in the neighboring town of Donaldsonville.

Bail was set at $500 cash, and we had no bail bondsman. This forced a major decision on me. Should I bail myself out and go to the march, leaving the others in jail? Many of them had planned to go to the march, too, but CORE certainly did not have the money to bail everyone out. I had the added pressure, however, of having been expected to make a speech at the march, as the head of one of the sponsoring organizations.

When, through my lawyer, I informed my office of my decision to remain in jail until the trial, pressure mounted on me to bail out and speak at the march. Those pressures came not from my staff, who agreed with my decision, but from some of the other civil rights leaders and others associated with the march. Apparently, some felt that my jail-in at this time was part of the SNCC-CORE campaign in the controversy regarding the nature of the march itself. Others reportedly felt that I was trying to upstage them by being a jailed martyr at the time they were making speeches.

I received a wire from Roy Wilkins and Whitney Young, strongly urging me to bail out immediately and come to the march. They indicated that my presence would be useful in maintaining the desired decorum in Washington.

My reply, of course, was negative.

A long-distance call came to me at the jail from Jay Richard Kennedy, a friend who apparently had some ties with some agency of the federal government. Jay Kennedy was planning a televised panel discussion among the march leaders following the march on Washington. He urged me to come out and speak. I declined.

For reasons of its own, the state of Louisiana seemed to agree with my decision not to be present at the march. It issued a summons for me on some entirely spurious charge, the nature of which I do not even remember. What it meant was that, if I should bail out, I would be rearrested as soon as I walked out of jail. By the time my lawyer was able to get the matter thrown out of court, the march would be over. The state thus ensured that I would not be present at the march on Washington.

In my Donaldsonville jail cell, I wrote a brief letter and asked CORE Chairman Floyd McKissick to read it at the march. I requested that the other march sponsors grant him that privilege in my absence, and they agreed to do so.

I learned that John Lewis had sent a draft of his speech to the committee set up to review all speeches prior to the march, and the committee had objected to certain parts of his draft. What they found particularly objectionable was a sentence calling for a "scorched earth policy." That phrase was finally removed. The phrase did not sound at all like John Lewis and I do not believe he wrote it. No doubt, some of the other SNCC persons had served as speechwriters on this occasion for John. He was far too gentle and compassionate a human being to even think in terms of scorching the earth he loved while people were hungry.

Some of the local black citizens of Plaquemine brought a small black-and-white television set to the Donaldsonville jail and the jail officials allowed them to bring it up to my cell so I could watch the march on the screen. All thoughts of the controversy over the kind of march it was going to be disappeared.

The awesome spectacle of over 250,000 persons—black and white, Protestant, Catholic, and Jewish, young and old, northern and southern, infirm and healthy—erased all doubts as to its worthwhileness.

I wept in my cell and actually regretted, momentarily, my decision not to go. When Mahalia Jackson sang and Martin Luther King, Jr., spoke, my tears disappeared and were replaced with awe.

The conscience of the nation could not be wrung any tighter. I believed then, and still do, that King's speech was an authentic American classic on a par historically with Lincoln's Gettysburg Address. There are times when divine inspiration so touches a person that he rises beyond himself. In that moment, at the march on Washington, Martin Luther King, Jr., was touched by a spirit that cannot be recaptured in our lifetime.

On August 31, 1963, three days following the march on Washington, all of us were released from the Plaquemine and Donaldsonville jails. Upon my release from jail, all hell broke loose!

CHAPTER 23

THE MANHUNT*

I HAD COME TO Plaquemine, which is the principal town in the Louisiana parish of Iberville, at the request of Ronnie Moore, a CORE New Orleans field secretary. CORE had targeted it for a voter registration drive because Plaquemine's city boundaries had deliberately been drawn in a horseshoe-shaped pattern in order to exclude the black community nestled almost in its center.

The black community had no municipal benefits. Roads were unpaved, and raw sewage flowed through its open gutters. A few of the local professional people—including the community's only black physician, Doctor Bertrand Tyson, also the principal of the local black school—had involved themselves in the registration drive at considerable risk to themselves.

When we were released from the Plaquemine and Donaldsonville jails, the spirit of militancy remained high in the wake of the successful march on Washington, and two days later, a group of young people organized another demonstration, this time protesting segregation in public places as well as the community's exclusion from the municipal boundaries.

They had asked me to lead the march, but I had declined because they had been charged with having been led by "outside agitators." I wanted this march to be led by local black citizens. I would remain behind, in the parsonage of the Baptist minister, Reverend Jetson Davis.

This time, however, the marchers did not make it into the town. The chief of police stopped them halfway, arrested the leaders, and held the rest of the marchers until state troopers arrived.

The troopers arrived on horseback, riding like cowboys, and they charged into the crowd of boys and girls as if they were rounding up a herd of stampeding cattle. They were armed with billy clubs and cattle prods, which they used mercilessly. Many of the youngsters who fell under the blows were trampled by the horses. The injured and uninjured fled from their pursuers back to the Plymouth Rock Baptist Church. I came out of the parsonage to give the terrified marchers as much comfort as I could, while a few nurses treated their wounds.

The gratuitous savagery inflicted upon their children immediately aroused the adults to a pitch of militancy much more intense than anything the organizational efforts of CORE had been able to achieve. The other ministers, who had previously hung back, united for the first time. Apathy or fear or whatever had caused the ministers' reluctance dissolved in outrage. The following morning, a Sunday, every minister in the black community preached a sermon extolling freedom and condemning police

*Excerpted, with revisions, from *Freedom When?* by James Farmer (New York: Random House, 1965), pp. 3–22.

brutality. After church, by previous arrangement, each minister led his congregation to Reverend Davis's church and they organized a massive march to protest against the rout of the previous day.

As the time approached for the march to begin, some of the ministers began to waver. One of them hesitated on his way to the front of the line. "Where's my wife?" he said, looking around fearfully. "I don't see my wife. I think I'd better just go on home."

His wife was standing right behind him. "Man," she said, "if you don't get up there in the front of that line, you ain't got no wife."

He marched, all right, but his presence could not alter the course of events. This time when the troopers intercepted the marchers, there was nothing impromptu about the confrontation. They did not even come on horseback; they came in patrol cars and the horses arrived in vans. The troopers mounted their horses and assembled their weapons as if the crowd of unarmed men and women before them were an opposing army. They then charged into the mass as they had done the day before, flailing with billy clubs and stabbing with cattle prods.

"Get up, nigger!" one would shout, poking a man with an electric prod and beating him to the ground with a club. "Run, nigger, run."

I was waiting at the Plymouth Rock Church. I watched the crowd come running back, those who could run, bleeding, hysterical, faint, some of the stronger ones carrying the injured. A nurse started to bandage their wounds and the rest of us began to sing "We Shall Overcome." The troopers rode roaring through the streets, right up to the door of the church (renamed Freedom Rock).

They dismounted and broke into the church, yelling and hurling tear gas cannisters, one after the other, poisoning the air. The gas masks protecting the troopers' faces transformed them into monsters as they stood and watched our people growing more and more frantic, screaming with pain and terror, trampling on one another in their frenzied efforts to escape through the back door to the parsonage behind the church.

When the people had finally escaped, the troopers set about destroying the empty church. They knocked out the windows, overturned the benches, laid waste everything they could reach, and flooded the gutted building with high-pressure fire hoses until Bibles and hymnals floated in the aisles. (A lone reporter remained, chronicling the scene, until he, too, was shocked with an electric cattle prod. When he later fled town, we were truly isolated from the outside world.)

Then they attacked the parsonage to which we had fled. The troopers sent tear gas cannisters smashing through the windows until all the windows were shattered and almost everyone inside was blinded and choking. The noise of the screaming was unbearable.

I caught sight of Ronnie Moore administering mouth-to-mouth resuscitation to a young woman. People writhed on the floor, seeking oxygen. A few managed to push through the rear door into the parsonage yard, but the troopers, anticipating them, had ridden around to the back with more tear gas to force them back inside again. Gas thrown into the parsonage forced them back out into the yard once again. All those men and women, who just that morning had resolutely banded together to reach out for freedom and dignity, were reduced now to running from torment to torment, helpless victims of a bitter game.

I tried to telephone the White House, the FBI, the Department of Justice, and my staff in New York. Every time I gave the operator the number to be called, we lost the connection. The operators were not putting through any long-distance calls from the black community that day. Within it, though, there was telephone service and several calls got through to us in the parsonage.

What had appeared to be a random and mindless brutality proved to have had a mad purpose after all. It was a manhunt. Troopers were in the streets, kicking open doors, searching every house in the black community, overturning chairs and tables, looking under beds and in closets, yelling, "Come on out, Farmer, we know you're in there. Come on out, Farmer! We're going to get you."

We could hear the screaming in the streets as the troopers on horseback resumed their sport with the cattle prods and billy clubs: "Get up, nigger! Run, nigger, run!" Holding their victims down with a cattle prod, they would say, "We'll let you up, nigger, if you tell us where Farmer is." Two of our group members, hiding beneath the church, overheard one trooper saying to another, "When we catch that goddamned nigger, Farmer, we're gonna kill him."

Spiver Gordon, CORE's field secretary in Plaquemine—who people say looks like me—told me later that he wandered out of the church into the street at this time. Sighting him, state troopers ran up, shouting, "Here he is, boys. We got Farmer. We got their motherfucking Jesus."

A trooper beckoned to a crowd of hoodlums who were watching nearby, many holding chains, ropes, and clubs. "What post we gonna hang him from?" said one.

After Spiver convinced them he wasn't me, he took a beating for looking like me. An officer said, "He ain't Farmer. You've beat him enough. Put him in the car and arrest him."

There seemed no prospect of aid from any quarter. We were all suffering intensely from the tear gas, and the troopers kept us running. In desperation, I sent two people creeping through the waist-high grass behind the parsonage to a funeral hall half a block away to ask for refuge. The owners of the hall agreed to shelter us, although I doubt they knew what they were taking on.

Dusk had fallen, and in groups of two and three, we were able to crawl on our bellies through the grass, making use of guerrilla tactics that some remembered from the war but none of us had ever learned as a technique of nonviolent demonstration, until we reached our new sanctuary.

Night had fallen by the time all three hundred of us were safely inside, jammed together like straws in a broom, into two rooms and a hallway.

The sound of screaming still echoed in the streets as the troopers beat down another black or invaded another house. The telephones were still useless.

Very shortly, the troopers figured out where we were. One of them, a huge, raging, red-faced man, kicked open the door of the funeral home and screamed, "Come on out, Farmer. We know you're in there. We're gonna get you."

I was in the front room. I could look down the hallway, over all the heads, right into his face. It was flushed and dripping with sweat; his hair hung over his eyes and his mouth was twisted. Another trooper burst through the door to stand beside him: "Farmer, come out."

I had to give myself up. I felt like a modern Oedipus who, unaware, brought down a plague upon the city. In this hall, their lives endangered by my presence, were three hundred people, many of whom had never even seen me before that day. I began to make my way into the hall, thinking that I would ask to see the warrant for my arrest and demand to know the charges against me. But before I could take three steps, the men around me grabbed me silently and pulled me back into the front room, whispering fiercely, "We're not going to let you go out there tonight. That's a lynch mob. You go out there tonight, you won't be alive tomorrow morning."

The trooper, meanwhile, had discovered a large black man in the back room. He shouted triumphantly: "Here he is, we got that nigger, Farmer! Come on in, boys. We got him here."

"I'm not Farmer," the man said. A third trooper came in.

"That ain't Farmer," he said. "I know that nigger." They went through his identification papers.

Suddenly, to everyone's astonishment, a woman pushed her way through the crowd to the back room and confronted the troopers. It was the owner of the funeral home, a woman who had previously held herself apart from the movement.

I can never know—she herself probably does not know—what inner revolution or what mysterious force plucked her from her caul of fear and thrust her forth to assert with such a dramatic and improbable gesture her new birth of freedom. A funeral hall is as good a place as any for a person to come to life, I suppose, and her action sparked a sympathetic impulse in everyone who watched as she planted herself in front of the first trooper and shook a finger in his face.

"Do you have a search warrant to come into my place of business?"

The trooper stared at her, confounded, and backed away. "No," he said.

"You're not coming into my place of business without a search warrant," said the owner. "I'm a taxpayer and a law-abiding citizen. I have a wake going on here."

I prayed inwardly that her valiant subterfuge would not prove to be a prophecy.

"This ain't no wake," the trooper said, looking around at the throng of angry, frightened people, crushed together before him. "These people ain't at no wake."

"Well, you're not coming into my place of business without a search warrant." The accusing finger pushed him back to the door.

He muttered for a moment to his men outside, then turned and yelled, "All right. We got all the tear gas and all the guns. You ain't got nothin'. We'll give you just five minutes to get Farmer out here. Just five minutes, that's all." He slammed the door.

The door clanged in my ears like the door of a cell in death row. "I'll go out and face them," I said. Once again, I was restrained. They would stick by me, these strangers insisted, even if they all had to die, but they would not let me out to be lynched.

Someone standing near me pulled out a gun. "Mr. Farmer," he said, "if a trooper comes through that door, he'll be dead."

"That may be," I conceded. "But what about the trooper behind him and all the ones behind that one? You'll only provoke them into shooting and we won't have a chance."

Very reluctantly, he allowed me to take the gun from him. It is hard for people to practice nonviolence when they are looking death in the face. I wondered how many others were armed.

Then my own private thoughts engulfed me. Reverend Davis was leading a group in the Lord's Prayer; another group was singing "We Shall Overcome." I was certain I was going to die. What kind of death would it be? Would they mutilate me first? What does it feel like to die?

Then I grew panicky about the insurance. Had I paid the last installment? How much was it? I couldn't remember. I couldn't remember anything about it. My wife and little girls—how would it be for them? Abbey was only two, then—too young to remember—but Tami was four and a half, and very close to me. She would remember. Well, damn it, if I had to die, at least let the organization wring some use out of my death. I hoped the newspapers were out there. Plenty of them. With plenty of cameras. At that point, I did not realize they had fled.

The five minutes passed. Six. Seven. Eight. A knock at the front door. My lawyers from New Orleans, Lolis Elie and Robert Collins, identified themselves and squeezed in, breathless.

The New Orleans radio had broadcast the news that a manhunt was in progress in Plaquemine, and they had driven over immediately. The community, they said, was in a state of siege. Everywhere one looked one saw troopers, like an invading army.

The two lawyers had crawled through the high grass to seek refuge in the graveyard, but when they got there, the place came alive. There was a black behind every tombstone. Apparently, everyone had counted on the dead to be more hospitable than the living. Apparently, also, everyone knew where I was, but no one was telling the white men.

The troopers, it seemed, had been bluffing. They could not be wholly sure I was in the funeral home. It occurred to me that my physical safety, in some elusive way that had very little to do with me, had become a kind of transcendent symbol to all these people of the possibilities for freedom and personal dignity that existed for them. By protecting me, they were preserving their dreams. But did they understand, I wondered, that through their acts of courage during this desperate night, they had taken the first great step toward realizing these possibilities? Did they sense that they had gained at least some of that freedom for which they longed, here and now?

Just as the lawyers finished their story, there was another knock at the door. I thought the troopers had come at last, until I remembered that troopers don't knock. The two men who entered were recently acquired friends from Plaquemine, and pretty rough characters in their own right. They were from an adjoining, unincorporated town. Fred and Bill were ex-marines who carried several guns in their car at all times. The troopers, they told me, had grown systematic. They had set up roadblocks on every street leading out of town. The men who had been waiting in the back had just driven off in the direction of the sheriff's office, presumably to get a search warrant. In short, if I did not get out right now, my life would not be worth a dime.

I told my lawyers to get in their car and try to drive out through the roadblocks. I thought the troopers might respect their identification as attorneys. If they got through, they were to call my wife and tell her I was all right, call Marvin Rich at CORE and have him get in touch with the FBI, and then call New Orleans to try to get some kind of federal protection. It was imperative that we make contact with the outside world.

Then Fred and Bill set forth their plan. The woman who owned the funeral home had two hearses, both equipped with shortwave radios. They would send the old one out as a decoy with just a driver. He was furnished with a hand-drawn map locating each roadblock. He was asked to drive to roadblock A, then back up fast, scooting toward roadblock B, and so on. The strategy was to get the troopers to leave their posts and pursue him. That done, he would radio back our escape route. Meanwhile, we would try to escape in the second hearse, which would be waiting, its motor running, in a garage we could reach without leaving the house.

Fred and Bill led the way to the garage, forcing a passage through the sweating men and women who murmured phrases of encouragement and good wishes as we passed.

I prayed that our departure would release them from danger, marveling once more at the courage and devotion shown by these strangers.

It was cool, briefly, in the garage, but the hearse soon became hot and stuffy. Ronnie Moore, Reverend Davis, and I crawled into the back and crouched down—three restless, nervous men huddled together in a space meant for one motionless body. Someone climbed into the driver's seat and we were off, speeding down the back roads toward New Orleans. Fred and Bill led the way in their car to the unmanned roadblock. They hit the wooden horses with their car, knocking them out of the way. They then made a U-turn and waved good-bye to us. Though I did not realize it at the time, both were heavily armed.

The driver of our hearse—a large man selected by Fred and Bill—was accompanied by an equally large companion. Both, I later learned, were similarly armed. Their instructions from Bill and Fred were, "Don't stop for anything and, if forced to stop, shoot." We took a winding route with countless detours over very rough country roads the blacks knew more intimately than the whites, because of segregated hunting. This was their territory.

Although you can drive from Plaquemine to New Orleans in less than two hours by highway, it took us four and a half hours, despite the fact that we were going very fast and did not stop at all.

Whenever a car approached, the driver or his companion would call back, "All right, Mr. Farmer, there's a car coming. Get your head down." Seconds later, they would say, "It's all clear now. You can sit up again." Our destination was another funeral home; our only protection was blackness, a color that had never before promised immunity to blacks in the South. At times during that wild ride, I thought I was already dead. I don't know what the others thought. But when at last we climbed out of the hearse into the hot New Orleans night, we were, by the grace of God and the extraordinary courage of many ordinary men and women, still very much alive. And not yet entirely out of danger.

I phoned Oretha Castle, head of the New Orleans CORE chapter; she knew there had been a house-to-house search for me. The last she had heard on the radio was that I was "missing." The two lawyers had passed the roadblocks and called the authorities in New Orleans, and the press had picked up the news immediately. They had also called my wife, before she had heard anything, to tell her not to worry. "Jim's all right."

"Oh," said Lula. "Why shouldn't he be?"

"There was a little trouble down in Plaquemine, but there's nothing to worry about now. He's out of danger."

Whereupon Lula turned on the television set and learned that there was a house-to-house search reportedly going on in Plaquemine, Louisiana, for CORE national director James Farmer, and, a little later, that James Farmer was reported missing in Plaquemine, Louisiana. She told me later that she turned off the news broadcast and took the children outside, where the voices they would hear were less ominous. Shortly afterward, when she went to call the press to find out more, she found they were already waiting for her at the house.

In New York, though, they never carried the complete story. Later that morning, I held a press conference at Oretha Castle's home. Newspaper and television reporters listened, mouths agape, and carefully took down all the details, but what they wrote never got farther than New Orleans. Even then, the story rated only a back-page item in the *Times-Picayune*, saying that CORE's national director, James Farmer, held a news conference yesterday and mentioned that there had been some trouble in the town of Plaquemine and that he had finally escaped in a hearse.

I announced at the press conference that I intended to return to Plaquemine the next day, for I had no intention of being a fugitive from anyplace in this country. I would appear at the courthouse at ten o'clock, in broad daylight, in order to be served with a warrant for my arrest—if there was one—and hear the charges, whatever they might be.

In the meantime, the assistant to the director of the Washington FBI office, Cartha "Deke" DeLoach, went to New York to find out the details of the incident from our national office. DeLoach walked into the CORE national office in New York, demanding to know "what the hell was going on in Plaquemine."

Val Coleman shouted at him, "Jim almost died in Plaquemine last night. He called us this morning to say that he is going back into Plaquemine tomorrow morning and will be at the courthouse at 10:00 A.M. You guys have got to protect him."

DeLoach replied, "The FBI is not a protection agency, it is an investigative body."

Val fairly screamed at him, "Well, goddamn it, if Farmer dies tomorrow morning, his blood is on your hands."

DeLoach said, "I repeat, the bureau is an investigative body. However, this is an extraordinary situation." He then turned and walked out of the office.

Our attorney, Lolis Elie, called the FBI regional office in New Orleans with the same request. I talked to the man in charge of the New Orleans FBI office, telling him of my close escape from a lynch mob.

"I was afraid of that," he said.

"What does that mean?" I responded.

"Nothing," he replied.

He told me he would "see" what he could do to help me.

With this ambiguous support, Lolis Elie drove Ronnie Moore, Reverend Davis, and me to Plaquemine the next morning. The city police were waiting for us. A large crowd of shirt-sleeved white men, women, and children stood to the side of the courthouse, waiting and staring.

To our relief, five or six FBI agents were on the steps of the courthouse. Two agents came over to me as soon as I walked up the steps. But, as it turned out, the state troopers had no warrant for my arrest and there were no charges filed against me.

Nor could we take any action against them, for their nameplates and badge numbers had been taped over during the manhunt. In fact, we learned that many of the men who had been riding that night were not even regular state troopers. They were ordinary citizens who had been deputized for the occasion.

I later learned that Bobby Kennedy cut short a vacation because of the incident, though to what extent he became involved I do not know.

Though I demanded that the FBI undertake an investigation, the sole agent who appeared in Plaquemine took statements from witnesses during the morning; then, saying he was going to lunch, he disappeared, leaving most of the three hundred witnesses who had made themselves available high and dry.

I asked Doctor Bertrand O. Tyson, who had many white patients, to find out what was up that day. Tyson told me three sources had revealed that "word had come down from high up" that I was to be killed that night. The state troopers were supposed to beat me almost to the point of death, at which point I would be turned over to a mob, which would then finish the job. My body was not to be found for a long time, if at all. I asked Tyson what "high up" meant, and he told me that either the people who had talked with him did not know, or were not telling.

I went back to New Orleans and spent the next day with friends, trying to relax. Then I boarded a plane for New York, destined to face internal problems with CORE that were almost as deadly, in an institutional sense, as those we had faced in Plaquemine.

CHAPTER 24

THE CANNIBALIZING OF THE MOVEMENT

"What!" I shouted. "why haven't I heard about this?"

"You're hearing about it now, Jim," Charlie Oldham calmly replied. "I decided a few months ago that it was time for me to step down as national chairman of CORE and give somebody else a shot at it. Marv Rich and I discussed it and decided that Alan Gartner would be the best person to succeed me. Alan has agreed to it, so it's all set."

"I'll be damned if it's all set," I yelled back. "This is entirely unacceptable. On something as vital to the organization as to who will become national chairman, the retiring chairman, a member of my staff, and a member of the National Action Council get together and make a decision on succession without even troubling to consult with the national director in the process. And now you present me with a fait accompli. It will never happen."

Charlie looked at me with mouth open, as though about to say something, but the words did not come. Marv looked at the floor. Alan Gartner reddened with embarrassment and anger.

"As national director of this organization, I am charged with the responsibility of guiding its destiny under the supervision of the National Action Council," I said. "I cannot guide its destiny if people are going to run around me and make critical decisions without even touching base with me. What do you think I am, your figurehead? There is no *way* that is going to be!"

Charlie Oldham tried to quiet things down. "Jim," he said, "Marv and I just decided that Alan is the best-qualified person to chair the organization through these troubled times, and we thought you would agree with that."

"Marv and you thought," I said, repeating his words. "Neither of you found it necessary to ask what I thought. Maybe you thought my opinion was irrelevant. Now, let me make it clear. Alan is a friend of mine and I have the highest regard for his intelligence and his abilities. He has served the organization well as chairman of the Boston chapter and as a key member of the National Action Council. But there is no way that a white man can be titular head of what Louie Lomax has called the 'Negro revolt' at this point in history.

"Further, as everyone here knows, this organization is under attack from black nationalists, both outside and inside CORE. Julius Hobson, has announced that he is running for national chairman.* If Alan's name is placed in nomination, all it will accomplish is the election of Julius Hobson. CORE will then become a hydra-headed monster at war with itself. I am not going to sit by and let that happen. Alan, if you allow your name to be placed in nomination, I will fight you on the convention floor and I think I will win."

What erupted was weeping, wailing, and gnashing of teeth. I was called a racist, a black nationalist, a Garveyite, a Black Muslim. One black member of the National Action Council, with tears literally rolling down his cheeks, stared at me and shouted, "This is not CORE. CORE is color-blind."

This meeting of a few key members of the National Action Council prior to the June 27–30, 1963, convention of the Congress of Racial Equality broke up in confusion. The chairman called for a recess, with the meeting to reconvene in two hours. Alan Gartner looked at me in absolute disbelief before walking out of the door with Marv Rich and Charlie Oldham. I overheard Oldham say to the other two, "If we give up this position, we will never get it back."

I remained alone in the room after everyone had left. I was greatly troubled. What I was doing—what I felt I *had* to do—tore me up inside. I had founded CORE and helped to guide its development as a "color-blind" organization; that was why it was "*of* Racial Equality" rather than "*on* Racial Equality." Now, however, CORE was being attacked by its enemies and even criticized by its friends as being basically a white-led organization with a black front. This was its Achilles' heel, and mine, even within the community of activist civil rights organizations. That picture

*In 1963, Hobson embraced black nationalism for a brief period in his life. He later moderated his views, finally returning to the integrationist position.

had to be changed if CORE was to consolidate its image as the cutting edge of the movement.

It could not be a black organization, but it had to be black-led. The chairman was the titular head but not the chief executive officer. The national director was. The chairman chaired convention sessions, National Action Council meetings, other major committee meetings, and conferences conducted by CORE. The titular leader, rather than the operational one, the national chairman was nevertheless vital to the organization's image.

Now that the attacks upon us for being white-led were mounting in the black community, I felt that the stand I was taking, tactical rather than principled, was the correct one for the organization.

When the meeting resumed, outrage had not subsided. If eyes could have killed, I would have died a sudden death. Charlie Oldham brought the meeting to order.

"Jim, we have been talking and have discussed it with some of the delegates coming in, and everybody has agreed that Alan Gartner is the best qualified and should be chairman. So I guess it will have to be Alan."

"Charlie, you are chairman of the nominations committee, and if you bring in a slate of nominees headed by Alan, I will be forced to take the floor and oppose it and propose an alternative. I will then proceed to fight for the candidate I present."

"But who else *is* there, Jim?" asked Oldham, raising his voice for the first time. "There is Julius Hobson and there is Alan Gartner. We can't think of anybody else."

"How about Floyd McKissick?" I shouted as the idea suddenly struck me.

"How do you know Floyd will run?" asked Oldham.

"McKissick's not even coming to the convention," interjected Marvin Rich. "How can there be a candidate who is not at the convention?"

"If Floyd is willing to run, I'll get him here," I said. I then asked for another recess, so that I might contact McKissick in Durham, North Carolina.

As people left the room, they were only slightly less agitated than after the first recess. It seemed to me, though, that the agitation now was more purposeful. They had not given up the battle. I asked Gorden Carey, one of my staff members, who apparently had not been a part of the Oldham-Rich-Gartner deal, to stay for a moment. Carey was a good friend of McKissick's and I wanted him to make the call.

"How many CORE chapters does McKissick have in North Carolina now?" I asked Gordon.

"Six or seven chapters, all growing out of the freedom highways campaign."

"That gives him a constituency. Call him and see if he will run. Tell him I want him to. If he agrees, ask him to take the next plane for Dayton."

McKissick agreed to run and said he would be on the next plane. When the meeting resumed, I informed the group that we had a candidate. McKissick, with six or seven chapters in North Carolina, was willing to run and would be present when the convention opened in the evening.

Stunned silence fell over the group. I asked Oldham if he would take the name before the nominations committee and bring out a slate headed by McKissick.

"I'll try," Charlie replied, with some hesitation.

Several hours later, just before convention time, Oldham came to me with some panic in his voice and said, "We've got problems with McKissick. I can't find anyone to make a nominating speech for him. We're in trouble."

"What the hell," I replied. "I'll make the nominating speech myself. Just bring in the slate, Charlie."

Floyd had not arrived by the time the convention opened, but he did get there. In the opening plenary session following a report of the credentials committee, and other housekeeping matters, the nominations committee brought in its report, presenting a proposed slate of officers headed by Floyd McKissick as candidate for national chairman.

Before I could rise, Lincoln Lynch, chairman of the Long Island CORE, hit the floor and said in his clipped West Indian accent, "I think we all know who Floyd McKissick is. We don't need a nominating speech for him. I move that attorney Floyd McKissick be elected national chairman by acclamation."

The motion was seconded and overwhelmingly passed by voice vote.

Floyd, who had just arrived, accepted his election with a stirring speech that brought the delegates to their feet in applause.

Alan Gartner, a brilliant and dedicated CORE leader, had his disappointment and hurt etched deeply in his face. I wanted words that would make him understand, but could not find them. He and I have worked together on many things since then, and he has shown no less dedication. I think he came to understand my decision intellectually, but I do not think he has ever come to terms with it emotionally. I believe that in his heart of hearts, he has never forgiven me for preventing him from becoming national chairman of CORE.

The scars from that fray remained. If, by my stand, I had beaten back an attempted nationalist takeover, I had by that same act softened the support I had hitherto enjoyed from many whites in the CORE machinery—staff and National Action Council both.

The clash of color was by no means the greatest of CORE's internal problems. After the Freedom Rides, its name became one of the best-known acronyms in the country, and its leadership a prize to be coveted. As we shifted our sights away from a primarily southern focus to the broad national scene, new problems rose to haunt us. In the South, the "enemy" could be personalized in a Bull Connor or a Leander Perez or a

George Wallace, and energies could be mobilized to combat him. In the North, though, the enemy was diffuse, scattered, and often concealed.

It was difficult to unite the forces and consolidate the attack upon so elusive a target. Thus, the boundless energies of the CORE movement, unable to zero in on a clearly defined enemy, focused instead on itself, and we devoured each other. Factions and caucuses multiplied. Minor differences of opinion on tactics became major political issues involving the direction and leadership of the organization.

There was, for example, the "stall-in" controversy triggered by an announced project of the Brooklyn CORE. The plan was to have automobiles run out of gas or become otherwise disabled on major expressways of New York on opening day of the 1964 World's Fair.

I opposed the scheme as being hare-brained and likely to achieve nothing more than irritation and the alienation of many CORE sympathizers. The New York press had a field day with that one for weeks in the spring of 1964. The Brooklyn chairman, Isaiah Bronson, was on the television news daily, hurling denunciations at the national director. CORE members lined up on either side: pro-stall-in and pro-Bronson, or anti-stall-in and pro-Farmer. The organization whose trademark had been moving on clearly defined targets was immobilized by internecine warfare behind the battle lines.

Non-CORE militants moved into the controversy on the side of the stall-in and kept CORE's internal pot boiling. I sent to our chapters a statement of my opposition to the stall-in plan and urged that their members not participate in it. I also suspended the Brooklyn chapter of CORE. Yet they expressed determination to go on with the project and claimed that they had lined up hundreds of cars to participate.

Since the issue had been presented to the press as a war between Bronson and Brooklyn CORE on the one side and me on the other, the success or failure of the stall-in loomed as a test of my strength within CORE. Consequently, the CORE national office announced plans for a counter-demonstration inside the World's Fair grounds in the New York City pavilion on opening day. Chapter members throughout the country were urged to come to New York to join in that project of the national office.

In early morning on the opening day, April 22, 1964, we sat glued to our radios, tensely awaiting news of the results of Brooklyn CORE's stall-in on the roads leading to the World's Fair. Only two cars showed up to participate in the stall-in, and no traffic jams materialized. A Brooklyn minister, Reverend Milton Galamison, a friend and adviser of Brooklyn CORE, who had become its chief spokesman, was on the scene to observe the results of his and the CORE chapter's efforts. Along with him was Dick Gregory.

Viewing the flopped stall-in, Reverend Galamison turned to Gregory and said, "Don't you think we had better go back to the church and regroup?"

Dick Gregory replied, "Regroup what?"

Inside the World's Fair, it was a different story. As I approached the main entrance gate with a long line of marchers, I observed uniformed Pinkerton policemen with walkie-talkies guarding it. Unknown to them, there was an advance contingent of CORE members inside the grounds, also equipped with walkie-talkies. One of our advance CORE persons, a teenager, was able to tune in on the Pinkertons' wavelength. He heard those guarding the entrance gate speak to their command headquarters: "Farmer's coming in with a big crowd of people. What are our instructions? Over."

"Stop them at the gate. Do not let them enter. Repeat, do not let them enter. Over."

The young CORE man inside the fair was in a panic. What should he do? I was not even going to get into the grounds, so there would be no counterdemonstration to the stall-in. He had to do something.

In a moment of inspiration, he spoke on the Pinkertons' wavelength to the guards at the gate: "Correction! There are new orders. Let Farmer and his group come in. Repeat. *Do* let them come in. That is all."

We marched right through the gates and the Pinkerton guards just looked at us in silence. We had picket lines and sit-ins at the pavilions of Louisiana and Mississippi, but saved our biggest for the New York City pavilion, which was neither completed nor open for visitors.

Bayard Rustin had joined me for this demonstration, and he and I sat down in front of the main entrance to New York City's showcase pavilion. We were blocking the entrance, but since the building was not yet open for visitors, we were in reality blocking no one.

Yet we were clearly violating the law against blocking ingress and egress to a public facility. That was a kind of civil disobedience little known in those years. It was not a bad law that we were protesting by breaking; it was a good law that we deliberately violated in order to bring the spotlight of public attention on other evils in New York, such as employment discrimination, housing discrimination, and de facto segregation in the schools. We were, in other words, a Socratic gadfly, courting arrest—even asking for it in order to gain a forum for discussions with the city on the issues of discrimination presented in our leaflets.

The Pinkertons had to act. They had their orders. Their orders appeared to be to try to get us to move, but to do everything they could to avoid arresting us. They did not want to give us the forum we sought.

"Mr. Farmer," said one of the Pinkertons, "you know you're blocking entrance to the building. Won't you please move over?"

My answer was no, and Bayard and I continued to sit.

The Pinkertons consulted and approached me again. "Mr. Farmer," they said, "Robert Moses, who is in charge of the World's Fair, does not want you arrested. We don't want to arrest you. So please move. Your picketing is all right and quite legal, but blocking entrance is illegal."

The answer was still no.

The policeman then asked, "Well, may we talk with you for a few minutes?"

"Of course, I'm listening. Go ahead and talk."

"I mean privately," he said. "Over there." And he pointed to several Pinkerton agents standing about forty feet away.

"All right," I said, "provided I will not be restrained from resuming my seat here after our conversation if I wish it."

"We'll agree to that," the man said.

The four Pinkerton agents sought gently to persuade me to leave my perch in front of the doorway, invoking the name of Bob Moses throughout the conversation. Their efforts were unsuccessful, and I went back to my seat.

The Pinkertons shrugged and told me softly that I was under arrest, and I should please come with them. I refused to move, so with pained expressions on their faces, they proceeded to move me. Two of them carried my legs, and a third held the upper part of my body. The agent holding the bulk of my weight said, "Gee, Mr. Farmer, you got to lose some weight."

I had to laugh as I took my easy ride to the patrol wagon. As they deposited me inside, one of them said, "Look out. Be very careful. Don't hurt him"

Along with scores of other demonstrators who were arrested on the grounds of the World's Fair, I spent two days on Hart Island, the "country club" of New York City's correctional institutions. We were housed in a barracks-type building with no bars on the windows and no locks on the doors and the cots were not too uncomfortable.

CORE bailed me out to meet with Mayor Robert F. Wagner at Gracie Mansion to discuss our grievances against the city. The meeting was successful; we got commitments from the mayor on several of our proposals. My committee and I urged that the city match jobless youths with jobs that needed to be done, such as cleaning up vacant lots and alleys. We asked that kids out of school for the summer be given New York City armbands and be put to work so as to keep them off the streets during the long hot summer months. Wagner agreed, but he moved slowly. The program did not materialize until after the Harlem riot. Had it come sooner, it is conceivable the riot might have been prevented.

CORE's public relations people, Marv Rich and Val Coleman, saw that the mayor's commitments were widely publicized. Following the meeting with the mayor, there was a well-covered press conference. The counter-demonstration had been a success; there was no stall-in, and CORE's reputation for focused demonstrations remained intact.

Much meaner than the stall-in controversy was another episode in 1964. On the recommendation and at the request of Bayard Rustin, I had hired a close friend of his, Norman Hill, the previous year. Norman was a young socialist then living in Chicago. I created a job for Norm as an assistant to Gordon Carey, then program director of the organization. Subsequently, I moved Carey into my office as assistant to the national director and promoted Norm Hill to serve as program director of CORE.

As a top-priority item, I asked the new program director to begin work on a series of rent strikes in Newark, New Jersey, slum areas in coordination with the local CORE chapter. After a period of exploration, Norm advised me that he would need a staff of about five persons to pull off the program and he had the five persons in mind. The CORE budget did not permit the hiring of five new persons at regular salary, so I agreed to take on the additional employees in a category we called "task force workers"— that is, persons hired for a specific project with expenses paid and a small weekly stipend provided. Among those hired for the project were Norm's wife, Velma, her brother, and three other persons.

The Newark rent strikes were not organized, but a caucus within CORE was. Reports I received from various chapters revealed that the objective of the caucus was my removal as national director. Their plan was to replace me with Bayard Rustin.

The caucus's efforts moved into high gear, and with feverish intensity prior to the 1964 convention of CORE. An active member of the downtown chapter who was a close friend of mine informed me that one of the task force staff members assigned to work with Norm Hill, Velma's brother, who was black, had said to him, "Farmer is an obstruction. He's got to be removed. If some members of your chapter will start a move against him, we've got some staff members who will back you up."

The chairman of our Columbia University chapter called to inform me that another staff member assigned to work with Norm Hill, this one white, had said to him, "Farmer's got entirely too much power. We are going to cut his balls off at this convention."

The chapter chairman told him that he had better be careful because I might fire him. The young man snorted, "Farmer doesn't have the guts to fire me."

I asked Norm and Velma about this, and they both denied that there was such a caucus or that they were seeking my removal. However, one member of the caucus, Blyden Jackson, defected and came to me with a sordid story of machinations and intrigue aimed at seizing control of the organization and replacing me as its head. The caucus meetings were held in various restaurants and at different apartments in New York. Among those who became involved in the caucus's planning, in addition to Bayard, were A. J. Muste and Max Schactman, the Trotskyite leader of the Socialist Workers' Party.

Blyden Jackson's involvement had been secured by promising him that the caucus would see that he became CORE's director of organization even before the coup was effected. Norm had sought unsuccessfully to maneuver that by seeking to get James McCain, who held the position promised Blyden, transferred to another post, southern regional director.

I did not know at the time why Hill had tried so hard to get McCain moved to another job, but it became clear when Blyden made his disclosure to me.

Blyden Jackson defected when the caucus failed to deliver to him what he had been promised. He expressed a willingness, even a desire, to expose the caucus and its maneuvering to the entire convention if the Norm Hill group made a move at that time. The convention was tense. The inner rumblings had spread throughout the organization and the delegates expected fireworks. Members of the caucus seemed jittery because of Blyden's defection.

At the very beginning of the plenary session of the convention, some delegate—I do not remember who—gained the floor, and said, "I think we all know that nobody can replace our national director, James Farmer. I move that this convention give Jim Farmer a unanimous vote of confidence."

The motion was seconded and passed by a thunderous voice vote—there were no nay votes heard. I had not engineered this vote of confidence, and had no idea that it was going to be proposed.

The rest of the convention went smoothly. Velma Hill told me that Norm's staff was meeting in one of the hotel rooms and asked me to attend. I agreed to do so, and at that meeting, Velma asked me if I would arrange for the convention to give Norm a vote of confidence. Naturally, I refused.

At a meeting of the National Action Council immediately following the convention, National Chairman Floyd McKissick asked a vice-chairman to take the chair so he could make a motion. In anger, Floyd shouted, "I move that we accept the resignation of Norman Hill."

I asked Floyd to withdraw his motion and let me deal with it in my way, and in my time. Still fighting mad, Floyd turned to me and said, "But these people are trying to kill you, Jim." I told Floyd that I was well aware of that, and I would deal with it, but that it was an administrative matter and not a policy matter. Consequently, it should be left in my hands. Reluctantly, Floyd withdrew his motion and resumed the chair.

As soon as the staff returned to the national office from the convention, I called in the caucus member who had said that I would not fire him. I told him that I had news for him: he was fired.

Velma and her brother came to my office and resigned. I called Norm into the office and asked him if he still maintained that he had no anti-Farmer caucus going in CORE. His mouth worked, but no words came out for a few seconds, then he said, "Well, when I first came here to work, I had no plans of starting anything like that, but I just kind of got swept up in something."

I did not press him for details. He resigned.

Not only was CORE eating away at itself in those days, infiltrators were chewing away at us, too. New members had come into various chapters apparently with umbilical cords from the past. We had neither the machinery nor the time to run exhaustive checks on new members. Clearly, some of those newcomers were agents provocateur sent in by police departments and government intelligence agencies.

Our Bronx chapter, for instance, was led by a bright and intensely dedicated young man, Herb Callendar.* Herb was certainly no wild man, but his chapter came up with some wild actions. On one occasion, Herb stood on the steps of City Hall until Mayor Wagner descended the steps, leaving for the day.

"Are you Robert F. Wagner?" Herb asked.

"Yes, I am," responded the mayor.

"Well, you're under arrest. I'm making a citizen's arrest on you," Herb said.

Bob Wagner went two steps back up the stairs while his policemen moved in and arrested Herb Callendar.

Several years later, when a group of American and Canadian left-wing militants were indicted for plans to blow up the Statue of Liberty and the Liberty Bell, there was a photograph on the front page of the *New York Times* of a black police lieutenant who had infiltrated the group, and brought about their arrest.

Looking at that picture with amazement, Callendar exclaimed, "My God, that man was a member of Bronx CORE. He was the wildest, most militant member we had. It was he who sold me the idea of making a citizen's arrest on the mayor!"

Surveillance and telephonic eavesdropping were also prevalent in those days. Evidence abounded that my phones were tapped at the office and at home. One illustration will suffice.

Making a call from my home to a friend one afternoon, I was astonished when the person who answered the phone at the other end of the line responded, "Department of Justice."

The number I had dialed bore no resemblance to the number for the Department of Justice either in New York or in Washington. Although I had nothing to hide and was, therefore, not unduly concerned about my phone being tapped, nevertheless I was outraged at the invasion of privacy. I wrote to the telephone company, the Federal Communications Commission, the New York City Police Department, the Department of Justice, and the FBI, telling them of my strong suspicion that I was being tapped. I asked that they either confirm or deny that such was the case. The telephone company denied that my phone was tapped. The FBI called me and asked why I thought I was being tapped and then denied they were tapping it. I did not hear from the others to whom I had written.

A short while later, an employee of the phone company made an unannounced and unofficial visit to my office. The young man informed me

*Callendar is now Makazi Kumanyika.

that he had seen my letter inquiring about a telephone tap, and that he had found that my phone was, indeed, being tapped through the master switchboard at the phone company's headquarters. He did not know who had ordered the tap, but it had to have been done with the knowledge and the consent of the telephone company. He asked, of course, that he remain anonymous.

In a whimsical moment, I decided to confirm my suspicions and laid a trap. I asked a CORE member to make a call to me at the office, informing me of a stupendous demonstration his chapter was going to conduct on the Brooklyn Bridge on a Thursday at 4:00 P.M. He was to say in that phone call that it would be a demonstration that would make all previous demonstrations pale into insignificance. He was to mention this conversation to no one else.

On Thursday, at 4:00 P.M., I walked to the Brooklyn Bridge. It was full of police cars with policemen on the bridge, under the bridge, and at each entrance. There was, of course, no CORE demonstration. Only the police demonstrated. We laughed at their predicament.

It was that ability to laugh that kept me going in those days when I was feeling put upon. And there was much to laugh about.

There was the time in 1964, for example, when I sent Jim McCain, our director of organization, to Mississippi to secure statements from a large number of blacks who had been denied the right to register to vote. The Justice Department was insisting on having documented statements rather than word-of-mouth reports from us. I had admonished McCain to safeguard the tapes with his life. He had replied, "Don't worry, Jim, I will get those tapes back here intact. Nothing's going to happen to them."

After he had gotten the statements on tape and was driving from the hinterlands of Mississippi back to Jackson in a rental car, he heard a siren and saw the sheriff's car pursuing him.

"Oh, Lord," Jim McCain said to himself. "They're going to find those tapes."

The sheriff's deputy pulled him over to the side of the road, searched him, searched the glove compartment, made him open the trunk, and saw the box of tapes. McCain's heart sank. The deputy unrolled one reel, examined it, and rolled it back again, repeating that procedure with a second reel, a third, and a fourth.

Then, he put the tapes back in the box, closed the trunk, and exclaimed, "Doggone, y'all sho do use a lotta scotch tape."

He let McCain go and the tapes were saved.

There was also much to cry about in those days. For instance, Marvin Rich had left CORE to head the CORE Scholarship, Education, and Defense Fund, an organization we had set up two years earlier to handle the tax-exempt functions of CORE, such as legal actions and educational activities. Immediately upon his leaving, the Scholarship, Education, and Defense Fund began making fund appeal to CORE's "tip top" list. They were more likely to contribute to a tax-exempt organization than to CORE itself. Marv and I had a talk, and he promised that the fund would, under no conditions, engage in direct-mail fund raising, since the direct mail was CORE's lifeline.

I was chagrined to discover a few days later that, at the very time that agreement was being made, the fund had a sixty-thousand-piece mailing going out from Brooklyn. I was astonished at what appeared to be a breach of faith. Subsequently, the name of the CORE Scholarship, Education, and Defense Fund was changed to Scholarship, Education, and Defense Fund for Racial Equality (SEDFRE), and it continued to do direct-mail fund raising.

Rich is a man of exceptional skills and he served CORE with competence from the late 1950s through 1964. Though I respected his abilities and opinion, we often disagreed. His growing disenchantment with CORE coincided with the rising demand within the organization for recognition and acceptance of black ethnicity, which flew in the face of the "color-blind" ethos into which he had been bred. When I complained to some members of the board of SEDFRE that such fund raising was siphoning money from the top of CORE's budget, they shrugged and made a reply to the effect that "business is business." CORE's budget was thus cut, and its activities weakened.

Another problem at this time was the deepening of the black/white clash within the organization. One day I received a phone call from a chapter officer in California, telling me that there was a war going on between blacks and whites in chapters throughout the state. I set up a meeting in a Los Angeles hotel, requesting all CORE chapters in the state to send some of their officers, white and black, to meet with me to discuss internal organizational conflicts. At that meeting, I urged the CORE staffers to let their hair down and speak frankly and bluntly, in the hope that we could get to the bottom of the problems that were plaguing them.

A black man jumped to his feet and said, "Brother Farmer, we have got to *dig* being black!" He repeated those words several times, and then went on: "There is no white man in this world that I trust completely. None whatsoever!"

A white man from the same chapter stood, dumbfounded, and stammered, "But I thought I was your best friend."

"You *thought*," replied the black. "I don't even trust you."

From that point on, the dialogue was bitter and remonstrative. Some voices broke as people spoke. There was even some crying. At times, the meeting became nasty. Another black man got to the floor and, gesturing animatedly, said, "Brother Farmer, those white bitches in my chapter are always trying to run everything and—"

A white woman on the other side of the room stood and, with unrestrained outrage, interrupted him. "Yes, I'm a bitch. That's why I'm sleeping with *you*."

For fully a minute, they stood, staring at each other as if looking at strangers, and then sat down in embarrassment.

I tried to get the meeting back to some semblance of decorum. I struck a middle course, and as is usually true of middle courses, satisfied no one. The whites at the meeting, like those in CORE generally, remained wed to the principle of a color-blind, raceless integration. Most of the blacks there were venturing toward a strident ethnicity—black pride tilting toward exclusiveness.

I sought a compromise, a synthesis, by arguing that interracialism was fundamental in CORE and that as long as I was national director of the organization it would remain so. There would be no expulsions, no one would be read out of the organization on account of race, and any chapter that could not accept this would have to relinquish the banner of CORE. The constitution was clear on that point.

On the other hand, I insisted, it was essential for blacks to come to terms with themselves, to find an identity and seize it, to know who they are. There was no inconsistency between the two ideas, I maintained, for if blacks felt black pride in their very bones, then they had nothing to fear from association with others of different ethnicity.

Obviously, most of those present found the words tepid and they rejected them. A few whites nodded their heads, but doubt shaded their faces. A few blacks shook their heads. The rest simply gazed in bewilderment.

Yet the meeting did get back on track; dialogue resumed, sometimes acrimonious, but civil. When I adjourned the meeting, most of those present—progeny of America's racial psychosis like most who walk this land—came up and shook my hand. They left, not friends, but at least talking.

As the chapter officers left that room, I felt that now there was more honesty between them, and that relationships thus could be realistic and less fraught with artifice. Like blacks and whites in the nation, their lives were intertwined, but their souls disparate.

Perhaps I was naive, not recognizing the depths to which white paternalism and black resentment—legacies of slavery—burrowed in the American culture. We are all victims of the race syndrome in America, and to some extent, its unconscious perpetrators. Even the most emancipated of us are not yet free.

CORE in California, like CORE in other states, continued to simmer over the fire of a widening racial clash and a strengthening of the spirit of black nationalism.

By late 1964, CORE was well on its way toward orienting itself to the problems of blacks in the urban ghettos, as well as in the South. The Civil Rights Act of 1964 was an accomplished fact. Jim Crow was legally dead, though rigor mortis had not set in yet. We had to move toward the problems that were national in scope as epitomized by those in the northern ghetto. The National Action Council (NAC) approved this change in focus, and I sent a directive to all the chapters, urging them to establish their offices in the heart of the ghetto and to begin recruiting from the ghetto slums as well as from churches, schools, and other middle-class institutions as we had done in the past.

On the express mandate of the NAC, I asked Jim Peck, the longtime editor of the *CORElator*, our official newsletter, to reorient that paper in line with the new CORE focus. I requested that the *CORElator* present fewer pictures and stories of blood-letting in the South, and more of the atrocities of urban slums—rats biting children, leaking roofs, flats without heat, and so on.

Peck opposed the change, stating that it was not CORE. The *CORElator* went on with its usual pictures of blacks with bloodied heads being beaten to their knees by white sheriffs, and stories in line with those photographs. This was good for fund raising among northern liberals, but did not reflect CORE's direction. The NAC complained about the dichotomy between CORE's official policy and the editorial policy of CORE's official publication and insisted that I do something about bringing the *CORElator* into line.

I explained the problem to the NAC. Jim Peck, who is white, had been editor of the *CORElator* since 1943. Being a man of much dedication and independent means, he accepted no pay for his work. In order to show its appreciation for Peck's commitment, CORE in its early years had made the editor of the *CORElator* a member of the NAC by constitutional provision. Peck, however, never attended the meetings because they were all talk and he was interested in action.

Yet, since the provision was written in the constitution, he remained a member of the NAC, not having to be elected each year by the convention. This was one of the structural flaws in an organization that had been small for a long time and then suddenly grew fast. As editor of the paper, he was technically a member of my staff and under my control, but as a member of the NAC, he was one of my bosses and not under my control. It was an awkward situation that could not be dealt with by any established administrative guidelines.

The NAC understood the problem, but said that I must deal with it. I then ordered Jim Peck to change the "line" of the *CORElator.* He refused to comply with the order. I could not constitutionally fire one of my bosses, so I took the matter back to the NAC, requesting its action. The NAC voted to cease publication of the *CORElator* after the next issue. The understanding, not stated in the motion, was that publication would be resumed at a later date upon reorganization of the paper. The motion to close down the *CORElator* was passed unanimously, with Peck, of course, not present.

When I informed Peck of the decision, he exploded in anger, accusing me of being the granddaddy of all black nationalists and black racists. He insisted that the only thing wrong with the *CORElator* was the color of its editor. I tried to reason with Jim, explaining that that was not the case. But he would listen to no views at variance with his own. For years after that,

Peck did not speak to me except to launch into a loud harangue, accusing me of having no principles, of having sold out to black nationalism, and of being the fosterer of race hatred in CORE. Whenever he saw my name on an organization's letterhead in any capacity, he would write a poison pen letter to that organization, attacking my integrity. It was only in 1982, nearly two decades later, that we made peace. In an accidental meeting on an airplane, he sat beside me and we had a friendly chat without either of us mentioning the issue that had separated us for so long.

Perhaps the most painful aspect of white/black friction in the sixties was the many personal tragedies that resulted, the bitter misunderstandings born out of differing conceptions of reality, and the collisions of divergent agendas—agendas that were often hidden even from those who were guided by them. Those misunderstandings will not be resolved, nor the clashing agendas brought together, until they are fully grasped by folk on both sides of the color line and wrestled with in the sunlight until that distant day when the color line loses its power to divide.

Not the least among our many problems was J. Edgar Hoover's hostility toward the movement and his downright hatred of Martin Luther King. The year after the march on Washington, 1964, was the time when many forces sought to capture, control, or destroy the civil rights movement. I received a call in my office from an editor of a New York daily newspaper one day. He said he had to talk to me. I replied that I was all ears.

"No, I am not going to talk on your phone. It's tapped," he said. (Nothing I did not already know.)

I suggested that he come to the office, where we could talk in person. He declined on the grounds that my office was bugged also.

"What do you suggest?" I said.

He asked me to meet him in an hour at a bar where we had had a drink two months earlier. (He did not name the bar over the phone.) We sat, with scotches and water before us, and he told me of a conversation he had had with a friend of his who happened to be an FBI agent. The agent was in New York, on a social visit. As they had passed by a newsstand, the agent observed the headline of a local paper: "HOOVER CALLS KING NOTORIOUS LIAR!" The man then read a portion of the story and said, "I guess the chief had to get it off his chest at last."

He then launched into a half-hour tirade against Martin Luther King, Jr., on the grounds of alleged sexual adventures, fiscal irregularities, and alliances with communists.

The editor asked me, "What am I going to do with this story?"

"You are not going to do anything with such wild and reckless allegations against King," I replied.

"I don't know how long I can sit on it," he said. "Somebody is probably going to pick up the story and run with it."

A day or so later, I received a call at home from Ted Poston, a black writer with the *New York Post*. He said, "I've got to talk to you, and I'm going to talk right here on this phone because whoever is tapping your phone, and possibly also mine, already knows this anyway. I just returned from Washington where there's a story being peddled by the FBI that smears Martin. They're trying to get somebody to publish it."

Poston then spoke of the same three allegations the newspaper editor had mentioned. Poston said that he had spoken with Whitney Young and Roy Wilkins and neither of them felt that there was anything they could do about it.

I said that I would check the story out and try to learn if the FBI, indeed, was trying to get King. I asked Poston to call me back immediately if he heard of further developments.

Back at the office, I instructed a staff member of mine to call his contact with the FBI and try to find out from him if the FBI was trying to get King, and why. The man told my staff member that, yes, indeed, they had the goods on King and were going to get him. He said that the chief was going to kill him before Oslo.* (I, of course, assume that the word *kill* was used in its political sense, not the physical one.) He then went on to say that Hoover had instructed him to have my staff member tell me there would be no attack on Roy Wilkins, Whitney Young, or me. It was just King they were going to get. Obviously, they wanted to isolate King and dissuade the rest of the civil rights leaders from coming to his defense.

Not many days later I got another call from Ted Poston, stating that the story was getting hotter, and it appeared that Fulton Lewis, Jr., the conservative columnist and commentator, was going to go with it. Poston said the deal appeared to be that if the journalist who broke the story got sued, Hoover would bring the files into court and testify for the defense.

"Okay," I said, "I'll have to get moving right away."

I then called Cartha "Deke" DeLoach, assistant to the director of the FBI. When I told him that I wanted an off-the-record meeting with him the next day, he asked me to come to his office. I declined to do that, repeating that the meeting had to be off-the-record, and suggested that he come to my hotel room in Washington instead.

DeLoach laughed and said, "I thought you said off-the-record. Hotel rooms are too easily bugged."

He finally suggested a cloak-and-dagger arrangement with an agent meeting me at the plane early the next morning, driving me in a limousine to a certain intersection, where he would join me in the back seat of the car. The glass partition separating the driver's side from us would give us privacy, he said. When I asked about recording instruments

*This conversation took place after King had been named the winner of the Nobel Peace Prize, but before he went to Oslo, Norway, to receive it.

in the car, he gave me his word there would be none. I told DeLoach that those arrangements were satisfactory, but that I might call him at home that night to cancel the appointment. He said he would understand.

I then called King, finally reaching him in Chicago at the home of the Reverend Archibald J. Carey, Jr. When I explained how urgently I needed to see him, he told me that he was flying into Kennedy Airport that evening, but had planned to go directly to Connecticut with friends before coming to New York. I prevailed upon Martin to change those plans and ask his Connecticut friends to wait for him while I had a staff member meet him at the plane and bring him to the VIP lounge, which I had reserved in advance for the two of us. He agreed to the arrangements.

King, it turned out, was unaware that the FBI was peddling the smear story about him. He agreed with me that such a story would do more than damage him personally; it would damage the entire movement, for he was its symbol.

I informed Martin of my off-the-record meeting with DeLoach to find out if it was the FBI that was spreading the smear stories, and if they were, to try to stop them. But I said I would not keep that appointment unless I had his permission to do so. For, if I met off-the-record with DeLoach and the smear story subsequently broke about King, and the FBI leaked to the press the fact that I had previously met with DeLoach, it would appear that I had been one of those seeking to knife King. Martin agreed with that assessment, but urged me to go ahead with the meeting and said that he would call me at my hotel in Washington for a report on what had happened at my meeting with DeLoach.

Martin subsequently decided that night to set up an "on-the-record" meeting with J. Edgar Hoover himself for the very next morning, in order to clear the air and try to stop the smear attempts. So, two meetings were held, one on-the-record and one off-the-record.

The meeting with DeLoach took place as scheduled. He alleged that the stories about King were true, but denied that the FBI was the organization peddling them, saying that "Dr. King has many enemies." He failed to say who the enemies were. In retrospect, I think what he may have been saying was that the agency was not peddling the story, but Hoover was doing it personally. DeLoach, however, gave me his word that FBI files would not be used in any such smear. I asked him if he was sure of that, and he repeated that I had his word.

DeLoach also called FBI headquarters from the limousine to find out how King's meeting with Hoover was going and found that it had just adjourned, and that now they were going out to meet with the press.

When Martin called me at one o'clock that afternoon, I told him of DeLoach's pledge that FBI files would not be used in a smear attempt.

Before I had left DeLoach, he had said that if we were finished with the King matter, the chief wanted him to bring another matter to *my* attention. He informed me that an individual who shall remain nameless had been sent into CORE by the Communist Party, USA, and that that person, now on my field staff, was running a caucus whose objective was to oust me as national director. The coup was to take place at the upcoming CORE convention in Durham, North Carolina, and I was to be replaced by a black minister the party considered more "controllable" than I. DeLoach showed me what he purported to be documentary evidence—photostatic copies of minutes of meetings.

My own investigation showed that there was, indeed, a caucus activity of the sort related to me by DeLoach. I fired the staff member in question and the caucus's activity magically ceased.

Through 1964 and well into 1965, the sweet smell of our victories was being dissolved in the bitter taste of internal snipings and power plays. That is the way it is with all revolutions, and this was a revolution, though a reformist one. Revolutions devour the revolutionaries. None but the tough and bloody survive.

Where there is power, or the appearance of power, there are always those who would go to any lengths to gain it. Only those with the gift and taste for it keep it. I always had the gift, but never the taste.

Retching from the daily fratricidal diet inside CORE, it was a respite to turn my sights to the Southland periodically, where the Klan sought my death. They were overt enemies who hated all that I loved and cherished that which I detested. Fighting them was exhausting, but it was also exhilarating—right against wrong. Fighting my colleagues and erstwhile friends was another matter.

CHAPTER 25

"TOMORROW IS FOR OUR MARTYRS"

IT HAD BEEN A calm day in the office, if any days could be considered calm in the frenetic atmosphere in which we functioned. There had been no major crises; no mass arrests or calls for immediate bail money; no libel suits had been filed against any of our chapters; no scandals were threatening to erupt in the press; the sky had not fallen that day. Such tranquility was rare, particularly in the freedom summer of 1964 when CORE and SNCC had drawn hundreds of young volunteers into Mississippi, blanketing the state with voter registration workers.

I went home the evening of June 21, 1964, with a sense of well-being, cherishing the night of easy sleep that lay ahead.

Gretchen, now an old dog, labored to get on the bed and snuggle in her favorite spot on the pillows between Lula's head and mine. ("I always knew some bitch would come between us," Lula had once said.) At 3:00

A.M., the bedside phone rang. Cursing the intrusion, I growled hello into the receiver.

CORE's Mississippi field secretary, George Raymond, spoke into the phone: "Jim, three of our guys, Schwerner, Goodman, and Chaney, are missing. They left Meridian yesterday afternoon to go over to the town of Philadelphia in Neshoba County to look at the ruins of the church where they had been teaching voter registration courses. You know that church was burned down a week ago. They were supposed to return by sundown, but they're not back yet. Can you come down right away?"

"Don't jump to conclusions, George," I said. "It's only been a few hours. Maybe they stopped to visit some friends for dinner and decided to take a nap before driving home."

"Face facts, Jim," Raymond shouted into the phone. "Our guys and gals don't just stop over and visit friends or take a nap without calling in. Those three are responsible guys; they wouldn't be nine hours late without calling us. That is, if they could call."

"Okay, I'll be on the next plane to Meridian," I said. "I'll call you back in a few minutes to let you know the time of arrival."

I wanted company going to Neshoba County, so I called Dick Gregory at his home in Chicago, waking him up. Before he answered the phone, I glanced at Lula and saw that she was wide awake, watching with no sign of emotion.

"Hey, big daddy," said Gregory. "What's happening?"

"Three of my guys are missing in Mississippi," I said.

After a brief silence, Gregory said, "Okay. I know you're going down there. I'll meet you there. What airport do I fly to?"

Meridian, though close to Neshoba County, was an island of relative sanity in Mississippi. At the airport when we arrived were a few dozen city policemen with rifles. They were there to ensure my safety. I was given a police escort to the small, unpretentious black hotel. Immediately, I was closeted with George Raymond; Mickey Schwerner's wife, Rita; and several other CORE people in Meridian.

It was early evening on the day after the disappearance, and still there was no word. We were certain our colleagues were dead. Rita, no more than five feet tall and less than a hundred pounds, was dry-eyed and rational. When Mickey had accepted the assignment, both of them were well aware of the risks. Mickey was a social worker from New York who had joined the CORE staff several months earlier. Rita intended to study law.

The local and state officials were showing no interest in locating the men or their bodies. We had alerted the FBI, but there was not yet any evidence of their involvement in the search. A nearby U.S. military unit had just been called in to search some of the swamps for bodies, but the results thus far were negative. The CORE car in which the men had been riding when last seen—a white Ford station wagon—had not been found.

As we discussed things that might be done to aid the search, Rita suggested that going through the ashes at the city dump where trash was burned might possibly yield some fragments of metal that could be identified as having belonged to one of the three men. Nothing more helpful than that came immediately to mind.

I told them that on the following morning, I intended to go into Philadelphia in Neshoba County to talk with Sheriff Lawrence Rainey and Deputy Sheriff Cecil Price about the disappearance of the men. Considering the racist reputation of the sheriff and his deputy, all agreed that one or both of them knew something about the disappearance of our friends.

George Raymond told us that Dick Gregory had called to say that he would be joining me in Meridian early the next morning.

"Good," I said. "Let's time my trip to Philadelphia so that Dick can go along with me."

Early the next morning, after Gregory's arrival, he and I sat in the small hotel office on the ground floor with Raymond and one or two other CORE staffers. There was also a lieutenant of the Meridian City Police. Outside the building were several uniformed policemen and two squad cars, with others ready if needed.

The police official asked me what our plans were and I told him of my intention to talk with Rainey and Price in their office. He let out a low whistle. "Farmer," he said, "you cain't go over there. That's Neshoba County. That's real red-neck territory. We cain't protect you outside of Meridian."

"Lieutenant, we do appreciate the protection the city police is giving us and we want to thank you for it. However, we're not asking for protection, and certainly not from the Meridian police, when we go into Neshoba County. Mr. Gregory and I will go to Neshoba County this morning to try to see the sheriff and his deputy. That is our right and our duty, and we intend to exercise it."

The lieutenant shook his head and then made a phone call to a Mr. Snodgrass, head of the Mississippi State Police. I knew Snodgrass and had always respected him. He was a conscientious law enforcement officer and, I felt, a humane one. At the various marches and demonstrations CORE had held in Mississippi, when Snodgrass personally was present, I had felt a little more at ease.

This time, I could hear Snodgrass shouting over the phone from ten feet away: "He can't go over there. They'll kill him in that place. We can't protect him."

The lieutenant handed me the phone. "Mr. Snodgrass wants to talk to you."

Still shouting, Snodgrass said, "Farmer, don't go over there. That's one of the worst red-neck areas in this state. They would just as soon kill you as look at you. We cannot protect you over there."

"Mr. Snodgrass, we have not asked for your protection. This is something we have to do, protection or not."

"Okay, okay," Snodgrass replied. "What time are you going?"

"We're leaving here in about an hour and a half," I said and hung up.

We left Meridian in a caravan of five cars, with an escort of city police cars. Dick Gregory and I were in the lead car. Our escort left us at the Meridian city limits.

At the Neshoba County line, there was a roadblock with two sheriff's cars and one unmarked vehicle. A hefty middle-aged man, stereotypical of the "Negro-hating" southern sheriff of that day—chewing either a wad of tobacco or the end of a cigar, I forget which—swaggered up to our lead car. He was closely followed by an equally large but younger deputy sheriff.

The middle-aged man spoke to me: "Whut's yo' name?"

"James Farmer, and this gentleman is Mr. Dick Gregory, the entertainer and social critic."

"Where yo' think you goin'?"

"Mr. Gregory and I are going to Philadelphia."

"Whut yo' gon' do there?"

"We are going to talk to Sheriff Rainey and Deputy Price."

"Whut yo' wanna talk ta them 'bout?"

"We are going to talk with them about the disappearance of three of the staff members of the organization I head: Michael Schwerner, Andrew Goodman, and James Chaney."

"Well, Ah'm Sheriff Rainey and this heah's mah deputy, Deputy Price. Y'all wanna talk ta us heah?"

"No. We want to talk to you in your office."

"Awright, folla me."

"Just a moment," I said, "let me pass the word back down the line that we're all going to Philadelphia."

"Naw. Jus' you and this heah man can come," he said, pointing to Gregory. "The rest of them boys'll have to wait heah."

I glanced at the unmarked car and saw that leaning against it was Mr. Snodgrass, watching the scene closely.

Gregory and I followed Rainey and Price into town. Outside the courthouse were several hundred shirt-sleeved white men, standing with assorted weapons in hand. Surrounding the courthouse, though, were state police with rifles pointed at the crowd. State police also flanked the sidewalk leading to the steps of the building.

Gregory and I followed Rainey and Price up those steps and into the courthouse. We followed them to an elevator, and as the doors closed behind us, we thought of the same thing simultaneously. We never should have gotten into that box with those two men. They could have killed us and said that we had jumped them and that they had to shoot us in self-defense. And there would have been no witnesses. But it was too late now. We shrugged our shoulders.

To our relief, the door opened on the second floor without event, and we followed the two men down the hallway to an office at its end. Rainey introduced the three men seated in that office as the city attorney of Philadelphia, the county attorney of Neshoba, and Mr. Snodgrass of the state police. Snodgrass merely nodded at the introduction, and looked sharply at the faces of the other men in the room.

Rainey cleared his throat and rasped, "Ah've got laryngitis or somethin'. This heah man will talk fer me." He was pointing at the county attorney. I nodded, but thought it strange that I had not noticed the impaired throat during our conversation at the roadblock.

The county attorney squinted his eyes, and said to me, "Well, we're all heah. What was it you wanted to talk to the sheriff and his deputy about?"

I told him that, as national director of CORE, I was charged with responsibility for the supervision of all members of the CORE staff. Three members of that staff had been missing for thirty-six hours. Mr. Gregory and I were there, I said, to try to find out what had happened to them and whether they were alive or dead. Specifically, I indicated I wanted to ask Deputy Price a question.

Price then sat upright in his seat. Deputy Price had given conflicting stories to the press, I pointed out. First, he had said he never saw the men, then he said he had arrested them and released them in the evening. I wanted to know the true story.

The attorney looked at Price and the deputy spoke: "Ah'll tell ya the God's truth. Ah did see them boys. I arrested them for speedin' and took them ta jail—"

"What time did you arrest them?" I said.

"It was about three or three-thirty. Yeah, closer to three-thirty when Ah arrested them. Ah kept them in jail till 'bout six-thirty or seven in the evenin'—"

"Why would you keep men in jail for three and a half hours for speeding?"

"Ah had to find out how much the justice of the peace was gonna fine them. The justice of the peace was not at home, so Ah had to wait till he got home. He fined them fifteen dollars. That colored boy, Chaney, who wuz drivin' the car, didn't have no fifteen dollars, but one of them Jew boys, Schwerner, had fifteen an' he paid the fine. Then, I took them boys out to the edge of town and put them in their car and they headed for Meridian. Ah sat in mah car and watched their taillights as long as Ah could see them. An' they were goin' toward Meridian. Then Ah turned around and came back into town, and that was the last Ah seen of them boys. Now, that's the God's truth."

"At this moment," I said, "I have about fifteen young men waiting at the county line. They are friends and coworkers of Mickey Schwerner, Jim Chaney, and Andy Goodman. They want to join in the search for their missing colleagues."

"What would they do? Where would they look?" the county attorney asked, rather anxiously, I felt. Could it have been he thought we might have gotten some clue as to where the bodies could be found?

"They would look anywhere and everywhere that bodies could be hidden or disposed of—in the woods, the swamps, the rivers, whatever."

"No!" he said. "We can't let them go out there by themselves without any supervision."

"Oh, they'll be supervised," I replied. "I'll go with them."

"And I'll be with them, too," Gregory added.

"No, no! I can't let you do that. This is private property all around heah and the owners could shoot you for trespassing. We don't want anything to happen to you down here," he said.

"Something already *has* happened to three of our brothers. I'll take my chances," I said.

"No, these swamps around here are very dangerous," the attorney said. "They've got water moccasins, rattlesnakes, copperheads, and everything else in them. Like I said, we don't want anything to happen to you. We won't allow you to do it."

"Then," I said, "I have another question. We heard over the car radio coming here that the car in which the men were riding, that white Ford station wagon, has been found burned out on the other side of town, the opposite side from Meridian. That automobile belonged to the organization I serve as national director, and I want to look at what is left of it."

"No," said the county lawyer emphatically. "We can't let you do that either. You might destroy fingerprints or some other evidence that will be useful to Sheriff Rainey or Deputy Price in solving this crime—if there has been a crime. You know, those boys may have decided to go up north or someplace and have a short vacation. They'll probably be coming back shortly."

Dick Gregory, who had shown masterful restraint thus far, rose to his feet. He began speaking to the assembled men, pointing his finger at them, looking at each one with sharp eyes, and speaking with an even sharper tongue. He made it clear that he thought someone there knew much more about the disappearance of the three men than was being told. He said that we were not going to let this matter rest but were going to get to the bottom of it, and the guilty persons were going to pay for their crimes.

I felt that this was neither the time nor the place to have a showdown with Rainey and Price. Yet, I was struggling with my own feelings. I was not Christ. I was not Gandhi. I was not King. I wanted to kill those men— not with bullets, but with my fingers around their throats, squeezing tighter as I watched life ebb from their eyes.

Back in Meridian, I called a meeting of the CORE staff and summer volunteers. Our embattled southern staff evidenced little of the black/white tension so prevalent in the North. At the meeting, I announced that I wanted two volunteers for an extraordinarily important and dangerous mission. The qualifications for the volunteers were that they had to be black, male, and young. I wanted them to slip into Philadelphia in Neshoba County in the dead of night, not going by the main highway but by side routes. They would very quietly disappear into the black community of Philadelphia, see a minister, and ask if he could find a family for them to stay with.

They would have to do all they could to keep the officials from knowing that they were there or of their mission. I believed that the black community would take them in, for that is an old tradition among blacks—the extended family. They would have to try not to be conspicuous, but to disappear into the woodwork, so to speak, until they were trusted by the blacks in Philadelphia.

In all probability, George Raymond and I believed, some person or persons in the black community knew what had happened to the three men. Someone in that community always does, but no one would tell the FBI or any city or state officials, for fear of retribution.

When accepted and trusted, our men were to begin asking discreet questions. When any information was secured, they were to communicate that to me. If they did so by phone, it was to be from a phone booth and not the same one each time. If by letter, the message should be mailed from another town, and without a return address on the envelope. If they had any reason to believe that Rainey or Price knew of their presence or mission, they were to contact me immediately by phone.

Practically all hands went up. Everyone wanted to go. When George Raymond and I selected two, most others felt let down and angry.

The two volunteers left the meeting, packed small suitcases, and surreptitiously moved into Philadelphia. It was about two weeks before I began getting reports. Those reports from eyewitnesses of various parts of the tragedy indicated a clear scenario, the stage for which had been set by an earlier report from another source.

A black maid in Meridian had told us of overhearing a phone call from a black Meridian man who was speaking in an open telephone booth. The man allegedly fingered the three young CORE men. The maid, of course, did not know to whom the call was made, but we suspected it was either to Sheriff Rainey or Deputy Price. The caller said that the three guys, two Jews and one colored, were in a white '62 Ford station wagon. He also gave the license number of the car. He said the three had just left Meridian, heading for Philadelphia.

The scenario as told to the CORE volunteers by various eyewitnesses was as follows: when Schwerner, Goodman, and Chaney entered Philadelphia, they were trailed by Deputy Price, who kept his distance. When they stopped at the charred ruins of the small black church on the other side of town, Price parked at a distance and watched them. As they got back into the car to drive on, Deputy Price, according to the witnesses, closed in on them.

James Chaney, who was driving the car, saw Price in his rearview mirror and, knowing Price's reputation as a "nigger killer," sped up.

Price then shot a tire on the Ford wagon and it came to a halt. The men were arrested and taken to jail, as Price had said. Also, as the deputy had told us, he took them out of jail about sundown, but there the similarity between the deputy's story and fact seemed to end.

He took them to the other side of town, not the Meridian side, and turned them over to a waiting mob in a vacant field. The three men were pulled into the field and pushed beneath a large tree. There, members of the mob held Schwerner and Goodman while the other mobsters beat Chaney without mercy. He was knocked down, stomped, kicked, and clubbed. Schwerner broke away from his captives and tried to help Chaney. He was then clubbed once on the head and knocked unconscious. Seconds later, he revived and was again held by members of the mob while the beating of Chaney continued.

By this time Chaney appeared dead, and the beating stopped. Members of the mob huddled, and then Deputy Price, who was also in the group, went back to his car and drove away. The mob remained there, holding Schwerner and Goodman and looking at the prone form of Chaney on the ground.

A little while later, Price returned and said something to the members of the mob. They then dragged Schwerner and Goodman and Chaney's body to a car and threw them into it. The car drove off.

The latter scene was allegedly witnessed by two blacks crossing different corners of the field at about the same time, on the way to church for a prayer meeting.

We turned this information over to the FBI.

It was weeks later—August fifth—when I received a call from Deke De-Loach, then assistant to the director at FBI headquarters in Washington, D.C.

DeLoach said, "Mr. Farmer, since Schwerner, Goodman, and Chaney were members of your staff, I wanted you to be the first to know. We have found the bodies. An informant told us to look under a fake dam. We drove in a bulldozer and with the first scoop of earth uncovered the three bodies. Though they were badly decomposed, there was every evidence that Chaney had received the most brutal beating imaginable. It seemed that every bone in his body was broken. He was beaten to death. Each of the other two was shot once in the heart."

Months later, on October 3, 1964, the FBI arrested a group of men and charged them with conspiracy to violate the civil rights of the dead trio— the only charge available to the federal government, since murder is a state charge. Mississippi never charged them with murder.

Among those arrested and convicted of conspiracy, in addition to Deputy Price, was a minister of the gospel. When he prayed to his God, did he feel remorse? Or had he silenced the still, small voice within his soul?

Evil societies always kill their consciences.

We, who are the living, possess the past. Tomorrow is for our martyrs.

CHAPTER 26

THE MUTING OF THE PIPER

"Jim, you'd better get your ass up here *fast!* Harlem is blowing like a volcano! Bottles and bricks are flying everywhere, and the cops are shooting like cowboys."

Those were the words spitting from the phone as I was awakened in my lower Manhattan apartment by a call from a member of Harlem CORE. It was about 1:00 A.M. on July 18, 1964.

There had been a classic case of police brutality. An off-duty policeman had shot and killed a black teenager who was engaged in childish horseplay with an apartment house superintendent and a garden hose. At some point, the policeman pulled out his revolver, and as the kid turned to run, the policeman shot him in the back. Eyewitnesses said that he emptied his revolver into the fallen youngster's back and then turned him over with the toe of his boot.

The policeman later charged that the boy came at him with a knife. A knife was produced. However, we were told by black policemen that the police often carried knives to plant on just such occasions.

CORE's investigation showed it to be an unnecessary killing, to put it mildly. At a press conference, I came as close as I legally could to calling the killing a criminal act. On the advice of CORE's attorney, Carl Rachlin, I said that it was an unnecessary killing, and that, in my opinion, the policeman should be tried for murder.* At the same time, I renewed my call for the establishment of a civilian review board in the police department and urged calm.

Nevertheless, Harlem erupted. Minutes after my sleep-shattering call, I was on the subway, bound for Harlem.

The CORE chapter office in Harlem was a second-floor walk-up over a storefront on 125th Street. I stood in front of the building. The acrid smell of gunsmoke hung faintly in the air. Glass from broken windows lay on the sidewalks. One could hear from side streets the shattering of plate glass, pistol shots fired in rapid succession, and the frenzied shouts of black youth. A siren wailed, and a dog replied with howling.

Otherwise, there was quiet on 125th Street, but an ominous scene approached. Coming westward toward me, was a crowd of several dozen black youth, walking slowly. Across the street, equal numbers of steel-helmeted policemen trudged along, keeping pace with them. The cops had in their hands riot clubs, and some had revolvers drawn. Each army eyed the other.

Hurriedly, I climbed the rickety stairs to the Harlem office. Sitting

---

*The policeman filed a libel and slander suit against me for about $2 million. The suit was later dropped.

around the office looking tense were about two dozen Harlem CORE men and women, a third of them white.

"It's a war," someone said.

"The cops are like occupation troops," said another. "They've gone crazy, shooting in windows and beating up women and little children."

I looked out the window to follow the course of the pending confrontation. The youths had stopped right in front of the building where our office was. The cops across the street had stopped also. The two armies—one white, one black; one with lethal weapons, the other with bottles and bricks—stood staring at each other.

I sent a CORE youth downstairs to mingle with the crowd and find out what they were planning to do. In a minute, he was back.

"You want to know what they're talking about? They're talking about raiding the CORE office. They say you've got some white CORE members up here."

It was going to be a long night. The chapter members and I went into a quick huddle to discuss strategy. Everyone agreed that the white women had to be gotten out of there and out of Harlem. Everyone agreed, that is, except the white women. Reluctantly, they consented to go.

But how on earth would they get out? I would leave the building first and walk into the center of the gang to draw their attention. I wouldn't be merely a decoy device; I would try to talk to them and defuse the situation, and seek some way to disperse them and get them to go home.

We moved quickly lest the gang outside move first.

Walking into their midst, I said, "Listen, you guys, I want to talk to you. I want to make a speech."

"Don't tell us about no nonviolence, Mr. Farmer," one of them said. "We don' wanna hear *that* shit."

"Right," another said, "We ain't gon' listen to none of that garbage."

Before speaking to this growing crowd that did not want to hear, a quick glance showed me that the four women had exited the building safely, surrounded by six black men, and were being taken to two cars halfway down the block, in which they would be driven home. The white men had remained in the office for the duration. The policemen across the street watched that maneuver, and they especially watched me.

Somewhere in the distance, a shot rang out and a woman screamed. I wiped my brow and my throat felt parched and dry. The canyon street seemed ghostly quiet and deserted now, except for the two battalions facing each other, and an occasional youth moving swiftly along the sidewalk to join the throng around me.

Bellowing loudly, I spoke of the great freedom movement, with King, and CORE, and SNCC, which was battering down barriers and was going to change the face of this nation. That approach was greeted with boos. I moved at it from another angle.

"Now, I'm bringing that movement north, so we can deal with the problems of the northern ghettos—the rat-infested firetrap housing; the garbage piling up because no sanitation trucks come by; the unemployment, when there are jobs for whites, but not for blacks; and the *police brutality.*" I fairly shouted the phrase.

They were beginning to listen now, and there was scattered applause. How could I have forgotten the most important thing of all? I would have to spring it now. I paused, and stared at their faces. They were absolutely quiet, waiting expectantly.

During the pause, Joe Overton, a Harlem labor leader and president of the New York branch of the NAACP, wormed his way through the crowd and stood beside me, slapping his hand on my shoulder in greeting. His formidable presence was comforting in this scene.

"Yesterday," I said and paused again, "yesterday, I met with the City Council president of New York, Paul Screvane, about the problems in Harlem."

There was loud applause, then another pause, and I went on: "The mayor, Bob Wagner, is out of the country—in Majorca, campaigning. I think he'd better stop in Africa and do some campaigning. He might learn something there."

The applause was even louder, and some shouted, "Right." There was even some laughter; I did not think those kids could laugh that night.

"In my meeting with Screvane, I demanded that the city set up a panel of civilians, not policemen, to hear the charges of brutality we bring against the police. It's ridiculous to have police investigating charges against the police."

The applause was deafening, and there were shouts of, "That's right, man," and "The cops just whitewash the cops."

"I said much more than that to Screvane. I told him that we wanted more black cops in Harlem."

There was sustained applause. Practically all the police assigned to Harlem were white. Black policemen had told me that they couldn't get assigned to Harlem because it was too lucrative a beat, with all the payoffs from vice and other crime. But I had not finished my speech.

"We know that black cops can be brutal, too, but we know that the black cop is not going to beat up our mothers and sisters and little brothers, because it could be *his* mother and sister and little brother."

They yelled their approval. I had them with me now, and I tried to wrap them up so that I could control them that night.

"I will meet again with Screvane and I will meet with Bob Wagner as soon as he gets back in the city."

Out of the corner of my eye, I was aware of a car window being rolled down, and a microphone thrust out of it. I went on: "Those were my demands; you heard them, and we will keep at it until we *win!*"

Applause almost rattled the windows of the buildings. The crowd moved closer to me.

"What can we do to help, Mr. Farmer? Tell us what we can do to help."

I had a strange sense of power, then; and, as always, I was uncomfortable with that feeling.

"There is only one thing you can do to help," I boomed.

"What is it, Mr. Farmer?"

"Get off the streets and go home!"

The answer came in a chorus: "No, we'll go home when those storm troopers go home. They stay, we stay! They go, we go!"

My heart sank. Joe Overton leaned toward me and whispered something. The plan he suggested was brilliant. Why hadn't I thought of it?

"All right," I shouted. "Line up. Everybody line up behind me. We're going to march!"

"Are you gonna lead us, Mr. Farmer? Are you gonna lead us?"

"Yeah, I'm going to lead you. Line up in twos."

They fell in line. I sent a young CORE worker across the street to tell the police my plan. I was going to try to turn a riot into an orderly demonstration. We would march west to Amsterdam Avenue, then north for a few blocks, then east, then north again, and then west, and so on. All along, we would tell them, "If we pass by your house, man, drop out and go home."

After a couple of hours, when everyone was tired, I would make another attempt to disperse them and send them home.

Two abreast, we marched, hands clapping rhythmically as we chanted, "We want justice. We want justice."

One kid behind me said to his partner, "Man, you're out of step. Get back in step."

The riot police followed, no more than fifty feet away. I wished they hadn't done that, but it couldn't be corrected now.

Joe Overton marched beside me. The ploy seemed to be working. The young men marching with us were drawn increasingly into the spirit of things; they were "helping" now by demonstrating peacefully, rather than striking out blindly in angry frustration.

Then, on Amsterdam Avenue, the sky fell. What sounded like the rat-a-tat-tat of machine guns caused the marching youngsters to duck and scatter, hiding behind parked cars. I moved to follow them, but Overton gripped my shoulder and said, "Jim, you can't run!"

He was right. I was a leader; I could not show fear.

Bottles and bricks started flying. Bullets ricocheted off brick walls around us and whined through the air. There were no machine guns, of course, but rapid fire from many service revolvers had the same effect. They were firing at windows and rooftops and answering bricks with bullets on the street. Some were reloading to join again in the shooting.

Four of the youths crouching behind cars rushed to surround me, holding their open hands around my head as a shield of flesh and bones. It was a futile but heroic gesture from street kids who hated nonviolence. There were young punks among them, no doubt, but that did not define them. Some were muggers, I'm sure, and maybe even rapists and possibly killers, and certainly there were haters; but the spark of humanity, scarcely born, had not yet died in them. Someday, a civilized society must learn how to blow the breath of caring on the flickering flame of compassion in its underclass.

Spotting a lieutenant, revolver drawn, pivoting around as he scanned windows and rooftops of tenement buildings, I went to him with the cordon of bodies around me and the hands riding my head like a hat.

"Why did you start shooting?" I asked. "Didn't you see what I was trying to do?"

"You tell those people to stop throwing those bottles and bricks at us," the police lieutenant shouted.

"I didn't see or hear any bottles and bricks being thrown before you started shooting," I responded.

The lieutenant repeated his words, as the shooting continued.

"Tell those people to stop throwing those bottles and bricks at us."

Now, it may well be that someone had thrown a bottle or brick from a rooftop or window behind our line of marchers and beyond my range of hearing. And New York's vaunted "tactical force," trained for riot duty, had panicked. True or not, there was nothing more that I could do to stop the Harlem riot of 1964. I walked back to the CORE chapter office.

Black male members went into the streets with orange-colored CORE armbands and makeshift stretchers to pick up the wounded. Those whose injuries were not serious were treated by a nurse at the CORE office and released. Others, after emergency treatment, were taken to Harlem Hospital.

One youth, brought in scarcely conscious and bleeding from head wounds, sat bolt upright as a white CORE member stood over him.

"What's that whitey doing here? Get 'im out of here! Kill 'im. Don't let 'im touch me!"

The injured man was in near hysteria. The white CORE member faded back into the next room.

"What you got whitey here for?" the man on the cot hollered. "I thought you was tryin' to *help* us."

"We are trying to help you," responded a black CORE member. "That's why we brought you here."

"Well, I don't want no help from you and your whitey friends," and with that, he got up and went down the stairs, and out into the hostile night.

Tortured by that hate, and the hate that spawned it, I went to the window and gazed out into the blackness.

Incredible tales of horror came to us from the wounded Harlemites. Cops, pursuing two brick throwers, for instance, charged into an all-night grocery store, swinging their clubs at random. When in an interview the next day, I told of that indiscriminate punishment of the innocent along with the guilty, a police spokesman said in reply that it was dark on the streets, and their men could not see the faces of the pursued, so once in the store how could they tell who the guilty ones were?

Time magazine, in a story on the riot the next week, implied that I had led the riot. I complained to the writer of the piece, Nick Thimmesch. He apologized by saying, "Well, now I owe you one."

Thimmesch paid that debt years later by doing a favorable story about me in his syndicated column.

* * *

It is doubtful that my posture on any issue during my leadership career was as incomprehensible to CORE's liberal friends and supporters as that on police brutality. The words they heard and the ink they read violated their credulity. In their childhood experiences and their adult communities, policemen were gentle with law-abiding folk, but firm with wrongdoers. They could not imagine the compassionate and friendly gentleman on the beat where they lived being brutal to any except those who were brutal to them and their community, which they protected. How could the man in blue whom they waved to each day and who called their children by name and helped them across the intersection—how could that fine man bust heads in Harlem or Bedford-Stuyvesant?

An individual here or there might break discipline and bow to the provocation, they thought, doing things unworthy of his uniform; but they could not believe that it was a pattern anywhere in this green land. Except maybe in Birmingham or Selma. But that was another world.

Some who had not believed us changed their minds at the time of the 1968 Democratic Convention in Chicago. There they saw policemen bloodying the heads of white youth.

As we said during those years, the wheel that squeaks gets the grease. I made loud noises in the media, and some grease was forthcoming. We got an integrated police force in Harlem and Bedford-Stuyvesant, and the black community applauded. We also got seminars for police in human and community relations led by social scientists and black leaders.

Yet the cost of those small concessions was high; contributions to CORE from liberal white supporters took another significant drop. Nor did my stance on police abuses endear me to New York's finest. Police officers, angered by the city's consideration of my demand for a civilian review board, announced plans to ring City Hall with a picket line of off-duty policemen. When asked by the press whether I thought police should be allowed to picket, I replied that, of course, they should; as American citizens, they had the same First Amendment rights I enjoyed. However, they should not have their guns on the picket line, I insisted. Mayor Robert F. Wagner agreed and directed that picketing policemen must leave their guns at home. That further insured that I would win no popularity contest among New York City policemen.

Walking around City Hall to observe their picket line, I was amused by the off-duty policemen lustily shouting a chant: *"Farmer is a rat-fink! Farmer is a rat-fink!"*

The attack on police abuse was no assault on the police function. That function is always needed most in the communities of the alienated of society. The need is perceived most by those who live there. Polls have confirmed polls, showing that safety in the streets is the number-one concern among ghetto dwellers.

The police function is appreciated by those who live in the ghettos, when police officers learn—as they are learning—that wrongdoing and criminality are individual qualities, not racial traits. A blue uniform on inner-city streets is becoming a sight more comforting than threatening.

That night on Harlem streets, however, hate confounded hate. White hate, black hate. I could not rid my ears of those "get whitey" cries. Black hate engendered by white hate; it was nonetheless hate.

For ten years, Americans had been fed a steady diet of white hate in the South, and the nation was retching. Whites were shocked by the explosion of anger in Harlem, stunned by the realization that most blacks were not as King had said they would be: long-suffering victims, loving so fiercely that hate would be overcome. The decent were agonized by the realization that haters in Harlem, like haters everywhere, made no distinction between the good and the bad; they, too, were victims.

Hate kills, and it was not done with its deadly work.

CHAPTER 27

TRYST WITH DEATH

THE SPECTER OF SUDDEN death was a constant companion in those years, riding with me on every trip. It was, therefore, no surprise when, one afternoon in 1964, a call came to my office from John Malone, the regional director of the FBI in New York.

"Mr. Farmer," he said, "I would appreciate it if you'd let me know the next time you're going to Louisiana. In fact, the next time you're going below the Mason-Dixon line."

"Why?" I asked.

"The Klan met yesterday in Bogalusa and decided that next time you come down there, you're going to be killed."

"How do you know that?" I asked.

"Routinely," he said. "We've infiltrated the Klan. We had a man there."

The threats of death came so frequently that they always had an air of unreality. I made a feeble attempt at humor: "Well, tell me, were there any dissenting votes?"

"I think you should be serious, Mr. Farmer," he replied. "The Klan is deadly serious. Until further notice, just have your secretary give me a call whenever you're going south, and let me know your itinerary."

"She won't have to call you. I can tell you now. I'm going down there tomorrow."

"To Louisiana?" he asked.

"Yes, to Bogalusa."

He sighed audibly and asked, "Okay, what airline? What flight? What time?"

After I hung up, I sat at my desk for a few minutes in contemplation. Should I cancel the trip, or at least postpone it? I had told the local black community in Bogalusa that I would be there in two days to address a freedom rally at the Baptist church. How could I cancel out of fear when they lived under the shadow of the Klan every minute of every day? I would have to go.

I called Lula and asked if she had paid last month's premium on my life insurance.

"Yes," she answered. "I mailed it yesterday."

When informed of the conversation I had had with the FBI regional director, she said, "Do you think you should go?"

Before I could reply, she answered her own question: "Yes, of course. You have to go."

I summoned key members of my staff into the office and brought them up to date. Someone mentioned something about a bulletproof vest and I rejected the idea out of hand.

"This is midsummer," I said. "Bogalusa will be like a steam bath even without that kind of paraphernalia. Furthermore, would we have similar protection for all the local people who'll be with me in that church?"

Before our meeting was over Marvin Rich said, "Although the Klan may be bluffing, I do think you should call the people in Bogalusa and alert them to the fact that this threat has been made. They may want to take some precautions of their own."

The flight to New Orleans was uneventful. After taxiing to the gate, the pilot spoke over the public address system: "All passengers whose destination is New Orleans, please deplane at this time. James Farmer, please remain seated."

When the passengers had filed out, a grim-faced, overweight man came aboard the plane and walked toward me, displaying his credentials as he approached. He was a captain in the Louisiana State Police Department.

"Mr. Farmer," he began, "our governor received a call from Washington informing him that your life could be in danger while you're in our state. Governor McKeithen called my boss, Colonel Burbank, who's state director of public safety, and ordered him to protect your life. Colonel Burbank has assigned me that responsibility."

The plainclothes lieutenant motioned through the window of the plane and four other plainclothesmen boarded and came toward me. I must confess to a bit of apprehension, since it had been the state police and deputized red-necks who had tried to kill me a year ago in Plaquemine, Louisiana, and the memory of that episode was still fresh.

The captain spoke again: "I'm assigning these four lieutenants as your personal bodyguards while you're in our state. They'll be with you at all times, except while you're sleeping, and even then they'll have all entrances to your room in view. They're well armed, they have a service revolver at their hips and small firearms strapped to their ankles—and they're excellent marksmen. They have two unmarked cars, one of which will transport you to Bogalusa.

"As you proceed to Bogalusa, there will be a helicopter overhead manned by state troopers armed with high-powered rifles in the event of an attempted ambush. The helicopter will be in radio communication with your four bodyguards. These lieutenants are entirely trustworthy. They're professionals who know their business. Please be assured that you can trust them implicitly. I'm holding them strictly responsible for your safety, as the governor is holding me responsible.

"Shall we go into the airport now?"

As the six of us walked to the airport, the lieutenant's eyes seemed to search everywhere danger might lurk. Inside the lobby, three black men who were standing near the entrance beckoned to me. They were friends from Bogalusa, members of the Deacons for Defense and Justice, a black self-defense organization that had been formed to shoot back when the Klan shot into homes of black citizens of Bogalusa. On a previous visit, they had told me of their plans to organize. They knew that CORE was a nonviolent organization and they said they accepted that while on CORE demonstrations. But when not on demonstrations, they would determine their response in consultation with their consciences and their God.

The KKK was said to have its largest per-capita membership in Bogalusa. On frequent occasions, carloads of white men would speed through the black community firing guns into homes, willy-nilly. The Deacons organized to fire back. After one night-riding venture by Klansmen, the Deacons returned the fire from inside their homes. The Klan cars sped away and the night riding came to an end.

I excused myself from my state police bodyguards, telling them that I wanted to talk to my friends.

"Jim," said one of the Deacons, "we don't trust those SOBs. We don't know which way they'll point their guns. We would feel much more comfortable if you'd ride to Bogalusa in our car."

"Let me work this out with the troopers," I said. "I'll be right back."

When I explained to the troopers that my friends from Bogalusa wanted me to ride in their car with them, the captain nodded.

"That will be all right as long as your friends' car is in the middle and one of ours is in front and one is behind. That way, the lieutenants will have you covered."

Our three-car caravan sped across the twenty-mile causeway spanning Lake Pontchartrain and down the concrete highway toward Bogalusa. The helicopter whirred overhead, searching the woods and hovering momentarily over roadside bars. Each time we approached one of these places, the lead car with the two lieutenants in its front seat accelerated. The Deacon driving the car in which I rode grunted as he floored his accelerator, trying to keep pace.

"Geez, that car can really fly."

Inside the town of Bogalusa, our caravan cruised to the address that had been given to the troopers. It was the home of the president of the Deacons for Defense and Justice. Before the troopers would allow me to enter the home, two of them went in and searched the house thoroughly, looking under beds, in closets, behind couches, behind drapes, in bathrooms—everyplace an assailant could hide.

Then, one trooper said, "All right, Mr. Farmer, you can come in now."

Two of the troopers sat in the living room all night; the other two remained in one of the cars parked out front, but positioned so as to give its occupants a clear view of both windows to my bedroom, as well as the front door. Two of the Deacons waited in the living room all night, too, sitting in one corner with their guns at the ready while the troopers sat in the opposite corner with theirs.

I retired for the night, secure in the knowledge that unless a bomb were tossed through a window, the Klan could reach me only if they were prepared to swap their lives for mine.

By morning, the Deacons and the troopers in the living room were almost fraternizing. It had been a long night for them, and they'd finally agreed that one of each pair would sit guard while the others napped.

As we drove to the church that afternoon, a pickup truck shot out from a side street and tried to intercept the car in which I was riding. The state police car behind me moved like a rocket out of the line and into the front of the pickup truck, crunching fenders with it and forcing it into a ditch. The driver of the pickup was pulled from the car and handcuffed, a pistol removed from his clothing, and he was taken away to jail. He was the leader of the local Klan organization.

Before the troopers would allow me to mount the platform at the church, they went up first, checking windows, doors, and other convenient hiding places. Two of the troopers sat in their car outside the church; the other two flanked the platform.

My address to the congregation went smoothly and I found myself whisked into the waiting car, which sped back to the New Orleans airport.

The plane had actually begun to taxi down the runway when the pilot spoke: "We are returning to the gate. All passengers will leave the aircraft immediately. Luggage will be taken off the plane and passengers will identify their luggage and search it in the presence of airline employees. We have received a call that there is a bomb aboard this plane."

No explosive was found, and in due time, we reboarded and flew uneventfully to New York.

A week later, as I returned to Bogalusa to lead a march, we went through the same ritual at the airport, with the captain introducing me to four lieutenants—two of whom were familiar faces, having been with me on the earlier visit. The other two, though somewhat smaller in stature, had huge, hamlike hands. The captain informed me that they were holders of black belts in karate.

"Why karate?" I asked.

"After your march was announced, the Klan said it was having a march the same day in Bogalusa, and it appears that the twain might meet."

The next morning, I received a call from Colonel Burbank, head of the state police.

"Mr. Farmer," he said, "I've come to town to take personal charge of your operation, because it appears it might be touch and go. After looking the situation over, it's my personal judgment that it will be very dangerous for you to be in the march this afternoon, probably suicidal."

"Colonel," I said, "I've told the local people that I'll be in the march, so I'll be there—on the front line."

"All right," he said. "We'll take all the precautions we can and I'll be in touch with you shortly."

A call came from one of the Deacons, informing me that one of their members had overheard two "crackers" talking downtown. One of them had said to the other, "This is 'D-Day.' That nigger Farmer dies today. We've got a trap set for him when his march gets downtown, and there's no way he can escape. By sundown tonight, that nigger's gon' be dead and in hell."

The Deacon said, "We'll understand if you decide not to be in the march today."

"I'll be on the front line," I said.

"Okay, Jim," he said. "We'll get some of our guys as close to every intersection as the troopers will let us, and if any trouble starts, we'll be ready."

Before noon, Colonel Burbank came to the house where I was staying.

"I want to let you know what we're doing by way of security," he said. "I've ordered seventy additional state policemen into Bogalusa. I've also learned that some segregationists are planning to come down from Mississippi and others up from New Orleans for the Klan march today. So we set up road blocks at every road leading into town. Nobody, but nobody will get into this town today who can't prove that he lives here. We've cleared our downtown buildings and are stationing state policemen at key spots on rooftops and at windows in downtown buildings, all armed with high-powered rifles.

"During your march, there will be two helicopters flying overhead, manned by state police armed with high-powered rifles and powerful sound systems. If any unauthorized persons proceed toward your line of march, said persons will be ordered to halt, retreat, or disperse—whichever seems appropriate. If they disobey, the state police in the helicopters will be prepared to shoot.

"Flanking your line of march will be state police, no more than ten feet apart, armed with rifles, shotguns, and submachine guns. Immediately in front of your line of march will be an automobile, in the front seat of which will be two of your personal bodyguards, the lieutenants. If any shooting starts, drop to the ground and crawl to that car. The back door will be swung open when you get there. When you're inside the car, it will take off at high speed.

"Immediately behind you in your line of march will be your other two bodyguards, the karate men. . . . I can't think of anything that we've overlooked. Good day and good luck."

I would be lying if I said that I was not afraid. I was more terrified than at any time since Plaquemine, or maybe since the Freedom Ride from Montgomery to Mississippi. I thought about begging out, but that was clearly out of the question now. I had to go through with it.

Usually, we sang while marching—"We Shall Overcome" or "Ain't Nobody Gonna Turn Me 'Round." This time, however, we were all too scared to sing. It was a silent march. The wife of one of the Deacons, a tiny woman of about five feet and weighting about ninety pounds, insisted on marching with me on the front line. She held my arm as we marched.

When we reached downtown, it was all that Colonel Burbank had said it would be. I spotted troopers on rooftops, rifles in hand. Silhouetted at many windows were other troopers with rifles. We encountered several bands of young white men standing in little knots. They were a leather-jacketed ducktail-haircut bunch, and they seemed as scared as we were. Any second, I expected to hear the crack of a rifle. Then I remembered that, if I heard it, it meant they had missed: bullets travel faster than sound.

Silently, we walked through the business district into a residential area. The tension inside me seemed to relax a little. I thought it more likely that a shot would be fired from buildings in the downtown area. At one intersection in the residential community, eight or ten white men were standing, leaning against parked cars.

As I came next to them, one of the troopers suddenly yelled, "Hey, look out! Get him!"

Two of the troopers flanking the line of march leaped on one of the young men, taking from him a metal pipe with a large bolt on the end, which he had just drawn from his leather jacket. They disarmed him, and arrested him. I do not know whether he had intended to swing it at me. If he had, it would have crushed my skull.

At the next intersection, a trooper shouted just as suddenly, and equally loudly, "Hey! Get him!"

The police flanking my line pounced on a man in the act of drawing from his jacket a pearl-handled revolver. They arrested him, too.

Then some fool among the white toughs set off a firecracker. The troopers flanking our line of march whirled, crouched, and pointed their guns in the direction of the sound. Thinking it was a shot, I debated with myself whether to drop to the ground and try to reach the car in front of us. I decided against it; some of the marchers might panic and run for cover, and the Deacons somewhere nearby might open fire. Then all hell would break loose.

So, I stood still, as still as the death I thought was imminent.

After a time—seconds or minutes, I don't know which—one of the state troopers shouted over a bullhorn, "Apparently, it was a firecracker. Proceed with your march."

I did not relax until I was in my apartment in New York, having a drink with several members of my staff who were waiting to congratulate me on my survival.

PART SEVEN

Cut Off at the Pass

CHAPTER 28

BETRAYAL ON THE POTOMAC

PRESIDENT JOHNSON'S GIANT FRAME leaned sideways over the arm of the leather upholstered chair in which he was sitting. His face was turned fully toward me.

"Mr. Farmer, I've got to get this civil rights bill through Congress, and I'm going to do it. If I never do anything else in my whole life, I'm going to get this job done. It won't be easy, but I'm going to do it. I have to get some of the Republicans on our side. You civil rights leaders can help me on that. You all should tell the Republicans that if they vote for this bill, you'll tell your people to vote for them. And I think you should, too; if they vote for this bill, you should tell people to vote for them. If I can't get the Republicans, then I'm going to have to get the Dixiecrats. That's the southern Democrats, you know. That's really going to be hard. I don't know how I'm going to do it, but somehow I'm going to have to break down their resistance. Somehow I've got to get my hand under their dress."

We were interrupted by several incoming phone calls—senators returning the president's calls. He twisted arms, threatened and cajoled, and then looked up to make sure I was duly impressed with his efforts on behalf of the bill.

Between the calls, I asked, "Mr. President, how did you get to be this way? You're a southerner, and your congressional record on civil rights was not very good. What changed you?"

"I'll answer that question by quoting a friend of yours," he replied. " 'Free at last, free at last, thank God almighty, I'm free at last.' "

What he meant by that reference to King's march on Washington speech, of course, was that, as president, he was freed from accountability to a southern constituency and could be responsive to the needs of all the people.

"The southerners tell me," he went on, "that they'll buy this bill if I take the public accommodations section out. But I won't do that. The public accommodations part is the heart and the guts of this measure, and I will *not* remove it."

I asked him how he came to view public accommodations to be so important and he related a story in response.

"One day down in Texas many years ago, my maid was going on vacation with her husband. Lady Bird—that's Mrs. Johnson, you know—told the maid to take our dog with her; we had a little beagle. My maid said, 'Mrs. Johnson, please don't make me take that dog with me. My husband and I will be driving across the South and it's going to be tough enough finding places to stay, just being black, without having a dog with us.'

"Mr. Farmer, that made me cry. Just to think that a wonderful woman like my maid couldn't stay in any hotel she wanted to. It made me mad. I'd lived in Texas all my life and I'd never thought about it before. Right then I swore that if I ever got any power, I would do something about it. Now I have some power and by God I'm going to do something about it."

I looked at him and said nothing. I found myself thinking of that terrible day less than a month earlier when President Kennedy's brains were blown out in Texas, and of the call I received from Johnson three days later.

"Mr. Farmer, this is Lyndon Johnson. I first wanted to call and tell you that I remember when you came to my office when I was vice-president. You made a good suggestion to me that helped me a lot. And I asked you to do something for me, and you followed through on that. I just want you to know that I appreciated that a lot."

"Thank you, Mr. President."

"Now, we're going to have to pick up this ball and run with it. I'm going to need your help in the months and maybe the years that lie ahead, and I hope I'll get it."

"If we're going the same way, Mr. President, we can go together."

"I'm glad to hear you say that. Next time you're in Washington, drop by and see me."

I knew that Johnson had to win the confidence of black leaders, for the absence of their trust had helped deny him the nomination in 1960. Nevertheless, I was flattered by what came to be known as "the Johnson treatment." Never before had I been called by a president.

Now, here I was in the Oval Office, still being buttered up by that flattery. The fact that I knew what was happening did not lessen its effectiveness.

He slapped his knee and drawled, "Well, Jim, I know you're interested in a lot of other things besides this bill. What else can I do to help your cause?"

I leaned back in the big chair and unbuttoned my collar and loosened my tie; I had gained weight and the shirt was not comfortable.

"Mr. President, there *is* one thing that keeps me awake nights. We've battered many doors open, and when the civil rights bill is enacted into law, many walls will come tumbling down. Yet, there are millions of Americans of all races who won't be able to walk through those doors or step across those fallen walls. The reason? A lack of basic educational skills; the inability to read, write, and compute."

The president nodded his head vigorously.

"I agree a thousand percent," he said, "but what are we going to do about it?"

"We have in the movement thousands of volunteers with intelligence, dedication, and boundless energies, who don't consider sitting-in, freedom riding, and going to jail to be the most meaningful things in the world any longer. They're standing by now, waiting for direction. Reading specialists can instruct them in teaching adults to read, and we can fan them out through the country. There are over twenty million adults who cannot read up to a fourth-grade level. I believe we can wipe out that functional illiteracy in ten to fifteen years."

"I think that's a great idea," said Johnson, "and we can make it work. I'll tell you what I want you to do. I want you to send me a memorandum describing your plan in detail. My staff will go over it carefully and give me their reactions. I also want you to send me a two- or three-page summary of your plan, and I'll read that myself.

"Now, the press is outside, and they're going to want to know what we talked about. You can tell them that you suggested a massive drive against illiteracy in this country, to teach people how to read and write and add and subtract and multiply. You can tell that as an old schoolteacher and former head of NYA* under Roosevelt, I'm enthusiastic about the idea. And tell them that we're going to follow through on it."

I nodded agreement, and at that moment a White House photographer entered and the president and I posed shaking hands.

As I headed for the door to take my leave, Johnson slapped me on the back and asked, "By the way, Jim—you don't mind if I call you Jim, do you?"

"Not at all, Mr. President."

"You may call me Lyndon."

"Thank you, Mr. President."

He continued, "What part of Texas do you come from?"

"Marshall," I replied.

"Marshall! Doggone, Jim, do you realize that's Lady Bird's hometown? Her father had a filling station there."

*National Youth Administration. Actually, he headed the Texas state chapter from July 1935 to February 1937.

When we parted, we shook hands warmly—two Texans reaching out across the invisible railroad tracks of the Lone Star State.

"Anytime you want to say something to me, Jim, just get on the phone and call. I'll see that your calls are put right through to me," the president said. "I'll see that your letters come to me, too, and don't get bottled up on somebody else's desk."

Johnson was a man of his word with regard to accessibility. Phone calls got through to him and written communications reached him without languishing on the desks of aides.

Gordon Carey, my assistant at CORE, was assigned the task of putting the memorandum on literacy together. After several months of exploring the question, he made contact with Dr. Myron Woolman, president of the Institute of Educational Research and a psychologist who had designed a programmed instructional system of proven effectiveness in teaching adults to read.

I met Dr. Woolman, whom we called Mike, and discussed the question at great length with him and his staff. Mike, a rotund and genial scholar of extraordinary brilliance, prepared the memo for the president. I summarized it in a brief paper for LBJ's personal perusal. The memo stressed the training and use of nonprofessionals in employing the programmed instructional method of teaching adult illiterates to read. It presented a carefully phased plan, starting with ten major cities, and proposed yearly expansion until the whole country was covered. There was evaluation built in each step of the way.

In October 1964, the memorandum and summary went to the White House. Johnson reacted promptly by suggesting that I get other civil rights leaders lined up behind it so CORE wouldn't be the only group pushing the project, and he wouldn't be accused of playing favorites. The president's suggestion was eminently sensible, not only for him politically, but also for the success of the literacy program, and for me. Without their involvement from the beginning I might encounter sabotage along the way.

So a nonprofit corporation, the Center for Community Action Education, was set up. Among the members of its board of directors were civil rights leaders such as Martin Luther King; Whitney Young, head of the National Urban League; Dr. John Morsell, associate executive director of the NAACP; Dorothy Height, president of the National Council of Negro Women; John Lewis, national chairman of SNCC; and such labor leaders as Jerry Wurf, international president of AFSCME; Stanton Wormley, vice-president of Howard University; Mike Woolman; Gordon Carey; and myself.

I touched base with the essential persons—Dr. Howard Howe, U.S. Commissioner of Education; Congressman Adam Clayton Powell, Jr., chairman of the House Labor and Education Committee; and Vice-President Hubert Humphrey. All three read the literacy proposal, which had been expertly prepared by Mike Woolman, and all three enthusiastically endorsed it. Humphrey, as was his style, became its ardent advocate.

Johnson was pleased and requested that I submit the proposal to the Office of Economic Opportunity (OEO). He said that he would tell Sargent Shriver, director of OEO, that the proposal had administration backing and should be given sympathetic consideration.

Humphrey told me that I should keep in close touch with Hyman Bookbinder, assistant director of OEO, who was "his man" at the agency, and Bookbinder would shepherd the program through to fruition. I believed that we were home free and went back to concentrating on CORE activities as we awaited funding.

CORE work went on and the excitement never ceased. Even more exciting in 1965 were certain events—fringe benefits of having been national director of CORE for four years. One of those events, dominating my recollection, was a meeting with a man who was, without a doubt, the most gifted human being ever produced by this nation.

When Lennie Seelig, a member of one of the New York CORE chapters, took me to a small Harlem apartment to meet Paul Robeson, I was awestruck as I faced that aging, huge, gentle man. It is incredible that any one person could have possessed such varied and superlative talents.

Robeson beamed as he looked down upon me and took my hand.

"Come in, Jim. For several years I've longed to meet you."

He had wanted to meet *me*. I mumbled appropriate words of gratitude as I stared at the seventy-year-old physique, which could still shame most of the athletes of the world.

Words were my trademark, but this time they failed me, and I just stared at Robeson. Here he was in the flesh. Rhodes scholar, smasher of academic precedents at Rutgers; all-American football player, breaker of athletic records; brilliant lawyer; greater singer; superb actor—his eyes smiled at the awkwardness I showed in his presence.

The baritone voice that crumbled spines and shattered crystal glasses in recording studios spoke: "Jim, my wife and I have watched you with admiration on television, on 'Meet the Press,' and 'Face the Nation,' and we have silently applauded."

"Oh, Paul," I interrupted. "All my life I've said if I could sing 'Old Man River' just once the way you sang it, I'd be ready to die."

The ageless giant, whose talents dwarfed his size, beamed and I added, "I can't even carry a tune."

There was no lull in the conversation as it drifted on into the night. In the course of it, I told him that although I disagreed with his politics—I was a Norman Thomas socialist akin to the European Social Democrats—they were *his* views and he had every right to them, and I deeply resented the efforts in our country to erase his greatness because he was a communist, and to make him a nonperson, a forgotten man.

Robeson nodded and murmured a resonant thank you.

I expressed the view that it was criminal for our kids to go through high school and college without knowing the name and accomplishments of Paul Robeson. I vowed that we would correct that.

The versatile genius again nodded his great head and his face seemed to leap out from a thousand playbills, concert programs, and record album covers as a big smile brought it to life.

Departing, I invited Paul Robeson to come to some CORE rallies and demonstrations, for we would be pleased and honored to have him. He said that he would.

Months later, when he had not come, I called to find out why.

"Jim," he said, "I felt that you had enough problems without being embarrassed by my presence."

Who among us, in the twilight of his career, would refrain from making a widely publicized appearance simply because he thought it would embarrass someone else whom he respected? Robeson had class.

In the second half of 1964 and through 1965, my relationship with Lyndon Johnson deteriorated and access to the White House became more difficult. The president's political career had led him to equate disagreement with disloyalty. Those who were not for him unconditionally were considered to be against him.

There were areas of major disagreement with Johnson. When he knew that Barry Goldwater would be his opponent in the election of 1964, he sought to still the turbulent waters of civil rights activity, fearing that a white backlash would help Goldwater.

Wilkins called a meeting at NAACP offices. In addition to himself and me, there were six others present: Whitney Young; Martin Luther King; Jack Greenberg of the NAACP Legal Defense and Education Fund; A. Philip Randolph; Bayard Rustin; and John Lewis. I did not know why we had been called together; I'd simply been asked by Roy to come to an urgent meeting on strategy.

Seated at the far end of the long table in his conference room, Roy chaired the meeting. He was always a masterful chairman, poised and polished. He began by articulating a concern that all of us shared—that Goldwater must not be elected. He ended his remarks by saying that he knew we all agreed that we must not do anything prior to the election that would help elect Goldwater president of the United States. Then he called on Randolph for a comment.

Randolph, then in his mid-seventies, had lost none of his grace and dignity. In stentorian tones and cultured Oxford accent, he described the disaster that lay in store for black Americans in the event of a Goldwater victory and the ascendancy of a right-wing philosophy to the White House. He expressed the belief that continued demonstrations might whip up the waves of a backlash on which Goldwater might ride to victory.

The grand old man then announced that he had asked Bayard Rustin to come along and read a prepared statement, which he hoped all of us could agree upon and adopt. Rustin read a statement calling for a moratorium on civil rights demonstrations in order to avoid helping Barry Goldwater in the November presidential election.

In the silence that followed, I perceived that all eyes were on me. It was only CORE, SNCC, and SCLC that had demonstrations as a major part of their operations. Really only CORE and SNCC, for SCLC demonstrated chiefly when King came to town and led a march. Glancing at the representatives of other organizations around the table, I had the sense that they were there to bring pressure on SNCC and CORE—mostly on me. My nature rebelled. Mentally, I tried to sum up the history and appraise the politics of the moment. This could blow CORE and SNCC out of the water.

I broke the silence and spoke: "I cannot go along with a moratorium."
Heads jerked upward and eyes showed shock.

"Announcing a moratorium," I continued, "would not halt demonstrations. My chapters have a great deal of programmatic autonomy. If I ordered a temporary halt to demonstrations, some of my chapters would demonstrate anyway. I could suspend them, of course, but the demonstrations would go on during suspension. There would be due-process hearings and appeals that would carry us far beyond the presidential election. If we said that we were calling off demonstrations and demonstrations went on, we would either expose our weakness or look like double-crossers. I think Martin is the only one who could call for an end to demonstrations and expect to get it from his organization. I can't speak for SNCC; John Lewis will have to do that. Further, even if I could call off demonstrations by CORE, I would not be inclined to do it."

Heads jerked again.

"Demonstrations are CORE's only weapons. If we talk to wrongdoers and ask them to change their ways, they'll laugh at us if they know we've given up our weapon. If we try to negotiate, we become an amateur Urban League. If we file suit, we become an amateur NAACP or Legal Defense and Education Fund. For CORE to give up demonstrations, even for six months, would be to give up its genius, its raison d'être. It might sound our death knell."

There was another reason, which I did not state. The Norm Hill caucus was, at that time, peaking within CORE. Had I agreed to a moratorium, I would have been clobbered.

John Lewis agreed with me and said that he and SNCC would not go along with a moratorium.

Randolph asked, "But what about the danger to the movement of a Goldwater victory? Do you want that on your conscience?"

"No, I don't," I replied to a man who was a hero to me. "But CORE people are politically motivated and activated. We're going to be out there getting people registered and turning out the vote for Johnson. Johnson will win the election."

Roy Wilkins cleared his throat and said that if everyone else agreed he would tell the waiting press that the civil rights leadership was calling for a temporary moratorium on demonstrations, and that two persons, James Farmer of CORE and John Lewis of SNCC, had declined to go along with the call.

The others agreed and the announcement was made to the press. Johnson, I was told, was furious that I had dissented.

After Johnson's landslide victory in 1964, he made the fateful decision to escalate our involvement in Vietnam, for in true Texas spirit, he was "not going to be the first American president to turn tail and run." In addition, he had been told by his military experts that if we flexed our muscles the North Vietnamese would fold like an accordion. The fact that I did not let CORE adopt a resolution calling for a unilateral U.S. withdrawal from Vietnam in no way softened his anger at my personal opposition to his Vietnam policy.

A tenacious friend to those who were "loyal," LBJ was an unforgiving enemy to the "disloyal." His animosity showed itself in petty ways.

After passage of the Voting Rights Act of 1965, a host of people, including all the top civil rights leaders, were invited to the signing ceremony. Arriving early, I positioned myself in the front row close to his desk, along with Roy Wilkins and Whitney Young. In the traditional manner, he used many pens in signing the bill into law, handing each pen as a souvenir to someone around him. It seemed everyone in the room got a pen as a souvenir except me. The president passed pens to my right, to my left, over my shoulders, but not to me, and all the while his eyes avoided mine. Finally, Wilkins spoke loudly, saying, "Jim Farmer, Mr. President, Jim Farmer. Give Jim a pen!" And he pointed to me. My fellow Texan seemed suddenly to have lost his hearing. Whitney Young took up the cry also: "Here's Jim, Mr. President. Jim Farmer. He hasn't got a pen yet." I was then given a pen without any eye contact.

No longer being close to the president did not, in itself, bother me. However, I viewed the future of the literacy program with some uneasiness. The OEO staff, though, and even Sargent Shriver himself, continued to be enthusiastic.

The literacy proposal was approved and championed by Shriver's entire processing staff and went to his desk for signature. Dr. Sanford Kravitz, associate director of OEO's community action program (CAP), remained in constant touch with Gordon Carey, Mike Woolman, and me and shepherded the proposal to Shriver's desk for signature. The sky did not immediately fall, but the rumbling sounds overhead were enough to cause Chicken Little to panic. The proposal already had the approval of Kravitz, Olga Boikess of the legal department, education specialist Jule Sugarman, and management director W. P. Kelly (for the hospitalized CAP director, Theodore M. Berry).

At 3:00 A.M., Christmas Day, 1965, someone called me and said, "Jim, get out of bed, if you're in bed. Get a copy of the *Washington Post*. There's a front-page article on your project. Get it right now!" I do not remember who the caller was.

Lula and the girls and I were in Washington visiting my family for the holidays. It was a holiday season I shall never forget.

The front-page *Post* announced that I was going to resign as national director of CORE in order to head up the literacy project that was soon to be funded by the OEO. The article gave full specifics of my program and was accurate in almost every detail. Obviously, it had been leaked to the *Post* from an OEO source. It was true that I intended to resign from my position with CORE in order to head up the literacy project, but that pending resignation was to be kept secret until the project had been funded. It was essential that the heaving and hauling over the succession within CORE not begin prematurely, and not begin at all if the literacy program failed to be funded.

Now it was too late for such caution. With the dawn came a plethora of agitated phone calls from CORE leaders and staff persons all over the country. They were being barraged by the wire services and local media for confirmation of the report that I was leaving CORE. It took CORE people by surprise, producing absolute chaos.

"What is this, Jim? Are you leaving CORE? We didn't hear anything about this before. Why didn't you tell us?"

"We feel like idiots being told by the media what's going on within our own organization. How shall we answer them? What shall we tell them?"

"Tell them 'no comment.'"

"No comment? But aren't *we* entitled to some comment from you? What the hell is going on?"

The pot continued to boil, and my phone was never silent in the days that followed. All of a sudden, I could not reach Sargent Shriver by phone or wire. I could not reach Lyndon Johnson.

Hubert Humphrey, who never really had Johnson's confidence, thought that the program had been funded. On January 10, 1966, he wrote me, saying, "Congratulations on your leadership and determination to bring this proposal through to reality. . . . I'm confident that your new assignment will produce . . . a truly historic contribution to our nation."

Humphrey was mistaken. It had not been funded. Shriver had not signed it yet. It was still on his desk. All Sandy Kravitz knew was that the staff work had been completed and it was awaiting Shriver's signature, as it had been for many weeks. I tried to reach Adam Clayton Powell, but he did not return my calls. I stewed while CORE people jumped up and down in confusion and anger.

Then came a column by Evans and Novak on the literacy program. The two journalists wrote that, very shortly, the federal government was going to fund to the tune of about $1 million for the first year a program to be headed by CORE's national director, James Farmer. This program, Evans and Novak stated, was to teach adult functional illiterates how to read. On the surface, they observed, it seemed like a meritorious program, but, they went on, that was just the "tip of the iceberg."

"Farmer," they said, "is not interested in literacy. He is a political animal. His plan is to build himself a political base in the major cities which he selects as pilots in his project. . . . His objective? . . . *To throw out the white power structure.*"

Congressmen were suddenly asking, "Why should the federal government fund a social revolution aimed at throwing us out of office?" Others queried, "Why the hell should we make Jim Farmer the savior of all the illiterates in the country?"

It appeared now that the program was dead. It was also clear that I could not continue leading CORE. I could no longer postpone taking action to smooth these waters and arrange for an orderly transfer of power.

I called an emergency meeting of the National Action Council in New York. At that late December meeting, I formally announced my resignation, to be effective March 1, 1966, and asked the NAC to set up a search committee, on which I wished to serve, to screen applicants for the job and present to the NAC two candidates from which they would make their selection. This action was taken.

At my recommendation, the search committee limited applications to those currently active in CORE. The two top candidates were Floyd B. McKissick, national chairman of CORE, and George Wiley, associate national director. McKissick had my support for the position. He was a friend and a good speaker, and I also believed him to have the kind of charisma needed at that juncture in CORE's history.

George had been my associate director for almost a year and a half and served as chief of staff, relieving me of much of the routine, day-to-day work of the organization. A former professor of chemistry at Syracuse University, he was a highly intelligent man, polished and cultured. Yet, I did not think he could relate to the young Turks in the Harlems of the country who were becoming more and more prominent in CORE. Nor was I convinced of his loyalty, to put it mildly. It was a truism that all number two's want to be number one's, but few were as open about their ambition as was George Wiley.

Prior to the 1965 CORE convention, for example, George had sent a message to the southern staff that upset me no end. Our southern field staff and task force workers were meeting in New Orleans. In a call to Rudy Lombard, CORE's vice-chairman, Wiley instructed him to "tell all the southern field staff and task force members to get together all their gripes and bring them to the convention. That will put Farmer on the spot." This message was passed on to me by one of our southern CORE leaders, who was present at that meeting. When I confronted Wiley with this breach of faith, he did not deny it, but merely said, "Now, you're accusing me of disloyalty."*

With my support, McKissick was elected in January to succeed me in March.

Once again, I went on the lecture circuit for a living. Between trips I still tried to get some answers regarding the stalled proposal at OEO.

In the meantime, Congressman Adam Clayton Powell had held a press conference that drove another nail into the coffin of my plan to teach illiterate adults how to read. At his press conference, the congressman sat blowing billows of smoke from his cigar. Occasionally, the billows were punctuated with smoke rings. Beside him, looking very uncomfortable, was Harold "Doc" Howe, the U.S. commissioner of education, who had been a champion of my program from the very beginning. Powell told the assembled newspeople that he did not think there was any need for a new agency to deal with the problem of literacy in this country because we already had the Office of Education, and that was its job. The Office of Education, Powell insisted, was well equipped with staff and experience to deal with such educational problems as illiteracy and was perfectly able to get the job done. Then he turned to "Doc" Howe and asked, "Isn't that right, Commissioner?"

The commissioner of education reddened and nodded his head. What else was he to do or say? Powell was chairman of the House Labor and Education Committee, which held the purse strings of the Office of Education.

After the news conference, Howe called me to apologize for what he had had to do. Once again, I vainly tried to reach Adam.

During this period, A. Philip Randolph, along with some other labor leaders, met with President Johnson. Randolph took the opportunity to bring up the matter of my literacy program.

"Mr. President," he said, "let me bring up another matter of great concern to me. Why hasn't James Farmer's program been funded? I ask this question not just because Jim is a good friend of mine, but also because I think his program is an excellent one that deserves to be operational. Is it going to be funded? If so, when? If not, why not?"

The president responded, "I'm all for Jim's program. I'm for it one thousand percent, just like I told Jim when he sat in that very chair you're sitting in now, Mr. Randolph."

"Then what's holding it up?" asked Randolph.

"Talk to the chairman," replied the president.

"What chairman?" Randolph asked.

"Chairman Powell," Johnson said.

*George Wiley went on to initiate the Welfare Rights Organization, which he led with imagination and verve. His death by drowning was a significant loss to the struggle.

"What does Adam have to do with it?"

"He's chairman of the House Labor and Education Committee. He controls OEO's funding."

When Randolph told me of that conversation, I asked him to call Powell, for I had not been able to reach him. Randolph had no more success than I.

I then asked Martin Luther King to call Powell, Baptist preacher to Baptist preacher, to find out why he was sitting on my program. King told me that he had spoken with Adam, whose response was: "I've got nothing against Jim's program. I'm all for it. Jim showed me the proposal before he submitted it to OEO and I thought it was a fine program and a good proposal."

"Then why are you holding it up?" King asked.

"The president told me to axe it," Adam said.

"Since when do you do what the president tells you?" King asked.

"Oh, well," Adam replied, "they're going to give me something I need very much; in fact, something I've got to have."

Martin said that Adam refused to say what it was they were going to give him in exchange for killing the literacy project.

Days later, Simeon Booker, the Washington bureau chief of Johnson Publications, who had joined us on the Freedom Ride, called me to say that he knew what it was they were going to give Adam. He said he had gotten it from one of Adam's top assistants. "They're going to get Adam off the hook on the bag woman libel case."*

When I told Simeon he had been reading too many conspiracy novels, he said, "No, Jim. Listen, there's only one person who can get Adam off the hook on that, and that's the judge who handed down the judgment against Adam in the first place. And there's only one person who can get the judge to do that, and that's Bob Wagner, mayor of New York City, who got the judge his job. The only person who can make Wagner do that is big daddy himself. Bob Wagner will call the judge, and presto, Adam will be home free."

I told Simeon that I didn't believe a word of it. A week later, however, I heard on the radio that the judge had reduced the judgment against Adam from approximately $169,000 to around $40,000. Powell should have paid the fine then, but apparently he wanted it reduced closer to zero.

As a partial consequence of Powell's failure to pay the reduced judgment, the career of the most powerful black politician in American history collapsed in ruins. He was found in contempt of court in New York and later was censured by the 90th Congress amid allegations of fiscal improprieties. Then, he was denied a seat by the 91st Congress and, ultimately, was rejected by his Harlem constituency in 1970.

---

*Powell, in a public statement off the House floor, identified a woman he said was a "bag woman" for the Harlem rackets. She subsequently sued him for libel.

Floyd McKissick invited me to address the CORE convention in July 1966. I used that as an occasion to blast OEO and Sargent Shriver, unaware at the time of LBJ's involvement. The CORE people were outraged at what had happened. One CORE leader, Ollie Leeds, chairman of the Brooklyn CORE chapter, remarked that it was "just like they used to do to the Indians—invite the chief to a pow-wow, and then shoot him." McKissick offered to share the leadership of CORE by setting up a codirectorship. I thanked him but declined.

I was intrigued by the effort to unravel the tangled web of events that had led to the demise of what was one of the most promising programs to come out of the civil rights movement of the 1960s. Only Adam Clayton Powell's tracks were visible; many others had been carefully covered over. Whose feet had fled the scene, leaving the body breathing its last? Who had made Adam the fall guy, and why?

Floyd McKissick visited Powell in Bimini after he had been expelled from Congress and asked him why he had done it. Powell told McKissick to tell me that he was sorry, but he had to do it. "They were supposed to give me something for doing it, but they didn't," said Powell. They just gave me the business."

Obviously, the president wanted Powell to posture opposition to the program, for that would prevent me from charging the White House with scuttling the project for racist motives. More than twenty-six million American adults living in this highly advanced and sophisticated nation cannot read or compute. Therein lies a tragedy that is at the root of many of the problems besetting the poor and the so-called "underclass" treading our concrete jungles.

CHAPTER 29

IN LIMBO

BEING UNEMPLOYED AT AGE forty-six after a lifetime crammed into five years had certain ironic advantages. My income more than tripled. As national director of CORE, my highest salary had been $13,000 a year. Lecture fees, which exceeded my salary, were given to CORE, as were royalties from my book *Freedom When?* Now, without any organizational ties, the lecture circuit was lucrative. The headlines from the stormy CORE years were still fresh enough in the public mind to place me in demand on university campuses all over the country.

In the fall of 1966, Lincoln University in Pennsylvania offered me a spot as professor of social welfare. Since it required only two days of my time per week and was within easy commuting distance, I took it. It was a chance to interact with young black minds at a time when those minds were volatile and angry. Stokely Carmichael had just made "black power" a part of the American vocabulary. The words had galvanized black youth all over the country. The bristling afro hairstyle became a badge of pride, dashikis the attire of ethnicity, the upraised clenched fist a salute, the medallion on the chain around the neck an insignia of blackness. Concealed firearms were almost as common as wallets. Humor was taboo. Jokes were viewed as a betrayal, and smiles as demonstration of weakness.

As Nixon tore across the country in 1967, gluing the Republican organization to his candidacy for president, I nailed a popular poster to the wall of my classroom at Lincoln. It was a hilarious takeoff on Nixon's campaign slogan. The poster showed a young black woman with an afro hairdo who was very pregnant. She had her hands folded under her stomach, and the caption read: "NIXON'S THE ONE." Two male Lincoln students glared at the poster, then at me. "Brother Farmer," one of them spat the words at me, "you are insulting black womanhood with this poster."

Carefully, I sought to explain the message of the poster, trying to draw a smile from the two students at its humor. I did not succeed.

"If that's the message, why don't you have a picture of a black body hanging from a tree with its eyes bulging and its protruding tongue swollen, with the caption 'NIXON'S THE ONE'? That would not derogate black women."

I, who had survived innumerable crises by cherishing the ability to laugh, found the intense and angry young faces almost unbearable. Yet, I understood them, so it was also a challenge to try to restore some sanity.

For all of its excesses of rhetoric and deeds, the fierce "blacker than thou" era in the Afro-American experience had much that was positive. Those who had rejected self and had referred to kinky hair as "bad hair," and straight hair as "good hair," and had bleached their skin and kept their lips compressed were now coming to terms with themselves and pride. It is good for one to love oneself. It becomes less good, though, when that love is exclusive.

Agonizing over that which was bad in the "black is beautiful" syndrome, I sought to herald that which was good and build on it, and put it into a proud partnership within a pluralistic culture—where we would be equal participants celebrating our identity while joining in the celebration of the other identities in that pluralism. Thus, when the Italian-American Veterans' Club in lower Manhattan, where I lived, invited me to become an honorary member, I accepted with a measure of joy, though I'm not a veteran and not Italian.

The seminars at Lincoln were slam-bang affairs with unfettered give and take. At the end of a semester, one of the sharpest of the young militants stood before me for several minutes. I thought he was going to smile, but he didn't.

"Brother Farmer," he said without emphasis, "you're all right. You fooled us in this class. We thought you were going to be a pompous, big-name stuffed shirt. We were going to puncture you and let the air out. But we were wrong. You're down to earth, man. I think you're wrong, but I'm willing to try it your way for a while; and when that fails, I'll do it my way."

"What's my way?" I asked. "And what's yours?"

"You want to play the game by the white man's rules, man. You can't play the game by his rules. He makes the rules. Anytime it looks like you're going to win, he's gonna change the rules on you, and if it still looks like you're going to win, he'll call the game on account of darkness. Now, my way is more realistic. I'll deal with this man in terms that he can understand. We gotta get control of our ghetto, man. We'll organize a black mafia. We'll go into those gyp joints on 125th Street in Harlem and say, 'Hey, man, this is a nice place you got here. We want this store. Here's a dollar. Bye.'"

"How far do you think you'll get?" I asked. "First, there'll be the police, then the national guard, then the army and the marines."

He said, "Isn't it better to die like a man than to live like a dog?"

I went to my office and sat alone for a while, pondering the inevitability of the woeful mood among black youth and longing for a glimpse of the light that must lay in the future, although at that moment I could not see it. On that day in 1967, Martin Luther King was still living, but nonviolence was already dead.

Sharing the tomb with nonviolence was the interracialism that had been the trademark of the movement. SNCC, under Stokely Carmichael, had put whites out. CORE, under Floyd McKissick, had not done that, but the black power rhetoric had made them uncomfortable, and they were rapidly drifting away. Interracial marriages were under open attack by blacks. Prominent blacks with white wives were dumping their wives and marrying black women with afro hairdos. American names were being exchanged for Islamic or African names. The times were most uncomfortable for anyone whose identification had been with integration and interracialism. Between 1966 and the early 1970s, such persons were salmon swimming upstream. When Lula and I walked together, we encountered more hostile stares than ever before in our marriage, most of them from blacks.

Walking on a Harlem street one day, I encountered four dashiki-clad members of the "Mau Mau," a new group taking its name from a group in Kenya that had terrorized the countryside, killing more blacks than whites in the violent struggle for that country's independence. The Harlem Mau Mau were led by a man who had adopted the name Charles Kenyatta, inspired by the great Jomo Kenyatta of Kenya. The four who confronted me fingered the handles of the machetes on their belts, and one of them said, "We're coming downtown after you next, Farmer, because you got that white wife down there."

Even Lula looked at me with some apprehension in those days, for I had elected to accentuate the positive in the mushrooming black identity, hoping to channel it into a creative cultural pluralism. The unasked question on her face was 'whether our marriage, like so many others, was doomed. Reading her unspoken words, I took her in my arms and assured her that nobody could tell me who my wife would be. She would just have to bear with me and understand while I sought to maintain contact with the strongest and angriest of my people. Those were scary days.

Once again, I lived in two worlds: the volatile and explosive one of the new black Jacobins and the sophisticated and genteel one of the white and black liberal establishment. As a bridge, I was often called on by each side for help in contacting the other.

Bobby Kennedy, then a U.S. senator from New York, was in a battle to the death with Tammany Hall, the Democratic machine in New York City. The issue was Tammany's choice for a surrogate judge in the city. Kennedy thought the machine's selection was dreadful, and he chose his own. An election was pending, and though the Kennedys never lost, it appeared that Bobby would lose this one. Tammany had Harlem locked up tight, as well as the "counterculture" votes in the Silk Stocking district and the counterculture votes in Greenwich Village.

Burke Marshall, a Kennedy intimate and former assistant attorney general for civil rights, called me. I must confess I was surprised to receive the call, because Bobby Kennedy and I had hardly been on speaking terms since the Freedom Rides of 1961. Marshall told me that the senator wanted to know if I would support him in the surrogate battle. I replied that I had just gotten back in town from an extended trip, and although I knew there was a surrogate fight, I was not aware of the issues or personalities involved. In fact, I didn't even know what a surrogate judge did. I would have to research the situation a bit before I could give him an answer.

"Well, how long will that take?" Marshall asked. "The senator needs an answer very quickly. The fight is touch and go, and he can't delay lining up his forces."

"Twenty-four hours," I replied.

"All right. I'll call you in twenty-four hours."

Twenty-four hours later, almost to the minute, Marshall called again.

"Well, Jim," he snapped, "what's your answer?"

"My answer is yes. Tell the senator I'll support him."

"That's fine," said Marshall. "Now, the senator wants to know if you'll ride with him in an open limousine through Harlem tomorrow and speak at an outdoor rally there, then ride downtown with him and speak in Greenwich Village."

"Of course. I'll be delighted."

I met Bobby at his East Side Manhattan apartment, and we drove up to Harlem and through Harlem's streets. The crowds recognized both of us, and people shouted, "It's Bobby with Farmer." We both waved, and Kennedy smiled constantly. I, however, was tense. The mood in Harlem, as in black ghettos throughout the country, was ugly. I feared possible action from hotheads, maybe even inspired by Tammany Hall. These were days when even routine political hissing and booing could produce disaster.

Working through my successor at CORE, Floyd McKissick, I had arranged for CORE heavyweights and street people to intersperse the crowds lining the streets and to be on the lookout for trouble at the rally and to alert me by hand signals. When we arrived at the site for the meeting at 125th Street, I spotted my monitors and they gave me a nod. A Harlemite who was a stranger to me came up to Bobby and asked him to please come up and have a chest X-ray as an encouragement to other people to do the same. He was very insistent with his request. Bobby merely sighed and said, "Okay, I'll do it."

As he left the platform and headed for the trailer, I spotted each of my monitors and with a motion of the head asked two of them to follow Bobby into the trailer. Then I decided that I would go in, too. Perhaps my apprehension was unnecessary, but the lessons of history had made me extremely cautious with those whose anger defeats reason. Consequently, along with the two heavyweights, I waited in the trailer until Bobby emerged and then walked with him back to the platform.

I spoke first and received loud applause. I then introduced Kennedy and the crowd gave him an equally thunderous ovation.

Afterward, we lunched together at Frank's Restaurant on 125th Street and then drove downtown. As we cruised along East Side Drive, some black kids playing baseball in a vacant field saw the limousine coming and immediately recognized Kennedy. One of them shouted, "*It's Bobby!* Hey, Bobby, gimme five!" The kid extended his hand, though he was fifty yards away.

Kennedy waved, smiled, then turned to me and said, "Give me five. What does that mean?"

The rest of the day included two other rallies, both of which went well. I gave some radio interviews for the campaign and Kennedy invited me to his apartment to discuss the political situation.

As we sat chatting, he said to me, "Jim, you're a stand-up guy. I only wish we had gotten acquainted a few years ago. Many things would have been different." He asked me how I thought he would do in Harlem during the election and told me that some blacks had assured him that he would sweep Harlem and take at least 90 percent of the vote. I told him that those persons were living in a dream world. The machine was far too strong for that; it had its way of turning out votes and controlling them. He might split the Harlem vote almost fifty-fifty, and if he did that, he could win—but it would be close. (It turned out that was precisely what happened.)

While his brother was alive, I always believed that Bobby thought in terms of votes with a mind like a cash register, counting those votes— tough and rather unscrupulous. Now, I really got the impression that he genuinely cared for the things he spoke about, though he would always be a politician who thought in terms of quid pro quos.

"Jim, you helped us a lot, and I appreciate it. Now, what can I do for you?"

I was shocked and sat up straight at the blunt "you scratch my back, I'll scratch yours" attitude, but that was the real world of politics.

There was only one thing that I asked him to do and that was to save CORE. He knew that I had left CORE and was surprised that this was the favor I would ask. He held out his hands in a gesture of incomprehension: "Save CORE? What does that mean?"

I told him that CORE was facing bankruptcy, that I had left the organization with a large debt partly because of the Freedom Rides and Mississippi's nearly successful efforts to put CORE out of business. On top of that, there had been the disaffection of many white liberals who felt that the problem was solved because of the Civil Rights Act of 1964 and the Voting Rights Act of 1965. Others had turned their interest away from civil rights to the Vietnam War. Still others had become afraid and had stopped giving. On top of that, there was the problem of CORE's tax-exempt arm, the Scholarship, Education, and Defense Fund, which had pulled away from CORE in 1965. With that breakaway had gone many of CORE's biggest contributors. Now the organization, led by Floyd McKissick, was fighting to survive, and I felt a sense of responsibility—not only because Floyd was a good friend, but also because CORE was my baby.

Kennedy asked whether the problem was creditors for goods and services who were demanding payment. When I said that that was essentially the case, he thought for a few minutes and then said, "All right. Have McKissick get in touch with my attorney. The two of them can work out the papers for a new tax-exempt arm for CORE. My guy will be able to facilitate the securing of tax-exempt status. Second, I would suggest that McKissick call a meeting of the creditors and offer them ten cents on the dollar and be prepared to go up to twenty-five cents if necessary. Then my guys will help McKissick run a fund-raising banquet in the biggest hotel in New York City, and we'll help fill the place at $100 a plate. Those things should take care of CORE's immediate problems."

I thanked him and prepared to leave. As he shook my hand on the way out, he said, "Jim, whatever you plan to do in the next few years—if it's politics or whatever—give me a call, and we'll see if I can do anything to help. I'll be glad to do it."

I continued to teach at Lincoln University for two years, until 1968. During the second of those years, as adjunct professor at the School of Education of New York University, I taught a course on U.S. social movements. I also gave a weekly lecture on the civil rights movement at NYU's School of Continuing Education. The ferment of ideas was always stimulating to me, but not entirely satisfying. After the blood and thunder and the constant pumping of adrenaline through my veins during the CORE years, anything else had to be anticlimactic.

The Liberal Party of New York, of which I was a member, asked me to run for Congress in the newly established twelfth congressional district in Brooklyn. I agreed to do so, provided it would not be just a token race. I asked that they be prepared to make a fight for it even though it would probably be a losing battle. The district was more than 90 percent Democratic, with a powerful tradition of voting along party lines. My party agreed to that condition, so I held a press conference in March 1968 to announce my candidacy and invited both the major parties to endorse me. The Republicans, who had already named a candidate, withdrew that person and endorsed me, for this would give them a chance to make a good showing in an otherwise hopeless race. The Democratic Party boss, Stanley Steingut, replied, "Hell, no! We don't need him. We can run Mickey Mouse against him, go on vacation during the campaign, and still beat him nine to one."

Under the laws of New York State since the days of Vito Marcantonio, who ran on all party tickets, a nonmember had to receive permission to run in any party's primaries. Through an emissary, I sought permission from the Democratic Party organization to enter its primary and was refused. Later, I learned that Steingut had looked favorably on my request, but that the black politicos in Brooklyn, having labored long in the party's vineyards, understandably resented an interloper coming in to seek the big prize.

The Democrats held their primary and its winner was not Mickey Mouse, but an extremely able state assemblywoman, Shirley Chisholm. A poll I had conducted showed that as far as name recognition was concerned it was no contest. I should win hands down. What the poll did not say was the extent to which we could translate name recognition and preference into actual votes, considering the tradition of voting a straight Democratic ticket, regardless of candidates.

Chisholm was a formidable opponent and an excellent campaigner. Even so, the name-recognition factor remained in my favor. My volunteers conducted a telephone poll of registered voters in the district; it promised a five-to-one victory for me.

"Ah, yes," I said to my volunteers. "But you told the persons you called that you were from Farmer for Congress headquarters. Now, conduct a poll representing yourselves as from Chisholm for Congress headquarters."

Even then, the results favored me by almost three to one. My young volunteers thought that we were sure winners, but I knew that not to be the case. Though we were banging away on how to vote for me on either the Liberal Party ballot line or the Republican Party ballot line, I had my doubts that the message would sink in. Sample ballots were widely circulated, clearly showing where they should be marked on my behalf. But I still considered it an uphill battle.

One month after my campaign was announced, the nation had been stunned by the news of the assassination of Martin Luther King. I was on a platform near Lincoln University in Pennsylvania, addressing a huge audience, when one of the wire services called for comment and asked that I be interrupted, no matter what I was doing, and told the news.

I stopped in midsentence when the news of the tragedy was whispered to me and asked the audience to wait while I took an emergency phone call. Told that Martin was dead, I returned to the platform, asked for calm, and made the announcement. I then adjourned the meeting. The county sheriff's car was already outside the building waiting for me when I came out. The sheriff himself gave me an escort to the home where I was staying overnight and left deputies there throughout the night. It seems that there was some fear that the murder of the symbolic leader of the civil rights movement might have been a part of a widespread conspiracy to gun down some others. I knew immediately what the reaction was going to be in the black communities throughout the nation; anger was certain to explode into violence.

Hardly had we stopped reeling from that blow when Bobby Kennedy died from Sirhan Sirhan's bullet. How much shock could a nation take in so short a time? Despite the twin tragedies, the campaign struggled on.

Now that my close associates and I were thinking politically, we began to speculate about who Rockefeller would name to fill the empty seat of the junior U.S. senator from New York. CORE people often made news, but seldom did we create it. Here was an exception. Val Coleman, who had handled public relations for me at CORE, had an idea he had not mentioned to me, but had whispered to the press instead. He told a reporter that Governor Nelson Rockefeller was considering naming me to fill the Kennedy seat. The reporter went with the story. Thus, new headlines with no basis in reality were born. Rockefeller had no thought whatever of naming me to the spot, yet it seemed a lively and exciting possibility to the national media. To most queries, I gave a "no comment" response. When questioned as to whether I would accept if offered the post, I told them that I would give it serious consideration. The speculation was cut short when the governor named Charles Goodell to the job.

Meanwhile, there was something that had been troubling me all along in my campaign. I was not bothered by appearing on the Republican ticket. I have long believed that blacks should not be wed to any one party. The thing that concerned me was the possibility that I might drain away enough votes from Hubert Humphrey in Brooklyn to throw New York State to Nixon in a close presidential election. That possibility I found unconscionable. Polls began to show Nixon edging ahead of Humphrey, with a strong likelihood of Nixon emerging the victor in the election. So, adding to the confusion already rampant in Brooklyn, I called a press conference and endorsed Hubert Humphrey for president. Naturally, that move angered many Republicans in Brooklyn and produced considerable foot dragging and withholding of funds.

My campaign went on. On the evening before the election, my staff of volunteers believed the election was in the bag. I took a walking tour through the streets of the twelfth district in Brooklyn, stopping in places where people congregate—barbershops, beauty salons, pool parlors, bars, and so forth. The response was overwhelmingly favorable. People rushed up to shake my hand, saying, "Mr. Farmer, don't worry about a thing. You got it, man. You're a shoo-in. Everybody in my family's voting for you. Everybody in my building's voting for you. Everybody I know is voting for you. You got it locked up, man. That's straight Democratic, ain't it?"

Or they would say, "Man, after all you've done for us, you know we've got to vote for you, and we're going to do it, too. And that woman, Cheese-home, she's on your ticket too, ain't she?"

I nodded, smiling, said yes, signed autographs, and went home. Nothing more could have been done at that late date. We had lost all.

But the Democratic machine was taking no chances. Later that night, one of my volunteers called me at home, crying, and said, "Jim, I can't believe this. They've got sound trucks out on the streets going throughout the district shouting, 'How can you vote for a man who comes over here every day and talks black, then goes home every night and sleeps with a white woman?'"

I told the caller and several other callers who followed with the same message to just forget it; that was politics. Knowing Shirley Chisholm as I later came to know and respect her, I do not believe she was aware of this chicanery.

Early next morning, the call from my campaign headquarters urged me to get there right away; there were irregularities at the polling places. First, there were no challenge sheets—those official forms on which you challenge persons seeking to vote who had voted earlier or who bore the names of persons who had died or moved away from the district. When my headquarters called the board of elections about this, they received the astonishing reply, "Tell him we're sorry, but we just didn't get them printed up in time."

At one polling place, our poll watcher had been asked by a policeman to show his credentials, and he showed his mimeographed Liberal Party poll watcher's license. He was then told, "That's no good here. If you don't get off the premises, I'm going to arrest you."

At another location, our poll watcher called to inform us that, in spite of the law that no electioneering could be done within one hundred feet of a voting place, there were opposition bumper stickers *on* the voting machines and *inside* them, as well.

At still another, our poll watcher reported that a representative from the board of elections was going into the voting machine with voters, telling them which lever to pull, and it was always the Democratic line. When the watcher complained about this procedure, he was asked, "Well, who are you working for?"

He replied, "I'm a poll watcher for James Farmer."

The woman responded, "Oh, he's a nice man. I'll give you five."

Then the next five persons she took into the machine were instructed on how to vote the Liberal Party line. Then she resumed her straight Democratic line instructions.

When all this information came to me, I asked my campaign manager,

Simeon Golar, who was a lawyer, if we could impound the voting machines throughout the district and challenge the election on the grounds of these irregularities. Golar replied, "Of course we could," if I wanted to waste the time and money. The case would doubtless go before a judge who was beholden to the party's machinery. Furthermore, "You would simply look like a poor loser; a defeated candidate whose nose is out of joint. My advice to you is to forget it and move on gracefully." I accepted the advice.

When the returns came in, I congratulated Shirley on her nearly two and a half to one victory and offered my help to her if ever she should need it. Subsequently, we became friends and worked together on many issues in Washington.

The irregularities that went on are no reflection whatever on the character and abilities of Congresswoman Chisholm. It was not her doing but the doing of an organization that would have won without it but chose to take no chances. Shirley performed well in Congress as the first black Congresswoman in history.

Many defeated candidates, in their defeat, find some kind of Pyrrhic victory; I found none. The name of the game in politics is not why you lose, but winning. I had not won. My adversaries did not confront me with Mickey Mouse; they put up Shirley Chisholm. They did not go on vacation; they stayed in Brooklyn and battled to the end. But they did not win by a nine-to-one margin; they won by only two and a half to one.

After my defeat, one good friend reminded me that I now had a most unique distinction; I was the first black man in U.S. history to be defeated by a black woman in a congressional race.

PART EIGHT

The Nixon Foray

CHAPTER 30

THE ROAD IN

"YOU'RE NOT SERIOUS! *ME* work in the Nixon administration?"

"I *am* serious, Jim," spoke Robert E. Finch, Nixon's secretary-designate for Health, Education, and Welfare (HEW). "I appreciated your serving on my advisory committee after I was nominated, and sitting in on the briefings I received from HEW officials. Your comments were very helpful. I would be very pleased if you would accept an appointment to a top post in HEW."

I sipped black coffee while waiting for breakfast in the dining room of a midtown Manhattan hotel. I had never met Finch before his nomination and I was a member of the Liberal Party of New York State, not a Republican. I had not supported Nixon, but had endorsed Hubert Humphrey, despite the fact that I had Republican endorsement in my congressional campaign. The invitation from Finch took me completely by surprise. I think I pondered for minutes those words he had just dropped on me.

"I will not reject it out of hand, Bob," I finally said, "but it will be a very difficult decision for me. Ninety-five percent of the blacks in this country are Democrats and Nixon is very unpopular among blacks. For me to work in that administration might be political suicide. I would be painting a bull's eye on my chest, my back, and both sides.

"However, I will give it some thought. For a long time, it has been my conviction that blacks achieve maximum political leverage by not being 'in the bag' for either party. Consequently, I see nothing wrong with working for a Republican administration. I need to know specifically what the job is that I am being offered. I also need to know what authority and responsibilities I would have, and the extent to which I will have the backing of the secretary in fulfilling those responsibilities."

"I'm glad to know you'll be open to consideration of an offer from us," he replied. "I'll get back to you regarding the specific job we have in mind."

A week later, Finch phoned to inform me that I had my choice of three jobs: assistant secretary for administration, deputy commissioner of education in charge of civil rights, or personal consultant to the secretary. The advantage of the assistant secretary's job, he pointed out, was that it had the sweep of the entire department, covering all the operating agencies. Along with it went considerable power and influence, since personnel actions would come across my desk for signature.

The deputy commissioner of education post had the advantage of a clearly defined jurisdiction and was an area in which I had much experience. He told me that he was unable to offer the spot of assistant secretary for education because Dr. James Allen, who was to be the new commissioner, had accepted that appointment on condition that the commissioner's job be combined with the post of assistant secretary for education.

The consultancy assignment would have the advantage of allowing me complete freedom of schedule since I would be paid on a per-diem basis. I would also be free to accept whatever lecture engagements and writing engagements I chose and the fees would be mine.

I told him I would get back to him within thirty days with my decision.

The month's delay allowed me to consult with many persons before deciding whether to accept a position at HEW and, if so, which one. I talked with Roy Wilkins and Whitney Young, and both of them urged me to take one of the jobs; they felt it would be a real advantage to have someone they could count on in a key spot at HEW. Although they were not pro-Nixon, it was their opinion that black Americans could not boycott any U.S. administration that would be in the seat of power for at least four years. I talked with my former colleagues at CORE and elsewhere in the movement, and the reactions were overwhelmingly positive. I then made a two-week lecture tour, speaking on college campuses in various parts of the nation, and used those appearances to touch other bases. Black college students, including the so-called militants, almost without exception urged me to take an HEW job. As some of them put it, "We have got to have somebody there who knows where the bodies are buried. Also, when we need funding for community organizations, we have got to have somebody in Washington who can point us in the right direction."

I met, too, with black community groups. Most of them thought I should go to HEW, but I was taken aback by a few of the responses. Many of the young people in the ghettos told me to tell HEW not to bus them to white schools. "If somebody has to be bused, they should bus the white kids to black schools. We like our schools and we don't want to go over there to those other schools. We've got the best football team in this league, and if we go over there, what will happen to all our trophies? They'll probably be locked up in some basement room where nobody can see them and our great coach will probably become the water boy." This flew in the face of conventional civil rights wisdom and led me to do some further thinking.

In early March 1969, I called Finch to advise him that I wanted to be assistant secretary for administration. He suggested a swearing-in date of April 1. I turned that down and suggested April 2. I did not want to hand the press ready-made April Fools' Day headlines.

President Nixon had a reception for me in the Oval Office, where we chatted and posed for pictures. Lula was invited down for the occasion. Since our money was tight, she came by bus, and when she arrived at the White House, she looked it. Her hair was in disarray, and her clothes were not her Sunday best. Although we agreed that I should take the job, I felt she was showing her contempt in nonverbal ways for the president's less than liberal record. Nixon asked for a picture with her. Reluctantly, Lula agreed, and the photo, in its way, is a classic. She was not shaking the president's hand. Indeed, she was not even looking at him. Her lip was curled upward, and on her face was the trace of a sneer. My wife clearly was not happy with the turn of events that now placed us in Washington, but her loyalty to me forced her to be at my side.

Ensconced in my ballpark-size office at HEW, having read the various documents briefing me on the office of assistant secretary for administration, and having taken a walking tour through the building, I called my first staff meeting. Sitting around the large conference table in an alcove at the end of my office were about fifteen persons, all white, all male, and all middle-aged and gray. One woman came in; she was Mary Campbell, the executive assistant to the assistant secretary. All the faces, except Mary's, seemed grim with lips tightly pursed. The expressions on those faces seemed to say in unison, "This, too, shall pass." I was sure there had to be one black, so I delayed the start of the meeting for a few minutes. Five minutes later, Sam Hoston, director of the Equal Employment Opportunity office, arrived. We were then ready to begin.

I made a short speech telling them who I was and asked that they go around the table, with each person introducing himself and giving a three-minute thumbnail sketch of the office he headed. We would then set a date within the next thirty days when I would be given an in-depth briefing by each office.

That done, I proceeded to detail some of the priorities the office of administration would have during the next year. I told them how happy I was before coming to HEW to learn that more than 20 percent of HEW's work force were members of minorities. Upon arriving, however, I had walked around the corridors but could not find them. Finally, someone aware of my puzzlement had laughed and told me I was on the wrong floors—I was on the carpeted floors. I should go instead to the basement, and there I would find the minorities. This information had proved to be correct; most of the 20 percent were low-grade-level employees, and many were doing the most menial of unskilled work, such as pushing carts and wrapping packages. That, I told the assembled staff members, all top-ranking civil servants, was going to be changed. We would develop an upward mobility program providing genuine training and real promotions for minority members of the work force.

In addition, I expressed serious concern about the management intern program, which was, and apparently always had been, virtually all white. That, too, would be corrected. We would see to it that an equitable share of the management intern slots were reserved for minorities. This was important, since the management interns, after their internship period, became eligible for mid-level jobs at HEW.

We would make moves, also, to ensure that highly trained and qualified members of minorities were brought into HEW and allowed to compete for top-level jobs, indeed, even super-grade slots.

I also told them that I was concerned by the fact that when I walked through the building, I observed there were few minorities holding decent positions even in the offices headed by those members of my staff now seated at that very table. We would work out some fair way of ensuring steady improvement in that situation.

The men at the table listened without moving a muscle, and then several of them spoke, each giving various reasons why the things I wanted to do could not be legally done. They were able to cite regulations issued by the Civil Service Commission and could even indicate the document in which such regulations could be found and the sections and pages on which I should look. They quoted executive orders from several presidents. They referred to directives issued by secretaries of HEW since the department began.

As they spoke, it was my turn to listen without moving a muscle. I thanked them for their opinions, reconfirmed the times and dates for the in-depth briefings by each office, and adjourned the meeting, asking Stu Clarke, an official of the office of personnel and training, to remain for a few minutes afterward.

Stu Clarke had not spoken at the staff meeting, but obviously had been deep in thought. I asked him for his assessment of the comments of the others near the end of the meeting.

He smiled and began, "Well, Mr. Secretary—"

I interrupted him to tell him that my name was Jim.

He nodded and continued: "These fellows have been at the bureaucratic game for a long time. They know their jobs backward and forward. Their quotation of regulations was entirely accurate, down to the dotting of i's and crossing of t's. Everything they told you was correct, but there is something they failed to tell you. That is, that for every regulation, there are always exemptions and exceptions built in. They did not tell you about them. Each one of those fellows could have told you precisely how to do those things you say you want to do, but they were not going to do that."

"Why?" I asked. "Are they racists?"

"Racists?" mused Stu. "Perhaps some are, but not all."

I asked what the real reason was for their failure to speak the unspoken. "As I said, they know their jobs. They can perform their duties blindfolded and with both hands tied behind their backs. But only if things are done the way they have always been done. With new guidelines, new marching orders, they are insecure and will be navigating uncharted waters. They will have to work much harder—and they are working hard already—and will be able to do nothing by rote, and will have to think about it each step of the way. Furthermore, in such unfamiliar waters, the ship of state may run onto reefs and spring a leak and sink. As good bureaucrats, they do not want the record to show they had any part in such a disaster if it occurs. Also, they are thinking of retirement and don't want to rock the boat. As you will soon learn, the message most civil servants carry in their heads is don't make waves."

My first real battle at HEW was over Head Start. The administration was committed to transfer or delegate Head Start from the Office of Economic Opportunity to HEW. The question was: where would it be placed in HEW? The two alternatives being considered were the Office of Education and the Children's Bureau in the Social Rehabilitation Service (SRS). In a memorandum to Finch, I suggested a third option, the creation of a new Office of Child Development (OCD) to house Head Start, the Children's Bureau, and other children's programs in the department. I suggested also that OCD report to the assistant secretary for administration.

Head Start was the jazziest, most highly visible program in the War on Poverty, so the issue of where it was placed and to whom it reported was viewed as critical. The deputy undersecretary, Frederic V. Malek, a Bob Haldeman protégé and, next to the secretary, the most powerful man at HEW, was my leading adversary.

The battle lines were drawn, and the struggle of flying memoranda raged over several weeks. SRS, of course, wanted Head Start and wanted to keep the Children's Bureau. Malek supported them. I felt, though, that in the SRS, Head Start would be no more effective than the Children's Bureau was. The Office of Education also wanted Head Start because, after all, it was an educational program. I feared that in OE, Head Start might become a downward extension of the public school system rather than the community action program it was designed to be. I thought I had persuaded Finch to go along with my views.

Malek then made contact with Capitol Hill on the question of the location of Head Start. Subsequently, the secretary informed me that Senator Russell Long, chairman of the Senate Finance Committee and a man of considerable power, had threatened to punish HEW if "Head Start were allowed to report to Jim Farmer." After all, Louisiana had been a site of primary CORE activity during the civil rights movement of the sixties and the Louisiana political establishment probably felt I should be the most hated man in America.

A threat from Russell Long could not be taken lightly, so Finch was forced to pause on the question of to whom the program should report. On the recommendation of an experienced bureaucrat on my staff, I suggested to Finch that he have the Office of Child Development report to the secretary himself "through the assistant secretary for administration." It was a device that seemed to be a distinction without a difference, since in my job I served at the secretary's pleasure and all my actions were as his agent. Yet it sounded like a real difference to Russell Long and others on the Hill. They bought it, and so did the secretary, though he knew that the distinction was an illusion.

My position at HEW became increasingly uncomfortable. I was not exactly inexperienced in dealing with bureaucracy, but my experience had been from the outside, prodding it for action. Trying to move it from within required the use of tools with which I had little familiarity. Most of my professional staff I had inherited. My deputy, Bernard "Bud" Sisco, had been acting assistant secretary before I arrived and had hopes that he would get the job. Being forced to step back into the role of deputy was for him a severe trauma. I think Sisco tried to play it straight, but his disappointment would not let him. I continually had to look over my shoulder. My executive assistant, Mary Campbell, however, became a close adviser and confidante. She, too, was an experienced pro. She caught many daggers in the air before they reached my back.

I brought onto my staff as special assistants two of the brightest persons who had been my associates in CORE: Ruth Turner Perot and Donald M. Wendell. Ruth, a former head of the Cleveland chapter of CORE and a member of the National Action Council, is a brilliant woman, sharp and tough. In CORE, she and I had frequently been at odds, and she was a formidable adversary, but she had integrity. Her assistance was to prove invaluable as my liaison with the Office of Child Development and as my eyes and ears and trusted adviser. A tiger with sharp claws, she worked to achieve the appointment of six minority regional directors for Head Start out of a total of ten in the Office of Child Development, and together we opened doors of contracting offices in HEW to minority firms.

Wendell had a labor background with the International Ladies Garment Workers Union before joining the CORE staff as field secretary, where he had been my top trouble shooter, finally becoming eastern regional director of the organization. It was he who had devised the concept of compensatory preferential treatment, which, when I presented it to Lyndon Johnson, became affirmative action. Don Wendell had a quick intelligence and keen political instincts, which were a perfect foil for my tendency to be overly trusting.

And then, of course, there was Sam Hoston, the department's EEO chief, who reported to me and became a staunch ally. Sam knew the labyrinths in that massive department as few people did.

Another who was well acquainted with the intricacies of the sprawling HEW complex was Stu Clarke, who, not long after my arrival, I appointed director of the Office of Personnel and Training and, thus, one of my two deputies. It was Stu who helped formulate the plans for the things I sought to do, and together, we did them. He prepared the papers requiring that 50 percent of management interns attached to the Office of the Secretary be members of minorities henceforth. Finch approved that, and with Stu's help I implemented it. As soon as a new departure was announced in the department, representatives of Hispanics, Asians, and Native Americans requested an appointment with me. I knew what was coming and welcomed it. They expressed delight that at least 50 percent of the management interns were to be minorities and politely informed me that they wanted their slice of the pie. We worked out an arrangement sharing the 50 percent equitably.

More difficult was the establishment of an HEW fellows program to bring in highly trained members of minority groups, including women, for ten months of orientation in the department, during which time they were to be attached to various offices—that of the secretary, the under secretary, the operating agencies, or assistant secretaries. At the end of the orientation period, they would have a choice: to return to the universities or industries from which they had come, to continue their service with the office in which their orientation had been served, or to compete for supergrade positions within the department. Several lengthy sessions were held with the Civil Service Commission while this program was in the conceptual stage. When commissioners asked questions about the philosophy of such a program, it was I who answered. When the questions were technical, about procedures and regulations, Stu Clarke carried the ball. To my surprise, it was approved. The commission only rejected our plan to call it a minority fellows program. Instead, it was to be called the HEW fellowship program, with the understanding that it was reserved for minorities.

Mrs. Marguerite Belafonte Mazique was brought in to administer the fellows program and it was off and running. The HEW fellows program has produced some outstanding upper-grade-level black professionals in the department.

A program I expected to be less controversial than that of the fellows turned out to be more so. The new careers concept of building into low-level jobs the necessary training and lattices for lateral and upward movement—a concept developed by Dr. Frank Reisman—seemed to me to be a natural for HEW, with its emphasis on human services and its large numbers of black and other minority employees congregated on the lowest rung of the employment ladder. I thought it would be easy to set up as an upward-mobility program for in-house staff members and stipulate it as a requirement for HEW grant programs. I spoke to Finch about the idea, and he encouraged me to pursue it.

I then invited Alan Gartner, formerly with CORE, who had in the past few years worked closely with Frank Reisman, to come in as my consultant and help devise new career systems for both the in-house employees and HEW grant programs.

In his first week Alan found literally scores of HEW job authorizations but the on-the-job-training directions were not outlined anywhere on paper. In fact, no one seemed to be aware of the fact that an integral part of these newly created jobs should include techniques for growth and development among low-level employees. In a memorandum, I asked the secretary to set up an Office of New Careers in my shop, which would coordinate and ensure the implementation of such components in grant programs scattered throughout the department. The new proposed office would also develop an upward-mobility program for lower-level employees working at HEW. The memorandum requested the secretary's signature of approval on the document, which was attached to it.

I knew from my earlier conversations with him, that Finch was sympathetic. Yet, my memo remained on his desk for weeks without response. Follow-up memoranda produced no answer. I, therefore, assumed that pressure was being put on him from some source.

It was only an accident of media questioning that finally produced action. Under Secretary Jack Veneman held a routine press conference. That conference was so routine several of the newsmen present complained, asking Veneman why he had called them there, for everything he had told them was old hat and nothing new had been announced. They had no story.

Veneman said, "Oh, there are lots of new things happening here. For example, we have set up an Office of New Careers to implement that concept in-house, as well as in HEW grant programs. That new office will be in Jim Farmer's shop. Details will be given to you later."

The reporters thanked him and left. Informed by a newsman of Jack Veneman's comment, I immediately sent him a duplicate of the document that was on the secretary's desk. Along with it went a covering memorandum expressing my delight at learning that the New Careers Program had been approved and asking that he sign the attached document, since the secretary had not yet gotten to it, so that it could be implemented. This he promptly did. An accident of the tongue had saved the day.

I do not know what had interfered with Finch's signing of the document, but I think it had to be political pressure. Bob Finch was an honorable and compassionate man and was not given to playing games, but he was also a shrewd and pragmatic politician.

In most cases, he was candid with me, as on the occasion of Mississippi Governor John Bell Williams's veto of Head Start grants in that state. That veto might have been a comic event, had the stakes not been so high. One of the reasons given by the governor for not wanting any federal Head Start moneys to come into Mississippi was that Head Start in his state was a segregated program! The governor was certainly no integrationist. Furthermore, whites who had been teachers in Head Start and parents of white children in the Head Start program had been so harassed and threatened by the Klan and other racists that they had been forced to withdraw and, in many cases, to leave town. Now, to kill the program because it was all black, when whites had been chased out by other whites opposed to racial mixing, had to make Governor John Bell Williams a candidate for "cynic of the year."

Upon hearing that news from Mississippi, I immediately called Finch to say that I thought we simply had to override the veto. It was the secretary's prerogative to do that. He replied that, since a Mississippian was one of the most powerful members of the Republican National Committee, he thought the decision on whether to override would be a political one and would be made "over his head." The message was clear, so I thanked him and put through a call to the White House, asking to speak to the president. To my surprise, Richard Nixon took the call.

"Mr. President, it is imperative that I have a chance to meet with you very soon, preferably tomorrow, on a matter of great urgency," I said.

"Well, how about first thing tomorrow morning, 8:30?" responded Nixon.

When I entered the Oval Office, the president was waiting. We shook hands and he motioned me to a seat. He faced me with jaw set and thrust out, waiting for me to speak.

"As you know, Mr. President, Governor John Bell Williams has vetoed Head Start funds for the state of Mississippi. You probably also are aware that the HEW secretary has the authority to override that veto. I am sure that the decision to override will be a ticklish political one for your administration, so I'm here to express my strong opinion that it is absolutely essential that we override."

"Just tell me one thing, Mr. Farmer," the president said. "Why do you consider this Head Start matter to be so all-fired important?"

"If the veto is allowed to stand, it will become contagious. We will have similar vetoes in Alabama, Louisiana, and possibly two or three other southern states. Head Start, the most important of the antipoverty programs, will be dead where we need it most."

Nixon nodded, and his eyes narrowed, but he made no comment.

"Mr. President," I said, "I feel it is my duty to tell you that if we do not override, I will be forced to consider my position at HEW to be completely untenable."

The Nixon eyes narrowed even more, and he nodded again. We shook hands and I left.

That afternoon, after lunch, Bob Finch called and said, "Jim, I think you will be pleased to know that I have just sent a registered letter to Governor Williams, overriding his veto."

"Thanks, Bob," I said.

"Thank *you*," Finch replied.

One morning shortly after going to HEW, I read in *Human Events,* a right-wing Republican paper, that J. Edgar Hoover, in testimony before a congressional committee, had been asked if it was true that I had been appointed and sworn into the job before a full FBI field investigation had been conducted. Hoover reportedly had replied, "Yes, he was appointed and sworn in even before a full field investigation had been requested." He had then gone on to make some statements full of innuendo, revealing his displeasure at my appointment.

I called Deke DeLoach, the FBI associate director with whom I had had contact while still head of CORE, asking for an appointment. DeLoach then called Robert Mardian, HEW's general counsel, to ask if he knew what I wanted to talk about. Mardian did not, but called me to find out. He then reported to DeLoach that I wanted to discuss Hoover's reported remarks before a congressional committee and to find out what kind of files they *did* have on me.

DeLoach brought an FBI press officer with him to our luncheon meeting. He showed me a full transcript of Hoover's remarks before that committee and his responses to questions about me and assured me that the FBI director had "intended" nothing derogatory. Although it was true, he said, that it was unusual procedure to make a high political appointment prior to requesting a full field investigation, that investigation was then in progress. DeLoach insisted that there had been many FBI investigations of me and my activities for quite a few years, and there was no derogatory information in the files. "We don't agree with many things you have done, and many positions you have taken," he said, "but there is no question whatever regarding your loyalty or your integrity."

When the field investigation was completed and sent to Finch's desk, he called to tell me that the FBI had given me a clean bill of health. However, in their letter of transmittal, they had brought to Finch's attention the fact that I had a pacifist background and that the Office of Emergency Preparedness for the federal government was in HEW and in my shop, reporting to the assistant secretary for administration. Since that office dealt with most highly classified and sensitive data regarding contingency plans for the government in the event of an attack on this country, they suggested that Finch might want to consider removing it from my shop and placing it elsewhere. I told Finch that I would take a dim view of such an action, and he informed me that he had no intention of removing anything from my office without my permission.

The Office of Emergency Preparedness remained under me, and sensitive and highly classified documents came to my desk for signature, yet I was sharply aware that, unlike my predecessors, I was never taken on a guided tour of the most secret contingency government facilities. I decided to let that ride and not make an issue of it.

Weeks later, I was at the White House again. This time, it was not to see the president but to keep a luncheon appointment with Daniel Patrick Moynihan, assistant to the president on domestic affairs. With me was my special assistant, Don Wendell. We sat in Pat's office for more than an hour, and just as we were about to leave, he came in with apologies.

I had requested the appointment just to touch base and try to clear the air. Moynihan and I were not close. I had been openly critical of some of the assertions and conclusions in his 1965 study of the "black family," written with Nathan Glazer, and Moynihan, like the proverbial elephant, neither forgives nor forgets. Wendell listened as Pat and I discussed the controversy surrounding the Jensen report, a study by Dr. Arthur Jensen, a psychologist, purporting to document the genetic inferiority of blacks. My host had asked me what I thought of the report and I had told him in no uncertain terms. Moynihan arched his brows sharply upward, straightened his bow tie, and remarked with no trace of a smile, "Well, Jim, what your people need are some of our genes."

I searched his face, looking for some sign that the man was jesting. I found none.

"Well, Pat," I said, "you've been giving them to us for three hundred fifty years now." Moynihan flushed slightly and changed the subject.

The rest of the conversation was short. I felt less than comfortable and thought that he did, too. We both wanted to get it over with.

Some time later, as I sat at my desk scowling at a pile of paper before me, my secretary, Dee Wilson, came in with another piece of paper in her hand. It was a sealed envelope addressed to me with a notation, "eyes only." There was no return address. When I tore the envelope open, I was puzzled to see before me a photocopy of an unclassified memorandum from Moynihan, addressed to the president, the vice-president, the attorney general, and the director of the FBI. The copy delivered to me was one that had a checkmark next to the name of Vice-President Spiro Agnew. Someone in the vice-president's office had made a copy of it and surreptitiously hand-delivered it to me.

I hit the ceiling when I reached a portion of the memo recommending a policy of "benign neglect" toward blacks.* I called my staff into my office and shared the contents of the memorandum with them. They seemed even more angered than I. The consensus was that such an outrageous recommendation to the president of the United States must see the light of day in public print. I agreed, but I had reservations of conscience in releasing any privileged information like this. Yet, it was such a shocking document that my conscience might plague me more if I did not release it.

For days, I sat on it, but could not force it from the front of my mind. George Schiffer, a lawyer from New York who had volunteered his services to CORE, came to town and I showed it to him. His argument that I had no right to keep that memorandum from the public was persuasive. I made a copy of the document and gave it to Schiffer with instructions to pass it on to Val Coleman in New York. (I had told the former CORE associate about the memo.) My message to Val was, "I have made my decision. See that this gets out."

---

*Moynihan subsequently explained that he did not intend this to be a policy for dealing with blacks generally, but only as the best way to deal with the irresponsible black militants who thrived on controversy and publicity.

Val called a *New York Times* writer, Peter Khiss, and asked for a lunch meeting at a place on Forty-third and Eighth Avenue. When Khiss read the memo, he was shocked beyond belief, and asked Val, "Are you sure this is authentic?" Val assured him that it was absolutely authentic. "Where did you get it?" Khiss wanted to know. Val responded, "Peter, you know I can't tell you that, but believe me, it is authentic."

When Khiss called Moynihan for confirmation or denial, Moynihan shouted into the phone an implied confirmation: "How the hell did you get hold of that?" Moynihan then went into an explanation about benign neglect being a phrase used in a Canadian report and having no negative implications.* He stated further that he intended it as a policy dealing only with black militants, not black moderates.

The next Sunday, March 1, 1970, the story exploded with a two-column headline on the front page of the *New York Times,* and it went all over the world via the wire services.

I am sure that many in the Nixon administration wondered how the memo saw the light of day. The person suspected of leaking it to the press was Leon Panetta, then head of the HEW office of civil rights. Panetta is a courageous man who had taken an uncompromising stand on civil rights enforcement, even when he was at odds with the administration. Pressure was put on Panetta to resign—not because of the memo, of course—and he finally did so in a celebrated withdrawal.**

Some may have suspected that the leak came from me. Shortly after the memo episode, my special assistants, Ruth and Don, observed an individual going through the in- and out-boxes on my secretaries' desks after we had left for the day. After seeing this happen several times, my special assistants began to stand guard at the main door to my office, which was not locked in the evening.

The person seen showing such an interest in what went in and out of those boxes was one of Nixon's men at HEW. This man danced in perfect rhythm—without hesitation, without misgivings, without second thoughts—to whatever tune his bosses played. Officially, he was a special assistant to the secretary, but actually, he seemed to report to Frederick Malek.

One evening at about 6:00 P.M., another Nixon loyalist came into my office. There was almost a reversal of stereotypical roles. He shuffled and scratched and said, "Yes, sir, Mr. Secretary; yes, sir, Mr. Secretary."

"Come in, sit down," I said. "What can I do for you?"

This was during the days when there was great media interest in the president's nomination of Judge G. Harrold Carswell of Florida to the U.S. Supreme Court. It was an extremely controversial nomination, and confirmation was by no means certain. Beginning to surface in the press was a record of hostility on the part of Carswell to civil rights issues in

*The Durham Report on Canada.
**Leon Panetta is now a Democratic congressman from California's sixteenth district.

Florida. I remembered the name from reports sent to my desk by CORE lawyers in Florida. Those reports indicated an animosity on Carswell's part to the goals CORE sought.

After Nixon's nomination of the Florida judge, various people from the press approached me for a reaction. I had to think fast and make a decision on the spot as to whether this was the time and the occasion for me to make a break with the Nixon administration. If I decided to do that, I would have to resign now and blast the president's terrible choice. That would mean many things I had in progress with HEW—a shaping up of the Office of Child Development; the New Careers Program, both in-house and out-of-house; an integrated management intern program; and the HEW fellows operation—would be lost. So I decided, on the spot, to say, "No comment."

It was a difficult thing for me to say in Carswell's case, and it stabbed at my conscience every time I said it.

Now, here was an administration toady sitting in my office, still nervously fingering some sheets of paper he held in his hands.

"What is it?" I asked.

He then stood and walked to my desk with the papers in his hand.

"Mr. Secretary, I have three lists of names of U.S. senators here. The first list is of those who are committed to vote for confirmation of Judge Carswell. The second is of those who will vote against confirmation. The third is of those who are yet undecided and the biggest question in their minds seems to be the judge's civil rights record. Now, we thought if you could call the senators on this third list and tell them that Judge Carswell is okay on civil rights, we would be home free."

He paused and looked into my face. I could not believe what I had just heard.

"When the press has called me on the Carswell nomination, I have said no comment," I told him. "I found that very difficult to do. But that is all that I can do for you. I will do no more. Now, please leave my office."

He gathered up his papers and said, "Yes, sir, Mr. Secretary. Thank you, Mr. Secretary," and backed out of the office.

Days later, when Carswell failed to win confirmation in the Senate, one member of my staff brought in a bottle of wine and some cheese and crackers, and we had a quiet little party of celebration.

Unlike most assistant secretaries, because of my prominence in the civil rights struggle, my job at HEW took on extraordinary duties beyond those that show up on the organization chart. I became a kind of unofficial ombudsman for minority and poor people seeking redress or funding from the federal government, as well as for blacks having problems in government that they perceived as being related to race. Most of the persons with whom I dealt in that capacity were not accustomed to calling or writing for an appointment. They were used to walking in and rapping with a "brother." They saw no reason to change that approach now, and if I forced them to change it by refusing to see them without a prearranged appointment, I would be bad-mouthed for having forgotten my roots, hobnobbing with the big shots, and refusing to see my people. This role became enormously time-consuming, but absolutely essential if I was to keep faith with my definition of myself.

My secretaries were driven to distraction by having people rush past them and into my office, ignoring their remonstrations. Sometimes they were old acquaintances or old friends, veterans of civil rights battles. They didn't care what I was busy working on, I always had to have time to see them or I had become a terrible guy. It was often a pleasant respite from the bureaucratic battles and mountains of paper. Sometimes, though, those unannounced intrusions became a crisis in themselves.

Bright and early one morning, into my office walked an old friend who had become the executive director of a community action program in Monmouth County, New Jersey. Along with him were four large Head Start mothers. As the entourage came in, I walked from behind my desk, embraced the brother, and we went through the "soul brother" hand-shake of that day, which usually took several minutes and involved contor-tions, slaps, twists, and claps of the hands. My friend then stepped back and beamed at me. "Hey, Jim, man, you're looking great and this office of yours, it's the size of a ballpark, even got a private bathroom, conference room, easy chairs. Oh, wow! It's nothing like the old CORE office, is it?"

I said, "Ah, you know the trappings of government, but it's great to see you, ole buddy."

"It's great to see you, Jim, and I got news for you, baby."

"Yeah, what's that?" I asked.

"You're our prisoner, man."

I laughed loudly, and he joined in the hilarity.

"It's funny as hell, isn't it, Jim?" he said. "But it's true."

The smile faded from my face.

"What do you mean, 'I'm your prisoner'? Is this some kind of a practical joke? Are you telling me you brought guns into my office?"

"Oh, no, Jim. You know better than that. I wouldn't bring any hardware into your office."

"Then how do you think you're going to hold me prisoner?" I asked. He motioned toward the door to where one of the women, built like a tank, was standing, arms folded.

"You're a pretty big guy, Jim. I know you could fight your way out of this office. But you're not going to do that. You know why? Because you'd have to push that lady around, and you're not going to do that."

I went back to my chair at the desk.

My friend said, "Uh, uh, Jim. I know you got a button under that desk that you can press to summon your security guards and have us busted, but you're not going to do that either, because if you do, we're going to bad-mouth you all over this country, man. I can hear it now: 'James Farmer has Head Start mothers busted.'"

"You haven't told me what it is you want," I said.

"We want to talk to Secretary Finch," he replied. "I thought you knew that."

"That's impossible," I said. "Finch is at a cabinet meeting at Camp David."

"Yes, I know. But we'll wait. When we get hungry, since we're your guests, you'll give us the money and one of these ladies will go out and buy sandwiches for all of us. You've got a beautiful bathroom with plenty of towels. What else do we need? And no rent to pay on top of all that."

"Well, look, let me call Camp David and talk to the secretary and see when he'll be coming back," I said.

"Fine, and I hope it's very soon, because I know you want to get home this evening, and we'd like to get home, too, but we're prepared to stay as long as necessary, and you're going to stay here with us."

I reached Bob Finch at Camp David and told him the problem. His immediate response was, "Well, hell, Jim, just summon the security guards and have them thrown out." When I explained why I could not do that, he understood.

"I see your point," he said. "This is a very important cabinet meeting, and I can't leave here, you know that."

"Which is more important, Bob, your cabinet meeting or my liberty?"

"Well, since you put it that way, let me go speak to the president; I'll be right back on the phone. Hold on."

Minutes later, Finch returned to the phone and said, "The president asked the same question I did, 'Why doesn't Jim have the security guards throw them out?' When I explained your reasons for not doing that, he thought for a minute and then told me I may take his helicopter and go into town and meet with those people if I want to. I'll be in my office within an hour."

About fifty minutes later, Finch's secretary called to tell me that Bob was at his desk, and my guests could come in. When I passed this good news along to my "guests," the community action program director said, "No, Jim, we don't want your security guards to intercept us in the hall, so you come along with us."

I led them into the secretary's office, and introduced them to Bob Finch, who smiled and met them cordially. Then I left. A half hour later, the quintet returned to my office, full of smiles, and once again we went through the soul brother handshake and they thanked me profusely.

"Jim," said the man, "I knew you were on our side, but we just wanted to help you do what we knew you wanted to do. We got commitments from Finch. You see, if we had met with you, Finch could have overridden anything that you promised, but the buck stops at his desk. So long, ole buddy, and thanks again."

I smiled as my guests departed.

One thing I tried not to be at HEW was a black buffer to take the heat off of those who were higher up. I did not want to be trotted out as the person to pacify unruly blacks whenever there was trouble. There is an almost unavoidable tendency for superiors to use a black appointee in that way, but in very short order it destroys his credibility and his effectiveness. I had discussed that with Finch and he understood my feelings.

In a subtle way, the man from Monmouth County understood that, too, and had devised an imaginative and unconventional plan, forceful as a sledgehammer, for making me his advocate rather than the secretary's buffer.

The media described me as the highest-ranking black in the Nixon administration. That was inaccurate. Sam Jackson and Sam Simmons, assistant secretaries for housing and urban development, and Art Fletcher, assistant secretary of labor, outranked me. They were executive level four, whereas, through a quirk in the legislation, the assistant secretary for administration at HEW was only executive level five, requiring no Senate confirmation.

Though I believed in the principle of Senate confirmation, I had been relieved to know that I would not have to face a confirmation battle. Thurgood Marshall, who had come from the moderate wing of the civil rights movement, had been cut up in the Senate hearings when he was nominated for solicitor general. He won the confirmation, of course, but he walked out of the Senate chambers bruised. I, having come from CORE, would have had a far rougher time in the hearings. Southern senators, especially those from Louisiana, would have lain in wait with press clippings of statements I had uttered in the heat of battle or pronouncements snatched out of context. I probably would have won confirmation, but the wounds might have been irreparable. As the best-known black in the Nixon administration, the White House got mileage out of my presence; and that fact gave me a good deal of leverage, which I was able to use for causes I was committed to. Yet there were the inevitable compromises, such as saying no comment on the Carswell nomination and my silence on the bombing of Cambodia.

For me, the months at HEW were a constant balancing act on the scales of my own conscience. Each morning, while shaving, I had to examine those scales as I looked into my own eyes at the beginning of another day.

CHAPTER 31

THE WAY OUT

LULA GOT HOME LATE from a picket line of the Women's Strike for Peace. She was exhausted, for her energy level was extremely low due to her battle with Hodgkin's Disease. Nevertheless, her mood was one of jubilation. She was pleased that one member of the family was free to say something about the atrocities we were committing in Vietnam. She had been photographed several times, she told me delightedly, and one of the photographers asked her name. We speculated whether he was from the press or the FBI. She didn't care. Nor did I.

Then the phone rang. It was Bob Finch calling.

"Jim, I want you to hear it from me before you read it in the *Washington Post* tomorrow morning. I'm leaving HEW and going to the White House as counselor to the president."

I told Bob that I had decided several weeks ago to resign but was just waiting for the time and the occasion to make the break. I explained further that my decision had nothing to do with his going or staying, and that I had enjoyed working with him and appreciated the support he had given me during the year or so we had been together.

"Oh, brother," he mumbled. "I didn't know you were thinking of leaving. My God, I had better tell Elliot about this right away. Elliot Richardson will be taking my place at HEW and I imagine he'll want to get in touch with you."

I got to the office early the next morning and it's a good thing I did. Five minutes after nine, I had a visitor. It was Elliot Richardson. He walked into my outer office and stood before my secretary's desk. Dee Wilson looked up at him in her most efficient manner, and asked, "May I help you?"

"Yes. I'm Elliot Richardson, and I would like to see Assistant Secretary Farmer for a few minutes."

"Oh, I'm terribly sorry, Mr. Richards," said Dee, shaking her head. "Mr. Farmer is extremely busy. It just won't be possible to see him without an appointment, and today he has appointments back-to-back all day long."

"Richardson," Elliot corrected her. "I know that I don't have an appointment, but this is a very important matter, and I am sure Mr. Farmer could spare a few minutes."

Dee, who had not read the morning paper, did not know who he was, so she continued to be her efficient and protective self. "I *am* sorry, Mr. Robertson. I wish that were possible, but it isn't. I suggest that you write Mr. Farmer a letter explaining the nature of your business and I am sure that he will reply, granting you an appointment as soon as possible."

"Richardson," he corrected her again. "I'm sure if you tell Mr. Farmer that Elliot Richardson would like a few minutes with him he will squeeze me into the schedule. Will you please ask him?"

"All right, Mr. Richardson, I'll ask Mr. Farmer, though I'm sure he won't be able to change his schedule."

Dee came into my office and told me that Elliot Richardson was outside. I, of course, dashed out the door and ushered him in. We shook hands and he said, "Where did you find her? She's great; I'd like to hire her as soon as I get over here."

"You can't hire before I leave," I said.

Richardson was an impressive man who exuded confidence, and he came right to the point.

"Bob Finch tells me you're planning to leave HEW. I hope that is incorrect, and if it is not incorrect, I hope I can persuade you to change your mind."

I told him that what Finch had said was true, and that my decision was firm. I stressed that my decision had been made long before I knew Richardson was coming to HEW, and it had nothing whatever to do with him. On the contrary, I knew of Elliot Richardson's reputation, his joining of King's march in Selma, for instance, and I had the highest respect for him as a person. The frustrations at HEW were just too great, and my decision was irreversible.

"Well, I hope you'll at least keep your mind open to rethink that decision. If you find your present job at HEW particularly frustrating, perhaps we can change that by shuffling the cards and moving you laterally to a spot more to your liking."

"I'm sorry, Elliot, my decision is firm. The frustration is so deep that no conceivable switch in jobs would eradicate it."

"Well, if you *do* leave, let me say that I hope you'll do it in such a way that the press will not draw the conclusion that there's some relationship between my coming and your going."

"Yes, I would want to do that," I replied. "But how do you suggest it be done?"

"First, the timing," said Richardson, his intelligent eyes glued to my face. "I would urge that you delay your leaving and any announcement of your leaving for a reasonable period of time. If you resign shortly after I begin here, the press is bound to jump to the conclusion that there is a causal relationship between the two events. Second, your resignation statement. It should be carefully worded to make it clear that you are not leaving to get away from me and to avoid giving the impression that I wanted you to leave. Of course, I still hope that you'll change your mind, and if you don't mind, I'll bring it up again and again in the hope that somehow you can be persuaded to stay."

"Certainly, I'll delay my leaving. I will also check with you after a reasonable period of time, so we can agree on an acceptable date. Whatever statement I issue at the time of my resignation will be shown to you in advance of issuance for comments. I'm delighted and flattered, Elliot, that you bothered to come by to see me so quickly after Bob spoke with you. I wish you well at HEW. If there's any way I can help while I am here, just let me know."

We shook hands and he left, pausing to smile and shake hands also with Dee Wilson.

It was necessary to tell my personal staff—the secretaries, the special assistants, and the executive assistant—of my decision to leave, and that though the departure would be delayed, it was definite. They had to be told so they could look around for new jobs for themselves in the department. There was no way to keep the word from filtering through HEW, but luckily, no leak to the press occurred in those first few months after Richardson became secretary.

Elliot Richardson and I got along extremely well. He's a good administrator, tough but fair, and possesses a finely honed mind. His thoughts were well organized and as clearly expressed as the intricate doodles on which he worked during every meeting, and for which he became famous. Several times he urged me again to stay and did everything within his power to encourage me to do so.

After a couple of months, I called him, suggesting that a reasonable period of time had elapsed, and that we should agree on a date for my departure so that the necessary steps could be taken to make it a smooth one. I proposed a date some two weeks in the future. He said that he would get back to me by the close of the day on that.

He called back to tell me that the president was going to be in San Clemente, California, on that date and wanted to be in town at the time of my resignation. He asked me to come up with another date if I was still not willing to change my mind on the question of resigning.

Later, when I suggested a second date, Richardson informed me that he was going to be out of the country on that date, and he simply had to be present when my announcement was made. A month or two went by before I named a third date, which seemed agreeable all around, but the week before, I came down with flu, so it had to be changed again. Finally I fixed a fourth date, and we agreed to keep it quiet until I was ready to hold my press conference on the day of resignation.

It is not easy to function in a bureaucracy when the word is out that you are a lame duck. During that interim of several months, I felt less like a decison maker than a document signer, just keeping the paper work flowing until the date of departure.

With only two weeks to go, I sat in my office one day, chatting with Bernard Shaw, a black reporter for Westinghouse News Service. He frequently dropped by my office unannounced just for a background chat about the state of the world, the civil rights movement, and any tidbits about HEW that I could pass on to him on-the-record or off-the-record, brother to brother, buddy to buddy. When things were told him in confidence, Shaw always honored that confidence. Now he asked me, "Jim, tell me honestly, off-the-record, how long are you going to stay in this place?"

Hesitating for a brief moment, I said, "Bernie, what I am going to tell you now has to be *strictly* off-the-record. Don't breathe a word about it."

"Jim, you know me. I'm your brother. This is strictly background information that I want. You have my word of honor. Cross my heart."

I then told Shaw that I planned to resign in two weeks' time. There would be a press conference, where I would make the announcement, but I did not want a word of it to get out before then. My frustration was so great, I said to him, that I simply couldn't stand it any longer.

Shaw wanted to know what my reasons were, just for background information, of course. I repeated my admonition that none of this was to be used before my press conference. Again he agreed, and so I related to him my various reasons for leaving: the slowness of the bureaucracy to move, the many paper-shuffling ways that the bureaucrats have of stalling and even preventing change, U.S. crimes against Cambodia, Nixon's nominees to the Supreme Court, the failure of the administration to take a firm stand on civil rights issues, the "don't listen to what we say, watch what we do" syndrome, the "southern strategy" devised by John Mitchell to win elections through appeasing the South by downplaying civil rights, and so forth.

I told Shaw that the Nixon record on domestic issues was not entirely bad. Some good things had been done, such as developing the "Philadelphia plan," requiring contractors receiving government funds to have an equitable share of minorities on their work force; and the family assistance plan, a proposal devised by Moynihan to encourage welfare recipients to work by allowing them to keep a share of their earnings as well as their welfare money until the income from both placed them above the poverty line; and the administration had provided a green light to Bob Finch's decision to override Mississippi Governor Williams's Head Start veto.

Yet, in my opinion, the administration had no conviction on these things and was merely playing a political game. The all-important moral leadership of the presidency was lacking.

Shaw thanked me for the background information and assured me he would be at the press conference.

The next day, on Westinghouse News Radio in New York, the story was out in full detail. Westinghouse News Service also sent a release to black newspapers throughout the country, reporting that I had told a good friend of mine, Bernard Shaw, of my plans to leave HEW within two weeks. The story also listed the reasons.

The wire services picked it up, and I was reached by AP or UPI (I don't remember which) while moderating an executive seminar for the Institute of Humanistic Studies at Aspen, Colorado. Immediately, I called Elliot Richardson to apologize for my stupidity in trusting a news-hungry reporter. I told Richardson that because of this unfortunate leak, I was postponing my resignation for a few more weeks in order to make Bernie Shaw out a liar at least on the point of timing. Richardson was generous and said, "Well, Jim, don't worry about it, these things happen."

Then I called Shaw to scream at him for his duplicity. He denied that there was duplicity at all, insisting that I had merely said "don't quote me," and he had not quoted me, but had only paraphrased what I had told him. He's a good newsman; though it was not an earth-shattering story, he *had* gotten a scoop.

The drama I had hoped to orchestrate in my resignation was no longer possible. Upon returning to Washington, I set a new date on which both the president and the secretary would be in town. Richardson called to inform me that the president wanted me to meet with him at the White House prior to making my announcement. That I agreed to do. Richardson expressed a desire to join me at the White House for that meeting, but he wished me to check with the president's office as to whether it would be all right with Nixon.

I called Leonard Garment, a presidential assistant known as the in-house liberal at the Nixon White House, and raised the question with him. Len's return call advised me that the president wished to meet with me alone, and I passed this information on to the secretary.

The statement I prepared for release at the press conference was very general and carefully worded. Of course, I did not criticize Richardson; I had the highest respect and admiration for him. Nor could I embarrass him by attacking the administration. Consequently, my statement was bound to be a disappointment to my Democratic friends. It merely stressed my frustration with the slowness of the bureaucracy and my strong feeling that my greatest effectiveness was outside the establish-ment, prodding it, pushing it, shoving it, rather than inside, trying to pull it forward. Richardson considered it excellent and told me that the presi-dent wanted me to hold my press conference at the White House, after meeting with him. That I declined to do, on the grounds that it would appear that the president was orchestrating the occasion, when it was entirely my show. I would, instead, rent a facility at a downtown hotel for the press conference.

Richardson subsequently suggested that I cancel the hotel reservation and hold the press conference in the Snow Room, a large conference room at HEW. He wanted to open the press conference and introduce me to the assembled newspersons. Though I was not pleased with this, I agreed to make the switch, for Richardson had been most cooperative in every way and this would assure the press that I was not leaving because of him.

The meeting with Nixon in the Oval Office on December 7, 1970, was friendly, though he seemed tense. Also present was Len Garment. I dis-covered that the president had a copy of my statement. He told me that he thought it beautiful and eloquent; that made me think that I should have said much more in it.

Nixon told me how much he regretted to see me leave his administra-tion and said he wished me well. If I had any suggestions, he hoped that I would pass them on to him through Len Garment in memorandum form. I made one suggestion at the time, that the administration establish an office of ombudsman so that community people needing or wanting to deal with the government would not get lost in the maze of departments and corridors, but would have one place to go where they would be directed to the appropriate agency or office. He thought that a good idea and asked me to send a memo through Garment on the matter.

Then he said, "Mr. Farmer, I assume you are still in support of the welfare reform system that we are working toward. You know, the family assistance plan."

I replied that I was indeed, and that I considered it a step in the right direction—too small and very late in coming, but a good move that could be improved as we went along. He expressed great pleasure that I still felt it was a move in the right direction, and then his eyes narrowed characteristically as he said that the press would be waiting outside to know what we had talked about, and I could tell them one of the things we discussed was the family assistance plan and that he, the president, said he was really going to fight for it in the next session of Congress. Then his jaw jutted forward, and he said, "If the Congress doesn't give it to me, there's going to be blood on the floor."

The press conference at HEW later that morning was well attended. Seated in the front row was Bernard Shaw. Elliot Richardson, as always, was masterful at officiating. Mostly, the reporters wanted to know what I was going to do next, where I would work. I told them, of course, that I was one of the few political appointees voluntarily to leave a good job without a soft place to land. I was leaving without a job to go to. As of December 28, 1970, the effective date of my resignation, I would be functionally unemployed. I did not expect to starve to death or to let my family suffer. As of the following month, I would be going on the college lecture circuit to fill engagements booked by a prominent speakers' bureau. That I expected would continue for a year or so, until the television images faded and the newspaper headlines became stale. Then I hoped to start a black "think tank" to try to get some unified sense of direction in the civil rights movement.

It was no real surprise that I made no friends by leaving. Many outside of government who had urged me to resign were now critical because I had left quietly. Some of my Democratic friends called me up and said in effect, "Man, I thought you were going to back out the door with both guns blazing, shooting from the hip."

Louis Martin, that great and durable black Democratic warhorse and power broker, wrote in an editorial in the *Chicago Daily Defender* that I had left far too quietly and politely and he wondered why. He said that people had grown to expect from me a careful cataloguing of the crimes and evils of the Nixon administration. They did not get it. They were "disappointed but not disgusted." I was pleased that Louie was prepared to give me the benefit of the doubt.

Many black Republicans were critical of me for leaving. "Only rats leave a sinking ship," one said. I had no idea how he knew that early, in December 1970, that the ship was sinking.

CHAPTER 32

FOOTNOTE TO WATERGATE

I WAS GONE, BUT not forgotten. Syndicated columnist Jack Anderson later informed me that the FBI bugged and tapped me for two years after my resignation from HEW. He said, further, that they had had me under electronic surveillance during the twenty-one months that I was with the government. He knew because he had seen the files.

That came as no surprise to me, for a telephone incident had alerted me to the possibility in 1971. Lula lifted the telephone receiver to make a call from home and heard voices talking. Motioning me to silence, she listened to the conversation. It was someone reading the text of a telegram to be sent by Western Union to the survivors of a newsman killed in a helicopter crash in Vietnam. At the end of the words of condolence, the party said: "This is signed, President and Mrs. Nixon. No first names, please."

Having been a student of statistics in college, my wife quickly calculated the probability that our line would accidentally cross a line from the White House in Washington, D.C. It was nil. She and I thought there must be a tap on our phone from some White House source. Later, on learning of the existence of the "plumbers," and the extensive wiretapping activity from the basement of the White House in search of sources of government leaks, the incident made sense.

An apparent break-in during an absence from my Washington home on Chevy Chase Parkway, also in 1971, had puzzled me because nothing was stolen. Lula, the girls, the dogs, and I had taken off for a few days to the Pennsylvania mountains. A frequent baby-sitter from the neighborhood, Bianca Mason, went to the house morning and afternoon to feed the cats and water the plants. One morning Bianca called me and insisted that someone had been in the house during the night. Furniture was not as she had left it, and a file cabinet drawer was partially open. The valuables in the house were still in their places and apparently nothing was missing. Police concluded that the intruders had entered with a passkey; there had been no jimmying of the locks. A quick check of my files revealed nothing missing.

The lecture circuit proved lucrative for a year and then tapered off. Money became hard to come by, and Lula's health was deteriorating rapidly. By 1972, she was forced to spend more time in bed than up and around. Her lungs were giving way; X-rays showed scars indicating that she had had tuberculosis. She had not been aware of it, and the disease apparently never had been completely cured. Now she was put on heavy medication to attack the TB. In addition, the massive radiation treatments she had undergone in the early years of chronic Hodgkins were beginning to take their toll. Her body had shriveled to ninety pounds. The once attractive face now looked strained and haggard. Hair that had gleamed was now dull and brittle. She was plagued with itching skin for which the dermatologists had no answer. There were few moments when this brave woman was without pain.

From somewhere inside, she dug deep and found the strength to go on raising our children and keeping the household going—and living.

With Lula's situation heavily on my mind, the precariousness of my income was frightening. I began seriously seeking funding for a black think tank, the Council on Minority Planning and Strategy (COMPAS), which Ruth Perot and I had started. As president of COMPAS, I went to the usual funding sources, the foundations, without success. Essentially, they said, "Jim, don't worry about thinking. We can do that. You're an activist. Act!" Two top officers of the Rand Corporation met with me twice, after expressing interest in COMPAS and in helping it to get under way. However, when I explained to the gentlemen that COMPAS, of course, would have to reserve the right to select the issues it would study, and would have exclusive control over the conclusions reached in those studies, the Rand Corporation people lost interest.

I went to Elliot Richardson. He drew his elaborate doodles on a pad in front of him while reading the COMPAS prospectus. Then he called into his office the assistant secretary comptroller, Bruce Cardwell, and asked him to examine the HEW authorizations to find out if there was any way to legally and ethically fund any part of the programs proposed in my plans for COMPAS. After a diligent search, Cardwell came up with a small authorization in the Office of Education (OE) division of developing institutions. Those funds were set aside for training. He explained to me that I would have to meet all of OE's requirements and prepare a proposal that would be entirely acceptable to them in order to be eligible to receive any of those funds. "You will have to meet every competitive test," Cardwell said.

The proposal was expertly prepared, largely by Ruth Perot. It was for a project to conduct a year-long series of seminars on public policy issues for a group of seventy-five participants, all faculty members from developing institutions* in the vicinity of Washington, D.C. The proposal underwent the usual revisions and polishing in consultation with OE staffers. Finally, it met all their criteria and was set to go through the various stages preliminary to a final decision on funding. The amount of money requested was $150,000.

After several months of silence from the Office of Education, I learned via the HEW grapevine that the proposal had been snagged "at the White House." Though I found it incredible that anything that small would get White House attention, I decided to go there and seek some answers. Whom did I know there? There was my former boss, Bob Finch, who was counselor to the president. But Bob would not be involved in anything of this sort and I was loath to draw him into it.

Then there was Frederic V. Malek, who was director of personnel at the White House. He listened to my description of COMPAS, read the prospectus, scanned the proposal, and said, "This looks meritorious to me. What's the problem?"

His eyes narrowed as he listened to my explanation. Apparently, my proposal had been snagged by someone at the White House and it remained stuck.

*The euphemism for a predominantly black college.

"Would you please try to find out where it's stuck, and what can be done to unstick it?" I asked.

"Surely. I would be glad to sniff around and see what I can do."

I thanked him and got up to leave, but he asked me to wait a moment. "Maybe you haven't heard, Jim, but I'm not in charge of personnel any longer. I'm now working for the Committee to Reelect the President [CREEP]."

"Oh" was my response. "In what capacity?"

"I'm in charge of ethnic groups."

I smothered a laugh and asked, "What ethnic groups?"

"All of them, including blacks, Hispanics, native Americans, Asian Americans, Italians, Irish, Polish—you name them."

"Well, good luck, Fred. You're going to need it."

"Jim, do you know Bob Brown?"

When I said yes, he continued: "Well, he's now with CREEP, dealing especially with blacks. Would you be willing to talk with him?"

"Of course, I'm always willing to talk to Bob. He's a decent guy and a friend of mine."

Malek called Brown and set up an appointment. The next morning, in Brown's office, we reminisced about the old days when I was at HEW and he was at the White House and we had gotten together on occasions to compare notes and lend mutual assistance when such was needed. Bob expressed outrage that my program had not been funded and promised he would look into it and try to find out what was holding it up and, if necessary, would crack heads to get it funded. I thanked him.

Then he asked if there was any way I could help them in the campaign. I told Bob what I am sure he already knew, that I could not possibly endorse or support the president in his bid for reelection. I explained that I was a registered Independent in Washington, D.C., neither a Republican nor a Democrat.* I elaborated further my views regarding the participation of blacks in electoral politics. For years, I had considered it a mistake for blacks to be "in the bag" for either party. The party that had them would consider them "safe" and would court those who were unsafe. The party that did not have them would ignore them, for they were beyond reach, and would concentrate on votes that were attainable. The road to political clout for a people in America was through the jungle of uncertainty—making it clear to both parties that their votes were attainable, depending on the programs offered, but were not a sure thing for either party. Only in such a climate would blacks or any other minority be taken seriously and listened to. I explained that in all my lectures I sought to make this point, as I had done in my unsuccessful congressional campaign in Brooklyn.

*Much later, in 1983, when I moved from Washington, D.C., to Virginia, I changed my registration from Independent to Democrat.

Brown nodded his head vigorously and said that if I pointed that out in my speeches that would, of course, help them, for it would loosen the death grip the rival party had on the black vote. I shrugged. Then he said, "Well, let's get down to specifics. Would you be willing to speak for the Republicans, making that point?"

"Not in campaign meetings and not in Republican Party meetings," I replied.

"Well now, Jim, we often get requests for speakers from groups such as the Lions, Rotaries, Kiwanis, women's clubs, church groups, and the like. Would you mind if we suggested your name to some of these groups in response to their requests?"

I pondered for a moment and replied, "Not at all. That's the way I make my living now, by lecturing for fees before such groups. Any invitation you refer to me will be considered on its own merit in the same manner that invitations from Democratic or nonpartisan sources would be considered."

"Great," said Bob. "We'll probably refer some requests to you. We think it would help us a great deal for you to express your political views honestly as you have outlined them to me."

We embraced and parted as brothers who had a simple understanding.

Many months went by and I heard nothing further regarding my proposal. Ruth Perot and I went to Cleveland and secured a $10,000 grant from the Schubert Foundation as seed money to keep the doors of COMPAS open while we refined our programs. It was not until the spring of 1973, and after the presidential election, that the proposal again began to move in the Office of Education. On May 1 of that year, we were funded through Howard University to establish the Public Policy Training Institute (PPTI) and conduct the program I had proposed to OE.

The weekly seminars were exciting and impressive, featuring a host of "name" speakers: U.S. senators Jacob Javits, New York Republican, and Edward M. Kennedy, Massachusetts Democrat; syndicated columnists Jack Anderson, James J. Kilpatrick, Robert Novak, and William Raspberry, pollster George Gallup, Jr.; General James M. Gavin, chairman of the board of Arthur D. Little Co.; Lieutenant General Daniel L. "Chappie" James; Dr. Charles V. Hamilton, professor of political science at Columbia; editors Howard Simon and Philip Geyelin, of the *Washington Post;* Simeon Booker, Washington bureau chief of *Jet* and *Ebony* magazines; U.S. congressmen Augustus V. Hawkins, California Democrat, and Charles C. Diggs, Michigan Democrat; lobbyists Clarence Mitchell, Jr., Washington bureau chief of the NAACP, and John Gardner, founder of Common Cause; James E. Cheek, president of Howard University; consumer advocate Ralph Nader; and journalist Daniel Schorr.

There was full attendance at each session of about seventy-five participants from faculties of "developing institutions" in Washington, D.C., Maryland, Virginia, Delaware, and Pennsylvania. As I was wrapping up the year's program in 1974 and preparing our reports for OE, a letter arrived from the Select Committee on Watergate, signed by Samuel Dash, general counsel for the committee.*

In his letter, Dash said that he had been informed through the White House and CREEP memoranda that the funding I had received for my program was politically motivated. Since this was within the purview of matters being investigated by the Watergate committee, Dash said it would be part of their report to the Senate. If I cared to answer the charge, he added, I could submit a sworn affidavit to the committee. If I wished to talk to anyone on the committee regarding the matter, he informed me, then I should call an individual he identified as a staff member of the committee.

I called the staff person. In a voice dripping with the arrogance of juvenile pretentiousness, he said, "Ah, yes, Mr. Farmer, we have received a lot of information on you in memoranda to the White House from CREEP and it is not a pretty picture. Let me read you a paragraph from these memoranda. . . . 'Farmer's program has been funded. He will now make speeches for the president's reelection campaign. He will also talk with leading blacks and line up their support behind the president.' Er, let me read you another paragraph from that memorandum."

I reminded the man that he had initially mentioned memoranda, and he had read a portion of one memo. I told him that I wanted to see the relevant memoranda.

"Oh! That will be quite impossible."

I hung up and called my lawyer, who advised me that under no circumstances should I send an affidavit attempting to respond to accusations that I had not been allowed to see, thus risking a charge of perjury. "How do you know," she asked, "that they do not have a half dozen witnesses who will swear that you are lying? And what makes you think a jury or judge would take your word over those of the witnesses?" My lawyer suggested that instead I write a letter to Dash, pointing out that the funding I had received for the Public Policy Training Institute (PPTI) was not political, and that there was no quid pro quo involved in the receipt of those funds. In other words, the grant I had received was not "payment for services rendered." However, I should offer to testify under oath before a closed session of the committee, and she would accompany me to that session.

I followed her advice to the letter and there was no reply from Dash or anyone else on the committee. No one on the committee or its staff contacted me again. I was not asked to testify.

Several months later, in 1974, I received a call from the *New York Times,* telling me that they had received a leaked draft report of the Senate Watergate committee to the Senate. The report had a section entitled "The James Farmer Matter." That section alleged that I had received

*The Senate committee chaired by Sam Ervin (D.-N.C.), which conducted the televised Watergate hearings.

funding for a program of mine in return for my promise to line up blacks
in support of Nixon in the campaign.

"I know you, Jim, and this doesn't sound at all like you. So what the hell
is the *real* story?" asked Tom Johnson, the *Times* writer.

I related to him the sequence of events in my quest for funding for
COMPAS—from the meeting with Elliot Richardson through the meetings with Malek and Brown.

He said, "Okay, I'll write the story. I think I have a clear perception of
what happened." The *Times* news article, published on June 12, 1974, said
in effect that the people at CREEP had tried to rope in prominent blacks
such as James Farmer and Jesse Jackson and had failed. I thought it an
accurate and fair statement.

The next day, however, I jumped out of my shoes when my secretary
burst into my office with the editorial page of the *Washington Post*. I read it
and immediately reached for a cigarette from her pack—it was the first I
had smoked in four and a half years. (It tasted so good, I went out and
bought a pack and was hooked again.)

The lead editorial in the *Post* had accused me of selling black votes to
Nixon. Nothing in the civil rights movement of the early sixties, nothing
in the battle with the Klan in Louisiana, nothing in the bus rides in Alabama and Mississippi had angered me so. If there was anything that was
my trademark, anything I treasured, it was *integrity*. Those who were my
heroes in life—A. Philip Randolph, Eleanor Roosevelt, Norman
Thomas—all possessed that trait. Nothing else—not money, not fame, not
power—could enable me to live with myself. Nothing in life is absolute;
like everyone else, I had done things that were not completely honest and
of which I am not proud. But the editorial that lay before me accused me
of being something I was not as no one or nothing else had in all my fifty-
four years.

The June 13, 1974, editorial was headlined "HOW TO BUY VOTES" and
read:

American election law, and the machinery to enforce it, was clearly not adequate to protect the country in 1972. The Senate Watergate Committee's
staff has now compiled an anthology of clear and obvious abuses. Many of
those abuses also appear to be crimes; the question of individual guilt can be
left to the special prosecutor and the courts. But the urgent need to safeguard the integrity of our democracy is Congress' business and the
voters'. . . .

Taken together, these transgressions constitute a warning that certain types
of tawdry but effective votebuying are getting easier to commit and harder to
detect because of the vast proliferation of federal grant programs. . . . Most
of the cases in this latest staff report revolve around the joint efforts of the
administration and the Committee for the Re-Election of the President to fan
support among the minorities. . . .

A White House memorandum casts a highly unfortunate light on the grant
the Office of Education gave to James Farmer, former assistant secretary of

Health, Education, and Welfare in the Nixon administration and, earlier, national director of the Congress of Racial Equality. The memorandum was written on May 2, 1972, by one White House staff member, Frederic V. Malek, to another, Robert Finch. It said, in part:

1. Farmer has been given a grant from OE to fund his project here in Washington.

2. He will now be able to spend a major part of his time on the above project while also making time available to the re-election effort.

3. He has agreed to do speaking on our behalf and also to talk to key black leaders in an effort to gain their loyalties. . . .

I jerked the phone off the hook. It flew out of my hand and onto the floor. My secretary retrieved it for me and I called the *Washington Post,* demanding to speak to Philip Geyelin, editorial page editor. In an uncontrolled voice and intemperate words, I shouted at him for the *Post*'s unconscionable, untrue, slanderous editorial. Rarely do I lose the reins on my discipline, but this time I did. I told him that the *New York Times* had been leaked the same draft report and they had called me long distance to check its accuracy. The *Post* had not troubled to call across town.

Geyelin screamed right back at me, "You're not attacking the *Washington Post,* you're attacking the Malek memo!"

"I'm attacking both the memo and the *Post.* The memo because it's a fabrication and the *Post* because it didn't even check the authenticity of the memo before rushing it into print! I'm sending a reply and I want you to print it."

"All right, send a letter to the editor and we will do what we can with it."

I sent a fifteen-hundred-word letter to the *Post* refuting the allegations in the Malek memo and criticizing the *Post* for not checking the accuracy of the material they had printed. More than a week went by without any word from Geyelin.

I called Joe Rauh, an old friend and a prominent liberal labor lawyer, and said, "Who's the best libel lawyer in this town, Joe?"

"I am, goddammit, if *you* need one. Who the hell are we suing?"

"The *Washington Post.*"

Joe Rauh gulped and asked, "Can you come right over?"

In his office, I showed him the editorial, which he had not seen, and my reply, to which the *Post* had not responded. He asked me if the editorial had accurately reported the contents of Malek's memo and was astonished to learn that I had not even seen it.

Rauh leaned back in his desk chair and became a lawyer advising his client. "Jim, you probably would not win a libel suit. The Supreme Court has held that the press can say almost anything it wants to about a public figure, which you are. In order to have a chance to win, you would have to prove 'malice,' which means they knew it was a lie before they printed it, and they printed it anyway with intent to injure. I don't think that can be proved. It is possible, however, that the *Washington Post* would settle out of court to avoid the embarrassment of your suit, which would get wide publicity. I doubt that they would do that, though. Newspapers don't like to settle such matters out of court for fear of encouraging a whole rash of libel suits from persons anticipating out-of-court settlements. Do you mind if I call Phil Geyelin?"

"Be my guest," I said. "I called him when I read the editorial and we had a shouting and screaming session. I am sure you'll do better."

When told that Geyelin was in an editorial committee meeting, Joe Rauh left a message: "Tell him that Joe Rauh called about the James Farmer matter."

Within two minutes, Geyelin had returned the call. "You didn't call to tell me that you're suing me, did you, Joe?"

"No, not at present. I called for information. Did your editorial accurately represent the contents of the Malek memo?"

Listening on an extension phone, I heard Geyelin reply, "Ask Farmer. He can tell you that our editorial quoted Malek's memo verbatim, though quotation marks were not used."

Geyelin was surprised to hear that I had not even seen the memo. He assumed that I had been interrogated by the Select Committee on Watergate or its staff. He told Rauh that he had before him the committee's draft report on the matter and would send it to Rauh's office by messenger immediately.

Rauh thanked him and told him that I wanted the *Post* to print my letter in a prominent place with a highly visible headline, and with a positive editorial note at the end of it. Geyelin replied that the letter was too long and would have to be cut. He asked if I would permit them to cut it to fit the available space.

I said, if it had to be cut, I would cut it myself and would bring the shorter version to him in person.

Geyelin asked Rauh if he would guarantee him that they would not be sued if they printed the letter.

"Hell, no," shouted Joe. "I can't guarantee that you won't be sued. I can't guarantee that Jim won't walk out of here and get himself another lawyer, so how the hell can I guarantee that he's not going to sue you?"

A week elapsed and the revised version of the letter had not appeared in the *Post*. On a Friday morning, I phoned Joe Rauh to let him know that I was tired of waiting. If the letter did not appear by the following Monday morning, I intended to sue, and if he was not willing to handle the case, I would find another lawyer. Rauh sighed and said that we should wait and see what happened.

On the deadline I had set, Monday morning, June 21, 1974, the letter appeared on the op-ed page under a large headline: "JAMES FARMER ON THE MALEK MEMO."* At the bottom of the letter was an editorial note: "We agreed that Mr. Farmer should have been given an opportunity to comment on the Malek memo before our editorial was written, and we are

---

*The full text of my letter appears in Appendix B.

pleased to present his view of the matter here. The editors." Frankly, I thought it a mealy-mouthed apology, but it was better than nothing.

The Malek allegations had self-destructed when my reply revealed that PPTI had been funded one year after the memo was dated and six months after the presidential election of 1972. It clearly was not possible for me to have made a commitment to campaign for an election that had been held six months before.

I do not know how Malek's memo could have been so wrong. I had spoken with him about the proposal in March 1972 and had called him on May 2, 1973, to invite him to speak at one of the seminars on the budget process in the federal government. The fact that the project had been funded was news to him at that time, and he asked when the funding had occurred. I told him that it was on May 1, meaning, without saying so, the previous day. Since my initial conversation with him regarding the proposal had been in 1972, he may have assumed that funding had taken place on May 1 of that year, prior to the election.

On the day my letter appeared in the *Washington Post,* I received a call from a high staff person of the Select Committee on Watergate, identifying himself as the author of the draft report. He said that he had read my letter in the *Post* and wondered if I would permit them to insert it in their report. I readily granted that permission, but he called back later to say that the general counsel of the committee had advised him that they could not insert the letter; they would have to have an affidavit from me. He wondered if I would care to come down to his office, read the draft report and the memoranda they had on file making allegations regarding the funding of the program.

I read the report carefully, as well as the several memoranda they had, including one to Fred Malek from Robert Brown following my meeting with him in March 1972. I was shocked to note that the section of the report on "the James Farmer Matter" ended with a misquotation of the final sentence from the letter I had sent to the committee in response to the one received from Sam Dash. What I had written was that my grant was not in "payment for services rendered." What the draft report stated was that I had said the money I received was not payment for "the campaign services which I rendered." Of course, I had rendered absolutely no services to the Nixon campaign for reelection.

The committee staff person who had authored the draft report apologized for the mistake of one of his assistants in refusing me permission to see those memoranda long ago when I had requested it. He said that the young man had committed an error and he was sorry that it had occurred.

After reading the material, I wrote in longhand a fifteen-hundred-word statement giving full details of the process that led to the funding of PPTI. I had the statement notarized and gave it to the committee for use in their final report to the Senate.

Some days later, I asked Bob Brown what contact he had had with the

Watergate committee. Bob let out a loud *whew* and said that they had called him in several times to interrogate him about me. Staff members had stood and shouted down at him, *"You made a deal with Farmer, didn't you? Didn't you?"*

Bob said that he had replied: "Hell, no. Nobody makes a deal with Jim Farmer!" He added, "I bet they didn't put that in their report." They had not.

I called the committee staff person to inquire whether the revisions in the draft report involving me had been made, and was informed that after reading my affidavit, the committee had sent the entire report back to the drawing board.

When the report of the select Senate committee went to the Senate, I am told, the section entitled "The James Farmer Matter" had been deleted.

Nevertheless, much damage had been done. Committee staffers had called on the OE division that had funded my program, presenting the allegations as irrefutable charges. The PPTI instantly became too controversial for further funding.

A successful and impressive educational program was scuttled.

The above sequence of events are of little consequence in the enormous tragedy of the Watergate conspiracy. There is no doubt that the "bad guys" in that terrible drama staining the pages of twentieth-century history were very bad indeed. Some of the "good guys," however, in their zeal to dig the bad out of their burrows, were themselves not without blemish.

PART NINE

Ebbtide

CHAPTER 33

COME BACK, LULA

THREE AND A HALF decades of pitched battles had left me war weary. At age fifty-six and in good health, I could not think of retiring. Like an aging prizefighter, I still found the shouts of the crowd aroused a pleasant nostalgia, resulting in a surge of adrenaline pumping through my veins. The wine of notoriety was a taste that still caressed my palate in memory.

But it was all just a memory, for I had no arena. CORE, under its new head, Roy Innis, successor to Floyd McKissick, was now less than a happy thought. COMPAS and its front, PPTI, were controversial and unfundable. Yet, I could not retire, for an ongoing personal war continued to drain Lula and me both financially and emotionally. For three decades, we had fought her illness, winning each battle along the way. Now we were losing the war.

Watching her brave retreat under assault from the enemy in her body, I knew that I had to do something. The feast or famine—largely famine—or free-lance lecturing would not pay the mounting medical bills. Nor would the irregularity of that income permit any budgeting or planning.

There was a stopgap. In 1975, my friend Morris Milgram, who for more than twenty years had been blazing trails in integrated housing, came to me with a novel idea. He would provide an economic incentive for smashing the pattern of ghetto living. I joined with him in establishing the Fund for an Open Society, a nonprofit company providing low-interest mortgage loans to persons of all colors who were making prointegration housing moves. Morris was its president, and I was chairman of the board.

I received a small stipend from OPEN, but it could not begin to support my family and me, even in good times. I would have to get a job.

It was to my old friend Jerry Wurf that I went. For over a decade, he had been international president of the American Federation of State, County, and Municipal Employees (AFSCME).

"Frankly, Jerry, I need a job. I simply have got to increase and regularize my income in order to deal with Lula's illness, which I believe to be near its terminal stage."

The man who was either loved or hated by all who knew him lowered his eyes to his desk, then looked up at me with genuine pain and said, "Jim, I'm sorry. Lula is a great woman."

The voice, which was usually shouting, screaming, and roaring epithets, now spoke softly: "I have a big union here now. I can find a spot for you or create one. It would have to be a job requiring a lot of administrative work, cracking heads, cracking the whip over staff members, and pushing paper. I'm not sure that that would be to your liking, but you tell me; I won't tell you."

"I don't think so. As you know, handling administrative details is not where I feel most comfortable. If there is no alternative, however—"

"There are always alternatives," he said. "Let me think aloud." He mumbled, "Two possibilities occur to me off the top of my head. I know you'll want something where you'll have some visibility and be able to use your great talents, rocking and rolling. One possibility is CBTU, tne Coalition of Black Trade Unionists. I would have to talk to Bill Lucy* about that; CBTU is his baby and he's president of it. Maybe he'd be interested in having Jim Farmer run it as executive director. AFSCME could put a little more money into it to cover your salary.

"The second possibility that occurs to me is CAPE, the Coalition of American Public Employees. It's a small coalition I started in 1972, and it brings together AFSCME, NEA, NASW, PNHA, NTEU, and ANA.** CAPE started out to be a Center for Public Employees, a kind of AFL-CIO in the public sector. I don't know where it's really going; we haven't decided that yet. Maybe you could help us make decisions like that. CAPE now does some lobbying, but mostly it's an advocate for the rights of public employees. I can't offer you the directorship of it; that job is already filled by a fellow named Harvey Zorbaugh, but they're looking for an associate director. I think this may be a better place for you than CBTU because I gather you need some security, and CAPE can provide that, whereas CBTU cannot."

*William Lucy is international secretary-treasurer of AFSCME.

**National Education Association, National Association of Social Workers, Physicians National Housestaff Association, National Treasury Employees Union, American Nurses Association.

Gratefully, I accepted the CAPE offer. Zorbaugh proved to be one of the finest human beings I have ever met, genuine and aboveboard, with no hint of meanness in his makeup. We worked well together. However, he could not get along with Jerry Wurf and resigned eight months after I joined the staff. I became executive director of the organization.

My sojourn in CAPE lasted six years, until Wurf's death in December 1981. CAPE went to its grave when he went to his. The organization survived Lula, though, by five years.

As we waited for the inevitable, I reflected on my losses. I had lost my mother in 1966 after a long struggle with Parkinson's Disease.

My brother had died of cancer in 1970. When all else had failed and his condition was terminal, I tried to secure government approval for the use, on an experimental basis, of that controversial and federally banned drug Laetril. A Navy physician had stood by to administer the medication, but the surgeon blocked its use, preventing the HEW assistant secretary for health and scientific affairs from making the necessary sign-off, which he was supposed to do.

Also in 1972, my sister's husband died, and two years later, she followed him to the grave.

Now, I was losing the woman who had been the mainstay of my life for nearly three decades. As she lay dying in 1976, all that this remarkable woman had meant in my life dominated my thinking. I devoutly wished that I had been a better husband and father. Wholly preoccupied with people in general, I had forgotten how to relate to individuals in particular. The movement was a mistress who had robbed me of the capacity to show Lula the attention and affection she deserved. I think Lula understood this, and since she, too, loved the movement, her own suffering in this regard was not an unbearable tragedy in her life.

Less bearable to her, though, was my neglect of our daughters. So intensely absorbed with the plight of children of the nation being maimed by hatred was I that my own children saw little of me, and I scarcely knew them. In the month that Lula lay in her hospital bed, I thus was haunted by deep and abiding regrets—not that I had given so much time to my people, but that I had found so little time for my family.

At Lula's request, she was cremated, and there was no funeral, just a small memorial service a month later with good friends. The service was not a sad affair; there was no weeping. There were anecdotes and there was humor. We laughed and remembered Lula. Evie Rich, Marv's wife, and a black woman, spoke of the gathering as a celebration, and that is what it was: a celebration of the life of one who, always in the shadow of death, had a great gift for living. Even Tami and Abbey, teenagers who had come to cry, were bathed in smiles. Lula would have loved it.

The nearest thing to inanity during that whole period was the cliché I heard repeated over and over: that time will heal all things and will heal this pain, too. No greater lie was ever told. Time heals nothing. It provides an opportunity for the wound to heal—or to fester and run. Pain was a predator, tearing at pleasant memories, growing larger as it devoured its prey.

Burdened by guilt for my own neglectfulness, the wound grew worse. Loneliness fed on itself and grew by the day, until it walked with me full-grown each day and through sleepless nights, a constant companion.

My closeness to Lula had possessed none of the impetuous, passionate, romantic love of the relationship with Winnie. It had been a calm, serene thing, and I took it for granted. Therein, I suppose, lay its greatest tragedy; knowing that it was there, and certain of its permanence, I came to ignore it and forgot how precious it was.

My correspondence at home and my financial records, which had been her domain, were now beyond my ability to reckon with. I could not face them. I walked past the desk in my study at home, looking away, while urgent matters piled up untouched. The very sight of them reminded me of her, and the memories tortured me. Dreams of the deceased springing back to life are a common occurrence, but when they recur with the regularity of the stars rising overhead, even the routine things of life are a crucifixion. I always saw her seated at that desk in the study, poring over papers and figures to free me for battles of greater moment. That house on Chevy Chase Parkway was her tomb, and the simple walnut desk in my study had become an ornate urn, encasing her ashes. I could not even look at it.

Looking this way and that, seeking a replacement in my life for her who could not be replaced, I was always vulnerable. A lonely, aging man, adrift from the moorings that for years had guided me, I now floundered. I squandered my limited resources on prospective brides, and even mindlessly approached the altar on two occasions, luckily stopping short before disaster.

It was a personal struggle for emotional survival. Perhaps, in some curious way, the fates tried to slow down my race with catastrophe. A rare eye ailment, retinal vascular occlusion, destroyed the sight in one eye in 1979. Four years later, it struck the other eye. Thanks to somewhat more advanced knowledge and the high technology at the National Institutes of Health, a modicum of sight was maintained in the left eye.

Having sold the house on Chevy Chase Parkway, losing my shirt in the process, I moved to central Virginia to complete this story while fighting blindness. Doing this book has been a kind of catharsis. It did not rid me of the past. Instead, it placed that which has gone before in perspective, bringing me to terms with the present, and I now face a future full of the beckoning sounds of battle.

The fight against blindness has been more difficult than the fight against the wildcats of the Klan or the termites within CORE. Many persons I know who can see less well than I cope much better. My tiny, aged Aunt

Sadie, for example, has made peace with near blindness and walks alone though the bustle of downtown New York with her aluminum cane and her enormous courage. So far, I have not been able to do that. Trying to cross a busy intersection in downtown Washington one day, after cursing the darkness and the inconsiderate drivers, I finally reached the opposite curb. A woman's voice spoke to me: "Mister, would you please help me across the street? I'm blind."

That of which the human animal is capable then rose up in me.

"Oh, yes, Madam, I would be delighted to help you across the street," I said.

Holding up my hand to stop traffic and holding her by the arm, we successfully navigated the dangerous terrain. I was like the man who cried because he had no shoes until he met a fellow who had no feet. Since then, I have been a little more at ease with my own disability.

A great comfort through all of this has been the fact that my daughters—thanks to Lula, not to me—have turned out well. Both are sensitive and compassionate persons, and that is a joy to behold. Both understand and celebrate the fact that I have other children, millions of others who sprang, not from my loins, but from my mind and guts. Most have never seen my face and do not know my name. From the early days in Holly Springs to the ebbtide years of the present, like all who have fought to cleanse this nation, I have helped to pave the roads on which America's black children walk toward new vistas that I shared in shaping.

Vast numbers of these black progeny of the movement know little of the past; they only know the present. Yet in some vague way, they know that the unknown past has made the greater hope of the present possible. They can accomplish much now and aspire to anything in this country. If I am one of their fathers, I am also one of the children of the many fathers and mothers who went before them.

Those who are not black are my children, too. The movement is as much a part of the American experience as is any other odyssey crowding the pages of the nation's past. No one who lives here, or who ever will, can inhale this air without breathing the breath of Schwerner, Goodman, and Chaney, Viola Liuzzo, or Reverend Leeb, or Medgar Evers, or Martin Luther King, Jr. All, the evil and the good, have suckled some of that experience from their mother's breast; in some way, great or small, they cannot be the same.

Living was tenuous in movement days, but the grasping at liberty, and the reaching toward happiness ennobled life for this nation.

Epilogue

THE DEAD WILL NOT return, and our martyrs will stay at peace. We survivors have got a second wind, and the young will draw their first.

Martin left us with a dream unrealized and a promise unfulfilled. Our nation deceives itself with the fiction that the task is complete and racism is dead and all is well. The myth surrounds us that America suddenly has become color-blind, and that all that remains is an economic problem.

No greater lie has ever been told, and the tellers of it, if they have eyes to see and minds to think, must know it.

The tired among us must recharge our batteries. The uninitiated must learn to gird their loins. We have not finished the job of making our country whole.

Jesse Jackson has given us the great promise of a restructuring of the political institutions. That promise must be fulfilled. The "rainbow coalition" has not come together, and it will not be driven into formation by expansive rhetoric. It will require careful and patient nurturing and sophisticated knowledge of how coalitions work.

Also, the late eighties and the nineties must see a rebuilding of America's black folk—a renaissance. Centuries of prejudice and poverty have wreaked havoc with folk of color. A new people in a renewed nation must face the new century.

But that is another story, whose telling must await another time—and another book. This time not for jailgoing and bleeding heads, but for long-range planning and sophisticated strategizing. There will be less demonstration and more cerebration.

The narrative of this odyssey has ended.

Appendix A

To: A. J. Muste

Feb. 19, 1942

From: James Farmer

Re: Provisional Plans for Brotherhood Mobilization

The plans suggested are but preliminary formulations to provide a basis for further discussion. Obviously, before any such program is put into operation, it must be discussed in detail by the National Council, or some committee which N.C. may designate, and should have much more elaborate and expert planning than went into this brief statement. Hence, any disagreement with certain points of the statement should by no means prevent a consideration of the general idea.

From its inception, the Fellowship has thought in terms of developing definite, positive and effective alternatives to violence as a technique for resolving conflict. It has sought to translate love of God and man, on one hand, and hatred of injustice on the other, into specific action. Leading naturally into a study of the Gandhian movement, this quest has been served mightily by the clear analysis in Shridharani's *War without Violence* and by the work of J. Holmes Smith.* New vistas have been opened, new horizons revealed. In general terms, we have spoken of the new technique as "nonviolent direct action."

There are two great fields in which our contemplations have rested: the industrial and the racial. For obvious reasons the former has been temporarily canceled as a field for great activity along these lines. But the latter remains, probably more urgent today than ever before since slavery. Several contemporary approaches to the problem, such as the NAACP and the Urban League, have proved their value from specialized angles, and must therefore be encouraged and supported. But they have also demonstrated their inadequacy in dealing effectively with the total aspects of a problem as comprehensive as that of race in America. Hence, the need for a virile and comprehensive program such as our study and experimentation in nonviolence should logically lead into.

---

*Jeff Holmes Smith, former Methodist missionary to India; then in the United States fostering Gandhian life-style and Gandhi-type action.

Regarding such a movement, we may venture a few general observations:

1. Certain societal and cultural differences between the United States and India, and certain basic differences between the problems to be dealt with in the two countries, militate strongly against an uncritical duplication of the Gandhian steps in organization and execution. The American race problem is in many ways distinctive, and must to that extent be dealt with in a distinctive manner. Using Gandhism as a base, our approach must be creative in order to be effectual.

2. If any such movement is to amount to more than a gesture of protest, however valuable such a gesture may be, it must seek to draw *mass* following. Therefore, the movement cannot be limited to pacifists but must try to "mobilize" all persons who want to see an end to racial discrimination in America, and are willing to commit themselves to a disciplined nonviolence in working toward that goal.

3. If such an endeavor is not to degenerate into violence and chaos, pacifists must serve as its nucleus, its moving force.

4. Such a program must be on a religious base if it is to possess genuine motive power and is to appeal to masses of people, black and white, Jewish and Gentile.

5. The difficulty in developing and utilizing mass discipline in unified action is so great that we would probably not attempt vital mass nonviolent direct action, except on an experimental scale, until discipline and training was perfected. There should be no hesitancy, however, in carrying out education and "moral suasion" projects from the very beginning. This, of course, is following the Gandhian and commonsense procedure of launching vital campaigns only when satisfactory discipline and unity is arrived at.

In light of the foregoing observations, I urge that the Fellowship of Reconciliation (in collaboration with the AFSC* if such collaboration is deemed feasible and can be worked out) immediately lay plans for launching a nationwide Brotherhood Mobilization, concerning which I offer the following specific suggestions:

TIME PLAN

There ought to be a time goal on the mobilization and preparation for effective mass action. I, therefore, suggest that the Brotherhood Mobilization be placed on a five-year or even a ten-year plan, after which, it is to be hoped, relentless noncooperation, economic boycott, civil disobedience, etcetera, will be thrown into swing wherever and whenever necessary.

Naturally, such a "time plan" would be outlined in successive stages, each of which would be given to a specific emphasis. For example: (1) Securing necessary initial finances and endorsements by strategic individuals and groups capable of supplying mass audience; (2) A vast enlistment drive; (3) Systematic organization for action, etc.

*AFSC, American Friends Service Committee, a Quaker service organization

APPENDIX 357

ORGANIZATION AND MEMBERSHIP

Such a venture, it seems to me, ought to be considered, in its early stages at least, as a semi-autonomous project of the FOR (and of the AFSC if possible). After a period of time—probably at the end of the five- or ten-year period—it may be wise to make the set-up of the movement thoroughly democratic. At such time, the FOR will doubltess to some degree find it necessary to "wean" the movement. Long before that time, however, it should become largely self-supporting.

SUPPLEMENTAL MEMORANDUM ON BROTHERHOOD MOBILIZATION

To: A. J. Muste

From: James Farmer

An extremely critical question in the effective execution of any such project as that suggested in the preceding memo lies in the vastly different inclinations to participation in various brands of nonviolent action, found among different groups in American society. A great number of people will doubtless be willing to work in a quiet manner to broaden the human fellowship and abolish all forms of racial discrimination, and will agree to utilize organized, persistent, and concerted *educational* and *moral suasion* methods toward effecting that end. Many others will go even further and participate in a thorough-going, nationwide, cooperative community, sharing cooperatively the burdens of the movement and the mutual destiny of its participants. Still others will be willing to engage in all-out-nonviolent direct action (economic boycott, noncooperation, pickets, demonstrations, civil disobedience, etcetera) whenever and wherever such action is necessary and strategic. How can the energies and talents of all those people most effectively be harnessed in the mobilization for brotherhood without eliminating any who agree thoroughly with the aims and objectives but are not inclined to participate in the more aggressive and demanding phases of the program, and without frustrating those inclined to the most direct forms of nonviolent action?

The most likely answer to that question seems to me to be provided by establishing different *levels* of membership or participation in the movement. Probably *three levels* are required. The first should be of the greatest possible mass constituency, including all persons who are opposed to every form of racial discrimination and desire to see it ended, and are willing to dedicate themselves to nonviolent methods in effecting that end. The second level, draws [drawn] from members of the first, should be composed of those persons who will participate in a carefully planned cooperative community which will provide the economic base for the movement, and will effectively apply some principle of mutual aid in providing for such persons as will be thrown out of jobs by virtue of their participation in the movement. The third level, recruited from the lower ones, should be composed of those persons who will take part in aggressive and relentless nonviolent direct action.

Obviously, the first level will be the largest of the three; the second, next in size, and the third, the smallest, most selective group. It should also be understood that in this suggestion the members of the third level would also be participants in the second level, and members of the second level would also be included in the activities of the first level. It should be hoped and expected that many members of lower levels could be induced eventually to enter higher levels. Thus, the lower levels would continually feed the higher ones with members—the ideal, however impossible, being that all members be participants of the third level, participating in all phases of the work of the movement. The three levels should work in a coordinated fashion, like the fingers on the hand or like three functional divisions of a military force.

By following such a pattern of membership, we should be enabled to exercise a wide membership appeal, to allow to devotees of direct action a maximum freedom of operation, and to avoid a perpetual wrangling over the validity or relative validity of various brands of actions.

Another critical matter deserving a great deal of special thought is the matter of a cooperative community to which I have referred in passing. This cooperative arrangement should be so planned, I think, as to serve the following four basic objectives:

1. To supply the social and spiritual comradeship which can be achieved only through true community.

2. To free participants of the movement, as far as possible, from dependence upon the capitalistic system.

3. To supply the basic financial needs of the movement, thus, as far as possible, rendering the movement as self-sufficient and serving as economic base.

4. To apply *mutual aid* in meeting the needs and sharing the misfortunes of participants in the movement.

Toward the building of such a cooperative community, I offer the following preliminary suggestions:

1. That *second level* members impose upon themselves a voluntary *income tax* consistent with each person's ability to help bear the financial burdens of the project.

2. That a network of interracial consumers' cooperatives (and wherever possible, producers' cooperatives) be developed on a nationwide scale among the *second level* members, turning a certain percentage of the dividends over to the *Brotherhood Mobilization*.

3. That interracial housing cooperatives, interracial cooperative farms, and interracial eating cooperatives be likewise developed with the co-op houses and farms serving as strategic local or regional headquarters for the total movememt, and the eating co-ops, like the producers and consumers co-ops, turning a certain percentage of their savings over to the movement.

4. That plans be developed for the cooperative production and cooperative marketing of *folk craft* and *art* by Negroes and whites alike. Flax can be grown, spun, and woven. Wool craft, pottery, glass work, sculpturing, coal carving, gourd work, wood carving, straw work, etc. will find a prominent place in such a project. Contrary to the usual opinion, silk can be grown in America, and thus, silk culture might well enter in the plan. Fine folk metalware is also a possibility. Such development of *folk craft* and *art* wold supply to participants a tremendous

spiritual value, by virtue of their working with their hands to produce useful objects. It could become a tremendous public relations and educational implement for the movement by providing an avenue for utilitarian and artistic expression. It might ultimately supplement industrialization by utilizing the labor of many *marginal persons** in our industrial society, and the spare time labor of others, in developing utilitarian and artistic objects of finer quality than those which can be produced by industrial mass production. It will enable many Negroes and poor white people to solve their unemployment problem through folk craft.

Obviously, to develop a meaningful cooperative community, we shall have to place great emphasis upon drawing in persons from lower classes, black and white. Far too many movements for racial justice have virtually confined their activities to the middle classes.

It is obvious that in order to develop such community, we must work closely with, and secure the counsel of the Cooperative League of America.

MEMBERSHIP PATTERN

A. The audience and membership of such a movement will, of course, be far wider and more heterogeneous than that of the sponsoring groups. The members will be united by devotion to the cause and commitment to nonviolence in working toward the desired end. There are literally hundreds of thousands of persons over the country who are opposed to racial discrimination, and many more who have no conviction in favor of it. Our task should be to persuade those without positive conviction to join the ranks of those opposed to discrimination, to mobilize and unite those people while persistently striving to enlarge their ranks and to provide them with a dynamic program and method. The membership therefore ought to proceed along the following lines:

1. It ought to be recruited from all sections of the country and from all ages, races, classes, and religions. In general, we can appeal to labor groups, church groups, schools, and social and civic organizations in addition to the unorganized and unaffiliated. I am certain that many church groups and labor groups can be tied up solidly behind it. Reaching the Negroes, however—and they will naturally comprise the preponderance of the membership in the southern sections—is a unique and even more difficult problem. Aside from those which will be reached in appeals to the above mentioned groups, the masses of Negroes can be reached only through the three following specifically "Negro" channels:

(1) *The Negro Church,* which is the only institution channeling the *hoi polloi.* I am now convinced that, if managed well, great support can be received from certain sections of the Negro church.

(2) *Negro Fraternal Organizations* (fraternities, sororities, lodges, etc.), in which tremendous numbers of civic-minded persons can be found.

*By "marginal persons" I mean those great masses of unsettled persons who are not established in our industrial society. It is not at all impossible that their numbers will consistently increase as industrialization becomes more complete.

(3) *Negro Schools,* through which the present and potential intelligentsia can be reached.

2. Members should be asked to contribute a small minimum fee of perhaps 25 cents annually. Eventually, it is hoped a cooperative arrangement can be perfected whereby members automatically bear the financial burden of the movement according to ability.

B. Regarding organization, I should think the cell idea ought to be considered basic, with FOR cells, wherever possible, serving as nuclei. The movement may well follow the pattern set by the FOR: regional, local, and cell. Much of the grassroots organizing can be done by a large number of volunteer organizers working in their own localities.

We might also consider the practicability of utilizing a technique similar to that employed by the AFSC in the past years. We might send out a nationwide call for volunteer workers with certain qualifications, or we might get key college professors to select one, two, or three good persons from the graduating class who would be willing to give the "after-graduation year" of their life to service in Mobilization for Brotherhood. (I am confident, after my November tour of southern Negro colleges, that the response to such a call in Negro colleges would be overwhelming.) The volunteers could be given three months of cooperative training for their task at a centralized point in the summer, and could then be sent out in teams or caravans for nine months of organizing and educational work in many parts of the nation. A large percentage of their expenses for the nine months may well be cared for by church groups and others in return for part-time work of some nature. It is indispensable that a movement as ambitious as this have some organ of expression. A page in *Fellowship* and a periodical mimeographed news bulletin may serve temporarily. But I think we should look toward the day when a small paper can be printed, and perhaps a quarterly journal providing the theoretical and critical approach.

AIM

Above all, the Brotherhood Mobilization must present a distinctive and radical approach. It must strive, for example, not to make housing in ghettos more tolerable, but to destroy residential segregation; not to make Jim Crow facilities the equal of others, but to abolish Jim Crow; not to make racial discrimination more bearable, but to wipe it out. In the words of the Twenty-Sixth Annual Conference of the FOR, we must "effectively repudiate every form of racism . . ." We must forge the instrumentalities through which that nationwide repudiation can be effected. We must not stop until racial brotherhood is established in the United States as a fact as well as an ideal. Ironically enough, the present unfortunate circumstances brought on by the war afford an excellent setting for immediate spadework in this direction.

Appendix B

JAMES FARMER ON MALEK MEMO

I agree heartily with the main point of *The Post's* June 13th editorial, "How to Buy Votes." Buying (and selling) votes in any way whatever, and for whatever purpose, is entirely reprehensible. Yet, I was surprised and disappointed that *The Post* did not seek my view of the facts before going into print with its assertions of my involvement in so venal an enterprise.

Frederic Malek's May 2, 1972 memo quoted by *The Post* is in error:

1. Your editorial reports the memorandum as saying that I had "been given a grant from OE to fund [my] project." The fact is, however, that my black think tank project, the Public Policy Training Institute, was not funded until a full year later, on May 1, 1973. It was not, to my knowledge, even approved for funding until March 1973—ten months after Malek's memo and four months after the election.

2. Your editorial also reports the memorandum as saying that I would therefore "be able to spend a major part of [my] time on the above project *while also making time available to the election effort.*" (Italics mine.) The fact is that since the project did not begin until a year later, well after the election, obviously I could not possibly have done that or committed myself to do it. The fact is, further, that I did not make any time whatsoever available to the re-election of the President.

3. The memorandum is further reported as saying that I made an agreement to "do speaking on . . . behalf of the re-election effort and also to talk to key black leaders in an effort to gain their loyalties." The fact is that I made no such commitment. And at no time did I do any speaking on behalf of the President's re-election. Nor did I speak to any black leaders or anyone else, in an attempt to gain their allegiance to that effort or to encourage them to vote for Nixon.

What I did do, at meetings with Fred Malek and other Republican officials, with Democratic officials in my writings, and in public lectures was to reiterate my basic theme—voiced publicly since 1965—that minorities achieve political leverage by being unwed to either party and by voting for candidates regardless of party label.

Since resigning in frustration as an HEW assistant secretary in December 1970, I have criticized the Nixon administration on many counts, including the weakening of desegregation guidelines, exploitation of the busing issue, nominations to the Supreme Court, and failure to support vital parts of the antipoverty program. I have also *credited* the administration with such positive moves as the Philadelphia Plan (later dropped), the Family Assistance Plan (also abandoned), and efforts to support minority enterprise.

I do not intend to weaken in my determination to build a private nonprofit "think-tank" on minority problems in order to determine where we go from here and how we can best attain minority goals in the complex days of the seventies and beyond. I believed when I left HEW, and I believe equally now, that the federal government has a responsibility to assist in supporting such an effort, for the "think tank" concept involves both a study of basic public policy and pursuit of the constitutional mandates of "ensuring domestic tranquility" and "promoting the general welfare." The precedents are numerous: the Urban Institute and the Rand Corporation, for instance, have become multimillion dollar research operations largely through government grants and contracts. I certainly see nothing sinister in their seeking and getting government funded projects to insure that we plan before we act.

In most public policy research, however, the minority perspective is largely lacking. This is one reason, in my opinion, why government policies affecting minorities have failed to achieve their objectives in education and welfare. That is one of the failures in our domestic policy which my associates and I seek to address, using research and planning as a catalyst.

The Public Policy Training Institute, a first step toward a minority "think tank" was funded on May 1, 1973, for $150,000 to train selected higher education personel in public policy issues with particular reference to developing institutions.

My associates and I will go on, of course, in our efforts to help in a small way to build a better and more equitable America as *The Post* must persist in its campaign to cleanse the body politic. In fact, both the building and the cleansing are parts of the same struggle to bring more decency to the nation's life—a struggle in which *The Post* enjoys a record of rare distinction which I applaud.

But neither the proud achievements of the past, nor the meritorious crusade of the present, justifies *The Post*'s failure to check the facts in the Malek memo or my purposes in establishing the Public Policy Training Institute.

Both the cleansing and the building, you will agree, require that we avoid at all cost "tarring with the same brush."

Index

Lomax, Louie, 224, 255
Lombard, Rudy, 302
Long, "Pops," 124
Long, Russell, 319–20
Louise, Aunt, 137
Lovestone, Jay, 85n
Lucy, Bill, 348
Lutov, Paul T., 135
Lynch, Lincoln, 257

M

Malcolm X, 34, 222–23, 223–33, 235, 236–38
Malek, Frederic V., 326, 338–39, 342, 343, 344, 345, 361–62
Malone, John, 285
Mann, Floyd, 4
Mao Tse-tung, 244
Marcantonio, Vito, 311
Marshall, Burke, 308
Marshall, Thurgood, 13, 74, 212, 221, 330
Martin, Louis, 336
Mason, Bianca, 337
Masters, Edgar Lee, 119
Masters, Mrs. Edgar Lee, 90, 96, 99, 102, 106, 194
Mau Mau, 307
Maxine, 49, 50
May, Alan, 326
Mays, Benjamin E., 134, 135, 143
Mazique, Mrs. Marguerite Belafonte, 321
McCain, James T. (Jim), 192, 195, 196, 197, 209, 261–62, 264
McDowell, Arthur G., 162, 165, 167, 168
McKeithen, Gov., 286
McKey-Pogue Realty Company, 114–15, 167
McKissick, Floyd B., 240, 242, 245, 256–57, 262, 302, 303, 305, 307, 309, 310, 347
McLaurin, Ben, 157
Melville, Nina, 140–41, 173
Mencken, H. L., 142
Milgram, Morris, 162, 347
Mississippi National Guard, 4, 5
Mitchell, Clarence, 127n, 239, 340
Mitchell, John, 333
Mittleman, Earl, 177
Montgomery bus boycott, 185–87
Moore, Ronnie, 246, 247, 251, 253

Morgan v. *Virginia* (1946), 165
Morsell, Dr. John, 188–89, 296
Moses, Robert (Bob), 179, 180, 259, 260
MOW (March on Washington) movement, 155, 156, 157
Moynihan, Daniel Patrick, 324–25, 334
Muriel, Cousin, 174, 175
Murphy, Michael J., 234
Muste, A. J., 74n 76, 86, 88–90, 94–96, 99, 102–103, 110, 111, 115, 116, 147, 150, 156, 160–61, 173, 190, 194, 261, 355–60
Muzumdar, Haridas T., 156

N

NAACP (National Association for the Advancement of Colored People), 13, 74, 93, 95, 99, 106, 109, 155, 178, 188, 189, 191–93, 209, 218, 219, 239, 242, 281, 296, 298, 299
NAACP Legal Defence and Education Fund, Inc., 212, 298
Nader, Ralph, 340
Nash, Diane, 203, 204, 205
National Action Council (NAC), 193–94, 208, 209, 254, 255, 256, 262, 266–67, 302, 320
National Association of Social Workers (NASW), 348
National Conference of Christians and Jews, 239
National Conference of Methodist Youth, 127–29, 132
National Council of Churches, 239
National Council of Methodist Youth, 129, 142
National Council of Negro Women, 134n, 215, 217, 218, 296
National Education Association (NEA), 348
National Federation of Committees of Racial Equality, 112
National Labor Relations Board, 164
National Negro Congress, 129, 132
National Treasury Employees Union (NTEU), 348
National Urban League. *See* Urban League
National Youth Administration (NYA), 295

Plume
 Meridian

DISSENT IN AMERICA

Ⓜ MENTOR

VOICES OF STRUGGLE

(0451)

☐ **BLACK VOICES edited by Abraham Chapman.** This exciting and varied anthology of Afro-American Literature includes fiction, poetry, autobiography, and criticism—reflecting a potent force in American writing today. With selections from Richard Wright, James Baldwin, Malcolm X, LeRoi Jones, W.E.B. DuBois, and many others. (622057—$4.95)

☐ **NEW BLACK VOICES edited by Abraham Chapman.** Here are stories, poems, and essays by some of the most acclaimed Black writers of today. Here are other, equally remarkable creations by Black writers who are making their first appearance in print, or have yet to reach a wide audience. This is extraordinary literary talent at work, as over eighty superb writers demonstrate that Black literature has truly come of age. (622928—$4.95)

☐ **THE BLACK WOMAN edited and with a preface by Toni Cade.** Black women speak out. A brilliant and challenging assembly of voices that demand to be heard. Included are stories, poems, and essays by Abbey Lincoln, Paule Marshall, Nikki Giovanni, Kay Lindsey, and many others. (623983)—$3.95

☐ **WHY WE CAN'T WAIT by Martin Luther King.** "I may not get there with you, but I want you to know tonight that we as a people will get to the promised land."—In his own words, Nobel Peace Prize-Winner Martin Luther King explains the events, the forces, the pressures behind today's—and tomorrow's—quest for civil rights. (621816—$12.95)

Prices slightly higher in Canada.

Buy them at your local bookstore or use this convenient
coupon for ordering.

NEW AMERICAN LIBRARY
P.O. Box 999, Bergenfield, New Jersey 07621

Please send me the books I have checked above. I am enclosing $_____
(please add $1.50 to this order to cover postage and handling). Send check or money order—no cash or C.O.D.'s. Prices and numbers are subject to change without notice.

Name_____

Address_____

City_____State_____Zip Code_____

Allow 4-6 weeks for delivery.
This offer subject to withdrawal without notice.

PL 27